Time to Know Them

❧ ✄ ❧

A Longitudinal Study of Writing and Learning at the College Level

Time to Know Them

A Longitudinal Study of Writing and Learning at the College Level

Marilyn S. Sternglass
The City College of
City University of New York

LEA LAWRENCE ERLBAUM ASSOCIATES, PUBLISHERS
1997   Mahwah, New Jersey   London

Lawrence Erlbaum Associates, Inc., Publishers
10 Industrial Avenue
Mahwah, NJ 07430

Cover design by Kathryn Houghtaling

Library of Congress Cataloging-in-Publication Data

Sternglass, Marilyn S.
    Time to know them : a longitudinal study of writing and
learning at the college level / Marilyn S. Sternglass.
        p.   cm.
    Includes bibliographical references and index.
    ISBN 0-8058-2722-6 (cloth). — ISBN 0-8058-2723-4 (pbk.)
    1. English language—Rhetoric—Study and teaching—Evalua-
tion. 2. Report writing—Study and teaching(Higher)—Evaluation. I. Title.
PE1404.S824   1997
808'.042'0711—dc21   97-12621
                                                    CIP

Books published by Lawrence Erlbaum Associates are printed on
acid-free paper, and their bindings are chosen for strength and durability.

Printed in the United States of America
10 9 8 7 6 5 4 3 2 1

This book is dedicated to my husband,
Ernest,
whose personal and professional support
has enriched my life

Contents

Introduction

I would like to conclude [this article, "What Happens When Basic Writers Come to College?"] by suggesting that we need a study of basic writers similar to that conducted by Perry—a series of interviews to tell us how they mediate between their home cultures and the academic culture as they move on through their college education.

—Bizzell (1986)

When I read Patricia Bizzell's article in *College Composition and Communication* and came to the statement cited above, I wrote a note to myself in the margin: "This is the long range study I want to do." Having joined the faculty at The City College of City University of New York the year before, I realized that the student population there, comprised of students from a wide range of racial, ethnic, and social backgrounds, would constitute a meaningful study population. Students from diverse backgrounds are rarely followed for extended periods of time. Knowledge gained from examining students' academic progress over their entire college experience contributes to rational decision making about educational priorities in a time of declining financial support for public higher education. Both writing development and the relationship between writing and learning can be best understood through longitudinal studies that consider all facets of students' experiences during their college years.

Bizzell's statement addressed my interest—in how the academic performance of the students would be influenced by their experiences outside the college, in their homes, in their workplaces, and in their communities. So, in my interviews over the years, I sought to have a full and rich picture of their development as "whole persons," not only as students in an academic culture.

Holloway (1993) also pointed out the importance of considering the complexities in the lives of urban students:

Today our classrooms are different. In them are those who were once only visible in our research data, and whose minority languages or economic disenfranchisement made them ideal research subjects *but masked their subjectivity* [italics added]. Our classrooms are populated by the "them" we once studied. Those we theorized about and universalized into subject populations and disaggregated from our objective data not only are in front of the classroom, but are its students. (p. 611)

In this study, the students' subjective lives are shown to be essential components of their objective lives, so that it is impossible to comprehend the nature of their academic experience or to contemplate educational approaches that will meet their needs without understanding how integrated these aspects of their experience are.

After 2 years of fruitless efforts to acquire foundation support to undertake a study with a large population, the foundations seeming to be interested in short-term studies with short-term results they could point to, I decided to reduce the numbers of students in the study but not to narrow the scope. In the fall of 1989, I became the instructor of three levels of composition, English 1, the lower level of basic writing, English 2, the second level of basic writing, and English 110, the single-semester freshman composition course. I explained to the students in these classes that I was interested in following them through their college years, interviewing them twice each semester, collecting copies of all the papers and examinations they wrote over their college years, and having a research assistant observe one of their courses each semester. Fifty-three of the students in the three classes initially agreed to participate in the study. In addition to the interviews, papers, and classroom observations, I collected copies of transcripts for the students each semester and copies of all attempts to pass the two writing tests required by the college.

Of the 53 students in the classes who agreed to participate in the study, 21 identified themselves as African American, 26 Latino, 4 Asian, and 2 White. Thirty were males and 23 were females. Twenty-five were born outside the continental United States, including 3 born in Puerto Rico. Students in English 1 and English 2 were placed in the courses on the basis of their performance on the college's Writing Assessment Test (WAT). Those placed at these levels had to retake the test before completing their 60th credit in the college in order to be allowed to continue in their majors. Students in the English 110 class had multiple routes into the course: initial placement on the basis of the WAT, completion of one or two semesters of basic writing, completion of one, two, or three semesters of English as a Second Language (ESL), or as transfer students who had not satisfactorily completed the English composition requirement.

Other longitudinal studies of college students have looked at large populations from a statistical perspective to examine issues related to student performance. The study most directly related to this study was carried out by Lavin, Alba, and Silberstein (1981). Lavin et al. followed for 5 years the progress of the first three cohorts of students who entered the City University of New York campuses after the implementation of open admissions in 1970. Their research was purely quantitative, examining such issues as numbers of credits earned and grade point averages. In their analyses of the data, Lavin et al. (1981) distinguished between what they termed *dropouts* and *persisters* and between *regular* and *open admissions* students. The students in my study who began their work in basic writing classes seem equivalent to Lavin's open admissions cohort, and those who started at the regular freshman composition level are equivalent to those labeled regular.

Further evidence of the importance of looking at a longer time frame comes from Lavin and Hyllegard's follow-up study (1996) of the first cohort of students admitted to City University of New York after the advent of open admissions in 1970. They found that the conventional 4- or 5-year time frame for graduation did not apply to the open admissions students:

> Nearly half needed more than four years to complete their bachelor's degree, 16 percent needed more than five years, 8 percent took more than seven years, and 5 percent went beyond nine years. . . .
>
> Ethnic differences in the length of time to graduate are striking. Among the senior college-entrants, only 15 percent of whites but almost 40 percent of blacks and a third of Hispanic graduates needed more than five years. Just how large time looms in the undergraduate careers of minority students is revealed by the percentages who took more than nine years to finish their bachelor's degrees: 15 percent took that long, compared with 4 percent among whites. Among open-admissions students, the proportions are even higher: one-quarter of Hispanic degree holders and almost a fifth of blacks went beyond nine years, compared with 7 percent of white open-admissions graduates. (p. 57)

With this follow-up study, it becomes easier to compare the persistence of the students in my study with those Lavin and Hyllegard followed from the classes of the early 1970s.

In my study, I could, of course, follow only those students who remained at the college and who agreed to continue in my study (like Lavin's *persisters* from the 1981 study), but I have tried to learn what has happened to those who have left the college (called *dropouts* in Lavin's earlier study). As of January 1996, of the 53 students who started in my study in the fall of 1989, 17 (32%) had graduated, 10 (19%) had transferred to other colleges, 18 (34%) had dropped out, and 8 (15%) were still continuing in the college. Thus, of this group, 51% had either graduated from the college or transferred to another college, 15% were still continuing at the college, and only 34% had dropped out of higher education. The difficulty with many statistical studies of retention is that either the time frame is too short or not enough information is known about students who leave the college. Those who transfer to other colleges are often lumped together with the true dropouts, thus increasing that number inappropriately. It is also important to note that the financial difficulties for the students beginning in 1989 were significantly greater than for those who started their college careers in the 1970s and more difficult than even for those who started in 1980. In those 10- and 20-year time spans, while the poverty level increased for minority students in the New York City area, the costs of a college education increased substantially. It is impossible to ignore these factors in students' lives when assessing their progress in the academic setting.

The purpose for acquiring all this data was to examine the ways in which the development of complex reasoning strategies was fostered by writing, to determine the role that writing plays in learning, and to understand how the multifaceted social factors in students' lives affected their academic progress. Such an examination also naturally included looking at the development of writing processes over time for students from different backgrounds and different levels of preparation and for students in different majors. Not surprisingly, changes over this 6-year time span occurred neither neatly nor linearly, as the data show.

The writing samples that are included are presented exactly as the students wrote them, without corrections of spelling or sentence-level features. I have occasionally inserted an intended word where the meaning of the passage would be clarified. I have not made any attempt to alter the punctuation from the original pieces.

PLAN OF THE BOOK

The importance of probing students' academic and life experiences over an extended period of time is presented in chapter 1. The argument is made that it is essential to have meaningful data on which to base decisions about what level of resources should be devoted to students who begin at basic writing levels. Previous research from longitudinal studies and writing-to-learn studies are reviewed. No previous studies have brought together the factors incorporated in this study: (a) examining writing and learning from a true longitudinal basis; (b) studying a multicultural urban population; (c) investigating the relationship between writing and learning by examining papers written over time for regularly assigned academic courses across a range of disciplines; and (d) taking into consideration nonacademic factors that influence academic performance. Because students in this study were interviewed twice each semester and copies of papers they wrote in all discipline areas were collected, a fuller picture of student development can be presented than in previous studies. Writing development is shown to be neither neat nor linear as instructional settings and social factors affect student performance. Examples of student writing are integrated within discussions of research issues.

Chapter 2 presents students' growing metacognitive awareness of the relationship between writing and learning. The role of writing in helping students remember facts, analyze and conceptualize, and discover new information is examined. As students are able to translate textbook and lecture jargon into their own language, they develop the ability to use writing as a means to critique existing materials and to develop their own insights.

The backgrounds and experiences of an urban, inner-city college population allow a reflective examination of the effects of race, gender and sexual orientation, social class, and ideology on the writing development of college students. In chapter 3, excerpts of student writing are presented that display the ability of students to apply knowledge gained through their life experiences to the beliefs in the academic fields they are working in. Researchers have shown that learning results in conflict, but the students' work also reveals that conflict results in learning. As students acquire analytical skills, they can examine their world views in relation to the new views they are being exposed to in their classes. The effects of extended outside working hours on the academic performance of students are set forth.

Composition instruction is presented in chapter 4 with particular emphasis on composition pedagogy, the effects of teachers' comments on student papers, the relationship between content and form in student writing, and the effects of composition instruction on writing in upper level courses.

Institutional testing has become a large factor in students' progress through their academic programs. The impact of placement testing, "rising-junior" requirements, and competency examinations required for graduation are discussed in chapter 5. The effects of second-language and second-dialect language patterns are analyzed in relation to issues of language development and assessment.

The association between instructional settings and writing development is explored in chapter 6. Using data from classroom observations in 20 disciplines over 6 years, instructional approaches are analyzed in relation to writing and examination demands made on students.

Chapter 7 presents case studies of individual students bringing together interview data, examination of student writing over the entire college experience, classroom observation reports, consideration of all attempts to pass required institutional writing tests, and transcripts indicating student performance in their courses. Factors influencing students' lives are integrated into discussion of their academic accomplishments.

The final chapter (chapter 8) presents the major findings of this study. Students are seen to acquire the ability to handle more complex reasoning tasks as they find themselves in more challenging intellectual settings and where risk taking and exploration of new ideas are valued. The integration of students' previous life experiences into their academic studies allows them to analyze, critique, modify, and apply the worldviews they held previously to their new learning. These changes are seen to occur over time with instructional settings and support providing key roles in writing development. Personal factors in students' lives present difficulties that require persistence and dedication to overcome. Implications for instruction and future research are also presented.

Appendix A presents a discussion of the methodology of this study along with the questionnaires that were used in the interviews.

Appendix B contains the assessment scale of the WAT.

BRIEF BIOGRAPHIES OF STUDENTS

Over the years of this study, I had the rare opportunity to watch a group of students grow—not only academically but in a personal sense as well. The most complete data in this study exists for nine students who started at the various composition levels. Brief biographies of the students are presented here to familiarize readers with their backgrounds and for easy reference. All names are pseudonyms. In these biographies, I provide a brief summary of the students' educational background, family history, travels through the academic disciplines, and accomplishments at the end of their college years. Data from the interviews and writings presented in the following chapters will demonstrate how these factors affected their performance as college students.

Linda is an African-American student who was originally placed in English 1. She received her elementary and middle school education on an air force base in Germany and her high school education in New York City at a school that sent approximately 30% of its students on to college. Her parents separated when she was 12, and she has lived with her mother and sister since that time. An aunt and cousin, who were "mean drunks," were frequent visitors to her home where they left the family "in disarray." Linda was a dedicated nursing major until her fourth year in the college when she became disenchanted with the program and the faculty. Her difficulties with math courses and chemistry left her uncertain about her official acceptance into the program. Feeling that the faculty had not taken any interest in her or attempted to provide her with support, she changed her major to psychology where she felt welcomed and was provided with assistance. Linda graduated with a degree in psychology in the spring of 1995 and began a part-time position in a drug abuse agency. She wrote to me in the fall of 1995, asking for a letter of recommendation for a master's program in social services at a private university in New York City, to which she was applying. But, by November 1996, Linda was working full time in an administrative position at the drug abuse center, and she had been accepted into a master's of education program in guidance and counseling that she expected to start in the fall of 1997 on a part-time basis. She eventually intended to work as a guidance counselor in a high school, helping students make career choices about higher education or vocational training.

When Linda began her academic experience, she realized that she was "not thinking as deep as they want you to." Through women's studies courses that she took, she began to have pride in her identity as an African-American woman. Her writing became more analytic as her reading skills improved, but she continued to need strong instructional support to be able to handle complex materials. When she transferred to the psychology department, Linda received the support and the prodding that was necessary for her to probe the materials she encountered more deeply.

Joan is an African-American woman who was 18 years old when she started in the English 2 class. All her preparatory schooling was in the Bronx. Joan was unprepared for the level demanded of college writing. She had not been taught how to take notes in high school, and her writing tasks had been mostly creative ones. Joan was disabled; she was in an accident at the age of 2 and as a result lost 70% of the vision in her left eye. She received therapy at the age of 4 and her eyesight improved. In high school, she pushed herself too hard, and the muscles in both eyes were weakened. She resisted letting the college label her "disabled," but, by the fall of 1991, when she was having academic difficulties with intense reading assignments in her upper level courses, she sought out that formal designation. But none of the labels applied to underprepared students could truly be said to characterize Joan's outstanding characteristic: tenaciousness. Success in college meant everything to Joan. It was her whole life. After 6 years at the college, Joan graduated in the spring of 1995 with a bachelor's degree in psychology. In a telephone interview in September 1995, she told me she had accepted a position as a counselor at the hospital where she had done an internship. Earning $25,000 a year in a unionized job, more than anyone in her family had ever earned, Joan was now planning to move her mother out of the projects into an apartment where, for the first time in her life, she would have, in her words, "a room of her own."

How does a "slow," "developmental," "disabled," "outsider," "novice" come to succeed in college? And what does success mean? For Traub, who wrote about Joan under another name in his book, *City on a Hill: Testing the American Dream at City College* (1994), Joan's progress did not mean that she had become an "educated person" by his standard: "[Joan] had not developed intellectual discrimination, and she certainly knew virtually nothing of philosophy and history" (p. 132). Traub spoke with Joan independently of my interviews over one semester, and, with her permission, had access to the papers she had written during her first 4 years at the college. What he failed to understand completely was that her difficulties and her life experiences combined with her college learning to prepare her to contribute meaningfully in the larger society. In fact, Joan told me that her family history helped the hospital that hired her consider her for the counseling position in a methadone clinic: "I came from a family where most members of my family had problems [with drug and alcohol abuse], so living through it gives you an indirect experience with families with these problems. I was a victim, and that gave me empathy, which is what the people in the clinic want."

Joan worked diligently on her college courses. Her writing was not laden heavily with grammatical errors, but she initially lacked depth in her response to college assignments, depending more on definitions and regurgitation of received knowledge. As her knowledge in the field of psychology grew, Joan became able to adapt findings from that discipline to other academic fields. Although she continued to struggle with abstract areas such as philosophy, she was able to bring significant understandings from her own experience to the needs of others. Joan's writing over the years revealed that she gained insights from the instruction she received and she was able to apply these insights to both practical and academic problems.

Ricardo is a Latino student who emigrated from Puerto Rico when he was 21 years old. Intellectually, Ricardo was able to respond in mature and thoughtful ways to his writing assignments, but he was placed into the English 2 level because of second-language interference patterns. Although he had aspirations to become a physician, when his parents separated, his father forced him to attend a vocational high school in Puerto Rico where he studied photography. Initially a communications major, in his fifth year at the college, Ricardo decided to revive his dreams of working in the medical field. Unable to afford the time or costs of medical school, he decided to prepare himself for a physician assistant program. He delayed his graduation so he could complete the necessary science and math courses. He enrolled in a physician assistant program after his graduation in 1994 and completed the program in 1996. He was 27 years old when he began his studies at City College.

Ricardo's experiences at the college dramatize how second-language interference patterns are used to hold back competent students by evaluators who do not know about issues of language development. Using the club of academic standards, assessors force students like Ricardo to take, and retake, and retake required writing assessment tests when their minds and energy could be usefully spent developing their intellect. Although Ricardo persisted, many others fall by the wayside, discouraged by these demands. Over the years, in his writing, Ricardo produced greater or lesser amounts of grammatical errors. But, far more important, he learned to temper his critiques and use his analytical powers to argue more effectively for the positions he espoused on social issues. His instructors showed him ways to be more successful in his arguments, and he flourished under such guidance.

Chandra is an African-American woman who was placed in the English 2 class because her placement exam was short. She lacked confidence in her writing, and she had had little practice in writing in high school, but she had no serious writing problems. A graduate of the Performing Arts High School in New York City, her ambition was to become an actress. She started out as a psychology major, but switched to communications in her second year. Chandra's interest in seeing Black women portrayed more honestly in the media led her to pursue production aspects of film and television as well as acting. After taking a year off to perform in a traveling musical company, Chandra returned to the college and graduated in the spring of 1995.

Chandra's experiences prior to her college years had led her to see herself as fully integrated into the larger society. As her sense of identity as an African-American woman grew, she began to apply perceptions gained from her personal experiences to the analysis of issues she confronted. In her writing, Chandra expressed her growing confidence that she could effect change in the attitudes of what she now saw as the dominant culture.

Delores is a Latina student from the Dominican Republic who came to New York and first began to study and use the English language at the age of 14. In her first semester at the college, her writing reflected her thoughtfulness and intelligence, but, like Ricardo's, it also demonstrated numerous sentence-level problems, for which she was placed into the English 2 level. Delores worked throughout her college years, first in her mother's restaurant in New Jersey and then as a receptionist in a doctor's office in New York City. Her work hours and commuting schedule placed tremendous pressure on her. Delores was accepted into a combined BA/MA program in psychology. She received her master's degree in psychology in the spring of 1995.

Through her studies, Delores came to see the significance of asserting pride in one's personal identity. Delores used the knowledge gained in her psychology courses to design studies that examined racial and gender issues important both to her field and to herself. She gained confidence in her ability to contribute new knowledge in psychological studies because she received support and encouragement from her instructors throughout her college years. She displayed initiative and fortitude in taking on complex original projects, even when her financial situation made excruciating demands on her.

Audrey is a White student, originally from Iowa, who came to City College as a transfer student in the fall of 1989. She had taken courses at the University of Iowa, but she told me that she had not taken her studies seriously there and she had not done well academically. She came to New York City shortly after leaving the University of Iowa. A few months later she decided to study more seriously and enrolled in courses at Borough of Manhattan Community College. By the time she transferred to City College, Audrey had accumulated 63 credits that City College accepted, but she was required to take the freshman composition course. Audrey graduated from City College in January 1993 in the field of geography. In March 1993, she wrote to ask me to write letters of recommendation for her application to graduate schools in the area of geographic information systems and computerized cartography. I do not know whether she was accepted into any of the graduate programs to which she applied.

By the time Audrey transferred to City College, she had transformed herself into a serious student. Audrey was not a risk-taker like Ricardo; rather, she was the "good student" who carefully and conscientiously carried out her academic tasks. Over the years, she acquired a more critical stance in her major field of geography, and she applied an analytical approach to her writing tasks.

Donald is an African-American student who was born in Jamaica and came to the United States when he was 5 years old. English was his first language. A graduate of the Art and Design High School in New York City, Donald at first selected engineering as his major. After 2 years, he decided to change his major to communications, even though he realized that the change would require him to enroll for an additional 2 years at the college. He graduated in the summer of 1995. When I spoke with him on the telephone in the fall of 1995, he was still sending out resumes but had not yet found a full-time job. By November 1996, Donald was working at an elementary school in New York City in the computer section, doing promotion for the school, teaching computer skills, and carrying out office responsibilities. Discouraged by the lack of opportunities in the field of communication, he was thinking of applying to a master's program in physical therapy.

Although he was placed directly into the freshman composition course, Donald's score on the reading test required him to take one semester of the second-level college skills course. In an interview in the middle of his first semester, Donald told me: "My easiest course this semester is college skills. This course is teaching me how to get by in college without much difficulty. And I am very attentive to such advice." This comment was characteristic of Donald's approach to his studies at the college. He was willing to do the required work, but he was interested in finding the most efficient ways to carry out his responsibilities. By the end of that first semester, he said he had learned "never to fall behind or it will catch up on you to give you great problems."

Donald changed his major because he had encountered difficulties in the required mathematics courses in the engineering program. He thrived in an environment such as the one he found in his world humanities courses where he felt free to "open up" about his sense of personal identity. Such opportunities led him to become reflective about the approaches used in advertising—especially those intended to appeal to African Americans.

Carl is a Latino student, born in the United States, of parents from Ecuador. Three of his older sisters were born in Ecuador, whereas his fourth older sister was born in the United States, as he was. Carl felt alienated from his family, becoming more "Americanized" than his parents or siblings. His homosexuality complicated his relationships with his family, but his pride in his own identity grew over the college years. A strong student from the beginning, Carl worked part time and then full time for the *New York Times,* dropping out for 1 year and then returning to complete the credits he needed for his degree in communications. In the spring of 1996, he was still taking courses.

Because of the Ecuadorian mores of his family, Carl had a difficult time finding a secure identity for himself. Once he asserted himself as a gay man, he was able to use his pride in that identity to see the public attitude toward homosexuality as an issue he would confront. With the support he received from friends and instructors at the college, Carl was able to use his course work as an effective outlet for analysis of societal perspectives.

Jacob, a Korean student who had received most of his elementary and all of his high school education in Australia, was the prototypical "insider" in my study. He was not required to take any remedial courses. He told me, in the fall of 1991, his third year at the college, that he knew exactly how to write papers for his college courses: "I read a book, make a long list of quotations, paraphrase some of them and quote others. I stick to what is in the book. I evaluate or give a critical analysis if that is what the teacher wants. I can figure out the teacher's feelings and don't cross him or her if the teacher feels strongly. I can be penalized if the teacher's opinions are different."

Jacob's cynicism toward his college work is evident. But, in the same interview, he acknowledged that he was beginning to see that in order to succeed, he would have to begin working harder. He said, "I have a history of being a 'general Renaissance man' who happens to know a little about everything, but when it comes to greater depth in a specific field, I'm not so confident I can succeed." Having changed his major from architecture (when he received his first "B" in a course) to physics, he reported that his performance in the math and physics course he was now taking would help determine how successful he could be in the field of physics. He had learned from his previous history that he starts out well but gradually falls behind. (He received a "B" in the math course and an "A" in the physics course and retained this major.) But his heart was not in these studies at all, as he spent most of his free time writing short stories, poetry, and a novel. After he graduated in the spring of 1995 as a physics major, Jacob returned for a visit to Australia. He had intended to return to New York and begin a master's program in computer science at a private university there in the spring of 1996. However, he remained in Australia where he took computer science courses. In November 1996, his sister told me that he had recently gotten married.

Jacob's story is a sad one. He was thwarted by family pressures and required to pursue a "practical" major. He fulfilled all his required writing tasks in a perfunctory way, realizing that he could perform credibly without much effort. His final studies in physics did not require much writing. By the time he graduated, he seemed burned out, by both his required course work and by publishers' rejections of the novel he wrote during his college years.

ACKNOWLEDGMENTS

Six years of research and 2 years of writing have left me with many individuals and institutions to thank for support of this work. When I first proposed the study in the fall of 1989, Dr. Paul Sherwin, who was then dean of humanities at the City College, enthusiastically made a commitment to me of a reduced course load each semester for the following 3 years. At the end of that time, Dr. Martin Tamny, the new dean of humanities extended that released time for an additional year, the last year that I made such a request. This released time enabled me to schedule interviews with the students and collect copies of their written work. I am very grateful for the college's support.

I also received support from two research foundations. The Professional-Staff Congress-City University of New York Research Foundation provided support for 4 years, and the National Council of Teachers of English Research Foundation provided support for two years. Grants from these foundations made it possible for me to hire research assistants to compile transcripts, make copies of student papers, and observe student classes.

I was very fortunate to have able research assistants, all of whom were graduate students in the MA in Language and Literacy at City College. Many thanks to David Marshall, Esther Bohm, Tara Cunningham, Qian Zhang, and Sharon Shambourger.

Colleagues and friends were willing to share their insights with me after reading a draft of the first three chapters of this manuscript. Their comments have helped me rethink and reshape aspects of my analysis of these materials and I am very grateful to them. My thanks to David Bleich, Barbara Gleason, Fred Reynolds, and Mary Soliday. Of course, I continue to take full responsibility for all ideas and materials presented here.

I also wish to express my appreciation to Linda Bathgate, my editor at Erlbaum, who was always available to provide support and encouragement for the book. In addition, at Erlbaum, Debbie Ruel, the senior production editor, was very helpful in preparing the book for publication. Amy Olener provided graceful and careful copyediting for which I am grateful. Kathryn Houghtaling's lovely cover design evokes the theme of the book in an especially effective way.

My deepest thanks are to my husband, Ernest, whose personal and professional support over the years has enriched my life.

1

Studying Writing and Learning
From a True
Longitudinal Perspective

Teaching in a time of declining resources in institutions of higher education, we grapple with how priorities are to be set for the limited resources available. Most vulnerable are those students labeled "underprepared" by the colleges and universities. Should we argue that the limited resources available ought to be used to support these students through their undergraduate years? And, if we decide that we want to do that, what evidence of their potential for success can we provide that will justify the use of these resources? Through longitudinal research that follows students who have been so labeled over all their college years we can begin to find answers to these questions.

In this book, I demonstrate that support for students who have been labeled "basic writers" should be forthcoming. This support should not be interpreted as advocating basic writing classes. Bartholomae (1993) argued that the strategic value of basic writing has been lost and that this is a productive time for professionals and students to think about what an introductory curriculum can profitably be. Soliday (1996) described an enrichment curriculum she and her colleague Barbara Gleason designed that mainstreamed formerly designated basic writers with traditional freshmen students in a 1-year program at City College of City University of New York. (I taught as an instructor in that program during the 1994–1995 academic year.) As Soliday (1996) described the curriculum of the enrichment program, issues of language and culture are foregrounded:

> Our curriculum begins with the language variety and cultural differences that City College students bring to the classroom. By foregrounding students' language experience and the everyday use of language in social contexts as resources for teaching writing (see Kutz, Groden, and Zamel [1993]), we try to enhance students' awareness of the complexity of their spoken language and its relationship to written language. (p. 87)

Although the students in my study were enrolled in the composition program at City College as it existed in 1989, with two levels of basic writing and one semester of freshman composition, those who were assigned to the basic writing sections had the same characteristics as the mainstreamed students in the enrichment program, while those placed directly into the freshman composition course were like those traditionally assigned to that level.

Stygall (1994) noted that the argument for retaining basic writing classes as a separate entity has often focused on the notion that both "regular" and "basic writing" classes are perceived as homogeneous entities. "Yet," she said, "as those of us who taught basic writing can attest, homogeneous basic classrooms are hardly the norm" (p. 339). Although attitudes about the placement and instruction of basic writing students are being strongly debated, the commitment to these students' potential for ultimate success needs to be strengthened.

The important role of the teaching environment is discussed in more detail in chapter 4, with attention to issues of composition pedagogy, the effects of teachers' responses to student writing in different courses over the years, the relationship between content and form, and the importance of discriminating between intellectual ability and grammatical structures.

NEED FOR LONGITUDINAL RESEARCH

The earliest call for longitudinal research came from Emig (1971) in her seminal study of the composing process. In her Implications for Research section, Emig noted:

> Another interesting approach would be to make longitudinal case studies of a given sample of students, following them from the time they begin to write in the earliest elementary grades throughout their school careers, up to and including graduate school. Such an approach would permit far more direct observations by investigators of how writing is taught and learned, with little reliance upon the memories of the subjects and upon indirect evidence of the teaching of composition experienced. More important, it would make better known the developmental dimensions of the writing process, both for the individual and for members of various chronological and ability age groups. (p. 95)

It is my hope that this study will provide some part of the data she requested.

In her pioneering work with basic writers at City College, Shaughnessy (1975) recognized that writing in particular would benefit from longitudinal research:

> Writing is a slow-developing skill that should be measured over longer periods than a semester, but no system for collecting longitudinal data on writing performance exists to my knowledge in any program. We lack information and the habit of getting information about individual students that would enable us to isolate outside influ-

ences such as previous training or career commitments from methods of instruction. (p. 146)

Another early call for longitudinal research on writing development came in 1980 from Bartholomae. In "The Study of Error," he called for research on charting "a sequence of 'natural' development for the class of writers we call basic writers. If all nonfluent adult writers proceed through a 'natural' learning sequence, and if we can identify that sequence through some large, longitudinal study, then we will begin to understand what a basic writing course or text or syllabus might look like" (pp. 267–268). Bartholomae's assumption here appears to be that this natural sequence will be relatively linear. He was correct in calling for such research to find out if such a sequence could be identified and described, but complex factors that have the potential to disrupt sequential learning paths, such as the nature of assignments, challenging or not, previous practice or experience with ana-lytical demands, or personal life situations that might interfere with the amount of time or concentration available to fulfill a task, also need to be considered. These latter factors, concern with how students mediate be-tween their home cultures and the academic culture, were the focus for Bizzell's call for longitudinal research in 1986.

Although they do not call specifically for longitudinal research, issues raised by Hull and Rose (1989) for study of "remediation at the community college, state college and university level" (p. 144) can best be examined through following the experiences of students throughout their college years who start in basic reading and writing courses in these types of institutions. According to Hull and Rose:

> We need further information on what it is that cognitively and socially defines an underprepared student as underprepared. What kind of knowledge does an under-prepared student bring with him or her to the classroom? How is the teacher representing the writing process and the writing task? How is the student, given her or his own background knowledge, representing the teacher's discussion of the writing process and the writing task? What occurs between the two in the classroom as they attempt to negotiate a common understanding of the task, and in what ways might that interaction further define the student as remedial? What happens when the student sits down to write? Researchers have few answers to these questions; there simply hasn't been a lot of research that addresses them. (pp. 143–144)

Through a longitudinal study like the one being presented here, there is time to examine these complex issues and their interrelationship: What actually happens in classrooms both in writing and content area courses? How specific are the descriptions of the tasks the students are asked to undertake? What kinds of responses have students received from their previous writing assignments, and what effect do these responses have on subsequent writing? Under what conditions are students doing their writing (at home—with what kind of privacy and with what facilities, in the library, in a computer center, while at work, etc.)?

Realizing that they must take into consideration the backgrounds and previous experiences of students, Hull and Rose (1989) recognized the need to develop further understanding of how and why students become labeled "underprepared." Finding appropriate terminology to describe or label students who are performing at levels below the norms for their grades at middle or high schools or academic years at colleges or universities has proved to be a vexing problem.

Haswell (1991) summarized at some length the dilemma of characterizing and labeling those students who are not performing as their respective institutions would like them to, students he called "bottom writers":

> One of the curiosities . . . , then, is why so unstratified a block of our population has attracted such a diversity of labels: "slow," "beginning," disabled," "deficient," "remedial," basic," "novice," "developmental. . . ." Are they laggard and in need of prodding ("slow"), fledgling and in need of orientation ("beginning"), lame and in need of prosthesis ("disabled"), lacking and in need of supplies ("deficient"), sick and in need of cure ("basic"), green and in need of expertise ("novice"), poorly equipped and in need of gear ("unprepared"), or immature and in need of catching up ("developmental").
>
> The answer is that bottom writers may not be any of these, or may be any combination of them. What they won't be is any one of them. 'Human cognition—even at its most stymied, bungled moments—is rich and varied,' agrees Mike Rose, warning of the 'cognitive reductionism' toward which each of these epithets lures us (1988, p. 297). Each label stands as a gist of a motive or narrative for the kind of writer who ends up at the bottom of verbal tests or holistic rating: they lack confidence, they fear writing, they are confused with an unfamiliar interpretive community, they trust everything to rules, they suffer from counterproductive cognitive styles, they suffer from a learning disability acquired at an early age, they operate from an inappropriate oral dialect, they are fixed in the security of an immature formative stage and can't cathect [i.e. invest with libidinal energy] or decenter or generalize or abstract or think relativistically or imagine any way but narratively. And, as Rose points out, often the epithet and the single rationale behind it are sanctioned by a single method of evaluation—whether it be a count of clause length, a test of writing anxiety, a spoken protocol, a Perry scheme, a holistic apparatus, or a measure of logical organization. And epithet, rationale, and method feed the interpretive tale that generates a single, monolithic reading. Compounding this danger is the other fact that the error-ridden and unstylish surface features of bottom writing *glares*, shielding the depths where the complexities are. Teachers agree on what constitutes the worst student writing not because they recognize it easily but because they simplify it.
>
> The transformative argues that in most bottom students these negative capabilities are mixed, and are further mixed with positive capabilities." (pp. 277–278)

Teacher-researchers in the Webster Groves, Missouri study of middle school and high school students described their dilemma as they designed curricular changes initially targeted at African-American male students in their schools:

> Amid all the good intentions are numerous signs that we implicitly accepted a "deficit model," locating the problem in the "low-achieving Black students." Soon we referred to "at risk" writers, and at first we saw the term as straightforward and not at all problematical. Gradually, though, we began to suspect that giving kids labels was actually part of the problem. Now when we are forced to identify the students who are the focus of our project, we prefer the term "underachieving" with its implication of untapped potential. But most important, as our research progressed, we began to talk less about "improving the writing of Black students" and more about increasing the cultural sensitivity and multicultural literacy of White teachers. (Krater, Zeni, & Cason, 1994, p. xi)

Researchers at the college level have proposed other nonjudgmental terms such as *novice readers and writers* (Dickson, 1995), or *insiders and outsiders* (Kutz, Groden, & Zamel, 1993).

In her study of freshmen college writers at Ohio State University at Marion, a regional campus offering the first 2 years of college instruction, Dickson (1995) searched for a label to characterize the student population she was working with. "After rejecting potentially loaded terms like *developmental* or *basic writers,* I decided to identify my students as *novice* readers and writers because many of the problems I discuss in [my] book affect *all* readers and writers who find themselves faced with comprehending and producing new and more difficult forms of written discourse" (p. vii). Dickson recognized the need to provide instruction over a long period of time, preferring a full year of reading and writing instruction rather than the two-quarter, 20-week teaching period offered at her campus. She noted that "most novice writers need time to develop: time to absorb what they learn and time to practice their skills. No teacher, no theory, no matter how brilliant either may be, can compensate for the abbreviated writing and reading requirements now in effect in most college[s] and universities" (pp. xi–xii). Even with her progressive plan for providing extensive instruction, Dickson failed to note the importance of the learning that continues after the formal period of composition instruction has ended.

Haswell (1991) also used the term *novice* as part of his characterization of an individual who can be characterized as a learner: "To qualify as learners, students must have a status of novice, nescient and receptive; to succeed as learners, they must achieve some set standard, say, writing three pages of prose that nowhere befuddles a reader" (p. 16). But Haswell argued that this definition is incomplete because it "omits a third term whose presence defines everything in learning anew: *change*" (p. 16). Haswell noted that the status of students change as a course advances. "It shifts again if we are talking about genuine learning and not grade earning, from adept to more adept. Learning so entails change that were the students in a course, even passing students, not to relinquish old ways and move to new ones permanently, their status would still change, from novice to dropout. What always qualifies any determination of status or standard in an act of learning is the sense of growth" (p. 18). This notion of learning as incorporating change is a crucial one, but Haswell appearred to suggest that it can occur in a relatively short time period (e.g., within a specific semester) and that this growth will be primarily progressive. Only through following the same students through more extended time frames and simultaneously in a range of learning environments can this thesis be evaluated.

In their study of first-year college writers at the University of Massachu-setts at Boston, Kutz et al. (1993) distinguish between student writers as "insiders" and "outsiders" (pp. 12–15). The "insiders" are those "who know their way around the university and understand the work that goes on there" (p. 12). When they reflect on their work:

> they know themselves as writers, as learners. . . . They see the shape of the whole project. They can trust that they will "end up somewhere—eventually." They are lost in the process, but only temporarily, and they can trust in the now-familiar experience of being lost and eventually finding a way out. (p. 13)
>
> There is none of the sense here . . . of hours, paper, words being "wasted." These students are patient with their own methods of negotiating ideas, concepts and language and thus can take some pleasure in them despite their intermittent bouts of anxiety. They are not afraid to take risks, to try new intellectual routes. (p. 14)

Understanding when and how to take risks constitutes one of the significant changes that occurs over the college years and is an identifiable charac-teristic of the change from outsider to insider status.

The insiders know their own competence, but "the students who are still outsiders . . . don't know the way out, feel trapped and lost, unable even to see the walls that inhibit them" (Kutz et al., p. 14). Outsiders are frequently first-year students in their first college writing course who are strongly aware of the outside constraints of the discourse situation they find themselves in. Such students may assume that "correctness according to the standards of 'pure English' will provide the most weighty measure of whether [they] have accomplished [their] task" (Kutz et al., pp. 11–12).

Hull and Rose (1989) emphasized the paucity of knowledge there is about how underprepared students go about the writing process:

> The small body of research that exists on what happens as such students try to write suggests that, for them, composing is a slow, often derailed process that proceeds via rules and strategies that are often dysfunctional. But that is about the extent of our knowledge. Teachers receive these students' essays and try to evaluate them and make inferences about what the students learned or didn't learn, what their cognitive capacity is, whether or not they're fit for the institution that already classifies them as marginal. And teachers do so with a pretty limited knowledge of the complex cognitive and social processes that produced the writing they read. (p. 140)

Characteristics of the writers themselves play an important role in how students interpret and respond to tasks (Brandt, 1992; Penrose, 1993).

Penrose pointed out that "students given the same assignment will, in effect, do different tasks—because they differ in reading and writing ability, in prior knowledge of the topic, in how they interpret the assignment, and in many other ways. Sometimes these differences are inconsequential; at other times they are large and important" (p. 56). Brandt's questioning of whether we can "treat all texts as accounts of their authors' reasoning process if authors lack the know-how to display those processes fully or accessibly in public, written language" (p. 350) is particularly germane to the examination of the writing produced by the students in my study since two thirds of the participants originally had been placed in basic skills level writing classes. Brandt suggested that "composition studies would benefit from assuming more competence on the part of the people typically studied. Instead of looking for flaws in [students'] reasoning, we might look instead for the grounds of their reasoning" (p. 350).

Longitudinal research provides the time it takes to get to know students and for them to be willing to share their experiences and the factors in their lives that have contributed in the past and continue to contribute in the present to their ability to respond to the academic demands being made on them as they simultaneously deal with the other claims on their complex lives. These factors are especially relevant in the lives of urban college students whose working lives and family responsibilities impinge strongly on time available to dedicate to the fulfillment of their academic tasks.

One illustration of the kinds of factors influencing academic progress comes from the experience of Ricardo, a Latino student originally from Puerto Rico, who started at the English 2 level at the age of 27. Financial problems plagued Ricardo throughout his years at the college. In December 1991, his third year at the college, he told me that it was becoming more and more frustrating to stay in college and survive. "I am very concerned to keep my academic standards, but cut backs [at the college] have depressed me. I could get 'Cs' with no effort because grades don't mean anything to others, but I do not want to diminish the quality of my own work. I have been on the honor roll for 3 years. But if I can't pay the rent and eat, who cares about grades? Financial aid has become worse, tuition has risen, and faculty can't pay as much attention to students as classes get bigger." Ricardo was forced to drop some courses for one semester to earn more money, but he continued his studies, graduating after 5 years in 1994.

In 1991, Haswell undertook a study of development in writing using data from different students representing different writing levels. He recognized the importance of following the same students over time, noting, "I know of no study that attempts to describe how individual writing styles develop over time. No one has taken the trouble to trace the history of such as the slow writer of Flower and Hayes [1981]" (p. 213). In chapter 4 (this volume), instructors' responses over a number of semesters to individual student writing are presented, thus providing a picture of how instructor comments can facilitate or impede student writing.

After following two case study students at the University of New Hampshire for 1 year, Chiseri-Strater (1991) also acknowledged the need for further in-depth studies of students' experiences. Two of her recommendations relate directly to this study: "[We need] more ethnographies of college students' literacies. I would look at the literacies of students of various ethnic backgrounds in a range of college settings and across the academic disciplines . . . [as well as] an ethnography of one college student, throughout all four years of education, considering every reading and writing assignment given" (p. 166). This study attempts to combine those elements.

Using different population groups as Haswell had, researchers in the 6-year study of middle and high school students in the Webster Groves School District in Missouri recognized that, by studying different students over the years of their study, they could not make meaningful comparisons of "mean scores of different years since the individual students are not identical nor are the prompts [prepared for the assessments]" (Krater et al., 1994, p. 369). Although the target students (African-American students achieving below the class level norms) improved over the years of their study, Krater et al. (1994) noted how they could not draw the same conclusions that could be drawn from true longitudinal research:

> As data from more years accumulates, it is tempting to look for longitudinal growth, to see if the target students improve as they move from seventh to eighth grade, However, since the target students are not the same from year to year, it is impossible to look at the data in this way. Longitudinal growth can't be deduced for all students either, since the prompts are different modes for the two years and different parts of the alphabet participate in the district's assessment each year" [half the alphabet one year, the other half, the next]. (p. 372)

The data in their study indicate that within each single year, the students' improvement on the posttest of 2 points on a 16-point scale brings them to the level attained as the mean for all students at the pretest level. Thus, the students, particularly in the middle school years, instead of "stagnating," are "closing the gap," now 1 year behind their classmates in writing achievement as compared with their previous 1½- to 2-year lag (p. 372). Although group differences may be inferred from such research, it is not possible to assess either long-term effects on individuals of particular instructional practices or the diverse set of developmental patterns that evolve for different individuals.

Flower (1994), too, in *The Construction of Negotiated Meaning*, called for longitudinal research that "could look at the durability of [students'] learning [and] the long-term effects of their newly designed strategies" (p. 256). She made the important point that "Literate actions emerge out of a *constructive cognitive* process that transforms knowledge in purposeful ways.

And at critical moments, this constructive literate act may also become a process of *negotiation* in which individual readers and writers must juggle conflicting demands and charge a path among alternative goals, constraints and possibilities" (p. 2). This process of negotiation became crucial for the students in my study as some sought out ways of making their controversial views acceptable for consideration while others searched for ways to articulate their new understandings.

In her book, Flower posed an important question that she never addressed in the study itself: "How do constraints such as gender, race and class, ideology, prior knowledge, strategic repertoire, goals, and awareness affect [the writing] process?" (p. 106). In her review of *The Construction of Negotiated Meaning*, Sullivan (1995) pointed out the limitation of analyses of writing processes that fail to consider the constraints Flower listed: "[In Flower's study], [t]he 'social' is reduced to context, context to situation, and situation to the immediate, temporally compressed circumstance in which Flower's students find themselves at the moment of inquiry. In *The Construction of Negotiated Meaning*, Flower is asking all the right questions of social constructivism. But her project doesn't answer and can't answer the more pressing questions it raises for literacy education. When the social is shorn from cognition, when gender, race, ethnicity, class, and ideology are rendered invisible to analysis, cognition is made to assume a burden of explanation greater than it can bear" (p. 956). So Flower raised again the questions that Bizzell introduced into the discussion in 1986, but she failed to address them in the study as it was carried out.

That the effects of gender, race, ethnicity, class, and ideology cannot be ignored in a complete examination of the literacy development of students is clearly exemplified by the students in my study. As the brief biographies of the principal students in my study (presented in the Preface) reveal, the students at City College almost all came from family backgrounds that made them eligible for scholarships and loans. They were also highly likely to work, from 4 to 40 hours a week. In a recent study, Lavin and Hyllegard (1996) researched the experiences of cohorts of students who started at City University of New York in the early 1970s, when the open admissions policy began, and those of students who started in 1980. For the students in both groups, working full time was a central factor affecting their academic progress and the likelihood of their earning a bachelor's degree. The students in the 1980 cohort were more likely to be from lower income families, attend school part time because of their work obligations, be forced more frequently to drop courses, and to accumulate fewer credits. Of course, a central factor in the increased difficulties of the 1980 cohort was that tuition was imposed at City University starting in 1975, and the latter group had to cover these costs as well as those for books and living expenses. By the time the students in my study started at City College in 1989, the tuition had increased markedly and the amount of scholarship aid had been reduced further, thus increasing the financial pressures on the students considerably above either the 1970 or 1980 cohorts.

Recognizing then the interwoven components that are involved in describing student performance during the undergraduate years, it becomes clear that only through following the *same* individuals over time, through *true longitudinal research*, taking into consideration the complex factors in students' lives, both personal and academic, will it be possible to determine the combination of elements that influence writing development. Attempts by other researchers to analyze changes over time in the writing performance of students are considered in the next section.

LONGITUDINAL STUDIES OF WRITING DEVELOPMENT

Although there have been many studies of the composing processes of writers at different age and grade levels, most of these studies have concerned themselves with short periods of time (from one or a few writing sessions, to a few days or weeks, or, in rare cases, over a single full semester's time). The first true longitudinal study related to language learning, published by Loban in 1963, was a study of the language of elementary school children. Wilkinson, Barnsley, Hanna, and Swan (1980), in England, also followed the language development of elementary school children, but, unlike Loban, they used different population groups at each level.

Until very recent years, studies of writing development of high school and college students have almost always compared the writing of different students who represent the various age and grade levels. Britton's study (Britton, Burgess, Martin, McLeod, & Rosen, 1978) examined the writing of high school students in England from ages 11 to 18, but separate groups of students' work were studied at each level. Similarly, Hays' study of college students at Skidmore (1983a) examined writing from a developmental perspective, analyzing the writing of different students representing each level. Perry (1968) followed the same students over their 4 years of college at Harvard in terms of their intellectual and ethical development, but he did not specifically investigate the relationship between writing and learning. Freedman and Pringle (1980) compared the writing of students in the last year of high school (Grade 13) with that of students in their third year at Carleton University in Canada in order to define indices of growth in writing development.

More recently, Haswell (1991) examined the writing of students at Washington State University. One set of papers used for analysis were written in class in 1 hour by freshmen on their second day of college classes for their freshman composition teacher (32 students, half male, half female, no ESL students, all 18 years old; pp. 20–21). On the same day, 19-year-old sophomores and 20-year-old juniors wrote diagnostic essays for an advanced composition teacher on the same topic, with the same purpose as the freshmen. This advanced course was required for graduation (p. 21). The topic for both groups was "a well-written essay offering to hypothetical researchers any opinion about one of two familiar subjects, American codes of conduct or American ideals of physical appearance" (p. 20).

Haswell (1991) made a case for choosing unrehearsed impromptu writing as the basis for analysis because "it comes closest to that most common occupational form of writing, the letter or short memorandum occupying less than a page of space and less than twenty minutes of composing time" (p. 223). But he acknowledged that "[i]t would seem better to ask how students and competent employees write under unforced conditions. That question would respect quality, show what a writer *can* do" (p. 222). He defended his decision to solicit the short, impromptu writings because sociological studies "of occupational writing . . . show quality and efficiency of production are rarely separated in the world of work" (p. 223). It is hard to accept this rationale when the writing samples were produced in constrained academic settings without any hint to the student writers that they should even think of the writing that they are generating as being analogous to what may be demanded in the work world. Thus, on two grounds, the adequacy of these samples for analysis of growth in writing falls short: They do not allow the students to produce the best work they are capable of, and they are posited as being samples of writing intended for totally different purposes than the ones for which they were actually produced.

Ackerman (1993) is also critical of the way that writing samples were collected in most of the writing-to-learn studies that he examined: "However, it is fair to ask just how 'extended' these experimental writing tasks are, because most of the essay tasks in the experimental comparisons were composed in one sitting and without collaboration. It appears that the constraints of designing a controlled and manageable study excluded the writing of multiple drafts or writing in more complex, social situations (see Marshall, 1987), models closer to everyday academic writing behavior" (p. 354). Although I agree with Ackerman's critique of the controlled writings as experimental samples, in light of his concern with writing development over time and the importance of considering the effect of institutional contexts on writing, I am surprised that he appears to value samples that could be analyzed in a "controlled and manageable study." It appears more valuable to confront the messy, real-world environment in which writing is actually produced for specific purposes in specific courses.

One example of a student who carefully "psyched-out" the writing situations he found himself in was Jacob, a Korean student, who would seem to be the prototypical insider in the college setting, in contrast with the less prepared students who have often been characterized as outsiders. Jacob received most of his elementary and secondary education in Australia. When his family immigrated there, Jacob was 8 years old. When he began at the college, he was placed directly into the freshman composition course. As described in the brief biography section of the Preface, he told me, in the fall of 1991, his third year at the college, that he knew exactly how to write papers for his college courses: "I read a book, make a long list of quotations, paraphrase some of them and quote others. I stick to what is in the book. I evaluate or give a critical analysis if that is what the teacher wants. I can figure out the teacher's feelings and don't cross him or her if the teacher feels strongly. I can be penalized if the teacher's opinions are different." So, although Jacob goes beyond the "knowledge-telling" strategy that Flower described in *The Construction of Negotiated Meaning* (p. 168), his cynicism toward his college work is evident. But, in the same interview, he acknowledged that he was beginning to see that in order to succeed, he would have to begin working harder. He said, "I have a history of being a 'general Renaissance man' who happens to know a little about everything, but when it comes to greater depth in a specific field, I'm not so confident I can succeed." Thus, Jacob's responses to his writing tasks varied according to the complexity of the demands being made on him. Where the task seemed easy to him, he could follow his algorithm easily but, when confronted with a challenging task, no neat formula existed to guarantee him success.

Haswell (1991) defined "*development*, in its broadest sense, as any human change that both lasts and leads to further change of a similar cast. Development then includes some but not all instances across the entire range of changes: physical accidents, experiential growth, physiological maturation, cultural maturing, skills expertise, book learning" (p. 5). Haswell went on to say that he saw

> writing development as three-dimensional, perhaps best pictured as an ascending spiral. It is not just an inner, maturational growth nor just an outer, social acculturation, nor even the interaction between the two, but an educational life-process or lifework composed of three main forces or vectors, all on the move. Where the developments of student, field of writing, and teacher meet and are furthered by the meeting, there genuine educational development takes place. (pp. 5–6)

From the intertwining of these perspectives, the relationship between development and longitudinal research can be seen most clearly. These factors can best be examined in the real settings of college courses where the instructional approach (as viewed through classroom observations), the teaching demands (as viewed through assigned tasks in different disciplines), and the students' stance and abilities (as viewed through interview data and written papers) can come together to provide fuller pictures of the complexity of writing development.

Through longitudinal research, it can be seen how individual students adapt and adjust themselves to the fluctuating currents in their own lives and the shifting requests made of them. For example, when financial problems become great and students have to work long hours at outside jobs, some find themselves unable to devote as much time to their studies as they would like to. Some even find themselves dropping out of the college temporarily. Other students, at considerable personal sacrifice, reduce their working hours so that they can devote the time they feel they need to their assigned tasks. As students progress into their major areas of study, the level of course work demanded of them increases, and they recognize the need to allocate more time to their assignments. Teachers, by their instructional approaches and the depth of their curricular demands, affect the students' engagement and commitment to the discipline. Some instructors may value "information transfer," while others encourage students to work toward critical analyses. All of these factors are variable in a given semester, in a given discipline, in a given moment in the students' life situations. Through longitudinal research, it is possible to see development as it occurs in relation to the factors affecting real students in a real educational setting. Development will be seen to be muddled, progressing at some times and regressing at other times. One or two of the factors posited by Haswell may dominate at one moment, while others play the central roles in specific settings. As Haswell's metaphor of the spiral suggests, development implies improvement, but time is required to identify the steps through which this improvement occurs and what factors can facilitate this direction.

Ackerman was skeptical of the way development is defined in relation to writing and learning at the college level: "First, developmentalism, as it describes the growth of child to adult does little to capture the socialization process of higher education. Universities, for better or worse, are defined by disciplines and specialties, with the mission to introduce students to domain specific literacies and intellectual customs. . . . Second, the insistence on writing as a unique mode of learning and expressive writing obfuscates culturally specific literate practices" (p. 350). He cited Ogbu's research (1978), which rejects "linguistic-deficit explanations for why Blacks fail in school" (p. 350). Rather, Ackerman posited the idea that cultural norms are assumed in writing to learn practices (p. 351). Students whose cultural values and routines differ from these norms may find their practices unacceptable in a particular classroom setting.

The experiences of Ricardo, the Latino student who started at the English 2 level, illustrate how cultural differences, including language patterns, affect the progress of students through their academic trials. Ricardo had had most of his early education in the Spanish language in Puerto Rico. In middle school, he had done a little writing in English "but not much effort was put into it." Although he had aspirations to become a physician, after his parents divorced and he was sent to live with his father, he was forced to enroll in a vocational school to study photography where he did little writing. At the age of 16, he started classes at a community college, but, unmotivated and using drugs, he was not successful there. He had wanted to go into a premed program, but he was refused admission because he had

had no chemistry in the vocational high school. His later ambition to become a physician was also thwarted because of the huge financial obligations required, and he eventually enrolled in a physician assistant program.

Because his education in Puerto Rico had not provided him with a good background in writing in English, Ricardo suffered from difficulties with sentence-level problems when he entered City College. He told me in the spring of 1990 that "one of my biggest drawbacks is that I can't transmit what I'm thinking in writing. Correctness of form is the problem, not lack of vocabulary." In a discussion of interlanguage development, Gleason (1995) explained how second-language students in an academic environment feel pressured to produce academic prose style, thus complicating their ability to express complex ideas effectively:

> What interlanguage development research suggests for writing instructors is that a writer's informal style is more systematic and in that respect a better indicator of the person's language acquisition while more formal styles represent a more complicated interweaving of writing development and language acquisition issues. The planned, more formal modes of writing will introduce new linguistic structures and rhetorical strategies and also new opportunities to lose control of written language forms—an outcome that may result from the dynamic interplay of factors such as complexity of cognitive task, test-taking or writing anxiety, and deliberately attempting to use a new language style ("academic discourse"). (p. 18)

The difficulties these pressures may have caused are highlighted by Ricardo's many attempts at passing the Writing Assessment Test (WAT), a college-wide (and City University-wide) writing test required before completion of 60 credits. He took this test eight times and, although his ideas were complex and well-thought out, he kept failing because of grammatical difficulties.

Some samples from Ricardo's attempts at passing the WAT over 5 years reflect the complexity of his thinking, his sense of social justice and political activism, and how his difficulties with producing the acceptable grammatical structures in a testing environment affected his score. In the initial placement test that resulted in his being assigned to the English 2 level, he wrote on the topic of "Winning isn't everything":

> I don't agree with the emphasis that this society place on winning. By placing so much energy and effort on just that, what they create is individualism; wich in noway helps the basic structure of society. A society is created by the effort of many and if you just from and early age teach children that they should win at any cost you are misguiding the future of the country itself. They don't develop that spirit of cooperation with each other; People won't get involved in issues that are important since they will not have anything to win & why bother? . . .
> Society should put more emphasis on cooperation. We must teach our childrens that teamwork is just as important as just winning. If everybodys works together don't you think we could make this a better world. I'm sure we could; and I hope we will.

Despite the difficulties with subject–verb agreement, spelling, and punctuation, Ricardo's intellect shines through in this first effort at producing acceptable academic prose. His use of syntax is remarkably strong, but the reviewers gave him little credit for that. In his second try at passing the WAT, Ricardo came closer to passing than in any of his subsequent efforts until his final success on the eighth attempt. In this second writing, at the end of his English 2 course, one rater gave him a 3 and a second rater gave him a 4 on a 6-point scale. (He needed a total of 8, 4 from each rater to pass the test.) If the third rater had given him a 4, he would have passed the exam, but he was given a 3 by that person. (The scale of the WAT is given in Appendix B.) On the topic of whether New York City should increase the subway fares or close the system down from 1 to 5 a.m., Ricardo concluded his argument that "the labor force cannot afford this rate increased either" by writing:

> I feel that any new fare increase will be unfair. That they won't solve the deficit in the public transportation system. The general public is being penalized by the inability of the MTA [Metropolitan Transit Authority] to find ways of making the system efficient at a reasonable cost to us.

Looking at the response to this exam question, it is difficult to understand why Ricardo failed to pass the test. A large part of the problem that he had in passing the WAT was that the readers of the exam were adjunct instructors in the English Department, most of whom at that time had no background in composition studies or second-language development. Students were assumed to be competent native speakers of English even though the population at City College was at least half non-native speakers of English and one quarter second-dialect speakers. I am not arguing here that students need not be competent users of formal writing style, but that considerations of language development are central to coming to a rational assessment policy. Because raters (representatives of their institution's unstated policy of "standards") are not cognizant of the changes that occur *over time* in language development, they are frozen into demanding perfection from the very beginning.

Ricardo's next five attempts to pass the WAT earned him total ratings of 6 consistently, both readers agreeing each time that he had not produced a passing paper. In one of his attempts during his second year at the college, he argued against the proposition that homework should be reduced because "it will created a double standard in the educational system that will affect in a very negative way the validity of our degrees." Despite the fact (which he pointed out in his paper) that he was a full-time student while working 20 hours a week in an inflexible work schedule, he opposed diminishing the academic requirements. Instead, he wrote, "The solution should come from the government. As a way of subsidizing the students and allowing us to study without pressures. When we graduate we are going to pay back with our work in society." This thoughtful response did not earn him success.

In his fourth year at the college, Ricardo responded to a question in the WAT about the treatment of homeless people in shelters in New York City. After graphically describing a personal visit he had made to a homeless shelter in a large armory in the city, Ricardo concluded his paper by writing:

> As a conclusion, I will like to say that I agree with the premise that homeless people should and must have the freedom to live any place or anywhere they wish. The visit to that shelter convinced me that the solution offered by the government is not the right one. Yes, they are homeless with mental problems and they must be given the proper medical care, But it must be provided in the proper environment, and not in a made up facility that may be more dangerous to them than our city streets.

This paper also received a failing grade.

So what was so different about the paper he wrote on October 10, 1992, the beginning of his fifth year at the college, that suddenly earned him a passing grade? The topic he wrote on was whether college education should be treated in the same way as public education at lower levels. Here is the section that I believe finally won him success:

> Also, as many more students from poor economic backgrounds achieve their educational dreams they will become role models for those coming after them.
> I will be an example of this. I am currently a pre-medical student and I am working two jobs to make end means. As a result of that my GPA which until now was 3.51 is going to drop, because I am not studying as often as is needed. I come from a poor family that cannot afford to help me financially. If my college education was part of the public education system I would not have to work two different jobs and I would have more *"free time"* to dedicate to my school work.

The reader here can judge whether the quality of Ricardo's thinking, so evident in his earlier attempts at passing this exam, is significantly different or whether his grade point average citation was impressive enough to overcome previous objections.

In his last semester at the college, Ricardo filled out forms in a stress management course he was taking that asked for lists of experiences that caused stress, the physical and psychological reactions to the stress, and the means of coping. One of the "stressors" Ricardo listed was taking the English Proficiency Test (required for graduation from the college). He cited his physical reactions as being "a rise in [his] blood pressure and heartbeat." The psychological reaction was anxiety. As a means of coping, he stated he would "talk about it, prepare. It will go away after taking it." He noted that he also used "images of waves and sound of soft music" to cope with the anxiety. The obvious stress of continual test-taking in writing was clearly having an effect on Ricardo, suggesting that Gleason's observations about stretching for appropriate academic prose would likely inhibit Ricardo's natural use of language. On his second attempt to pass the proficiency test,

Ricardo wrote an impassioned paper on the topic, "Is It Worth Immigrating to the United States?" He first described some of the hardships that he as an immigrant endured, and then he presented the advantages of his decision to come and remain in this country. Although his paper still contained some verb form lapses, his essential argument apparently won over his reader. His conclusion gives a sense of his paper:

> I want to conclude by saying that I may not like what I call a money base society. I do say to many of my friends and family that if I have to do it all over again, I would not hesitate. The level of maturity not only intellectual, but also emotional that I have reach is worth every single one of my last eleven years in the United States. If someone ask me if they do it? I say Yes! But be aware of who you are and above all don't loose the ties with your past. That's in many instances is what going to keep you going. It's worth it!

The sentence-level problems evident in so much of Ricardo's writing continue to be in evidence in this test-writing. Nevertheless, the passion of his ideas shines forth, and that may account for this paper receiving a passing score. These examples of Ricardo's stressful pathway through the college's required writing exams highlight the difficulties that students whose cultural values and routines differ from the mainstream suffer as they struggle to overcome the hurdles frequently placed in their path by assessors who are not competent in understanding issues of language development central to the students' possibilities for success.

Although Haswell's major emphasis (1991) was on growth between the writing produced in freshman courses and the writing produced in advanced writing courses, he did analyze the development of the freshmen writing from the beginning to the end of the semester, the one true longitudinal aspect of his study since the writing of the same students was examined. There is some difficulty, though, in assessing even these changes since the papers came from only some of the sections represented in the full study and the final papers were written for a grade rather than a diagnostic purpose (pp. 315–316, footnote 1). Haswell found that the "main concerns of the freshmen at the end of the course seem to be length, support, and explicitness" (p. 317), not surprising "[s]ince these concerns were the writing tactics the course probably emphasized" (p. 317). Freshmen students were found to improve most in support and organization, least in ideas (p. 315). There was an increase in comma splicing, rote five-paragraph themes, simple collection organization, and stative as opposed to process verbs (p. 316). "Higher production is achieved along with some simplification of organization, fuzziness of word choice, and increase in error" (p. 316). These and other changes led Haswell to conclude that there is a trade-off between features that teachers seem to value and regression in features such as syntax and no improvement in ideas (pp. 315–317). The absence of improvement in ideas serves as a cautious warning to composition instructors who emphasize instruction in form more than in content. Characteristics of essays that changed from freshman to sophomore or junior year included organization, specificity, coherence, diction, syntax (Haswell, pp. 23–24).

In 1989, Wolcott (1994) began a 4-year longitudinal study of reading and writing of special-admissions students at the University of Florida. Of the original 139 students who began in the study, 6 participated throughout the full 4 years. Five of these were African American (four females and one male) and one was a White female. Students were paid $25 to $35 each year for participating in the study. Data collected included one 50-minute essay written late each autumn using the Hoetker and Brossell (1986) paradigm (e.g., "a book/that many students read/that may benefit them beneficially"). At the same time, students also took a standardized Nelson–Denny Reading Test and completed a questionnaire on their reading–writing practices. During the last year of the study, students also took a multiple-choice test of writing skills, identical to the one they had taken their freshman year for placement, and met with the researcher "for an interview about their reading and writing experiences rather than completing a questionnaire" (p. 17).

Wolcott recognized the limitations of her study: The number of participants was very small, consisting of self-selected students. (This limitation extends to my own study but, as in Wolcott's case, whether you start with 139 or 53, as I did, you have no way of knowing at the beginning which students will continue throughout the entire study period.) A more serious limitation to her study is the nature of the writing samples that were collected, one on-demand, 50-minute writing once each year. Wolcott acknowledged this problem: "It did not allow students to engage fully in the writing process with multiple drafts or with access to resources. Moreover, the use of one essay cannot be considered a reflective measure of any student's overall writing ability since it is limited to one mode and one opportunity that may be marred by chance circumstances" (Wolcott, 1994, pp. 17–18). Another limitation of this methodology, of course, is that the writing is obtained in a sterile, purposeless environment, unlike writing that is assigned through real academic tasks.

Wolcott noted that she was troubled by whether the payment influenced the students' participation: "How motivated they were to do well on each test or writing sample remains unknown" (p. 18). In my study, I had no financial resources to pay the students who continued to participate beyond the semester they were in my classes. My hypothesis for an important reason why those who remained continued to do so is that they were proud that they were doing well or for some, surviving, in the college and they wanted to share that pride with someone who knew them well. Over the years, I wrote many letters of recommendation for the students, some to colleges where they sought to transfer, and others to recommend them for jobs or scholarships they were applying for. I was a rare individual who knew the students well in a largely impersonal setting where students who have work and family responsibilities have little time to get to know their professors or to participate in extracurricular activities, and where faculty are burdened with large classes and increased teaching loads.

Wolcott also acknowledged that she would have been better off to have collected writing portfolios from her students, had she known that so few would persist throughout the entire period of the study. Of course, the writing portfolios would have provided a more representative view of the writing that her students actually were called on to produce. So, even without anticipating what the final numbers in a research population will be, it is advantageous to collect the best possible material from the very beginning. (Appendix A presents a detailed discussion of the methodology of this study and the questionnaires used in the student interviews.)

The analysis of the writing produced in Wolcott's study revealed that the four students initially appearing the weakest made some small gains or remained the same. The improvement for the weaker students was "neither consistent nor linear" (pp. 23–24). The two students who were initially screened out of the developmental writing course scored lower in each of the following 3 years than in their original assessment (pp. 23–24). When the essays were scored analytically, using a scoring guide that addressed rhetorical elements of thesis, organization, development, content, diction, grammatical elements of sentence style, sentence structure, and usage and mechanics, improvement again was found not to be linear (pp. 24–25). But Wolcott's most interesting finding, in relation to the controversy over whether writing fosters learning, supports the view that writing does foster analysis: "There was no steady progression of analytic scores for any student. Nevertheless, all students showed an improvement in total analytic scores from the first paper in 1989 to the last paper in 1992" (p. 25). It is not necessary to argue for neat, linear improvement to demonstrate that writing fosters critical thinking when an extended time frame is examined.

As can be seen from this review of writing development through a range of study types, much can be learned from examining the actual writing of students at different points in their educational experience. But much more can be learned from following the same students over time and incorporating the complex factors in their lives into an analysis of their writing development.

RELATIONSHIP BETWEEN
WRITING AND LEARNING

One of the central issues in examining the relationship between writing and learning has to do with how *learning* should be defined. Some studies define learning as recall (primarily of facts), others as the ability to organize and synthesize information, and still others as the ability to apply information to the creation of new knowledge. Another issue that has been raised concerns the appropriate time in the educational sequence when writing becomes useful as a tool for analytic learning. Examining these issues through a longitudinal study can help determine when and how writing becomes most useful for different kinds of learning. After reviewing the issues raised by researchers who have looked at the relationships between writing and learning, I provide examples from my students' work over the years that will illuminate the usefulness of writing as a means of developing complex reasoning strategies for use in new learning environments.

Reviewing a series of earlier studies, Langer and Applebee (1987) concluded that "any manipulation or elaboration of material being studied tends to improve later *recall* [italics added], but the type of improvement is very closely tied to the type of manipulation" (p. 92). In their own study of ninth- and eleventh-grade students over 3 years, Langer and Applebee found that note taking and responding to study questions facilitated the remembering of discrete facts and that analytic writing fostered better understanding of concepts and relationships between ideas, although students' ability to recall particular information from the source text was more focused and thus more limited (pp. 130–131).

Newell and Winograd (1989), in a reexamination of the data collected in Newell's 1984 study, concluded that both responding to questions and writing analytic essays enabled students "to *recall* [italics added] the overall organizing frames of the original passages more often than when they engaged in notetaking" (p. 210). Recall of gist was best fostered by analytic writing. Newell and Winograd also found that note taking was least effective for recall, suggesting that simply "translating" information in prose passages into lists of facts does not lead to the building of relationships among ideas (p. 206). These studies then suggest that writing leads to a higher level of recall, that of meaning, rather then just the remembering of discrete facts.

The relationship between writing and learning has been examined frequently from a cognitive perspective. Spear (1983) argued that "cognitive development follows a hierarchical sequence of stages [, which] suggests that a curriculum can be sequentially organized to promote cognitive development" (p. 47). This belief resembles Bartholomae's (1980) idea, noted earlier, that learning may follow a natural developmental sequence. This perspective could be supported more strongly, assuming that students were neatly exposed to gradually more challenging tasks, were it not true that other factors inside and outside the instructional setting affect students' abilities to carry out the tasks assigned to them. Schumacher and Nash (1991) also believed that the varying kinds of cognitive operations writers engaged when doing different types of writing tasks account for the different kinds of learning. I do not intend here to minimize the importance of appropriate sequencing of tasks that challenge students to practice more complex reasoning strategies, but do need to point out that this is not the only factor in the learning situation that must be taken into consideration.

Studies emphasizing the importance of cognition to the exclusion of other factors have examined discrete academic tasks with little knowledge of the writers, except for their level of prior knowledge about the topic being addressed. Such limited background information about the writers makes it difficult to assess the basis of their reasoning because of lack of data about what Brandt (1992) called "cultural resources" (p. 350). Brandt offered a definition of *prior knowledge* wider than simple background information. She defined it as "methods of experiencing, methods by which a person 'rounds out' an isolated event so that it can appear sensible, typical, normal or whole" (p. 329). This approach led her to define a sense-making model as one that "can capture wider cultural considerations that writers should attend to, considerations that arise from sources other than a particular writer–reader relationship or the rhetorical exigencies of a particular occasion" (p. 350).

Berlin (1988) also critiqued strictly cognitive models of rhetoric, noting that their scientific orientation reinforces a meritocracy of the middle class wherein a body of knowledge is constructed that supports current expertise in the marketplace. In place of this model, Berlin proposed a social–epistemic rhetoric in which knowledge "is an historically bound social fabrication rather than an eternal and invariable phenomenon" (p. 489). Writers then seek out an understanding of their own selves, building a "social construct that emerges through the linguistically-circumscribed interaction of the individual, the community, and the material world" (p. 489). Such an approach argues, then, that characteristics of students' lives such as race, class, and gender need to be factored into an assesment of their responses to varied tasks and disciplines. These issues are considered in detail in chapter 3.

Citing research on middle and high school students by Copeland (1985), Langer (1986), Langer and Applebee (1987), Durst (1987), and Newell (1984) and on college freshmen by Penrose (1992), Geisler (1994) argued that writing is not useful as a way of acquiring specific knowledge and that students who use analytic writing rather than other study methods will perform more poorly "in answering questions requiring simple recall and application" (p. 46). Drawing on a review of the literature in the field of writing and learning by Schumacher and Nash (1991), Geisler concluded that "analytic writing is not a good way for students to acquire the kinds of information routinely tested in school" (p. 47). She did, however, acknowledge that "if students are required to make significant selections and transformations of knowledge, extended writing may be of benefit" (p. 47). It is surprising that Geisler's critique of writing as a way of learning discrete facts does not support critical analysis as the appropriate goal of instruction in schools at all levels.

Although I do not have writing samples from my students prior to their college work, their responses to the college tasks suggest that they would have benefited greatly from opportunities to practice analytic writing during their high school years. This lack of practice in writing was apparently not compensated for by instruction in strategies for taking examinations that addressed knowledge of "facts." Thus, students had been short-changed by a lack of preparation both for test-taking and writing. The students repeatedly told me that taking short answer or multiple choice quizzes or exams at the college did not provide them with sufficient opportunities to demonstrate what they understood and what they had learned. The students themselves were dissatisfied with the regurgitation of "accepted facts." (This issue is discussed more fully in chapter 2.)

According to Geisler, it is only in late undergraduate school or in graduate school that students begin to understand that "texts are now seen to have authors, to make claims, to be acts that can be understood only within a temporal and interpersonal framework. Some issues are hot, some issues irrelevant, some issues settled. Some authors are credible, some discredited; some irrelevant. People write texts not simply to say things, but to do things: to persuade, to argue, to excuse" (p. 87). Geisler claimed that "development does not appear to be the result of any direct teaching but rather the result of hours of individual effort at hands-on problem-solving" (p. 86). Although this is likely to be true, it downplays the role of writing assignments designed to foster analysis and synthesis that prod students to engage in the complex reasoning processes required to fulfill the tasks, the factor emphasized by those who focus on cognition as the most salient factor in learning. The teaching environment cannot be ignored; neither can it be raised to an exalted or exclusive status.

In her 1992 study, Penrose asked 40 college freshmen to read two source texts and to write a report on one and study for a test for the other "using whatever study strategies they thought were appropriate" (p. 470). The order of the two experimental tasks was counterbalanced. The students had 1 hour for each task and they provided think-aloud protocols in both conditions (p. 470). Penrose found that "the advantage of studying over writing on simple recall was consistent across the two passages. Students were more likely to remember individual facts from their reading if they had directly studied the text than if they had written an essay about it, suggesting that writing may not be the best choice of learning activity when the goal is simply to gather factual information" (p. 476). The larger question remains: Should learning be considered the accumulation of factual data without questioning or analysis?

Penrose (1992) discussed the problem that students' "written notes were not a good indicator of their level of engagement with the task" (p. 486). She cited Durst's (1987) study in support of her findings: "[He] observed a similar contrast between students' protocol comments and their written texts in his study of analytic writing. He reported that students frequently made connections 'in their minds' that did not appear in their analytic essays" (Durst, 1987, p. 373), a gap that he attributed to the "difficulty of analytic writing and students tendency to rely on more familiar narrative forms" (p. 486). Another explanation for this difficulty may be Brandt's concern (1992) that some writers may have difficulty expressing their complex thoughts in formal, written language.

The difficulty of assessing students' responses to writing tasks is highlighted by Penrose's 1993 report of her 1992 study of freshmen students' responses to the same writing assignment. She interpreted the range of responses to suggest that students who paraphrased the source text might have been "able to answer factual questions correctly but be unable to recall the author's main idea or author's argument. Students who wrote analyses should be better able to answer questions about the author's point of view or the type of evidence used in the argument" (p. 64). In his review of writing-to-learn studies, Ackerman (1993) was critical of those studies that preferred "quantitative measures, such as factual recall, over more qualitative measures of knowledge change" (p. 355). In this longitudinal examination of student writing, preferences for specific responses to tasks regardless of the assignment (e.g., paraphrase or summary even if analysis is requested) have been found, as has been found a developmental ability (even if not neatly linear) to learn to respond to more complex reasoning demands through analysis and synthesis. When students responded with descriptions, for example, when analyses were called for, instructors frequently prodded them to reflect more deeply on causes and reasons for behavior or ideas they were examining. Such prodding helped students move beyond their initial responses to higher levels of critical thinking.

What is surprising and disheartening about Geisler's analysis of the value of extended writing for precollege students is her disdain for the important role that writing plays in transforming knowledge. Her review of the literature rewards the value of what she calls "the standard knowledge-transmission purposes of the schools" (p. 48) as the acceptable way of acquiring knowledge in the precollege years, rather than gradually acquiring the ability to evaluate and synthesize ideas presented through reading and writing activities. If one believes, as I do, that the value of education lies in the ability to learn to question "facts," then the transmission model at every level subverts the true purposes of education. If analytic writing can be shown to foster questioning and critical examination of ideas, then its value becomes apparent. Students need to practice these processes from the earliest phases of education.

Support for this perspective comes from Dickson's (1995) study of college freshmen at the Marion campus of Ohio State University. Dickson contended that college instructors value inquiry and design tasks that will push students into this perspective:

For the academic, *inquiring,* if not completely synonymous with *learning,* represents the first step in constructing knowledge. The students who choose to enter the academy cannot escape the necessity of engaging in inquiry. And here the struggle begins. Novice writers and readers resist inquiry; their teachers resist received knowledge. Because the goals of the instructor and the goals of the novice student seem too removed from one another for learning to take place, students and teachers seem at an impasse. Eventually, however, students who refuse to accept the need to question and inquire about all phases of experience will lose—the teachers set the rules in the context of the academy. (p. 33)

Kutz et al. (1993) believed that "it is full participation in the work of the academic community that will enable [students] to learn to think and write in the ways that are valued there" (p. 55). They argued that "just as it is not through memorizing forms but through engaging in meaningful conversation that people acquire new ways with words, it is not through learning facts but through thinking, working with others, and having the opportunity and the need to perform certain intellectual operations and see things in new perspectives that people come to value their own knowledge and to acquire new ways of thinking" (p. 55).

Haswell (1991) noted that teachers examining the papers of the students in the advanced composition classes he studied (sophomores and juniors) at Washington State University may be disappointed that the student papers do not have more concreteness. But he pointed out that the teachers may simultaneously be failing to see that there is a "presence of complex ideas" (p. 38).

In 1987 and 1988, at the University of New Hampshire, Chiseri-Strater (1991) followed two students for a year through a common upper level prose writing course and separate courses in art history and political science. The instructor of the prose writing course told Chiseri-Strater that "We will use reading and writing to find out what we have to say—what we think about a subject" (p. 4). Social interactions and revision were built into the course. However, in the political science course, Nick, one of the case study students, treated each paper "as a separate assignment, a completed product, finished and then abandoned" (p. 110). Chiseri-Strater concluded that Nick cannot use writing as a way of learning "because he does not invest in the process of revision" (p. 110). Linking revision to the ability to use writing as a way of learning highlights the difference that reflection can play in extended writing while not occurring in note taking or responding to assigned questions, particularly those of a factual nature. (Some students in my study used note taking in a more complex way, as is discussed in chapter 2.)

Ackerman (1993) has been skeptical about the value of "writing to learn" because he believes that the British model of Britton and others has been translated too literally into the American educational system in both "process writing" and Writing Across the Curriculum adaptations: "The

British model grew out of a specific culture, time, and educational setting and was intended to liberate, through the exercise of self-expression and discovery, students and teachers in British school systems. In translating this model, writing specialists in this country found in it their own linguistic and semiotic biases by claiming the uniqueness of the technology of writing, the inevitability of learning as its companion, and the value of personal discovery" (p. 361). Given the increasingly diverse student populations, Ackerman believes that "the challenge remains to link process instruction and cross-curricular instruction and research with institutional, disciplinary, and cultural practices" (p. 361). These diverse student populations will often find that learning "result[s] in conflict, not harmony" (p. 361) and that different disciplines "may differ in important ways from the communicative competences and values of students" (p. 361).

Many of the examples of student writing cited in this study will illustrate precisely the role of conflict in the writing of the diverse student population at City College. Whereas Ackerman pointed out that learning results in conflict, it is also true that conflict results in learning. When students took up issues that clashed with their own experiences and their sense of social consciousness, they were moved to produce elaborate analyses to support their views. Student examples of such writing are presented in chapter 3.

Although not explicitly calling for longitudinal studies, Ackerman (1993) noted that "the host of advanced, abstract, intellectual skills promised by 'strong text' advocates will come only with time, repeated effort, and social confirmation" (p. 362). An empirical examination of this thesis can best come from an analysis of the writing produced by individual students over extended periods of time, particularly those from a diverse set of backgrounds. Ackerman also supported the importance of investigating "a different model of writing and learning: more social than developmental, more situational than conceptual, more tied to activity than knowledge" (p. 362). This study attempts to address these concerns through a broader examination of the context of the students' experiences, both the personal constraints they faced and the academic environments in which they participated.

Penrose (1993) proposed "four key variables in the relationship between writing and learning: the type of learning desired, the nature of the material to be learned, the nature of the writing task, and characteristics of the writers themselves" (p. 53). Penrose's analysis agrees with Geisler's review that "writing holds far greater potential as an opportunity for higher level learning than as an aid to factual recall" (Penrose, 1993, p. 54). When the writing tasks were connected with difficult source text material, writing proved to be more effective than simply rereading and studying for high school students (Langer & Applebee, 1987; Marshall, 1987, cited in Penrose, 1993, p. 54). Noting the many studies that examined the effects of analytic writing (e.g., Durst, 1987; Langer & Applebee, 1987; Marshall,

1987; Newell & Winograd, 1989), Penrose concluded that "the assignment we develop is a critical variable in the write-to-learn process, and it is the only variable the teacher can directly control. These early findings suggest that the type of writing assignment we choose to give our students will—to some extent—determine the type of learning they engage in" (p. 55). A longitudinal study of the type presented here provides a unique opportunity to examine the same student's response to a wide range of assignments over an extended period of time. Thus, evidence can be presented that illustrates the varied responses to varied tasks and the varied responses to similar tasks over time. For example, in an earlier paper, the case study of Linda, an African-American student who started at the English 1 level (Sternglass, 1993) was presented. Linda wrote a range of papers in several different courses about the role of women in society. In relation to a paper for an upper level psychology course, Linda told me: "The more I wrote, the more I understood what I was writing about" (p. 248). Similarly, a White male student in Krater et al.'s study (1994) told his teacher that "surprises were frequent: Things pop into your head as you're writing and you just put it down. Sometimes you can make something really good just with a really crazy idea" (p. 399).

Over the period of their college years, students reported in interviews that they came to realize that writing provided them with opportunities to rethink and reexamine their understandings of complex reading materials and writing tasks that had been assigned to them. The interviews and papers reveal that students used writing in the ways that writing and learning studies have pointed to: to help them remember facts and meanings, to analyze concepts, and to construct knowledge that was new to them, even if not always new to the discipline. Students' growing metacognitive awareness of the role that writing plays in learning is presented in the next chapter.

CONCLUSION

Studies that have looked at writing development and the relationship between writing and learning have contributed important insights in these areas. But none of these studies has combined the factors brought together here: (a) examining writing and learning on a true longitudinal basis, that is, following the same students; (b) studying a multicultural urban population; (c) examining the relationship between writing and learning by probing papers written over time for regularly assigned academic courses across a range of disciplines; and (d) taking into consideration nonacademic factors that influence academic performance.

Only through examining the interrelationship among these elements can we see the true complexity of writing development. We need to look in greater detail at the experiences students bring to their college years, as Hull and Rose (1989) pointed out, as well as the changes that occur during the college years. We need to consider how academic preparation, personal life factors such as working hours and family responsibilities, instructional settings and approaches, and the nature of instructional tasks interact as students respond to the writing demands placed upon them. Only then will it be possible to present the true complexity of writing development, nothing that will likely fit into a neat flow chart.

2

Developing Metacognitive Awareness of the Relationship Between Writing and Learning

In chapter 1, the three most commonly cited ways that writing is viewed in relation to learning were briefly described: writing to help remember facts and meanings, writing to foster critical thinking through analysis, and writing to construct knowledge new to the learner. The claim was made that these ways of using writing to foster learning did not develop neatly nor linearly for students. In this chapter, the factors that influence and shape these different uses of writing are presented.

CHANGE FROM UNCONSCIOUS TO CONSCIOUS USES OF WRITING

In an earlier book, *The Presence of Thought: Introspective Accounts of Reading and Writing* (1988), I drew on the research of Ericsson and Simon (1984) to make the argument that the reports of graduate students at Indiana University describing their reading and writing processes could be considered both valid and reliable. One of Ericsson and Simon's points about the ability of students to report on their reading and writing strategies is germane to this study. Ericsson and Simon noted that if individuals are experienced in carrying out particular types of tasks the processes may become automatic and not accessible to conscious examination and verbalization. Thus, there must be attention paid to the process before the individual will be able to report on its use. Like the proficient graduate students described in my earlier study when they had tasks that were not challenging, the students in the present study had also internalized the processes by which they initially responded to the reading and writing demands made on them, using their prior experiences with similar tasks as models. However, unlike the graduate student population, the City College freshmen were not adept at producing responses to the assignments that gained them approval. It was when the students began to realize that they would have to change their approaches that writing became a more consciously complex tool in their academic arsenal.

Flower (1994) also recognized the significance of bringing writing strategies to conscious awareness:

> *Literate action opens the door to metacognitive and social awareness.* . . . First, seeing literacy as action lets us focus instruction on the points of conflict that make writing problematic—on those moments when a student's personal goals, available strategies, or history as a writer come in conflict with the expectations of a reader or teacher, the practices of a discourse, or social and cultural conventions. Some conflicts are public and social; others go on within the mind and goals of the meaning maker in the inevitable play of competing possibilities. By making such points of tension a subject of inquiry, we might better help students understand and negotiate the circle of possibilities, constraints, and expectations they face.
>
> Secondly, this view of literacy asks students to step back from their own decision as writers and develop great *metacognitive awareness* of the discourse practices they are entering, of how those practices differ, of how they as writers switch among them, and the strategies they use. Texts and their conventions are no longer rules and formulas, but tools writers use and options they can take. Metacognition allows writers to reflect on the choices they made.
>
> Third, we can encourage writers to step back even further and see how their rhetorical actions are themselves situated in the larger circle of social and cultural assumptions, some of which can empower a writer and some of which, as unexamined language and unquestioned premises, exercise tyranny. Reflecting on one's own thinking and actions within this broader context is, in part, an ethical act. It is a way to recognize the structures of authority that shape our meaning making and to resist the patterns of racism, sexism, and prejudice that are shot through those structures. Such reflection is also a means to empower writers who feel excluded; it opens a search for alternative ways of constructing one's world and for seeing the authority of one's own voice (pp. 27–28).

The students in my study reflected on the ways that writing affected their learning as they advanced through their college years. There was development within the categories of remembering, analyzing, and discovering, as well as development between categories. But, again, none of this can be pictured as sequential. There were too many factors involving the experiences of the individual students to paint a simplistic picture. Factors previously mentioned, such as the nature of the task or the student's particular work–life situation at a given time could influence progress or regression. Considerations of issues of racism, sexism, and prejudice occurred frequently in their responses to assigned tasks as will become evident through excerpts of the students' writings presented throughout this book. (Particular attention is paid to these matters in chapter 3.)

Over time, students became more able to articulate what the role of writing was in helping them understand the increasingly complex reading materials they were assigned and the increasingly demanding analytic tasks required of them. In this chapter, I present examples of their verbalized insights and examples of their responses to the writing tasks assigned to them.

In his study of the writing development of college students at Washington State University, Haswell (1991) pointed out the significance of students' coming to an awareness of their present writing strategies before change could begin: "For writing to advance, old and less mature procedures must be made conscious" (p. 146). Haswell also cited Perry, for whom "'meta-thought' is the most critical moment in the whole adventure for both student and teacher" (1981, p. 85), "when the learner uses reflection to break free from an old automatized and hence unconscious frame" (p. 146).

WRITING TO HELP REMEMBER FACTS

A familiar refrain heard from students in the study was that writing helped them remember facts and ideas. This assertion seems to contradict Geisler's claim, discussed in chapter 1, that writing is not a useful way of acquiring specific knowledge. Instead of placing analytic writing as an obstacle to learning factual information, the reports from the students present a more complex picture. Writing appears both to help students remember hard facts and to simultaneously assist them in seeing the relationships among the facts and ideas, thus facilitating the practice of analysis. Students did differentiate between studying for exams that they knew would ask for short answers and preparing for exams or papers that would require the application of more complex reasoning skills. Interestingly, the weakest students preferred to take examinations that required extended written analyses or the opportunity to write prepared papers over the taking of multiple-choice or short answer exams.

Students who started at all the different levels of composition instruction recognized that the opportunity to write papers or responses to questions in essay exams provided them with much better chances to demonstrate their knowledge to their instructors than short-answer quizzes or exams allowed. Support for this understanding comes from a study of 10th- and 11th-grade African-American students from inner-city Minneapolis schools carried out by Oliver (1993). Oliver argued that even students who performed poorly in areas such as reading comprehension, vocabulary, and mechanics should be provided opportunities to demonstrate their capabilities through writing (pp. 2–3). She found that her students' writing capabilities surpassed those that might have been expected from their "skills level" work (p. 12). She noted, "If given the opportunity to write, instead of being judged by indirect measures not relevant to composing activities, students will often surprise us in most positive ways" (p. 12). Similarly, White and Thomas' (1981) study found that minority students performed poorly on multiple-choice usage tests while in an essay test their writing was distributed along the whole range of scores.

Although Oliver's study was aimed at convincing prospective teachers of the necessity of including writing in the curriculum, the insights she fostered for the teachers came over time to the students in this study. In her fourth year at City College, Linda, who had started at the English 1 level, said: "I do better on exams that require writing. I can break things down, show the teacher I learned. I'm writing and telling them, this is what I know." In almost the same words, Joan, who was in the initial English 2 class, told me at the end of the fall semester of her sixth year at the college: "Writing helps me learn because I just know how to write a format in a paper. I stick to my concepts; it helps keep the thoughts well organized—the structure. I used to have trouble getting my thoughts together—how to get away from paraphrasing and putting thoughts in my own words. When I write papers, it helps me get better grades. I might have a midterm 'C+,' but a paper gives me a chance to develop my own thoughts and prove myself more." And, at the beginning of the spring semester that sixth year, Joan added: "Writing helps me 'regurgitate' back what I learned, not to mimic back to the professor but to apply what you learned from readings. . . . Writing helps me remember things because I have to apply concepts." In her third year at the college, Audrey also pointed out the difference for herself between preparing for examinations and writing papers: "There is more thinking involved in writing papers than in taking exams. Papers allow me to select something of my own interest to write about."

At the college, Jacob continued to use a technique he had developed in high school, what he called "revision," the condensation and summarization of material he needed to study for exams in his courses. In a journal entry for a freshman orientation course in his second semester at the college, he wrote about the differences between preparing for short-answer exams and those requiring more analytic responses, thus calling into question Geisler's view that writing is only useful when preparing for more analytic responses. Jacob's comments illustrate that writing is useful for both, but the types of preparation would differ:

> I had my first quiz today, a sociology one, and I fear I did not do very well. I think it was in part the fault of the teacher though because his choice of questions was poor (he seemed interested only in stumping us with peripheral questions outside the textbook and ignored entire huge areas of central importance we had gone through and which I spent the bulk of my time revising). As well the test, which was supposed to be multi-choice in format, had several diagram and open-ended questions which were worth a lot of points. It would have been better if he had warned us of these because the whole process of revision drastically changes depending on whether the test is open-ended or closed-ended.

As the insights of these students illustrate, exams that equate learning with memorization of discrete facts leave many students frustrated when they feel they would be able to demonstrate their level of understanding, their ability to see meaningful relationships, and their discovery of new insights much better through opportunities to write analytic papers or take essay examinations. Multiple-choice test questions were most frustrating for students who frequently felt the test choices were either deliberately selected to be confusing or were on obscure points.

At the end of her first year at the college, Linda began to recognize that writing could be helpful to her. She said, "My classes require a lot of thinking. I think, but not as deep as they want you to. I have to clear my mind and get serious, think about what the teacher wants. For example, What is Communism? What were they trying to achieve? I didn't have opinions before. I can express myself more in writing. I can go back to revise, especially introductions and endings. I write a draft, see something that doesn't sound right; I have to change the phrasing to make it clear." In the fall of her second year, Linda was staying close to the language of her texts. For a world humanities course, she wrote a paper on *Sundiata,* using definition as a way of responding to the task of what constitutes a warrior: "A warrior is loved and hated. He is considered a hero to some, an enemy to others. A warrior is also considered a special man because he is protected by the gods. The warrior is a man that is feared and respected. A man whom I admire and consider a great warrior is Sundiata." By the end of her second year, Linda told me that writing papers gave her the opportunity to demonstrate to her instructors what she had learned far better than did short-answer examinations. She said, "Writing helps teachers discover more about a person—how mature the student is and what the student is learning. I consider that I've progressed. I like the writing and the progress I'm making. Teachers like the points I make—I come up with new ideas." In a paper Linda wrote for a women's studies course at the end of her second year, she questioned the depiction of heroines in children's fairy tales:

> Take our classics such as Little Red Riding Hood, Sleeping Beauty, Snow White and Cinderella. These young, virginal, fair-haired, white-skinned women who were considered epitomies of beauty were always the scared, gentle, feminine, shy and quiet types. They were never strong women who could protect themselves. A man was always present to save "screaming damsels from distress." Women in these stories were never encouraged to bond as a strong group. Instead, they are pitted against each other with strong and disturbing hatred which lead to the demise of the other female.

The women's studies course provided Linda with opportunities to assert her identity as a strong African-American woman who would not allow herself to be diminished by the stereotypes of society. In settings like this, Linda's background enabled her to assert authority in her judgments. Soliday (1996) stressed the importance of encouraging students to build bridges between their own cultures and the academic culture.

In her second year at the college, Joan said that writing helped her understand ideas better, but at this point writing and speaking seemed to be exactly the same. Writing helped her get her thoughts on paper while her brain was filled with many ideas. Her major mode of writing was to supply definitions in response to examination questions, carefully using the language of instructors or textbooks. For example, in a paper for a sociology course during her second year at the college, Joan wrote: "Sociology is referred to as the systematic and objective (scientific) study of human society and social interaction. Sociology is more or less the study of interaction within groups in society. A sociologist never studies an individual. He or she may observe or study an individual's interaction within a group or groups." As has been noted by Belenky, Clinchy, Goldberger, and Tarule in *Women's Ways of Knowing* (1986), Joan was relying on "received knowledge," with authoritative definitions her basis for response. Writing helped her remember these definitions, but she was not yet ready to go beyond them. At this point in her education, Joan was still using writing to help her memorize points for examinations.

The complexity of using writing as the basis for transitory memorizing was described by Jacob, who told about his experiences in preparing for examinations in Australia while he was a high school student. In a journal entry written for a freshman orientation seminar in his second semester at the college, he wrote:

> I dislike doing work and I always leave things to the last minute so I have a lot of experience tackling tremendous amounts of revision [his term for writing concise summaries] in a pitifully short period of time. I remember high school when I used to take all the notes of two years worth of classes for a subject and revise them during the fifty minutes ride to school and the ten minutes before the exam began. I systematically focus on the points I feel is important and cram them into my mind by repetition. Using this method doesn't let you "memorize" anything but it can stay in your mind for 10 minutes which allows you to get into the exam hall and write them all down before you forget them.

Although I would not wish to make an argument that real learning has taken place in this setting, nevertheless the student must be able to expand knowledgeably on the items or ideas listed through his efforts at condensation, or the process would not have been worth the effort to begin with. So the "revision" activities have served more than one purpose, allowing him to have the key terms available for responding to examination questions and seeing the required relationships between these terms and ideas. Otherwise he could not have decided which ideas were the most important ones.

Other students also described the role that summarizing ideas played in helping them to remember information and to understand it better. In an interview in his third year at the college, Carl said: "Writing helps me remember material better. If I'm having problems, I try to write in a concise form. That helps my understanding." Joan, too, recognized this relationship between remembering and understanding. In her sixth and last year at the college, she told me: "Writing helps me understand the material in my courses better because when you write, you get a chance to gather your thoughts as you're writing. Hearing, you don't always interpret it in the right way. The mind is flowing in writing and developing thoughts and you won't forget them."

Students saw these relationships between remembering and learning in more complicated ways over the years. At the end of her freshman year, Delores said, "Writing makes you get more into the subject and then remember more about it." By the fall of her fourth year, she saw writing as playing a more complex role in her learning: "Writing helps you conceptualize more. When you dedicate time to task, you become more attached to it. You remember more after you've written something. You read about something, you can't remember it, but if you write about it you can explain it more, structure it more." And in her fifth year at the college, now enrolled in the combined BA/MA program in psychology, she noted: "When I write, it's visual. Information gets more to my brain. I'm able to comprehend more when I do research on a topic. Once I do a paper on a topic, the information is there forever. It helps my memory."

The role of note taking has frequently been downplayed as a significant factor in learning because it is assumed that students simply use the notes taken from lectures or textbooks to study rotely for examinations. But students have not usually been asked what they actually do with these notes when they prepare to study for exams or to write papers. Some of the students in my study made a clear distinction between the taking of the notes and the preparation of the notes for use in their academic work. The most striking distinction came in discussions about the difference between listening and analyzing with the claim being made that these two processes could not operate simultaneously. For example, Jacob told me in the fall of his fourth year at the college, "Especially in my physics courses, I write as the professor talks and hope to make sense of the notes from class later. I integrate these notes with material from the textbook and rewrite the notes. Rewriting helps me understand better. In order to write it out, I must organize [information] in my head. The process of writing forces me to understand. I have to have some idea myself." Ricardo made a similar point in an interview at the beginning of his second year. He emphasized the importance of his having learned to take notes on lectures without immediately analyzing the ideas. He said, "Later I analyze and think about it. I don't miss out on information that way. Analyzing interferes with listening."

He said that in his world civilization course, he would write out answers to the questions at the end of the chapters and then read the material over to make certain that the answers were right. He took notes in all his classes and reviewed them on the subway train to class. He developed the habit of making analytic notes about the informational notes he had taken in class. He used these notes to review for exams and for writing papers. So, both Jacob and Ricardo were starting with what Jacob had earlier called *revision* when he described his method of studying in high school. The step beyond the informational note taking to the analytical stance moved note taking beyond its traditional role of information transfer.

A crucial transitional point for students in the study came when they recognized the importance of being able to take textbook or lecture "jargon" and translate the ideas into their own language. In her first year, Delores noted, "My writing is too repetitious. I need to vary my vocabulary. I take notes from textbooks and lectures." At this point, her sense of repetition in writing was limited to word-repetition. By her second year in the college, Delores was still having problems with repetition, but by then she recognized that the problem concerned a higher level of thinking: "I'm learning through doing research. Writing makes me put things in my own words. I find myself restating ideas rather than developing them." One of her instructors had specifically pointed this problem out to Delores in responding to a paper she had written.

Two crucial realizations grow out Delores' comments. Writing research showed her that she had to pursue greater depth in her thinking, leading to awareness that she had to develop ideas rather than restate them. Second, and perhaps most crucially, she was beginning to recognize that she had to move beyond a dependence on textbook or instructor formulation to putting ideas into her own words to demonstrate to herself that she under-stood the difficult concepts being presented. Almost all the students in the study articulated this important concept to me at one time or another. Hayes (1990) pointed out, "Only when the words of others are translated and transformed through the thoughts, words, and syntax of the individual mind do those first words become truly original thoughts" (p. 9). Other examples of students who shared this insight with me include Ricardo, who said at the end of his first year, "After reading a chapter, I have to write notes to show that I understand it," and Linda, who said in the spring semester of her second year, "I formed my own sentences so I could understand what the author was saying. Put it in your own words. If you don't do that, you have a problem." Donald, a student placed in the freshman composition level, told me in the spring semester of his third year, "I find that textbooks are professional and full of jargon. I break things down in my language. Then I summarize it. Then I understand it much better." And in the spring of 1991, her second year at the college, Chandra said: "Writing [something] down and explaining it back to the professor means I know it. Writing in class and outside helps me know something better. It provides a test of my ability to explain something. Putting ideas in my own words is a test for me."

This process of translating technical language or jargon into the student's own language appears to be the transitional link between using writing as a means of memorizing or remembering material, perhaps best used for short-answer quizzes and examinations, to using writing to promote more active learning. What needs to be stressed here is that the varied uses of writing in academic settings demand different cognitive strategies, and only when students are required to go beyond textbook or instructor formulations do they begin to see writing as a useful tool for analysis. But this development is neither neat nor linear, and it is strongly influenced by the demands placed on the students. Writing can become the tool that moves students beyond regurgitating uncritically the material that has been presented to them; it can begin to provide the basis for assessing one's true understanding of the complex ideas being encountered. This is the crucial step toward using writing for analysis.

WRITING TO HELP ANALYZE CONCEPTS

Various ways of characterizing "growth," "development, "maturity" in writing have been proposed. Haswell (1991) described what he characterized as "the normative steps with which the craft in the *field* of writing is acquired, given the ways mentors instruct and students appropriate today's discourse goals" (p. 297):

> As writers continue applying the trade of writing in college, they gradually move toward more fluency, flow, and literary self-assurance. They shift toward a more technical vocabulary. They build on a growing meta-cognitive awareness of certain techniques, such as enhancing readability or shaping introductions and conclusions. Other tactics become more automatic: explicit coherence slowly gives way to tacit, concentration on form loosens with a greater attention to ideas, closed organizations yield to more adventurous and progressive ones. Certain concerns precede others: ideas move in advance of syntax, errors precede mistakes, the testing of new repertoire in organization and vocabulary attracts before the polishing of old repertoire. Everywhere writers progress toward a grasp of greater complexity: clauses, sentences, logical segments, and essays grow in breadth and depth. Writers move from a more piecemeal or hard-wired facility with discourse toward a fuller and more integrated one. And all along, regressive sequences take place: final free modification grows along with comma splicing; bound modification increases along with embedding and reference errors; students quicken their writing pace and raise their rate of production mistakes, attempt more midstream improvisation and write more awkwardly, focus more on ideas and less on specificity. (p. 298)

The writing of the student population in this study evidences many of the characteristics Haswell presented. In particular, since two thirds of the population started at one of the basic writing levels, it is not surprising to find that surface errors continue to appear, especially when students confront complex ideas. As Brandt (1992) pointed out, such student writing needs to be given extra consideration in attempting to determine intent as well as clarity in conveying meaning. Development, in other words, reflects simultaneous progress in confronting complexity and potential for regression in stylistic features.

Haswell (1991) was cautious about the underlying assumptions of a frame of growth and realized that questions must be posed and examined: "Is the change [over time] adopted by the students a change in the right direction? Up to this point, I have avoided words implying that the natural development of students is necessarily a change for the better, words such as *advancement, progress, improvement.* Growth may not be unlearning or deterioration yet may still be warped, or misguided, the students mislearning" (pp. 61–62). Or, is growth not neatly linear, as factors such as complexity of task, instructional settings, and students' lives affect academic performance?

Analytic writing has been presented by researchers as having a variety of characteristics. In this chapter I cite some of these characteristics and illustrate them through excerpts of student writing. "Peter Elbow (1991) describes as central to his concept of academic discourse 'the giving of reasons and evidence rather than just opinions, feelings, experiences; being clear about claims and assertions rather than just implying or insinuating; getting thinking to stand on its own two feet rather than leaning on the authority of who advances or the fit with who hears it' " (p. 140, cited in Kutz et al., p. 35). Analytic writing demands appropriate evidence and thoughtful interpretation of that evidence.

In a midterm take-home exam for U.S. Society 101, in the fall of 1991, his third year at the college, Jacob responded to the following exam question: "Do you think European–Indian relations could have turned out differently than they did? Whatever position you take, provide a convincing explanation." After discussing the early Spanish and English encroachments on the lives of Natives Americans, Jacob turned to how cultural differences brought about the conflicts between the English and the Native Americans:

> Once firmly entrenched in the new land, the [English] settlers who had remained faithful to their original purpose by continuing to look for new sources of wealth, discovered tobacco. One of the Native American contributions to the Europeans, it changed everything. While before nothing more than trading posts were needed to utilize the economic potential of the land, now the more land they cultivated for this new crop the more wealth they would gain. And tobacco needed more land than other crops since it quickly used up the nutrients of the soil. The English discovery of the tobacco was inevitable, since it was widely used by the Native Americans, and once they had established it as a source of capital there was little to dissuade them from encroaching steadily on Indian territory.
>
> How could they take the land that belonged to the Indians, one might ask? Might they not have had the scruples to restrain or at least limit their greed? Alas the promise

of wealth was more important, and besides this fact there was also the genuine problem of cultural differences between the two people on both sides. Anytime two cultures meet, there are bound to be misunderstandings and misrepresentations as people judge others by their own standards. The English though the Native American as being a lazy hunter. Since hunting was regarded as a sport and not real work, who oppressed the women with field labor that Englishwomen were not expected to do. The Native Americans on the other hand considered fieldwork the duty of women, and considered the English rather feminine for occupying themselves with it. What was most important of all however was the idea of property ownership. For the English, property was a piece of personal possession that one could fence up or sell as one pleased. The Native Americans on the other hand had no real personal property but shared land with other tribes at different times of the season according to need. And since the Native Americans were more hunters than farmers, and the English did not respect hunting, it meant that they did not regard taking over seasonal hunting grounds as being equivalent to stealing what rightfully belonged to someone else. Only land cultivated designated property owned, because they had done something with the land to change it and mark it as their own.

Following Elbow's criteria, Jacob provided the evidence necessary to support his analysis of the conflicts between the English and the Native Americans. Perhaps his own cultural transactions, first in Australia and then in New York City, sensitized him to the potential for cultural misunderstandings.

Jacob described his approach to writing such papers in an interview the following semester. "When writing a paper," he said," I write about a specific thing. I have to know it to write about it. I can hide problems in my writing; it is more planned than speaking. When I write, I can pick a calculated way to present my ideas through my editing. I often don't plan ahead—I just plunge in. I try to do just one draft as a matter of pride." Jacob also said that he felt lazy and wanted to use the least effort he could to get by with. He felt pressured by his family, especially his mother, to get high marks. For Jacob, college "wasn't really the place to learn information." He said he preferred to read novels on his own. He told me that he had been writing a novel and had completed seven chapters and a draft of the whole novel. Now he was rewriting the novel because the original was rough and compressed. He needed to flesh the ideas out and convert each chapter to two chapters. (The novel was later submitted to several publishers but not accepted by any of them.) The short stories and poetry he shared with me were consistently dark, almost morbid.

Kutz et al. (1993) proposed three ways of thinking that are necessary for students "to make any sense of what goes on in their classrooms" (p. 52): analytical thinking, dialectical thinking, and figurative or metaphorical thinking. A series of papers written by Chandra over the years illustrates the first two of these types of thinking.

"Analytical thinking allows students to appreciate the nature of a proof when it is offered to them, to do classificatory thinking, to see the implications of the things they are reading and learning about, to see the importance of providing explanations, and to appreciate the fact that they are being offered explanatory material when they read" (Kutz et al., pp. 52–53). Analytic thinking also allows students to "conceive of the nature of theories and to take critical stances with respect to them: to identify the elements of an argument, to recognize which parts are premises and which conclusions, and to see the relationship of evidence to those conclusions. It enables students to devise strategies for solving problems" (p. 53).

In a midterm exam for World Humanities 103 in the spring of 1992, Chandra explored the meaning of *war* for the Greeks. After explaining the causes of the Trojan war and how Achilles came to be involved in it, she concluded her paper by considering how Homer ended *The Iliad*:

> *The Iliad* ends here, an odd ending, indeed. If a reader was seeking an ending with a strong closure and an ending of this disastrous war, he or she was disappointed. However, thematically, the ending has resolution. Achilles discovers that although we are all autonomous individuals with our own goals and desires, our decisions coincidentally affect the group in which we are a member. Individualistic as they were, the ancient Greeks saw war as a part of life. War was not fought for "just causes," as twentieth century wars are fought. War was an opportunity to advance personal gain. Achilles and the gods in *The Iliad* were a direct reflection of Greek society. Everyone sought self-worth and the way one went about it became irrelevant. At the end of *The Iliad* Achilles discovers that he played a destructive role in the Trojan War because he could not see past his own anger. However, by then it was too late because the damage was done.

Neither hostile nor sympathetic to the character of Achilles, Chandra demonstrated her ability to see the implications of the reading, to "go beyond the information given," as Bruner (1973) described this kind of thinking.

Dialectical thinking, according to Kutz et al. (1993), "allows people to see one position in relationship to another, to see from different perspectives, to respond to different contexts, and to tolerate ambiguity and multiple meanings. It encourages an appreciation of complexity and controversy, of challenge and dialogue. It also supports reflexivity and an awareness of the self as knower" (p. 53). "Context sensitivity is one of the most important aspects of this kind of thinking" (p. 53).

In only her second semester at the college, in the spring of 1990, Chandra demonstrated in a psychology paper the open mindednes s and reflexivity that characterized her thinking and her writing. She carried out an experiment in her psychology class on the topic, "Does Gender Have an Effect on a Person's Helping Behavior?" She assessed the credibility of her findings in the conclusion to the paper:

> I don't think the results of this experiment [on gender behavior] was accurate enough for us to determine the answer to the initial question. As an observer, I found it difficult to be unbiased and completely unprejudiced throughout the experiment. I tried to obtain general answers from the students but I think my own prejudices interfered. I

connected their responses with their personality without taking any of their situational influences into account. I tended to imply if they were helpful they were kind and if they were not helpful they were unkind. Possibly I committed the Fundamental Attribution Error: the tendency to overstate other's dispositional influences and underestimate their situational influences. Whether the students' responses were due to what previously occured to them, their personality or the manner in which I sought their help I cannot determine. It could be possible that my efforts to eliminate situational influences was not accurate enough, therefore we cannot come up with any facts.

Her harsh self-evaluative analysis of her methodology in this study demonstrates the open and honest approach with which she undertook all of her studies. She was able to adequately distance herself from her methodology to present her report objectively.

Chandra's communication course in ethics at the end of her third year made a strong impression on her. In an interview on February 27, 1992, she told me that she loved the course, but she was discovering that "there isn't always a right answer to every question." She said, "I can't react emotionally but have to critically think things out and come up with a rational answer. This course makes me question my beliefs—it's challenging." In a paper titled "Death Watch: An Invasion of Privacy?", which she wrote for the ethics course, she considered how a television program intruded on the privacy of a young woman with a terminal illness without obtaining her permission. The producers of the program publicized the woman's reactions to her personal tragedy:

Legally, Catherine could have sued this television network for [appropriation]. The NTV representatives did not take into account the impact that their invasion [of privacy] would have upon this individual. The Network used Catherine's name and picture in their billboard ad, strictly for their own purposes. They wanted ratings and more viewers, using immoral tactics to achieve their goals. They pretended to have a legitimate concern for Catherine, saying "the public needs to share this time with you," but it is clear that they did not. Supporters of Kantian's theory, the deontological theory of moral duty would say that a person's privacy should never be invaded for the sake of the sensational. This act was illegal and therefore it should not have been committed. If one approached this dilemma from a teleological perspective, the ethically correct decision would be the one that produced the best consequences. First of all, a person's private business is not the public's concern and therefore it would not produce the best consequences for the public nor Ms. Moman. Finally, if one tried to come to a conclusion by using Aristotle's "Golden Mean" theory, he or she would discover that the only median would be to ask the dying individual if he or she would like to be a part of their program. If he or she declines, then they should respect that person's privacy and leave him or her alone.

In this excerpt, Chandra demonstrated the context sensitivity integral to Kutz et al.'s (1993) idea of dialectical thinking as well as the willingness to challenge the decisions made by the media executives. (Carl and Ricardo also took this ethics course and critiqued the media in papers that are excerpted later in this chapter.)

The third kind of thinking Kutz et al. (1993) proposed is figurative or metaphorical. It is the kind of thinking that may occur in narratives and sees "particular events or things as pointing to something else" (p. 53). Figurative thinking involves diving "beneath the surface of experience and pull[ing] out meaning" (p. 54). Kutz et al. believed that the significant difference between this kind of thinking and analytical and dialectical thinking is that "it is problem *finding* in nature, rather than simply problem *solving*" (p. 54). This type of thinking will be considered in the next section of this chapter on constructing knowledge.

Chiseri-Strater (1991) is sensitive to the problem that occurs when the ability to do close reading of assigned texts is "an 'assumed' college literacy skill, based on very little evidence of students' reading abilities, and with no guidance offered on how to accomplish this" (p. 160). She highlighted the problems that arise when a mismatch occurs between an instructor's assumptions and a student's fitness:

> The traditional assign/evaluate model presumes that reading is a purely cognitive, meaning-based activity, rather than an affective and social process. Most college coursework disregards the social aspects of reading, implying that interpretations of texts take place in isolation, ignoring students' background knowledge as an aid to making meaning and discouraging students from working together to construct meanings from texts. Little personal interchange about the course readings even takes place between the teacher and the student; instead, instructors offer their interpretations or readings without much disclosure of how these were arrived at over time. (p. 161)

The problem with understanding complex readings can be clearly illustrated by examining papers that Linda wrote for world humanities courses two years apart. At the end of her first year at the college, Linda expressed the view that she was still having difficulty in doing academic tasks: She reported a problem she was having in a freshman psychology course: "I'm not certain what the teacher wants. I didn't use concepts in analyzing the story in the way they wanted." This difficulty carried over to her first level world humanities course in the fall of her second year. She had serious problems with reading the required world classics even at a literal level. As described in an earlier paper (Sternglass, 1993), Linda was unable to explain in a written assignment how it was that Macbeth became king. She was confused by the actual events within the play and, in this instance, could not write her way out of her dilemma. She was unable to recall factual information correctly, and she apparently was not receiving the amount or kind of instructional support she needed within the classroom (p. 254). She wrote:

> In the play *Macbeth* by William Shakespeare, Macbeth wanted to become king. In order to become king, Macbeth had to get rid of Banquo who was in line to become king. One night when Banquo and his son Fleon [sic] were traveling the roads, some thieves came upon them. Banquo was killed but Fleon escaped somewhere else. Since that event happened, Macbeth was given the title of king.

Although her instructor corrected the factual information in her paper through his comments, it was clear that Linda's difficulty with reading had been at the level of frustration, rather than the level of challenge at which she might have had a better opportunity to engage with the material. In such a situation, writing could not overcome the difficulties. Linda was suffering because she was not receiving assistance at what Vygotsky (1978) called the "zone of proximal development," in which she would have gained knowledge from proper instructional assistance.

By the time Linda took the next level of world humanities, in the spring of her fourth year, she was much better prepared to analyze complex literary works. She explained that by then writing was helping her comprehension of assigned reading materials: "With writing it's easier for me [to understand the material in my courses]. I can explain things more easily in writing than in talking. You can remember things more. It's like an outlet." In an essay exam on *Pride and Prejudice*, she responded as follows to this question: "Indicate four or five themes you consider to be present in the works we have read. EXPLAIN WELL. DEFEND YOUR ARGUMENTS":

> The five themes I considered present in the work are love, spite, pride, boredom, and escape. . . . In *Pride and Prejudice* by Jane Austen, *love* took on a meaning in two different ways. In one incident, love was only for status, wealthy prestige. Yet, on the other hand one had actual love from one person to the other. For example, Lydia really loved Wickham. Even though Wickham didn't have the same feelings for her. Elizabeth finally fell in love with Darcy when she saw Pemberley. *Spite* also played a role in Elizabeth acceptance of Darcy's proposal. This occured because Lady Catherine didn't want the marriage to happen and she insulted Elizabeth very badly. Because of Elizabeth's *pride*, she didn't accept Lady Catherine's venemous threats and counter-attacked her for insulting her family's name. The woman who did get married wanted to do so because they wanted to *escape* their family life. They never realized that their cycle of *boredom* would continue after their marriage.

In contrast to her inability to make sense of *Macbeth*, here Linda asserts her authority to select appropriate themes and to support her claims with evidence from the novel.

For Ricardo, as for others who took the ethics course in the communication department, the course provided students with opportunities to examine cultural and social issues and come to their own conclusions. In the spring of his third year at the college, Ricardo wrote an analysis of Spike Lee's film, *Do the Right Thing*, drawing on his own background knowledge and experience:

Do the Right Thing presents an excellent study of media stereotypes. The director, Spike Lee claims to be a different kind of filmmaker and that he brings a new vision to Hollywood cinema. In the movie he presents one stereotype after another. His depiction of women as defenseless, or as in the case of the Latina, he used the old Hollywood extreme stereotype of either too hot or too virginal; in this case she was hot. His portrayal of the Black males included the Black Coon (Radio Raheem), the drunk (Ozzie Davies), and the handicapped (a stutterer). The young Latinos hanging in front of their building drinking and listening to music is also a stereotype. From the very beginning we are presented with one stereotype after another.

. . . The ethical dilemma is: Was it ethical for Spike Lee to use all those negative stereotypes in the making of this movie?

A stereotype is defined in the book as a "fixed mental image of a group that is frequently applied to all its members." Starting from this point, Spike Lee already has the responsibility of not using stereotypes that will perpetuate the preconceived ideas that his audience may already have. By portraying most of his characters [as] these stereotypes he reinforces and perpetuated those ideas which in turn robs whole ethnic groups of their dignity and humanity.

In many of his writings over the years, Ricardo revealed a sense of moral outrage when he felt members of racial minority groups or women were being denigrated. But, in a sign of his maturation as a writer, here he had learned not to use language that would alienate his readers. Rather, Ricardo shaped his style to influence his readers on the suitability of his views. At the beginning of his fifth year at the college, he spoke to me about how his awareness developed that he had to change from a confrontational style to a more reasoned one:

I do revisions of everything I write . . . I'm writing—listening and analyzing. I write and then I read it over and try to make sense of what I wrote. I am much more careful, more careful about presentation—what I write. My ideas must be good, relevant. I watch syntax and grammar. My style is not as confrontational as I used to be. I present ideas in a more subtle way. They are better received. My words are more carefully chosen. One professor said my words are too political. He suggested I should find different ways of saying things. That is working better.

Joan attempted an analysis of Nora from *A Doll's House* in a paper in her fourth year at the college. She told me in an interview about the role of writing in this world humanities course. She said, "The professor is a very worldly person." She felt that the way to succeed was to have good structure in her writing and expand her vocabulary. The task was to decide whether Nora was entitled to a divorce from her husband. Joan included some thoughtful analysis of the relationship between Nora and Torvald: "Torvald not only stripped Nora of her pride and dignity as a person, but he also assisted in the degrading of her character by taking advantage of her childlike ways." The instructor admired this insight and wrote "nice" in the margin. Joan inserted her own opinion about the relationship when she stated: "Moreover, to deprive a mother of contact with her children is appalling to me. Torvald phorbids his wife to even physically look at her children which is downright cruel." Applying first an analytical and then a subjective stance, Joan both understands and identifies with the problems of Nora. Since Joan's most important relationship is with her mother, who encouraged Joan's efforts to get a higher education despite the dismal lives of many of the other children in the family, it is not surprising that Joan is repelled by the idea of children being separated from their mother. In a poignant interview in her fourth year at the college, Joan described how she tried to reciprocate her mother's support and encouragement by teaching her five new words each day.

In a paper for World Art 101 on *The Joy Luck Club* in the fall of 1993, her fifth year at the college, Joan drew on the concept of empathy (from her psychology classes) to ground her analysis of the film: "the filmmaker wants us to empathize with the mother, by observing her, not as an antagonist, but a victim of circumstance, as she sees no choice but to abandon her children, hoping that someone would have the heart to help return them." Had Joan taken this core course in world art earlier in her academic program, she would not have had psychological terms to assist her in her analysis. Her instructor is pleased with the insight and writes "good" in the margin of the paper. Again, Joan's sympathy with the dilemma of the mother is highlighted.

But seeing the improvement in analytic writing as a pure developmental process is muddied by what actually happens in different instructional settings. Two papers, both written in the second semester of Delores' freshman year, illustrate how different tasks can bring out different levels of response. In a paper written for an introductory philosophy course, Delores explained some ideas of Henry James, while staying carefully close to the academic language of her texts:

> In his piece "Pragmatism," William James discusses the truth of ideas. In his work, James made a mere distinction between pragmatists and intellectualists view about the truth of an idea. For intellectualists, as James describes, the truth of an idea is an inert and at the same time stationary property of an idea. Intellectualists supposition is that once an individual has reached the truth of anything the process of searching for the truth is discontinued.

It seems likely that Delores' unfamiliarity with the concepts of the philosophy course motivated her to protect herself by incorporating the text-jargon into her paper.

In a paper written for her freshman composition course that same semester, Delores ventured further into an analytic stance. Writing about Orwell's "Shooting an Elephant," Delores offered her own interpretation of the effects of subjugating others on the "tyrant" himself:

Orwell says, "A tyrant needs to wear a mask." Orwell in his essay "Shooting an elephant," is referring to the kind of behavior that the tyrant must display in front of the people they oppress. Even though they might as well behave differently following their own feelings, they have to behave as expected by the people. Even though tyrants subjugate the people, in some way or another they are also subjugating themselves by having to let feeling [be] suppress. And at the same time robbing themselves.

While clearly hostile to the behavior of the tyrants she described, Delores also revealed a compassionate sense of understanding the impact of such behaviors on the individuals involved in such acts. Although not yet deeply involved in her major of psychology, she possessed a sense of empathy that would assist her in her future studies. And, in a composition setting in which the primary readings were literary ones, critical interpretations of such texts were highly valued.

By the end of her third year at the college, Delores was writing longer and more analytical papers for her psychology courses. She wrote a lengthy paper on the role of social support groups in the individual's life in which, as part of the paper, she explored the roles of race and gender on an individual's ability to function in the society:

> . . . Thus far, we have seen the influence our immediate social support groups have on our health (psychological and physiological health). But it is not only our immediate social support group influencing our health, the group to which we hold membership and the status in which our group is regarded by society also influences important [aspects] of our lives. Our membership in groups which are regarded as high "status" or "low," "inferior" or "superior," influences the way we feel about ourselves and by the same token influences our health . . .
>
> Through the history of the United States, we have seen how different groups (Native Americans, African Americans, Jews, and Latinos) have been the victims of racism, prejudice and discrimination. Research have shown these minority members as having significantly lower self-esteem when compared with members of the majorities. Ethnic identity has prove to be very crucial in the reversing of negative prejudice against one's group and developing positive evaluation of oneself and that of the group. Therefore, we can clearly see who we are is a direct function of the groups to which we belong.
>
> Silverstein and Perlick studied the effect of holding a minority status in the mental health of the individual. They studied how being a woman and the perception that women are minorities affected women. Their study is [particularly important] because contrary to the common belief that gender inequality would affect women who are the most limited by their status, they found that women whose desire was to excel in male dominated fields were the ones who experienced the real effect of gender inequality . . .
>
> Society has denied women prestige—being regarded in high status, the scarce resources men usually possess. Women have also being denied the opportunity of excelling academically. One could ask oneself, what happens to the little girl who is told she is to keep herself clean, who sees that her beloved daddy gives more attention to comments of [her] little brother than hers [when] they are talking. What happens to the adolescent who encounters herself with the sad reality that if there is money to

go to college, it is her brother who will go. In a company, a woman sees the position she has been waiting for years after the retirement of her supervisor was given to a man who is less experienced than her. . . .

We have seen how important are support groups to our well balance as individuals. In the work of Silverstein and Perlick we saw, once again, how the presence of a good support could protect oneself from the diseases and psychological distress of belonging to an "inferior" group. In their work, Silverstein and Perlick documented of some women, who by having the support of their fathers, did not show evidence of the symptoms of anorexia or disordered eating.

In sum, we have seen the influence of groups in our personality. We could be influenced negatively or positively by our membership in groups. In a more specific way also the social support group are crucial to our well being. Through examples, we have seen how crucial social supports are to our (psychological and physical) health. . . .

As future clinicians, parents, [spouses], brother, sisters, students, friends, we need to realize the importance of social support groups and how others and ourselves could benefit from having support groups. Personally speaking I do not have [any] idea what would be of me without my mother, my sister, and my friend; there would not be such a person as [Delores], who although I feels would go insane sometimes, they are there to rescue me.

In this instructional setting, Delores was clearly been made to feel that it was appropriate to point out the relevance of her academic studies to her personal life. Delores' family history no doubt influenced her strong belief in the value of support groups. After her parents divorced when she was a young child, Delores saw her mother resolutely take up the responsibility for supporting, caring for, and motivating her children. (In a paper for a psychology course in the fall of 1993, she wrote: "My mother is the most important person in my life, whom I admire, and respect for her strong sense of endeavor. My mother unlike my father has sacrificed all her life in order to give us the best life possible.") Delores' hostility toward men as supporting influences was grounded at least partially on her own experiences, since her father played no role in her life after her parents divorced. Furthermore, in an interview with me that same semester, she commented on the weakness of her brother, who was not even mentioned as part of her support group. Like several others in my study (Linda and Joan, in particular), Delores' mother served as her principal role model.

Among the men in the study, the mothers played a greater range of roles: Carl could confide in his mother but not his father about his homosexuality, but he received no emotional support from her. Jacob was dominated by his mother who demanded that he have a "solid" career rather than become a writer, while his father remained in Australia, an unmentioned figure in his life. Ricardo's parents divorced, and he was reared by his father in Puerto Rico who discouraged his intellectual dreams. In one of his papers, Ricardo vividly described the cruelty of his father, who attempted to deny medical care to one of his sisters and who physically assaulted his mother. Among this group only Ricardo felt compelled to defend the rights of women when issues of gender arose for consideration. (Audrey, Chandra, and Donald spoke less openly about their family relationships with me, although Chandra did talk about moving out of her family home variously to live with her sister, a girlfriend, or, for a short time, a boyfriend.)

Haswell (1991) noted findings from other studies that show changes in writing development that occur over the college years (p. 298). Hays (1983b) pointed out that students grow in their abilities to consider their readers. In a paper for a communications course, Carl examined the treatment in the press of the woman who accused William Kennedy Smith of rape, a topic also considered by Ricardo in a paper excerpted in this chapter. In the fall of 1991, Carl wrote on the following topic: "Should reporters take sides on the issues they are covering?" After providing definitions and discussions of journalistic objectivity, Carl critiqued the handling of the Smith case in *The New York Times* starting with a quotation from A. M. Rosenthal: "So now we have freedom of press. Now all we need is freedom of conscience." Carl picks up on the latter phrase to begin his analysis:

> Freedom of conscience. Fox Butterfield, also from the Times, was missing both conscience and objectivity in an April 1991 article. The article featured an in-depth look at Patricia Brown [Bowman is the correct name]. Ms. Brown is the rape victim in the West Palm Beach Kennedy case. Mr. Butterfield uncovered her past and presented a less-than-complimentary view of Ms. Brown. The way the article was written, it was as if Ms. Brown was on trial, that she was the one who committed a crime. Her past history should have remained just that—her past. Mr. Butterfield seemed too eager—too aggressive in his coverage. It was as if he took it upon himself to decide her guilt or innocence. The poor woman never had a chance.
>
> Yes, there were protests. Yes there were apologies made. All that came later, after heated debates. The apologies, unfortunately, never received the spotlight the damaging article did. Fox Butterfield considers himself a journalist. His job then is to inform the people. In this case he took it upon himself to decide for them. Why he wrote the article the way he did does not matter. There can be no valid excuse. As a journalist, he should have been impartial. As an American, he should have remembered the basic right of innocence until proven guilty.

Carl hoped that his position would resonate with his readers who were perceived to be sympathetic to the difficulties inherent in such cases for female accusers. The ethics course provided the appropriate environment for reasoned critique. The paper also gave Carl an opportunity to demonstrate his literary style, effectively using the rhetorical form of parallel repetitions.

Jacob also recognized the importance of considering the needs of his readers. In a paper on Kuhn's *The Structure of Scientific Revolutions* for a world civilization course in the spring semester of his first year, he examined Kuhn's arguments by summarizing the major points and then evaluating them. After discussing Kuhn's use of the term *paradigm* as "normal science," that is, "research firmly based upon one or more past scientific achievements" that are acknowledged as supplying the foundation for future practice, Jacob considered how paradigms are used by scientists:

> So the presence of paradigms is indicative of a mature scientific society. A paradigm makes sense of the immense infinity of nature, it allows the scientist to build on prior experiments without the time consuming need to reiterate the rudiments for fellow practitioners (at the same time it created a gulf between the educated layman and the members of the scientific community as papers on the sciences began to assume shared and established knowledge and therefore became unintelligible to the general public), it provides the rules, standards and concepts of normal science and it allows for more precise and detailed experiments—since a paradigm determines which data is most worthy of unearthing, the scientist feel confident in devoting much time and money to procure much more in-depth results than his pre-paradigm counterpart. (A relevant contemporary illustration can be drawn with the proposed building of a superconducting supercollider in Texas which would be completed around the year 2000, has a circumference of 54 miles and is expected to cost between $7 billion to $8 billion. Such a commitment would be unthinkable except for the Big Bang theory which suggests that such an endeavor would unlock the secrets of the origin of the Universe.)

Realizing that most of his discussion had been at a very abstract level, Jacob provided a concrete example to show his readers how the public could be influenced to support expensive scientific experiments if they could be made to understand their significance. He did not want his paper to be "unintelligible" in the way he critiqued other scientific writings.

Another kind of change that shows up over the college years is that students develop the ability to see both sides of an argument (Whitla, 1981) and to present their positions from more reasonable perspectives. In a paper for a political science course in the fall of 1991, his third year at the college, Carl took on the complex issue of American responses to the war in Vietnam. He specifically addressed the following topic: "How America was Affected by Vietnam":

> Vietnam. The undeclared war the U.S. waged against Vietnam has been over for more than 15 years but the remnants of the war are still evident in America. The haunting memories of the War continue to be relived in motion pictures from "Apocalypse Now" and "Born on the Fourth of July" to books and television documentaries. Historians, philosophers and everyday Americans have postulated the "what if" scenarios, and struggled with the bitter memories, scars, and nightmares that the war produced. The military sought to influence the "hearts and minds" of Americans into supporting the war. It is a new generation of "hearts and minds" that have attempted to scrutinize the war and how America was affected by it. . . .
>
> One particular question, about the conduct rather than the purpose of the war, is raised by Americans even as it confuses them. They wonder how a "backward" country like North Vietnam "won" the war against a military superpower with advanced technological capability. The North Vietnamese knew their own land better than the Americans. The Vietnamese had another advantage. Unlike many Americans, the Vietnamese knew what they were fighting for. U.S. troops and a majority of people on the home front wondered why we had gotten involved. It's a question that is still unresolved. Nevertheless, the Vietnamese won. Their persistence, coupled with

America's changing attitudes at home, forced the U.S. to withdraw from the small country. American policy makers accepted the loss but have refused to officially recognize the country. This failure drove the people of Vietnam to depend even more on the Soviet Union. The U.S. policy was to contain communism wherever it existed. American leaders ignored the strategic attributes that Vietnam possesses because of bitterness, spite, and guilt over there previous actions...

America was strongly affected by the Vietnam War, some chose to ignore the lessons it taught, while others will forever remember the tragic, senseless loss the war instilled on the nation. Vietnam taught the American people to think critically, to ask questions, and to challenge its elected officials when damaging events occur. Vietnam also taught Americans something on manipulation, that some people will follow blindly and that others will take the government at its word. All in all, Vietnam showed the importance of debate, the fallacy of under-estimating your foes and your people, and importance of answering diplomatic problems with something other than military force.

From the ambiguity of the Vietnam war, Carl drew lessons that he hoped would guide future decision makers as well as the general population in making judgments about commitments to waging war.

Audrey felt the need to show her readers the complexity of issues that many individuals may not have information about. In the fall of 1990, she told me: "Writing a research paper makes me think more—how to relate ideas to earlier materials and other sources." In a paper for an economics course on "Employee Stock Ownership Plans" that same semester, she began to analyze more deeply the causes and effects of issues that she had been content to describe in earlier academic papers:

The third element in ESOP [Employee Stock Ownership Plans] law, the Doctrine of Non-discrimination in Employee-benefit Plans, is double talk. Because a company and its managers can define what an employee is even before the ESOP takes effect, they can discriminate against groups of employees by age, sex, or race. The problem lies with who has the authority to apply the definition of discrimination. An ESOPs nature can be completely transformed through variations in the definition of a worker, voting rights, structure, unallocated stock voting provisions, formula for allocation of ownership, vesting schedule, annual contribution commitment, cost and class of stock, percentage of co-ownership, future co-ownership provisions, employee distribution plans, composition of the board of directors, identity of ESOP trustees, and amount and attended voting rights of non-ESOP employee-owned stock. If a higher number of non-salaried employees are excluded, and many salaried or highly vested employees are included, the ESOP will falsely appear to be democratic if the stock is one vote per share.

Understanding how such programs can be manipulated to favor one side, Audrey chose to gather pertinent evidence that she believed could be used to sway public policy.

Another marker of students' increasing analytic ability is the capacity to write papers in which they can counter opposing arguments (Hays, Brandt, & Chantry, 1988). Addressing the issue of whether it was ethical for the news media, particularly NBC, to identify the rape victim in the William Kennedy Smith trial (the topic also addressed by Carl in an earlier excerpt about *The New York Times* coverage), Ricardo's social consciousness came to the foreground in a paper he wrote for a course in ethics in the communications department in the spring of 1992, the end of his third year at the college:

> [There] are not easy answers to very difficult ethical questions. This is one of them. But, as I weigh the reasons provided by those involved I feel compel to reject the "Libertarian Theory" and respect the privacy of Ms. Patricia Bowman. It is clear that a major news organization like NBC has to be preoccupied with ratings. The pressures on a news organization to achieve higher ratings and maintain their competitive edge is being lived by those news organizations on a daily basis. It does not justify the outrageous intrusion on a victim's right to privacy. It is the victim's decision to come forward to denounce the crime. It is not the network's right to further victimize a rape survivor by invoking their First Amendment Rights and their Freedom of the Press. The long-term harmful consequences of this action are greater than the reward. And even after Ms. Bowman was named, she said in the NBC interview that "The statistics show that after I was named, the amount of rape cases charged diminished substantially." That it's too negative of a consequence for a rape victim to suffer. The 1972 edition of the Webster's Dictionary defines rape as, "to seize and take away by force." That is what naming a rape victim without her consent does. It robs and takes away the right to remain anonymous and not suffer the consequences of becoming an unwilling public figure. Nobody has the right to do that to a victim. For the few victims that potentially would be willing to go through a biased legal system in search of justice, they are going to be thinking they will outright refuse to denounce such a violent crime for fear of being victimized for a second time. But this time the perpetrator will be the news media.

While Carl berated the media for its lack of objectivity, Ricardo's focus is on the human dimension, as he applied an analytic stance to the harm done to the individual he felt had been treated unfairly. Ricardo's writings over the years were particularly sensitive on issues pertaining to the treatment of women.

Carl focused on the human dimension when an issue arose to which he felt personally committed. The ability to include more situational information in persuasive discourse (Beach & Anson, 1988) is seen as another marker of student improvement in the ability to examine issues analytically. In his world humanities course, Carl found an instructor who would "allow for more creativity" in his writing. He said, "Writing makes me think about things more. It makes papers more interesting unless the topic is boring. In world humanities, [the topics] are open ended. In other courses, they are more defined. For example, in my world civilization course, I have less free rein to do what I can do." On his own, he said he was doing some creative writing, "parodies of other things." He said he shows them to his close friends. He told me that he might like to do creative writing, but he was not sure he had the talent.

An example of the openness Carl found in his world humanities course came when his instructor accepted as one of the assigned papers one that Carl had written on his own. It was an autobiographical piece, describing a conversation between Carl and one of his female colleagues who also worked the evening shift at *The New York Times* with him. As the encounter developed, Carl revealed his sexual orientation to his friend as they discussed an article that had appeared in a gay magazine. "'You know, I'm gay too,' I said in astonishment. I did not believe I was admitting something I had hidden so long." His friend's positive reaction encouraged him to share his deeper feelings:

> "I do that a lot [testing people]. Sometimes it's pretty hard to keep all this inside. The worst part about it is that I can't talk to my family about it. I'm willing to risk friendships, but when it comes to my family I'm afraid to even hint at anything. I'm glad that you didn't freak out or anything. It's nice to be able to talk to someone about it at work."
>
> . . . [At Howard Johnson's after work] we ordered (what would later become our usual order) milkshakes and discussed work; the people there, more about her feelings toward P___, and more about me. We must have spent about three hours there. It was wonderful to just talk, being fully honest about everything and having someone so understanding to speak to. That taught me to relax about myself a little, not to worry so much about what people think, and not to get worked up if they find offense in what I am. It's such a small part of me; I shouldn't make such a big deal about it in my mind. Being gay should not be the issue that makes or breaks me. It is merely one aspect of me. That is something that I always should have known, but I've never bothered to realize.

By sharing this paper, first with his instructor, and then with me, Carl took a further step toward establishing his public pride in his identity. His world humanities instructor wrote a note to him on the paper: "I'm glad to see that you have been able to find your way back to yourself. Being estranged from oneself is so common and so deadly to life happiness." Carl clearly expected this affirmation from his instructor or he would not likely have shared the paper with her. My receipt of the paper was his first acknowledgment to me of his being gay, but in interviews we had later he elaborated to me on the difficulties he had in communicating with his parents, especially his father. He said he could never tell his father he was gay.

Bringing life experiences into student writing led to more careful reflection on societal issues. In a paper for a psychology course in her second year at the college, Linda expressed her views on a subject that was meaningful to her:

> I want to talk about a topic which is not talked about often—childless women. Believe me, there are women out there who do not want children just as much as women who do. Childless women aren't equally respected as their maternal counter-

parts. They are considered selfish women who are not doing their duty. They are also considered not to be total women.

   . . . For example, I have a 40 year old cousin who is a junior high school teacher. Prior to that job, she used to travel across the U.S. performing in broadway plays. My cousin has been in and out of relationships and never thought about having children.

   She chose that decision because she felt her lifestyle wasn't ready to fit a child in. Today, she still feels that her life is too comfortable and stable to start thinking about any children. Her mother, however, is still hostile and angry because her daughter hasn't bore her any children. She consider her daughter to be selfish.

Linda's instructor put a check beside this comment of analysis and indicated to Linda that he wished she would provide more evaluations of the examples she provided. He wrote on her paper: "Good points. I think that if you had used more specific examples of prejudice against childless women, and analyzed these prejudicial attitudes (e.g., their origins and underlying assumptions), your essay would have been stronger." Encouraging the movement toward further analysis with these kinds of comments tailored to the particular task enabled Linda and students like her to understand how analytical processes could be applied to writing.

In her sixth and last year at the college, in a paper for a psychology course on the history and evolution of transvestites, Linda's writing demonstrated the growth she had acquired in analytical abilities and her capability in delving beneath surface features: "There were also some differences as to why each gender cross-dressed. The women who cross-dressed were poor and lower class while the men came from a higher class background. The women cross-dressed as a mean to escape their restricted lives as women. The men cross-dressed as a form of sexual gratification and as a release from societal's views of masculinity as being ideal in their noble class setting. Regardless of one's sexuality, cross-dressing cut across all boundaries." This analysis of the differences between the motivations of the women and the men gave Linda an opportunity to demonstrate her awareness of the complexities in this topic and to show her professor that she was not satisfied with easy generalizations.

No claim is being made here that the examples of analytic writing in this section of the chapter are consistently profound, but what is being asserted is that engagement with writing has moved these students to reflect more deeply on the materials and ideas they have encountered and to develop a critical consciousness that they will be able to apply to future intellectual and life settings. In addition, particular instructional settings are seen to provide support for students to take risks in producing analytical responses to tasks. Such settings not only facilitate attempts to undertake complex reasoning tasks, they make it clear that they value such undertakings. The task alone will not provide the incentive. The student must believe that the instructor will respect and respond to the student's efforts and struggles. (The role of instructional settings is presented in chapter 6.) These movements toward analysis demonstrate the ability to apply concepts to data, to examine critically the causes of events and behavior, and to critique the presentation of purportedly unbiased information. The next logical step is to go beyond such analyses to propose new solutions to existing problems or to create new relationships between existing ideas.

WRITING TO CONSTRUCT KNOWLEDGE NEW TO THE LEARNER

The difficulty for undergraduate students in attempting to construct new knowledge is that they are fully aware that they are working in fields where a great deal of expertise already exists. It is difficult for them to imagine that they can create knowledge that will be new to a discipline. Studies carried out by Martin, D'Arcy, Newton, and Parker (1976) concluded that the high school students they were working with felt more comfortable proposing new ideas or interpretations when they were communicating something that was "drawn from their own observations" (p. 77). But it was "far more difficult for pupils to feel either confident or committed to information when it is really someone else's knowledge that they are drawing on and not their own" (p. 77). Part of this difficulty, Martin and her colleagues believed, is related to the issue previously considered in this chapter of remaining tied to textbook or lecture jargon, in contrast with finding one's own words to express ideas. In dealing with personal experience, students must rely on their own formulations while researched material can make the student dependent on the language of the source. Although such dependence might appear to make the writing "easier," it conflicts with the ability to create or present original ideas (p. 79).

Martin and her colleagues offered a definition of *imagination* that is appropriate for the kind of constructive learning that this section is involved with: "that mental process which enables a person to make his own connections, whether this happens to be in the sciences or in the arts" (p. 86). They go on to point out that such "moments are rare when an 'imaginative leap' opens up new patterns and new perspectives for others" (p. 86). They noted that this kind of writing helps "to take the writer further into real insights about himself and his world" (p. 96).

Therefore, this section deals with the construction of knowledge that is new to the student even if not always new to the field. When students perceive the significance of the information they have acquired and make new connections for themselves, a crucial aspect of learning has been achieved for them.

There were three primary ways students constructed new knowledge for themselves: (a) applying concepts from one discipline to another, (b)

integrating material from personal knowledge or experience into the analysis of informational materials, and (c) carrying out original quantitative or
qualitative studies to answer research questions they had formulated for
themselves.

Constructing knowledge took different forms with different students. For
Joan, in her fourth year at the college, constructing knowledge manifested
itself through the integration of her studies in one discipline with those of
another. As a psychology major, Joan had learned many terms that she had
used in the analyses of psychological cases. Now, in her world humanities
course, she brought in a psychological concept in the analysis of Candide's
optimism. Joan wrote: "Pangloss inspired Candide's Optimism because he
attributed what we would call in Psychology, a Halo-effect to every experience in life, meaning, there is good in everything and everyone."

In an argumentative paper on a proposed medical treatment bill written
in his first semester at the college, Jacob took issue with "Right to Life"
proponents who argued against what he called "Death with Dignity" provisions of the bill. To bolster his position, Jacob drew on knowledge of Shaw's
play, *Saint Joan*, to support his belief that quality of life should determine
one's views about the sanctity of life:

> The word "Life" has a positive effect on us, much like virtue, light and purity; "death"
> on the other hand is related to negative words as night, black and hell. Like "love"
> which means two quite different things when referred to ice-cream or another person,
> "Life" also covers a wide area, and its boundaries are not very clear at times. This is
> of the greatest benefit to people like those at Right to Life who uses the positive effect
> of this word in every occasion, no matter how appropriate. An excellent example of
> the different aspects of the word "Life" is given in George Bernard Shaw's famous play
> "Saint Joan." Joan has just decided to recant before the Inquisition because otherwise
> she will be burnt at the stake, and because she has been promised that elusive concept
> of life. She soon discovers however that her "life" will actually be life imprisonment,
> she rages at the court with venom. "You promised me my life; but you lied (indignant
> exclamations). You think that life is nothing but not being stone dead." I suppose Mrs.
> Tighe [president of the Right to Life organization] would be having a fit when she
> discovers that Joan did not chose to live to "a ripe old age" but in a sense, committed
> suicide by deciding not to recant. Her definition of life would be very similar to that
> of the court I suspect, simply "not being stone dead"; but there is much more to it
> than that, like the quality of living. The prison that Joan so feared (more than death)
> is here with us today, whether it be in the form of physical pain, depression,
> disillusionment, or whatever—then life would no longer be "life" as Joan saw it, but
> a living hell. . . .

In these last comments, Jacob moved to his own perspective on what the
quality of life entails; as his poetry and his comments to me over the years
indicated, his own dreams of a "quality life" as a writer have been thwarted
by the practicalities of making a sound living that have been thrust on him.
In addition, he told me that since he was the only son in his family,

"important accomplishments" were expected of him. In his private writings, he was absorbed with despair about the meaninglessness of life.

In his fifth and last year at the college, Ricardo wrote a paper for a psychology course in which he integrated personal knowledge into his analysis. His paper dealt with a comparison of the diagnosis of "hysteria" to Anna O., a patient of Dr. Joseph Breuer in the 1880s, with the treatment of contemporary women. His discussion contrasted the "extremely restricted" world of women in the late 1800s with the "greater freedom" of women in the 1990s. But rather than painting a stark comparison of the conditions of women in these different times, Ricardo pointed out that women in our present time are also subjected to social pressures. He wrote:

> Even with all the freedoms that today's women enjoys they are still restrained by societal rules. An example of that is my little sister. Even thought she is a woman of this generation and she wanted to do with her life what she believed was her right, to move in with her boyfriend, she was force to marry him by the pressures exerted by my mother and aunts. They were worried about what the people in the community will think of her/them. She was forced into a situation that was not decided freely by her. In this case it was societies rules exerting their power all over again. But even with those little flashes of societies interference [it] is a lot easier for today's women. They have more choices and more freedom to achieve their goals and aspirations.

Through this analysis, Ricardo demonstrated how he has understood that complex social changes do not come about easily or consistently. These realizations moved him beyond uncritical acceptance of notions of "progress" in the status and lives of contemporary women.

Similarly, Chandra brought her own experience in the African-American community to bear on her analysis of the way African Americans are portrayed on television. She discussed the importance of doing this in two interviews with me, the first in the spring of 1990 and the second in the fall of 1991. In the first interview, she said: "My creative mind is starting to open up. When I relax my mind, ideas start to flow and I can write non-stop. I didn't realize I had that within me before. I can also remember things better now. Before, I didn't make connections to my own life—I was just memorizing facts." She carried this idea further in the next interview: "Now the professor wants more of your thinking in advanced courses. They want a step further than understanding. They want to know how this [idea] applies to your life. You need to know a little more." With this kind of encouragement, Chandra and other students were made to understand that their contributions to knowledge were legitimate and valued. Furthermore, new apprehensions could be generated by bringing new perspectives to the issues and fields they were working in. Applying insights from her own life in a paper for a communications course, she argues that although the portrayal of African Americans on television has changed somewhat, there is now a more subtle form of discrimination going on:

. . . Blacks are not portrayed fairly and the Black Experience is not realistically explored. The stereotypical images of Blacks and the type of roles available for African American actors has [gone] through a tremendous moderation since early television. However, the content of these shows do not reflect realistic behavior of Blacks and the subliminal messages within these shows have replaced direct negative images, reinforcing negative ideas of African Americans.

. . . *True Colors* is a sitcom about an interracial marriage between a White woman, who has a teenage daughter, and a Black man, who has two teenage sons from previous marriages. The husband is a dentist and the wife is a homemaker. The sons speak in slang terms, while the daughter always has something intelligent to say. The wife always makes all the major decisions in the household, while the wife's mother, who lives there with them, struggles to translate anything the sons say to her. How can this family realistically exist in this society today? The race issue is never addressed and everyone seems to be color blind. The slang that the boys speak is not the kind of slang I hear in my neighborhood; furthermore, I do not think this father would send his sons to the neighborhood High School and allow them to speak like illiterates while he speaks so elegantly.

. . . Are the creators of *True Colors* trying to say that a successful Black man can only find happiness with a White woman, after one marriage with an African American woman failed? Only the creators and writers of these shows know the answers. However, viewers should open their minds and ask themselves these questions.

We need more Black shows on television to capture the whole range of Black experiences. Although television was created to depict fantasy, it should also contain some realism, or at least realistic portrayals of people of all cultures.

The analysis presented in this paper explains Chandra's decision to expand her view of her own role beyond that of acting, her original goal, to also function as a director, a position in which she could have greater influence on the depiction of African Americans on television. It also demonstrates her growing sensitivity to issues often raised in women's studies courses as to how women have been positioned in society and have frequently not questioned the universally accepted norms for their behavior (Ritchie, 1990, p. 251).

Carrying out original quantitative and qualitative research also led students to new insights. In her second year at the college, Linda said, "I'm able to come up with new ideas in writing." A few months later, she said, "Writing helps teachers discover more about a person—how mature a student is and what the student is learning. . . . I like the writing and the progress I'm making. Teachers like the points I make. I am coming up with new ideas and teachers like that." In her fourth year at the college, for a psychology course, Linda carried out an experiment to determine young women's attitudes toward older women. One of her major points concerned the attitudes of African-American women, her research population. She wrote:

If one looks at impression formation from a cultural standpoint, one will find out that there is indeed an age bias. People of color tend to put a more positive light on the older woman. Being that she is older she will overcome her problems faster than a younger woman. The community would conclude that the older woman may have suffered similar symptoms during her younger years. At this stage in her life, they may feel that she has a better chance of coping with them. On the other hand, the younger woman is seen as someone who couldn't possibly cope with all that stress. They'll say she is too young and most likely she will suffer more because she has no previous experiences. Therefore, she wouldn't know how to cope. They would look at situations more negatively. No matter how identical their situations may be. The fact that she's younger immediately puts her in a negative view.

This paper is an example of the kind of writing Martin and her colleagues (1976) considered when they described works students did that was drawn from their own observations. Even though Linda is close to the subject and the subjects, she is able to retain objectivity in her writing. Her interviews with the African-American women led her to these insights. Linda's instructors continued to encourage her to move further in her analysis: "You raise interesting points about cultural differences! Why do you think people of color have more positive attributions to older women? Good work!" Probing teacher comments of this type were often instrumental in helping students move to more analytical stances as the discussion of this topic in chapter 4 reveals.

Delores' absorption in the relationships between race and gender was transformed into a concern with the relationship between skin color and self-esteem in a study she did titled "Skin Color and Its Impact on Self-Esteem of Latino College Students—Dominicans and Puerto Ricans (A Bronx Study)" which she carried out in 1993 through a special enrichment program at Lehman College of the City University of New York in preparation for writing her master's thesis. In an interview in the fall of 1993, she described how writing this report made her feel: "I create it. It's my paper—my ideas, like a birth. There wasn't anything like that before." The hypothesis in her paper was that skin color was related to self-esteem among Latino college students and that darker skinned Latino college students would have a more negative sense of self-esteem than lighter skinned ones. She also hypothesized that her population of Dominican and Puerto Rican students would differ significantly from each other in their sense of self-esteem.

Delores administered a self-esteem inventory and a demographic questionnaire to her subjects. She found that her Puerto Rican subjects rated themselves significantly lighter in skin color and that they had higher self-esteem than the Dominican subjects. In addition to the relationship between skin color and self-esteem, Delores sought out other possible causes for the Puerto Rican students' evaluations of themselves. Among possible other causes, she considered the possibility that lighter skinned Puerto Ricans might "feel more attached to the Anglo Americans for the virtue that they share similar physical traits with the dominant group." She also considered that time spent living in the United States could be a factor:

"Puerto Ricans have lived longer in the United States with a length of stay of 18.76 [years] on the average, while respondents from the Dominican Republic had an average length of stay of 8.89 [years]. Perhaps the longer the stay the more one is acculturated to the customs and norms of the United States, the better English one knows, the better an economic position one has secured for oneself." She also considered the fact that Puerto Ricans have greater status in the United States as members of a Commonwealth of the country, and they are thus entitled to certain services that Dominicans did not qualify for. Since Dominicans appear to be disadvantaged in all these areas in relation to Puerto Ricans, Delores understood that no single factor could account for her findings. She ended her paper by looking forward to her further research in her master's thesis in which she planned to explore more fully the symptoms influenced by skin color, "depression, anxiety, low self-esteem, low achievement threshold, vulnerability to stress that might be accounting for the differences in self-esteem of Dominicans and Puerto Ricans."

Through this original study, Delores started to establish herself as a researcher able to generate worthwhile areas for investigation and able to identify confounding factors that affect the interpretation of her results. Her ability to handle complex, interwoven factors in this study prepared her to go to the next level in her master's work.

The examples in this section illustrate students' attempts to explore new understandings. In some cases, as when they relate information from one discipline to another, they are able to apply insights that lead to more astute understandings of the material they are examining. When they integrate personal knowledge and experience into their studies, their ability to critique existing beliefs is heightened. And, when they carry out original studies, they begin to have the potential to add information to existing fields, adding not only knowledge but perspectives that may have been previously ignored. As Chandra's study of the portrayal of African Americans on television and Delores' examination of the relationship between self-esteem and skin color demonstrate, the addition of perspectives frequently absent from consideration add depth and insight to an increasingly complex multicultural society.

CONCLUSION

As students used writing to achieve different goals, their awareness of the role that writing played in learning grew. When they were required to study for short-answer or multiple-choice tests, they used their classroom and textbook-based notes to assist them. But the transformation of these notes into analytical appraisals of the information served far more important needs as they were required to respond to essay examinations or to write prepared papers. Students increasingly found "objective" tests far less satisfying as means for them to display their understanding of the materials they were working with. Opportunities to write formal papers, and to rewrite them if allowed, gave them better possibilities to manifest not only their knowledge, but their ability to reflect on, analyze, and evaluate complex ideas. As they advanced into the major areas, students brought insights from other disciplines to bear on issues in their fields. They were challenged to design original studies that had the potential to contribute new knowledge to the fields they were working in. Their consciousness of the role that writing played in moving them through these levels of engagement with their academic studies reinforces the point that metacognition improves students' abilities to use writing effectively for diverse purposes.

What these descriptions reveal is that development of complex reasoning strategies over time does not produce consistent improvement. Students who have been functioning at an analytical level in some areas may find themselves reverting to definition and textbook language when they are confronted with new complex materials or when the instructional demands restrict them to reciting the "facts" that have been presented to them, frequently in "official jargon." The ability to translate textbook language into their own language leads to the development of true understandings that can be built on. Reflective analysis leads to the possibility of the discovery of new findings, both for themselves and for their disciplines.

3

Effect of Complex Social Histories on Academic Performance

It is not surprising that in a diverse population of students who enter a college like City College issues of race, gender and sexual orientation, class, and ideology should affect their approaches to undertaking academic tasks. In this chapter, I discuss how these aspects of their lives influenced their responses to the demands being made upon them. It is crucial to recognize that inclusion of background knowledge does not diminish the analytical perspective the students present in their critiques of existing conditions and viewpoints. Rather, their lived-through experiences enhance their ability to assess the frequently unquestioned assumptions of the larger society. In an article, "Diversity Opens Doors to All," Beckham (1997) argued that even the so-called literary canon is still "unsettled and contested," and thus, it "continue[s] to animate students and entice them into critical thinking about current concerns" (p. 58).

Chin (1994) considered the complexity involved in examining how contextual factors affect student writing. She noted the importance of reflecting on "the ways in which each individual writer's reading of the social, emotional, political, economic and cultural texts plays into the construction of [the students'] own social text for writing" (pp. 476–477). "Writing," she contended, "can be seen as an experience encompassing both material and mental worlds" (p. 477). Lu (1992) lamented the absence of attention to conflict and struggle in the instructional approaches used in basic writing classes since the advent of open admissions at the City University of New York in the early 1970s: "We also need to gather more oppositional and alternative accounts from a new generation of students, those who can speak about the successes and challenges of classrooms which recognize the positive uses of conflict and struggle and which teach the process of repositioning" (p. 910).

Holloway (1993) also pointed out that personal identity factors should not only be explored but valued:

> Eschewing the criticisms of those now feeding off their own alarm at the academy's disarray, I suggest that we embrace to our own ends the identity politics—the perspectives of race, culture, gender, and ethnicity—inherent in language. We can

claim the power of our voices, and their complexity, *and their complexions* to assert the dimensions of our concerns, to call attention to our successes in vitalizing the community of the university—both its faculty bodies and its student bodies. (p. 617)

Not surprisingly, the environment in an urban, inner-city college like City College can provide the longitudinal data through which such accounts can be presented and examined. As is seen here, students reposition themselves in terms of their personal identities and in their relationships to the mores and values of the dominant society.

Previous research provides a basis for understanding the need for studying a population like the kind found in an inner-city college like City College. In her study of correspondence among 6 White middle-class teachers enrolled in her graduate course on teaching basic writing with 6 White working-class women in an adult basic education class, Brodkey (1989) expressed concern that "an approach to teaching and learning that many educators share in this country . . . insists that the classroom is a separate world of its own, in which teachers and students relate to one another undistracted by the classism, racism, and sexism that rage outside the classroom" (p. 139). Students are frequently accused of having cognitive deficits, being emotionally or intellectually immature, being ignorant, or lacking cultural literacy. Such accusations distance the knowing teachers from their unknowing subjects (p. 139). Brodkey's findings in a study where all the participants were White suggest that in integrated settings where backgrounds of race, gender, and class differ to a somewhat smaller extent between instructors and students, the possibilities for less misunderstanding exists. That students in my study from the wide diversity of backgrounds felt comfortable and free enough to explore issues of race, gender and sexual orientation, and social class in their writing is a credit to the environment created in many City College classrooms, where the proportion of minority instructors is greater than at many other City University (or nationwide) campuses, but still far less than the 83% non-White undergraduate population at City College in 1987, just before this study began (Harlston, 1987). Delores described the educational environment she found in a paper she wrote in her second semester at the college for her freshman composition course.

> It is not a surprise to anyone that when people of different ethnic, racial, religious and economic backgrounds meet and work together in an atmosphere, problems will arise. However, City College of New York has been quite successful in bringing all these different groups together to form a safe community, where they interact together in harmony.
> The classrooms, for example, are the most common places where students and professors from different ethnic, racial and economic backgrounds meet and work together in unison in order for them to achieve their goals. In the classrooms, both the students and professors work in mutual respect. There is cooperation from the students and the professors as well. Students contribute to the development of the

class by exposing their points of view to the whole class. They can learn from the professors and from each other. For example, a student from Asia may have a different opinion from a student from the Caribbean about the same subject. Through the discussions in class, the students will learn the different points of view of students from other countries and cultures.

Delores' sensitivity, even as a second semester freshman, to the advantages of a multicultural learning environment stand in strong support for settings where such exchanges such as those she describes from both professors and students enhance the intellectual environment wherein they are interacting.

Not surprisingly, gender and race frequently influenced interpretations and analyses of assigned tasks. In arguing for the value of personal disclosure through writing and classroom discussion, Bleich (1995) emphasized that "[d]isclosure should be distinguished from confession and revelation, which take place respectively in either completely private or completely public contexts" (p. 48). Instead, disclosure "refers more to telling things in intermediary contexts, like groups, subgroups, classrooms, and lecture halls, where estimations need be made about appropriateness and helpfulness to others as well as oneself" (p. 48). Although Bleich's emphasis was on the contribution of disclosure in interpersonal settings, he was sensitive to the role that institutional settings can play in determining students' willingness to offer disclosure to their classmates or their instructors. He cited an article from the *Chronicle of Higher Education* by Swartzlander, Pace, and Stamler (1993) in which the authors expressed hesitation about what "students of color feel ready to share: if a classroom is majority white or if the teacher is white, shouldn't minority African-American students be permitted to decline an assignment if a safe atmosphere with regard to race has not yet been established?" (pp. B1–B2, cited in Bleich, 1995, pp. 45). The willingness of the students in my study to disclose personal experiences and attitudes spoke well of the instructional environments in which they found themselves. Bleich valued, as I do, the students' "tendency to integrate accounts of lived experience into their critical commentaries and responses" (p. 55), rather than limiting themselves always to references to external texts and authorities.

Ideology can hardly be separated from considerations of gender and race, since students' social consciousness is an integral part of their sense of personal identity. Issues of social class arose most powerfully in relation to the student's socioeconomic conditions: The greater the number of hours per week that students had to work, the less time that was available for preparing for classes, exams, and writing assignments. Ingenuity and doggedness often compensated for the shorter available hours.

The importance of gender, race, class, and ideology in students' academic lives is not presented as a defense or an excuse for bringing personal knowledge and experience to bear on their responses to the academic demands. Rather, it becomes crucial to understand the context of the students' lives from which they are able to enter into the academic world. Horner (1996), too, delineated aspects of the lives of basic writing students in inner-city urban colleges like City College, considering the conditions that give rise to the problems many basic writing students bring with them to college: "health problems, lack of child care, inadequate financial aid, and a history of inadequate [previous] schooling" (p. 215) as well as the "ongoing family, economic and social pressures on these students" (p. 215).

Jones-Royster (1992) pointed out that "blacks and Hispanics" are frequently regarded as a monolithic group "of unsuccessful learners, inexperienced readers and writers, and sometimes eager but always underprepared low achievers" (p. 8). But, she argued, closer attention must be paid to group members who do not fit into those categories:

> The fact is that learners, despite the specifics of their possible marginalization, can cover the full range of academic potential and achievement from the very top of the scales to the very bottom. In addition to unprepared and underprepared students, there are also well-prepared ones, average ones, some who are prepared in some areas and not in others, all of whom could conceivably be nurtured in ways which could encourage higher levels of performance and achievement. As professional educators, therefore, we must be much more consciously aware of cultural, social, political, and economic complexities so that we can recognize negatively charged assumptions which point us much too often toward minimal expectations, strategies, and measures rather than maximum ones. (p. 8)

And Fox (1993) contended that "standards" for writing need to be considered more carefully and that they need to be seen in relation to social and political change (p. 43). He proposed a set of standards by which writing should be considered. First on his list is a call for "writing that interrogates cultural/political commonplaces, that refuses to repeat clichéd explanations for poverty, racism, sexism, homophobia, and all the other diseases of our society" (p. 43). Because of the interrelatedness of these factors, it becomes difficult to separate them for discussion as discrete factors influencing students' responses to writing tasks. In the examples presented in this chapter, I sometimes make an arbitrary decision that one factor assumes more importance than another in assigning it to a category for consideration.

RACE AND ETHNICITY

The use of terms like *race* and *ethnicity* as categories for identification is fraught with difficulties. A marker like skin color clearly does not hold up, as Keating (1995) pointed out:

> The status of so-called "blacks" and "whites" is, perhaps, even more problematic [than that of Asians or Hispanics]. To begin with, the terms themselves are almost entirely

inaccurate. "White" is the color of this paper, not the color of anyone's skin. And people referred to as "black" would be more accurately described as they are in Nella Larsen's *Quicksand* [1928] as "taupe, mahogany, bronze, copper, gold, orange, yellow, peach, ivory, pinky white" or even "pastry white" (p. 59). Furthermore, although many "Hispanics," Native Americans, and "Asian Americans" have lighter skin than some so-called "whites," they are not classified as such unless they are passing. (pp. 911-912)

Support for the complexity in using skin tone as a racial marker comes also from Delores' study, cited earlier, wherein she investigates the relationship between skin color and self-esteem. If there were not differences in skin color among the Latino population she studied, such an investigation would never have occurred. In this study, the basis for assigning a student to a racial group is the student's own decision to so identify himself or herself on a demographic questionnaire distributed to the participants in the first few weeks of the study.

Of the 53 students in my original cohort, 21 identified themselves as African American (39%), 26 as Latino (49%), 4 as Asian (fewer than 1%), and 2 as White (fewer than 1%). Of the 9 students for whom I have the most complete set of data, 4 are African American (44%), 3 are Latino (33%), 1 is Asian (11%), and 1 is White (11%). Therefore, all the groups present in the original classes are represented by the smaller set. Although the percentages of Asians and Whites were greater than were in the original group, each of these categories is represented by only one student.

In recent years, researchers have become increasingly sensitive to the impact of students' full lives on their academic performance. For example, in their study of middle and high school students in the Webster Groves school district near St. Louis, Krater et al. (1994) reflected on their increasing understanding of nonacademic factors as their 6-year study progressed:

> This book [*Mirror Images*] tells the story of our six-year journey that we as teachers and students took together. By learning as a research team, we began to view the "problem" from a new angle—the intersection between race, gender, class, and age. More than a linguistic clash, might the problem be the cultural estrangement of Black teenagers, particularly, males, from the world of White females reflected in the school? Was our students' alienation in the classroom a mirror image of our own alienation from their world? (p. 14)

The population of students that Krater et al. (1994) studied consisted of five suburban municipalities with about 4,400 students, of whom roughly 1,100 were African American. Most families had incomes in the broad middle range, although the population varied "from marginal workers living in subsidized housing to descendants of the wealthy" (p. 21). They concluded that "neither dialect nor social class explained why African-American students were failing to thrive in [their] classrooms" (p. 24), an assertion hotly debated in early 1997 over the valuing of Ebonics as a separate language. Searching research "that dealt with Black students' learning styles, composing processes, and cultural preferences and with basic writing in general" (p. 25), Krater et al. set "global goals that might create a context for writing improvement: self-esteem, role models, teacher expectations, and cultural awareness" (p. 25).

Just as Bizzell (1986) was concerned with how basic writers would mediate between their home cultures and the academic cultures, Fox (1994), too, explored the effects of the academic setting on students with cultural backgrounds "that value styles of teaching, learning, communicating, and understanding the world . . . in . . . ways that are radically different from the ones most U.S. faculty are familiar with" (p. xiii). Some of these differences include "strong traditions of communicating indirectly and holistically, learning by absorption, valuing the wisdom of the past, and downplaying the individual in favor of the group" (p. xiii). Fox noted that these differences can

> affect the way students interact with their professors and classmates, their attitudes toward the books they read, and the problems they are called upon to solve. . . . They affect how students understand assignments, how they study, and how they comment on their classmates' papers. But most of all, these differences affect the way they write. For writing touches the heart of a student's identity, drawing its voice and strength and meaning from the way the student understands the world. (p. xiii)

Fox quoted one of her graduate students from Chile who articulated exactly the issue framed by Bizzell. She told Fox about her resistance to learning "a new way to write":

> You said it was just a technique, but what I discovered was that it meant I had to look at things differently. Real differently. And in that sense, my world view has to change. You know it's so powerful when you start to see things from a different perspective—the whole meaning of the world changes. So how am I going to change? Or would it make sense to me? All my life and everything is going to make sense in a different way. There is so much changing! And that's powerful. You see? I mean, that's incredible. That's so strong. (p. 44)

Although Fox's emphasis was on students who came from other countries to study in the United States, she recognized that her findings applied to students from a wide range of multicultural backgrounds. Of the central group of students reported in this study, three were born outside the continental United States (Ricardo, Delores, and Jacob), although Jacob's primary education was western (in Australia). In addition, although Carl was born in the United States, his major cultural influence was Ecuadorian—illustrating how muddy and elusive categorizing students' cultural influences can be. And, of course, the cultural influences on the African-American students—Linda, Joan, Chandra, and Donald—were central to their sense of identity, as were the Latino backgrounds of Ricardo, Carl, and Delores, regardless of where they were born.

At the college level, the advent of open admissions (at City University of New York in the early 1970s) coincided with an increased focus on multiculturalism and women's studies perspectives in the humanities and social sciences. Lavin and Hyllegard (1996) questioned whether these changes in the curriculum affected "a softening of standards":

> If one could isolate these various influences, could any consensus be reached about how the changes reflected on academic rigor? We do not have the data that would be required for such evaluations, and if we did, we doubt that there would be much agreement on what they signified. Multicultural influence on the curriculum is one of the most controversial issues in higher education today. (p. 206)

The data from this study are obviously too limited to come to any consensus about the relation between multicultural perspectives and grading standards. However, what is evident from the work the students produced over the years is that opportunities to deal with topics that encouraged a wide perspective generated not only enthusiasm but careful reflection. When given opportunities to bring their own knowledge and experience to bear on their consideration of assigned topics in fields such as composition, world humanities, psychology, women's studies, and communications, students' examination of traditional perspectives enhanced their ability to bring analytic perspectives to bear as they recognized assumptions that needed to be questioned and "facts" that warranted further investigation.

In a study of literacy narratives, Soliday (1994) focused on the role of cultural experience in influencing interpretations of diverse materials and experiences:

> Literacy stories can give writers from diverse cultures a way to view their experience with language as unusual or strange. By foregrounding their acquisition and use of language as a strange and not a natural process, authors of literacy narratives have the opportunity to explore the profound cultural force language exerts in their everyday lives. When they are able to evaluate their experiences from an interpretive perspective, authors achieve narrative agency by discovering that their experience is, in fact, interpretable. In my basic writing classes at an urban college [City College of City University of New York], I have found that literacy narratives can expand students' sense of personal agency when they discover not only that their own stories are narratable, but also that through their stories they can engage in a broader critical dialogue with each other and with well-known texts. (pp. 511–512)

Soliday pointed out that there was some disagreement as to whether students in basic writing classes who usually had minority, immigrant, and working-class backgrounds should be acculturated to academic language (p. 512). (This is an issue also raised by Min-Zhan Lu, 1992.) Although the students in my study were not assigned the writing of literacy narratives by their instructors, they did use their writing in the way Soliday suggested, enabling them "to ponder the conflicts attendant upon crossing language worlds and to reflect upon the choices" they must make, especially when they were also speakers of minority dialects and languages (p. 512). By following the students into their core courses and their major discipline areas, it is possible to see how their power of reflection grew as their sense of personal identity was strengthened.

Examining research that has been done over a long period of time can reveal surprising insights about one's own teaching. Only after I had pulled out examples of writing about racism and ethnicity that the students in my study had done did I realize that fully two thirds of the samples had been written in the writing courses I taught the students during the first semester of this study. Because my approach to teaching writing consciously uses readings as one basis for writing, the selections I made frequently led students to examine their own backgrounds in relation to the individuals they were reading and writing about. These comparisons often led students to begin to critically examine their own knowledge and experience. Although Hairston (1992) would strenuously critique my choices of subject matter for freshman composition, an issue discussed more fully in this chapter in the section on ideology, I offer no apology for providing students with these opportunities for reflection early in their college experience. The students' responses to related opportunities to consider these issues in their upper level courses demonstrate their growing ability to analyze and evaluate the conditions of the world they inhabit.

In their papers that considered issues of race and ethnicity, students wrote their ways into and through issues of personal identity and cultural assimilation, stereotyping, and racism. Once again, these cannot be seen as discrete categories, as consideration of one issue clearly segues into another.

Personal Identity and Cultural Assimilation

In the Preface to this book, I pointed out that Joan was the subject of a chapter in Traub's book, *City on a Hill*, in which she was characterized as a "miraculous survivor." I claimed that Joan's tenacity was a prime factor in her ability to overcome her difficult family background, her visual disability, and her poor previous educational experiences. But, as Joan's writings before Traub's book appeared and an interview subsequent to its publication demonstrate, her pride in herself and her own accomplishments were an important basis for her continuing efforts, along with the support and encouragement she received from her instructors. In early 1994, before Traub's book was published, Joan wrote a paper for her World Humanities 103 course on *The Narrative of the Life of Frederick Douglass*. In this paper Joan highlighted the importance of education in Douglass' being able to achieve his freedom and "devote his time and efforts to spreading his self-obtained knowledge, as an educated black man, no longer oppressed through *Ignorance.*" In a direct use of her voice as an African American, Joan asserted a prime value of education for herself: "In closing, reading, *The Narrative of the life of Frederick Douglass,* one can conclude, education was, and still remains, the key element involved in overcoming oppression. One should *never* forget that knowledge is the one tool that can be used to overpower the white man." Inside Joan, not evident in her quiet demeanor, resides the pride that has carried her throughout the difficulties of her personal life and her college life to this point of achievement, within grasp of earning her undergraduate degree in the next year. She, too, will not allow herself to be oppressed through ignorance.

In an interview at the end of that year, Joan told me that the most significant thing that happened to her during the last semester was reading about herself in Traub's book. In this book, Traub concluded, after talking with her and reading the papers she had written in her first 3½ years at the college, that by his standards she would never be an "educated person" (p. 132). At first, Joan said she was really depressed about it, but at the end of the year she said it did not really bother her. "I don't have the time. At first, I worried about my family. They didn't have much of a reaction. My degree confirms that you are capable of doing what you want to do." The most important thing she learned from her experience with Traub was, "You just can't be nice to everybody. You can't trust everyone." She said that Traub's book really surprised her. It took a while for what he said to sink in. She believed that Traub was inaccurate in some of the things he said about her. For example, Traub had said that she knew no one who had succeeded, but she contended that although she did have friends who were on the wrong track, she also knew successful people. A counselor at the college who knew Joan well told me that Joan had initially taken Traub's assessment of her capabilities quite hard, but that her determination and pride in herself gradually re-emerged and seemed likely to sustain her. As Joan said, her degree would confirm her capability to herself.

Aronson (1992) raised the important issue that for some individuals there is a sense of multiple identities within an individual student. She asked, "How do students manage, or fail to manage, the multiple identities they bring into the classroom? How do their multiple and sometimes conflicting identities affect them as writers?" (p. 1). Aronson looked at how identities are established, through, for example, gender, race and ethnic group, regional and national associations, class, and so on. She noted that because individuals have many identities, they are plural and not singular, causing tensions, conflicts, and contradictions. Chandra tellingly pictured her recognition of her complex identity in a paper she wrote during her first semester at the college:

> Similar to [Richard] Rodriguez, I felt that when I became a student I was "remade."
> The language I was used to speaking was based upon slang terms. All of the schools I

attended allowed me to speak and write with incorrect English. I learned the correct pronunciations of words in drama class. Recently, here at City College, I have gained a new identity which I feel that I don't identify with. I am referred to as an African-American. Similar to Rodriguez experiences, I've never connected myself to this racial minority so I feel guilty representing a culture I knew nothing about. I spent all of my life trying to overcome my race and color in order to produce as a part of the American society. But I have realized, one cannot move forward unless they know where they have been. Now, I feel like I've missed out on something since I don't know anything about African history or African culture. My peers always viewed me as a "wanna be" white girl because I tried correcting my speech and speak intelligently. When I tried to imitate the slang later in my teens, everyone could always tell I did not belong.

I always believed that I had to give up my culture to be taken seriously as an intellectual, I later realized that I didn't.

For Chandra, issues of gender and race became more strongly intertwined as she went through the college years. Factors that influenced her decision to move beyond acting to a more influential role directing movies or television shows are presented in the next section on gender and sexual orientation.

Ricardo's cultural background strongly influenced the social values he espoused. In an autobiographical paper he wrote for his English 2 class early in his first semester at the college, he almost lyrically described early experiences in Puerto Rico that shaped his value system. He affirmed the qualities of the people and the culture he had known as a child in Puerto Rico:

> I met a lot of people during my childhood. People who held different jobs from doctors to mechanics, from housewifes to teachers. They taught me lessons that until this day are a very important part of my life. One of the lessons I remember the most came from a fisherman who told me once that in order to eat fish, you have to go fishing but at the same time you must care for the ocean and that [you must] never throw any garbage into it since by doing that I will kill the fish and we wouldn't have anything to eat.
>
> Thanks to my grandparents I was exposed to the backbone of my culture. I learned that all of these people were important not for their money or professions, but for their honesty and caring.
>
> The legacy that I hope to past to my children, from their ancestors is to love the land the ocean and respect it for what [it] is worth. It gives us food, provide us with shelter and sustaining our existence in this fragile environment. They will learn from me as I did from my eldest, to respect people no matter who they are. To look after their friends and families and care for those who can't.
>
> And a beautiful but important lesson to be proud of who you are, be proud of your heritage and above all try to do a work or job wich you love and honor, because that alone will bring you happiness. . . .
>
> The main drawback of going to a vocational school is that they put more emphasis on the vocation or trade, [than] on preparing you to college. As a result of that it makes it harder on people like me to be proficient in college. We lack the studies that will make us better students and that's something that is affecting my life as a college student.

Along with the value system he internalized, Ricardo demonstrated his acute awareness of the disadvantages that his past level of education were inflicting on his present attempts at undertaking college work.

Issues of cultural and personal identity are frequently tied closely to questions of the desirability of assimilating into the dominant culture. One student who grappled with the intersections of these matters over the years was Carl. As his papers reflect, he distanced himself from the cultural practices of his Ecuadorian family, partly, it appears, to become more Americanized himself, but also as a way of protecting his identity as a homosexual from his parents, from whom he anticipated a hostile response. In this section of the chapter, I present excerpts he wrote for papers in the freshman composition course his first semester at the college where he overtly discusses his conflicting feelings about cultural identity and assimilation. In papers written for later courses, and in interviews I had with him after he left my classroom, he more openly confronted the implications of his homosexuality for himself and his relationship with his family. (Excerpts from these papers are presented in the later sections of this chapter on gender and sexual orientation and ideology.)

Initially, Carl presented himself as understanding of the reasons why he and his parents found themselves with differing cultural perspectives. In an early paper, he explored generational differences between immigrant parents and their children:

> Becoming educated in the new country is harder for the parents. For the most part the parents must go directly to work in order to support their family. [Mario] Puzo and [Richard] Rodriguez both wrote about how hard their parents worked and I can echo their writings. My parents joined the work force as soon as they arrived. The immigrants' children normally go straight into school unless the situation is so critical that they are forced to work as well. For those who can go to school, if completed, they will undoubtedly be better educated than their parents and have more options to move on to. . . .
>
> "Going with the flow" of things would certainly be easier for the children than their parents. Even after living here 25 years, my parents are still shocked by customs that I take in stride. They expect my married sisters to slave in front of the kitchen to feed their husbands. My response to this is "this is the 80's. It's okay for women not to be their husbands slave." They give me a disgusted and shocked look and the conversation ends. Going to school, I learned what was acceptable in terms of behavior and attitude and what was not. I learned, somewhat, what to expect from life. I became an "American," not knowing what it really means while my parents still struggle to keep part of their culture by pretty much ignoring the one I accepted. By becoming "American" and speaking the language, I have opened more doors that I would have by "remaining" Spanish.

Even while espousing assimilation as his savior, Carl provided a rationale for his parents' adherence to their traditional ways.

In another paper, the break between Carl and his parents was pictured as widening as he discussed why the children of immigrant parents drift apart from their families more frequently than do children whose parents were born in the United States. Carl forcefully described his current relationship with his parents:

> In my own experience, I can see the barrier education has created between my parents and myself. Our conversations must be short and on uncontroversial topics. Once a debate begins, the yelling starts as well. I *dismiss* [italics added] their opinions because they are Spanish opinions or I'll say, "This is America, if you don't like it go back to Ecuador."
> . . . Unfortunately, when it comes to social attitudes, immigrant parents can be narrow minded, at least in my experiences. I have dealt with Spanish friends and relatives who are so prejudiced that I have trouble speaking to them without getting angry. This has been one reason I keep my friends away from home. I would not subject them to that. This causes the break in social situations. I will not associate with my parents or their friends nor will I bring friends to meet them. We are from two different worlds when it comes down to the people we associate with.

Carl had no desire to attach himself to the cultural community that provided comfort and support for his parents. At this point, his disregard for his parents' views was unabashed. He was not yet as secure and open about his homosexuality as he would be in the next few years, so it was safer to keep himself distanced from his family. He later told me that he could confide some things to his mother (like his homosexuality) but never to his father.

In still another paper in which Carl compared his experiences with those of Richard Rodriguez, he pictured himself as an outsider in his family life, the price he was willing to pay to assimilate to the dominant culture.

> Speaking to Spanish relatives has been as difficult a task for me to do as it is for Richard Rodriguez. I feel uncomfortable when I'm forced to visit with friends or family from Ecuador because I am unable to answer their questions so my parents must act as a go between to bridge the gap in our communication problem. . . .
> What separates Richard from myself is that he seems to feel guilty for the drifting. I feel uncomfortable and at times wish Spanish friends or relatives would never come over *but I never feel guilty* [italics added]. My attitude has always been—this is the U.S., you have to speak the language and go with the flow of things. This has been a constant source of argument with my parents and three of my sisters, all of which were born in Ecuador. I feel my youngest sister who was born here 4 years before me is more comfortable in English situations than Spanish though her Spanish is better than mine. In comparing the two of us I see that she has not drifted as far away from the family as I have.
> Part of the blame of my lack of ability in being able to communicate could be placed on my parents. They never forced or even asked us to speak Spanish around the house so with each year my ability to speak the language got worse, though I can understand most of it. I don't blame them for the way I am but then they can't blame me for answering their Spanish spoken questions with my English spoken answers.

Although Carl offered language differences as a partial cause for the estrangement between his family and himself, even he acknowledged that this was only one factor among many that had led to both a cultural and emotional detachment. Writing allowed Carl to reflect on his relationship with his family and the choices he was making, although at this point he saw his possible choices as extreme polar ones, requiring him to reject his family's culture and values in order to project a specific identity for himself. Carl's determination to be identified as an "American" showed up even more strongly in his later writings, as he seemed oblivious to the dangers of stereotyping entire groups, since he was so certain that such characterizations could not apply to him. (Carl's papers on the issue of stereotyping are presented in the next section of this chapter.)

Delores' attitude toward her family was quite the opposite of Carl's. Even though she, too, was separated through her educational attainments from her family, particularly her mother, her admiration for her mother's fortitude in keeping the family together and supporting Delores' efforts to gain higher education increased her affection and respect for her family. She wrote about this in a paper for the English 2 course in which she compared her experience of assimilating into American culture with Richard Rodriguez's:

> In summary, both Richard Rodriguez and I had similar experiences in assimilating to the American culture. It can be seen clearly that both Richard Rodriguez and I were forced or expected to behave in certain way. Richard Rodriguez was expected to speak only in English at home. I, on the other hand, was encouraged to speed up my learning process by listening to American music and watching only American television. Furthermore, I learned the language and assimilated to the culture, yet I didn't detached myself from my Hispanic background. On the contrary, Richard Rodriguez did assimilate to the American culture, but also went through feelings of detachness from the family structure.

As mentioned elsewhere, Delores' closeness to her family allowed her to retain her cultural identity, but simultaneously she was acquiring the knowledge and education that would allow her to become a respected member of both her own community and the larger society, without a sense of alienation to either one.

Issues of cultural identity and assimilation are also closely connected for Jacob. Born in Korea but moving to Australia at the age of 8 and receiving most of his elementary and all of his secondary education there, Jacob had a "western" approach to education by the time he enrolled in City College as a freshman in the fall of 1989, but he was still influenced by the Korean cultural traditions practiced in his family life. In a paper for his freshman composition course in which students were asked to assign themselves to suggested categories in relation to degrees of assimilation to American culture, Jacob wrote that he believed he fell into the "Anglo-Conformity model."

> In that all my acquaintances outside of the family are white and I do not participate in the "society within a society" of expatriate Koreans. However, Gordon's definition for my individual case would need to be modified, for I have not been so totally

"absorbed" as to have lost all allegiance to my past. I still identify with Koreans to an extent, participate in some traditional Korean ceremonies with my family, eat ethnic Korean food and mix up my English (at home) with a splattering of odd Korean words. I would therefore fit into a more lenient version of Anglo-Conformity, not totally isolated from my native culture but basically "Westernized."

It is notable that he mentioned here only sporadic participation in cultural customs that essentially had no meaningful impact on his identity as an individual. He continued to assert an identification with his Korean culture, as the next paper excerpt demonstrates but deep within his life, there were other cultural traits, not mentioned here, that seriously impacted his free choice in deciding the direction of his future.

In his final paper for the English composition course, Jacob wrote about the novel *Mama Day*, which had been assigned to the class. His thesis for this paper was that "assimilation requires commitment, not sacrifice." In the paper, Jacob contrasted the urban and rural experiences of the two main characters, George and Cocoa, and then raised the question of whether one must give up one's culture in order to assimilate:

> [This] naturally leads us to the question of what can be done to remedy this situation. How does someone like George or Cocoa, or an immigrant like Maxine Hong Kingston, assimilate into the new society? Is Richard Rodriguez, the son of Mexican-American parents, correct when he describes how one can successfully be assimilated into the student life of a new country in the following way:
>
>> For a time, the scholarship boy may try to balance his loyalty between his concretely experienced family life and the more abstract mental life of the classroom. In the end, though, he must choose between the two worlds: if he intends to succeed as a student, he must, literally and figuratively, separate himself from his family. . . . To succeed in the classroom, I needed psychologically to sever my ties with Spanish. Spanish represented an alternate culture.
>
> Does one need really to sacrifice one's native "culture" in order to assimilate into a new one. Does ignoring and discarding your past experiences and connections lead necessarily to assimilation? Most veritably this is not the case.

Here is Jacob's most direct assertion of his own view on retaining some semblance of one's own culture. Although he had previously described himself as "not totally isolated from my native culture but basically 'Westernized,'" here he more strongly claims that discarding one's past does not inevitably lead to assimilation. Yet, in an earlier paper written that semester, Jacob opened the issue of family pressure on academic and professional life choices, an issue having strong cultural roots in his own family.

In a paper comparing the educational progress of minorities with immigrants, Jacob revealed the pressures he felt from his Korean family and culture:

> When we see the family environment too, we are aware of a contrast that supports the educational discrepancy [between immigrants and minorities]. In a 1988 article

titled "The Model Minority Goes to School," a 10th-grade Vietnamese immigrant to the U.S. describes the pressures she faces from her family to excel in class. I can personally vouch for the accuracy of the description of the push for Asian immigrants at least to not only do well, but to beat everyone else. Not necessarily so in my family [a disclaimer he rejects in interviews over later years], but Koreans in general that I see around me, push their children without mercy from the beginning. Success not only brings personal glory, but is said to improve the image of the community of Koreans as a whole, a need to prove ourselves in our new home. . . .

Like Carl, Jacob had distanced himself from the cultural community of his mother, but his continuous disillusionment with college life can likely be traced to pressures to succeed academically. He was required to be a source of pride to his family and community in professions they would find acceptable, especially because he was the only son in his family. His travels through academic majors that he consistently disliked—from architecture to a brief flirtation with the social sciences to physics to computer science—forced him into studies that not only did not interest him but committed him to a life without joy or enthusiasm. Writing was his real life.

Stereotyping

The issue of stereotyping was a sensitive one to most of the students in my study. However, their responses to these kinds of characterizations varied. As Chandra's and Ricardo's writings in this chapter reveal, their reactions were to rebut such views. Carl's acquiescence to ethnic stereotyping can perhaps be understood as a defense against the potential for stereotyping him in relation to his sexual orientation. If he could be more American than the Americans, perhaps he could be better shielded from some societal judgments about his identity as a gay man.

Carl wrote two papers in the freshman composition course that dealt with how stereotyping was applied to individuals with a Latino background. In both papers, he took no offense at derogatory characteristics being applied to those of his background, since he believed himself to be so totally Americanized that none of the epithets could possibly apply to him. In the first paper, Carl recounted an experience he had had in high school:

I've never been stereotyped as a "typical hispanic" in a mean-spirited way. In high school, the lunchroom was filled with racial jokes. There I was typecast as a "typical hispanic" which meant I was on welfare, that I came from a big family, that there was numerous possibilities on who my natural father was, that I carried a switchblade, that I wore lots of multicolored outfits and that I stole car radios in my spare time when I wasn't eating rice and beans or dealing drugs on the corner. The guys saying these things meant it as a joke and I took it as one. These things don't bother me as anyone who does feel that way is not going to change.

It is striking that Carl genuinely seems to take no offense at these stereo-typical characteristics, believing that since they do not apply to him, it was harmless to apply them to others. He also has no commitment to change the stereotyped views in those who hold them.

In the second paper that semester, one dealing with the stereotyping of minorities, Carl focused on education and job discrimination, with some references to his own experiences. Again he denied that he could be included in any group that "does poorly and can barely speak English," ignoring the malice behind such blatant group characterization. He demonstrated some sensitivity in this paper to the danger of an entire group being stereotyped by the actions of a few, but he remained distanced from this problem, seeing safety in his own exclusion from such characterization. However, he did acknowledge that stereotyping could be harmful to some, citing his knowledge of an experience that a "darker skinned Black" friend of his had, although the implication here was that the prejudice was entirely caused by her darker skin color:

> [John] Ogbu also points out that "black education has usually been inferior and often separate" (p. 85). The white kids had the better facilities, teachers and materials for their school, while blacks had to settle for less and for the most part, had to travel to the designated "black" school. People, in my opinion, have never put me in the category of being a typical "dumb spic" who does poorly in school and can barely speak English. . . . There will always be blacks and hispanics who do poorly in school, drop out and deal drugs on the corner. Even a small number is enough to give a tainted view of a whole race or group. . . .
>
> Even when minorities are hired for jobs there are still negative stereotypes to deal with. My manager [in a stock job at Bloomingdales] once told me that she and a friend both worked as waitresses to help pay for college. My manager was never allowed to wait on the front tables, where the better tips were usually received. The owner's reasoning was that it was better to have the other girl up front because she was [a] light-skinned black and as such, she gave the place a better look. The stereotype that light-skinned blacks are somehow better than darker-skinned blacks is still around today. . . .

Although these papers suggest that Carl had some sensitivity to the danger of stereotyping for those who were so depicted, his need to separate himself from any minority ethnic or racial group dominated his rhetoric, implying as he had said in other papers that his Americanization and his academic accomplishments should be obvious to others so he personally would never find himself in a position where he could be denigrated by others. Because he recognized that his homosexuality could lead to potential negative characterizations of himself, he must be so "American" that his background cannot provide anyone with other reasons to criticize him. By resolving one aspect of his background in a way that was satisfactory to himself (his ethnicity or lack of ethnicity), he set himself free to resolve his sense of personal identity. (This may be an "overanalytic" interpretation on my part, because he apparently separated himself from his parents' culture at a very young age; yet, his suspicions of his sexual orientation apparently also came to him at an early age. Carl's first statement of his knowledge of his sexual orientation came in a play he wrote for a creative writing course in 1992 in which the main character, Brad, told a friend that he knew he was gay since he was 10 years old. An excerpt from this play is presented later in this chapter.)

In a midterm examination for a communications course in the spring of 1992, Ricardo's third year at the college, he was asked to analyze readings that dealt with how minorities are pictured by the media. For each of two essays, he was also to select a salient quotation. In one of his essays, he focused on how Blacks are stereotyped in films:

> The Black experience and the Puerto Rican experience is very similar. Even though we [Puerto Ricans] did not serve as slaves the process by which Blacks are oppressed are the same. In the essay by Donald Bogle titled *Toms, Coons, Mulattos, Mammies, and Bucks*, we see how Blacks had being Excluded, Dehumanized and Discriminated in the jobs that they [are portrayed in] in the mass media.
>
> The first [Black] characters that were portrayed in the movies were played by whites. This was the beginning of the process of dehumanization. That Black women were always shown as Mammies or prostitutes and the Black man was either a Coon, a Buck, a Tom or a Mulatto serves the purpose of oppressing a whole race. That when Black filmmakers and actors started to develop their film industry and take some control over the kind of film they would make, they used the same stereotypes had being used against them. An example of that even thought [it] was shot by Vicente Minneli is Cabin in the Sky. In this film we see all the same stereotypes done by Black actors, but the quality of their acting is good. I am not condoning the use of those stereotypes, but they were seeing [seen?] in control of their work. From that movie we can jump to others like Super Fly and Shaft that used the Bucks as their platform. The main problem with this type of cinema was that they never dealt with real problems, but they gave the audiences an artificial [portrait] of the Black experience. Quote from the article: "Blaxtaploitation film, a movie that played on the need of Black audiences for heroic figures with answering those needs in realistic terms" (p. 242).

The quotation he selected illustrates his awareness that the filmmakers were consciously portraying their Black characters as superheroes because they believed that these portrayals would earn them bigger audiences and bigger profits. As Ricardo was aware, the term *Blaxtaploitation* carries the strong meaning of intentional exploitation of audiences that were being stereotyped just as the actors' roles were.

Carl's and Ricardo's writings demonstrate students' awareness of stereotyping being applied to racial and cultural groups. Although Carl denied being implicated in such typecasting, his easy recognition of the characteristics assigned to Latinos reveals how widespread such characterizations are. He may not take up the battle of overcoming the use of derogatory traits directed at his cultural group, but he became an impassioned fighter against negative stereotyping of another minority group with whom he gradually developed a proud identification, homosexuals. Resolving these parts of his identity gave him the freedom to pursue the academic and professional goals he desired. Ricardo's fight for justice was more broadly based, encompassing all groups that are discriminated against. Both students' writing reflect that conflict leads to learning, although not all of the lessons learned are equally desirable.

Racism

In their courses over the years, students had opportunities to reflect on how racism affected their lives and the lives of others. Reading and writing assignments brought them opportunities to contemplate how they could best reconcile their native cultures with the often socioeconomically more privileged cultures they were exposed to. Such openings authorized them to scrutinize attitudes and practices that they believed needed to be changed.

In an interview in December 1992, her fourth year at the collge, Joan told me that her mother was 58, disabled, and had an eighth-grade education. Joan gave her mother five words a day to learn. After experiencing problems with Joan's siblings, her mother had pressured her to succeed. She told her that she had made mistakes with the other children and she wanted to take time with her. Joan also said that at age 20, a year before this interview, she had had her first experience with racism. Someone pushed her and called her a nigger. From then on, she had had a wall of hate, and she felt she shouldn't talk to certain people, Whites, Asians, Hasidic Jews, anybody that she felt was prejudiced toward her. She said it took her a year to get it out of her system. She also said that she wanted to get into clinical psychology so that she could deal with troubled teens, especially those who were into narcotics. She promised herself that she would never turn out like her brothers and sisters. Being at college was her life.

The next semester, in a paper for U.S. Society 101 on "The Flawless Constitution," Joan raised the issue of slavery:

> The Declaration of Independence was constructed to help all individuals establish the right to life, liberty and the pursuit of happiness. However, peoples lives were constantly taken, which violated the life issue. People owned slaves which were considered 3/5's of a person each. Moreover, these slaves were chained, over-worked and beaten which helped to violate the liberty and pursuit of happiness issues. It will never be believed by anyone that slaves could possibly be happy being chained like animals, and constantly worked.

This last sentence in particular expressed Joan's analysis of what she had been studying. But, for her instructor, this discussion of slavery appeared to be a digression. The instructor commented: "Also, you wander from this theme when you discuss slavery. Now, slavery could be incorporated if you wanted to talk about how slaves were never given due process in that their masters determined guilt and punishment." Thus, her instructor attempted to move Joan away from her response toward a more legalistic stance, ignoring the experiential analysis Joan was attempting.

In his first semester at the college, Donald wrote a paper for his English composition course comparing the discrimination leveled against minorities with that leveled against immigrants in the field of higher education. Drawing on his own experience as an African American, he described the advice given to him and other minority students by his guidance counselor:

> Under personal experience in high school, my guidance counselors many times tried to discourage minorities from applying to well-known and respected colleges. Even with an acceptable grade point average, they were told it would be impossible to be accepted. After this belief from my counselor was issued many went on their own and applied. And to their surprise, they were; well many were accepted. And to our surprise many non-minorities with poor grade point averages were encouraged [to apply].

Although Donald's voice was muted in this discussion, his sense of personal outrage at this type of treatment is apparent. Furthermore, his experience provides just a small window into the obstacles that many minority students face as they attempt to negotiate the "system" that is often closed to them.

But Donald's outrage was transformed to pride in his racial identity as a paper he wrote for his World Humanities 103 in the fall of 1994 demonstrated. In this paper, he analyzed several poems of Langston Hughes. He concluded the paper as follows:

> The final and strongest example that expresses this survival theme is "African-American Fragment," the first poem of his selected writings. It starts by saying black history and culture is being maintained through fragmented history books and songs. And we must cling to what is available. Once these items are remembered, our existence will continue.
>
> Music is such a powerful medium. It is able to convey or create a desired emotion: happiness, sorrow, anger, fear. At one time, the drum was a major part of our communication. The poem says that the drums of our past has been silenced, yet when we hear it, a special bond is formed. Feelings of our ancestral home is evoked, and as strange as it may seem, we are brought closer to our heritage.
>
> The history of the black community has been so distorted throughout time that this poem pleads with its reader to save what little memories are left. The history of our people was once relayed through music and song, since many of our ancestors were unable to read or write. Therefore, we must save the songs and memories of our ancestors; acknowledging them will maintain our present existence.
>
> These songs makes us aware of our past and therefore we are able to direct our future. We are able to find strength and self worth in ancestor's accomplishments. For if a man or a people knows their past, they will be able to learn from the previous mistakes.
>
> As long as the black man exists, he will always be faced with the struggle of survival. He was persecuted throughout slavery and he overcame that obstacle. He is persecuted today and he still finds strength within himself. Equality is a dream that will one day become a reality.

Here we see that the student who would not accept the racist recommendations of a high school guidance counselor has come to the point where his entire cultural history informs him so that he can fight to overcome obstacles such as the ones he confronted earlier in his life.

In a paper he wrote for the English 2 class his first semester at the college, Ricardo described a personal incident that occurred after he emigrated to New York City and began to work in a camera shop:

> While in my job, I became one of the best salesman for the company. I was making over $25,000.00 a year at the age of twenty two. But I was uneasy at this job. The racism and prejudice that was evident was making me look for ways to get out of it. And finally one day a manager saw me in the stock room pulling merchandise for a sale that I was working on. He came to me and shouted "that I was the same as all the other Puerto Ricans, that I was a thief." I have never killed anyone but he got very close to be the first one. I had never been insulted like that in my life. I told the manager what had happened and he laughed in my face. That made me mad. I presented a complaint to the store manager and he said to forget about it and he apologized on behalf of the other. I left that job a couple of months later when I found a job at another camera store. Several jobs followed until I decided to change my career.
>
> It hasn't been easy to start all over again. I'm giving it the best I got. The financial responsibilities and the cost of living in New York are obstacles that are making it very difficult. I plan to get my degree in Film & Video. I want to be able to use my art to educate people, and prepare them to fight against the injustices and the prejudices that bear all over us. You don't need weapons to create awareness. You need books to eliminate ignorance. We can only do it, if we have the education.

In another paper he wrote for this same course, Ricardo demonstrated the activist part of his nature. In discussing Maya Angelou's *I Know Why the Caged Bird Sings*, Ricardo concluded his discussion by considering the larger issue of racism considered in the autobiography:

> Due to Maya Angelou determination, sense of pride and activism she was able to break new grounds not only in the streetcar system in San Francisco [as the first female operator] but on the struggle to maintain her identity and self respect as a black person. This story could had happen in any period of time from the 1930's to the late 1980's. But no matter what period of time it take place, we have to take charge and be active in order to produce changes that would eliminate the bias and racism forever.

Unlike Carl, who sees stereotyping and racist comments as harmless because he assumes they cannot apply to him, Ricardo not only felt the impact of racist behavior toward himself personally, but he was able to see beyond his own situation to how the larger society would be impacted by such attitudes and behaviors. Ricardo always had a mission to help others; at this point, early in his academic career, he saw the field of communication as an outlet that would allow him to fight against the "injustices and the prejudices that bear all over us." Later, disillusioned by the lack of opportunity in the field of communication, he returned to a more personal ambition of being a positive force by becoming a physician assistant and working in poverty communities.

Ricardo's awareness of how stereotyping leads to racism is evident in another part of his response to an essay examination in his communications course in the spring of 1992. In this section of the examination essay, Ricardo analyzed how stereotyping led to oppression and subordination of minority groups. Despite some persistent grammatical problems, Ricardo had developed a forceful rhetorical style:

> Welcome Home, Richie Perez article about the negative stereotypes of the Puerto Rican Community in El Centro really hits right at home. As I said before the only difference between the Black experience and ours is the fact that Blacks were brought into this country as slaves over 200 years ago and that Puerto Ricans were flown over to do the same jobs as harvest croppers. The way Hollywood excluded the Puerto Ricans reality is not a new thing. It was started against the Black community. Neither is the Dehumanization of a whole ethnic group by using the same negative stereotypes over and over again. Sound familiar. Also the fact that when we appear in a film or in television we are always represented by the same stereotypical jobs. We are either building superintendent or factory workers.
>
> That we don't hold any powerful position in the media industry is not alarming. After so many years of that kind of negative stereotype, *who the hell want's to employ a Puerto Rican.* When our people are offer roles in the media those roles are as in the case of our female actress, a hot blooded latina or a virginal innocent wimp. Both of them the extremes. In the case of our male actors, they are basically thieves or junkies and they always are [seen] carrying knives.
>
> This whole process has being done with the purpose of oppressing my ethnic group. As in the case of the independentista movement is done to suppress dissension and to confuse the community. To restrain us in a subordinate position against white domination, and they try very hard.
>
> Quote from the article: "The effect is to deprive our children of positive role models, and to rob our people of our history, culture, sense of pride, and self-respect" (p. 9).

Ricardo is proud of his identity in a Puerto Rican–Latino culture. His own upbringing, his sense of values, and his moral courage led him to condemn injustice and to design a life for himself that will not only bring pride to him personally but meaningful deeds to his cultural community. For Ricardo, social justice for all is the most legitimate goal one can strive for.

In their consideration of the ways that race and ethnicity impacted their lives, the students in my study demonstrated how they were mediating between the academic culture and their background cultures. Not surprisingly, they evidenced strong feelings about issues of personal and cultural identity, assimilation, stereotyping, and racism. But, as can be seen from their writings, there was not a monolithic view on these matters. Each individual took on him or herself the right to reflect on these questions and respond to them. Carl's detachment from his family and Delores' strengthening attachment to her mother present one strong contrast in views on assimilation. Jacob's attempts to deny that his family pressures force him into academic and occupational areas he dislikes contrast with the true support and encouragement that Joan receives from her family. Even though one supports the child's own desire, whereas the other places obstacles in the path of personal goals, it could be said that both mothers want the same thing for their children.

As the students bring their own experiences and knowledge to bear on the readings, topics for papers, and essay-examination questions they confront, they display raw honesty and integrity in presenting their views and analyses. The papers demonstrate that the students expect fair readings and hearings from many of their instructors as they grapple with bringing their cultural heritage into a meaningful relationship with the academic culture. Certainly an environment like the one at City College is more familiar with and more conducive to valuing such explorations than some other academic settings might be, but this does not diminish the accomplishments of the students who benefit from the opportunities to grow more proud of their identities and cultures as they become more analytical about the mores of the larger society.

GENDER AND SEXUAL ORIENTATION

Lavin and Hyllegard (1996) pointed out that college graduates "tend . . . to move from traditional conceptions of gender roles to more egalitarian views about women's roles and opportunities" (p. 177). Such awareness can be seen to develop in the students in this study as they progressed through their education. They became not only more sensitive to how women should be viewed, but also developed the ability to see men's roles as more complex than the traditional "macho" image fostered in much of the popular culture.

Considerable attention has been paid to women's orientation to knowledge in recent years. Two of the most influential studies have been Gilligan's, *In a Different Voice* (1982), and Belenky et al.'s *Women's Ways of Knowing* (1986). Gilligan argued that because women take into account particular circumstances as well as abstract principles, they are not necessarily less morally developed than men. Belenky and her colleagues noted that women are more embedded in particular social contexts and relationships and that this perspective influences their thinking over the college years.

In her early study of the composing process of twelfth graders, Emig (1971) found that her female subjects were more comfortable than the males in writing in the reflexive mode, which "focuses upon the writer's thoughts and feelings concerning his experiences; the chief audience is the writer himself; the domain explored is often the affective; the style is tentative, personal, and exploratory" (p. 4). The males in her study were more comfortable writing in the extensive mode, which "focuses upon the writer's conveying a message or a communication to another; the domain explored is usually the cognitive; the style is assured, impersonal and often reportorial" (p. 4). Since the writing excerpts presented in this section deal with gender and sexual orientation issues, the writing the students in this study did differed from the styles cited by Emig, as her subjects wrote about open topics. All students were reflecting on their complex social contexts and backgrounds, thus essentially obviating the differences that might be found in samples of other types of writing. Being embedded in a social context does not mean that the writer is less cognitively active nor astute; it suggests, instead, that the writer is bringing dimensions of personal knowledge and experience to bear on the analysis of the issue under investigation.

Jones-Royster (1992) pointed out that even in the mid-1980s, African-American women were not being talked about "as intellectuals in any systematic way" (p. 9). Instead, they were nurtured as "achievers, as creative and ingenious beings, as leaders, but not really as thinkers, as scholars, as intellectuals. Fortunately, for us times and images change" (p. 9). As the illustrations from the students' writing in this section demonstrate, the African-American women in this study (Linda, Chandra, and Joan) did come to see themselves as "thinkers," as did Delores, a Latino woman. The writings of Carl, Donald, and Ricardo explored ways in which the traditional images of men need to be reassessed. Audrey demonstrated how a White woman must assert herself to fulfill her potential as a woman. Only Jacob, of my central group of students, did not consider his gender role in his writing, although as was pointed out in the previous section, as the only son in his family, he is "destined" to fulfill his mother's ambitions for "success," not his own. Jacob never acknowledged this conflict in his academic writings; he only revealed these problems in the interviews we had over the years.

The issues students investigated in relation to gender and sexual orientation are closely related to those they examined in relation to race and ethnicity. Attention was paid to support or lack of it in their gender roles, the complexity of asserting an identity, how pride grew in their assertion of their identity, the pressure to conform to majority standards, and how gender influenced their opportunities in the future.

Support in Gender Roles

Papers written by two women students poignantly illustrate how their sense of self is fostered by family attitudes toward the roles of women. In a paper for a psychology course written in the spring of her second semester at the college, Linda described how she was encouraged by her mother to be a strong and independent person:

Finally there is my need for motivational drive of achievement. My goal is to become an honor student at City College. I am very ambitious and expect a lot of life. This is a goal that comes [from] deep within me which I want to openly express in my schoolwork. This ambition [was] started early is my life by my mother who let me handle my own responsibilities. Since I had such independence when I was young, I carried it over to my schoolwork.

Linda is a student who started at the English 1 level, hardly a predictor of much success from traditional perspectives. Eventually recognizing her difficulties with the chemistry courses in her original major, nursing, she changed her major to psychology, in which she not only found herself academically more prepared but also in an environment where she received additional nurturing and support from the faculty in the department. Although never achieving honor roll status, she graduated with a respectable 2.7 average.

Even though Joan received strong support from her mother, as she described in a paper she wrote for the English 2 class her first semester at the college, she never recovered from the hurt of her father's rejection of her. In the paper, she tells how her father wanted a son instead of a daughter when she was born. She feels that her being a girl helped cause the rift between her father and mother. She wrote, "Every time they spoke, they would argue about me. Then I would hear 'If this was my son.' I often heard this phrase and I tried to ignore it, but every time I heard it, it would hit me right in the heart. I've held back my feelings for many years." In an interview several years later, Joan, who by then was working several part-time jobs to sustain herself, told me that the only time she heard from her father was when he wanted to borrow money. She was unwilling to help him. As in Linda's and Delores' cases, Joan's mother was the primary supporter who believed in her goals.

In an interview at the end of her second year at City College, Audrey described her evolving relationship with her family, indicating how sibling relationships can complicate family ties. She openly described her changing relationships with her family to me: "The first time [at a smaller college in Iowa] I didn't study hard enough. In the second year, I transferred to a bigger school [the University of Iowa] where my sister was. I didn't do too well when she was around. My sister is the perfect child; she got excellent grades. She was what my parents wanted—a genius. Anyone else was worthless. Only intelligence counted; only school work was valued. My parents feel better about me now. I'm getting good grades and I'm on my own. They respect me for that." Perhaps being away from her family gave Audrey the independence she needed to convince herself of her own capabilities.

As these excerpts from papers and interviews from three women students reveal, the presence of a supportive environment enhances their likelihood to succeed. When discouraging factors enter their lives, they must muster within themselves the strength and determination to carry on. I have said elsewhere that I am not arguing that the population in this study is a representative population of inner-city students:

> It [is] not surprising that in an urban, inner-city public college like City College, many of the students in the study are in the first generation of their families to attend college, but it was also not uncommon to find students with siblings who either already attend college or plan to. So, although most of the students' parents have not had higher education, there is clearly an "education ethic" that is strong in many of the families. Such a finding suggests that students who are considered to be high risk because of their economic and educational backgrounds may in fact be a select population who have been encouraged by their families to achieve professional and financial success as have previous generations of immigrants and individuals from poor economic straits. Thus this study will not claim to make broad generalizations about the writing and learning processes of urban, high-risk college students in general, but it will attempt to account for the kind of progress that is possible for students of this background. (Sternglass, 1993, p. 241)

As the extended presentation of the student's experiences in this book reveals, the students who persisted at the college were a highly motivated group who had both academic shortcomings and economic setbacks to overcome before they could achieve their goals. (Their economic difficulties are described more fully in the section on class in this chapter.)

Complexity of Asserting Identity

Most frequently, gender issues of identity are associated with women with labels that are interpreted negatively, such as "too aggressive" or "immodest." But stereotypes of men are equally damaging, and when physical appearance suggests a particular kind of acceptable behavior, men, too, have difficulty acquiring the courage to assert their right to behave as they deem appropriate.

Donald is a tall, muscular but not heavy young African-American man, who looks like he could be a superb athlete. In a paper for an advanced writing course titled "The Man in the Mirror," written in the fall of his third year at the college, he reflected on the effect his physical appearance had on others:

> Is the man in the mirror really me, or is he just a figment of my vast imagination? Am I still the same individual, who once started out so innocently? Or have I grown to be someone or something else, for my ever changing society?
> In these times, it is very difficult for an individual to remain in single state of being. He is approached time and time again by different characters in his or her life, that for each new personality he comes across, he adds another section to his being. I too am caught up in this ever changing cycle. I am more times looked upon as a strong and stable individual because of my size; but in reality I am putting forth an act, to hide my insecurities.

People believe I should have great confidence because I am able to intimidate others by my size. Well one night a few friends and I went to a gospel concert, and were later approached by another group of young men wanting to rob us. We all stood our ground, showing no fear and they backed off. My friends later told me, that if I was not there, they would have been scared out of their minds. I too was afraid but I felt that I had to live up to the stature that they placed me in.

Another personality that most people are unable to see is the sensitive and artistic side of me. Most people look at me and see the athletic side. They say, "Oh, you must play basketball, football and all those kinds of things"; in which I do, but I am also a great big softy. In my spare time my artistic side emerges from its slumber. I many times seclude myself and then begin writing poetry or painting. These were the only activities in which I was capable of expressing myself without fear. . . .

Through fear, my true personality must take on the form of the stature called machismo. I many times go along with the crowd upon an issue, because I am afraid of the negative attitudes that will be geared towards me. Unless they are true friends, I have nothing to hide; and true friends are quite rare. But I usually use my comical side to hide the present insecurity. But there was one incident in my life, which I vividly remember, in which these two personalities clashed. One day while hanging around with a few of my friends, we viewed a dog, which was despised by most of the neighborhood, get crushed under the wheel of a speeding car. Most of my friends laughed and cheered about it, but I was almost torn apart. I didn't want to look like a big softy in front of my friends, but the animal-lover part of me, brought tears to my eyes. They began laughing at me, but [I explained] to them that I was man enough to show my true feelings. I felt real good about myself, but the fear still remains. I guess it is just a fail safe device that my body has created, to keep me from opening up too much and getting hurt.

It is quite hard as well as difficult, for most people to express themselves, because their actions usually, do not fit the accepted norm(s) created by society. Once one oversteps the boundaries in which man have constructed, you are considered abnormal in the eyes of the followers. Man must learn to accept the diversity in the cultures. For until we are able to show our true selves, our true reflection and inner being, we will all be displaced into the state of multiple personalities. We must learn to accept the individuality surrounding us, for in time, the real personality will be smothered by its counterparts, never to be seen again.

In this paper, Donald's concern was that he would be stereotyped by his physical appearance and that his caring nature would be subordinated and perhaps even lost if society denied him the right to be the complex individual he wished to be. He became the youngest deacon in his church, thus asserting his right to have a caring nature.

Pride in Asserting Identity

Over her years in the college, Delores grew steadily more confident of her identity as a Black Latino woman. Through interviews and papers written in 1993, her fourth year at the college, she described the problems that had complicated her life as a student and the factors that strengthened her in her determination to succeed. In an interview in May 1993, Delores told me:

My personal life is not going the way I'd like it to. My boyfriend for three years got another girl pregnant, and I ended the relationship. Financially, it's not so easy for me. My mother sold her business, and finances are tighter than they were. My mother, brother, stepfather and I are all working. After all these problems, I keep hanging on. Problems get to me, but I have the ability to get around them. I can have problems, but I still do decent work. It takes a lot of energy. I have lost a lot of weight.

When asked whether she felt she was a different person from the person she was when she started at City College, Delores said:

The first semester I went through a period of extreme anxiety and depression. The first semester in school was a big thing—my first actual year in college—a big thing.

Looking back, every year I try to analyze what happened. I have come to understand that I'm here, I'm a woman. Back then my English wasn't so well. I was taking remedial courses—things didn't feel so good.

The project in Lehman really made me know—I tested myself. I could do it or I couldn't. Fifteen started, nine finished. I had no doubt I could do it. I got up at 3 A.M. to do that paper and other work and two jobs.

I know myself a little better. I know I have the perseverance to do what I want. I feel different. I'm a woman, a Latino woman, a Black woman.

I don't have doubts I can do these things. My family always supports me. I have a lot of good friends.

Without being the way I am, I couldn't do it. The main part is coming from me—the motivation. My financial situation is not good. I always see my mother struggling. My parents divorced when I was 5. My only identification was with my mother struggling—like her, I'm trying to struggle. All men who have passed through my life have disappointed me—my father, boyfriend, stepfather (I'm not proud of him), my brother is not a strong male figure. All male figures have failed me in my life. Only my mom doesn't disappoint me. My mother went through a lot—so can I. My mother's hard work tells me a lot.

Like Joan's father, Delores' father had not provided her with a positive male image, nor had the other men in her life. Delores' trials did not defeat her; they strengthened her. Her pride in being a Black Latino woman doubtless influenced her decision to study the relationship between skin color and self-esteem. Unlike the subjects she studied, her self-esteem had not been diminished by her own skin color.

Delores most directly stated this pride in her personal identity in a paper she wrote for a women's psychology course in the fall of 1993:

Theories of Social Psychology stress the individual in the social setting; social scientists argue that there is such anything as an individual aside from the social context. I could say that the way I have been socialized has shaped my sense of a woman. My parent's divorce and the fact that I was raised by my mother and have not received any moral or financial support from my father have taught me how to struggle in life and be proud of it. My arrival to the United States has affected me in the sense that I could not describe who is [Delores] without defining me as a black Latino woman. The goals that I have set for me, my way of thinking, my sense of self and my self-esteem have been the result of interaction with other people who I regard as role models, starting from my mother to my college professors. . . .

As I have mentioned before, one is affected by the environment in which one lives. I have felt that there have been other events in my life that were crucial in shaping my sense of a woman. The education I am getting has influence my sense of a woman. I feel that education has given me the self-esteem and the confidence that I need to go on in life. Education has open my mind to the world and make me want to explore life issues concerning me and my place in society. Through education I have become to realize that I am an important part of the coming generation, the generation who will be making the policies, and the important decisions that will affect the lives of others. A college education has made me become more self-aware of my humanity, and of my womanhood. . . .

Finally, living in the United States not only has strengthen my sense of a woman, but also my sense of ethnicity and the color of my skin so that I do not only see myself as a woman, I also see myself as a Latino black woman. Woman in the sense it is my gender and I will do my best to enhance it and work for the advancement of other women. A Latino woman in the sense that I am a Hispanic person in this country and I would work for the advancement of the Latino woman, which up to the present lacks recognition. A black woman because as the Latino, the black woman is lacking the recognition deserved.

No clearer statement of how a student's world view and academic experience come together to shape the individual personality could likely be found. This must surely be the synthesis that Bizzell (1986) was seeking.

Chandra's identity as a proud African-American woman also grew over her college years. In interviews and papers written between 1991 and 1993, she demonstrated her growing awareness of the characterization of African-American women in the media, and she came to resolve to change those stereotypes. For an introductory communications–film–video course in the fall of 1991, Chandra reviewed the film *Boyz in the Hood,* drawing on her own experiences to evaluate the depiction of African-American women:

"Boyz N the Hood" can be viewed as an educational film based upon real life events that occur in inner city black communities. As an African-American woman living in a crime infested neighborhood, I speak from experience. Many crimes in my neighborhood are not reported, therefore no legal action is taken. John Singleton, the director decided to take a stand, by addressing these issues, giving the audience an insider's view of what goes on in the "hood."

. . . For the most part, the director of this film should be commended. However, if there is one thing I could change in this movie, I would include some positive images of black women. Each woman in this film was depicted as being either ignorant, addicted to drugs, negligent mothers or referred to as "bitches, hoochies or ho's [whores]." Even the actress who plays Tres "educated" mother did not know how to make a U-turn or park her car.

Her complaint echoes that of Jones-Royster (1992), who had objected to the depiction of all Blacks and Hispanics as a monolithic group in a negative way. Chandra's sensitivity is directed particularly to the way that African-American women are portrayed, but the same argument can be applied that Jones-Royster argued for: "closer attention must be paid to group members who do not fit into those categories" (p. 9).

In the fall of 1993, Chandra wrote a paper titled, "The Media Image of Black Women: Mammies, Sapphires, and Jezebels." In this paper, Chandra argued that "television perpetuates and reinforces cultural stereotypes. Thus, viewers must become critical thinkers and decoders of this information that we are force-fed every day." Then, she went on to ask, "But who controls what we see?" Arguing that television programming is controlled by "white males," she questions how "black women are portrayed in situation comedies." Seen as "Mammies" (servants responsible for domestic duties and rearing children), "Sapphires" (talkative and sassy), or "Jezebels" (shapely seductresses who use their sexuality to get their way), "blacks were locked into stereotypes" as the only way of even being included in television programs. Citing the research of others, Chandra noted that television has "evolved from just being a tool for escapism to become the myth makers, the story teller and the passer of old cultural ideas." She also argued that "television's unspoken motive was to sell the 'American dream,' a white way of life and values to the American public." Here we see that 2 years after Chandra expressed her initial indignation at the stereotyping of Black women, she has moved to a critical analysis of the effects of such stereotyping and its damage to women like herself.

It was not surprising, then, that in an interview later that semester, Chandra told me that she was now considering becoming a director rather than an actress: "A director is more in control, hires others. I'm unhappy with the images of Black women in film. I either want to be on camera or behind it—in a decision-making position, creating images." Chandra had come to recognize that positions of power were essential to bringing about change in the way race and gender were depicted to the larger public. As she had become more confident about her own identity as an African-American woman, she sought to create the images that would depict her and others like her.

In a paper Audrey wrote for the freshman composition course, she described her journey from Iowa to New York, from failure in one academic setting to success at City College. She also considered the different potentials in her life as a result of decisions she made:

> I grew up in the midwest, where people don't have to lock their doors and install window guards to feel safe at night. At the University of Iowa, I neglected my schoolwork to run around with sorority pledge sisters, and later to mend a broken heart. I found myself on academic probation, unable to activate my sorority, and therefore, unable to remain a student with so much failure stacked up behind me. I got myself a job as a nanny for a New York City family, thinking I might be interested in the fashion business. My escape led to yet another escape since the nanny job didn't work out, so I found a tiny little apartment to share in Park Slope, Brooklyn. I was then forced to find my way around a big bad city, pay my own bills, take myself to the doctor, and buy my own groceries. In the process, I toughened up, stopped letting people take advantage of me, and opened my eyes to the real world.

I missed my family and home way of life. I had trouble meeting friends in the working world as opposed to a college campus. As rough and lonely as it all was, I convinced myself to stay in New York which has resulted in meeting my future husband and getting my grade point average up at the Borough of Manhattan Community College. I am now studying geography here at City College.

Had I stayed in Iowa, I would have muddled my way through school, married some guy, raised tons of children, and looked back on my life with disappointment. Instead, I am proud to say I'm not as bad as I thought.

Having proven to herself that she could survive and even thrive in the "big bad city," Audrey could now concentrate on her academic studies and look forward to a life that would be personally meaningful. I don't believe she meant to denigrate the life of the woman who chooses to stay home with a family, but rather that she wished to assert that she had created the conditions that allowed her to choose the future direction of her life for herself. And, furthermore, she had built her confidence level to a point where she now believed she could succeed on her own.

In a series of interviews and papers written from the spring of 1992 through the spring of 1993, Carl increasingly asserted his pride in his sexual orientation and his commitment to the community of homosexuals, something he had earlier been reluctant to do. In an interview in the spring of 1992, Carl told me that he was taking a creative writing class. He said, "It took me a while to really settle in and have total strangers read [my writing]." For this class, he wrote a short story that allowed him to examine his feelings toward publicly acknowledging his homosexual identity through a character he calls Brad. In this excerpt, Brad and another character, Fray, are having a conversation in a gay bar in which Brad has expressed feelings of uneasiness:

Fray gets up from his stool and approaches Brad. "Come over here," he motions off to the side. "I want to talk to you."

"Okay," Brad responds, with the uneasiness magnifying.

"You have to loosen up, Brad. Relax. Can I be honest with you?"

"Sure," Brad answers wondering where the conversation was going.

"Did you come out recently?" Fray asks.

"Last year," Brad whispers, trying to ignore the imagined stares. "Last year," he repeats a little louder, the burning sensation on the back of his neck lessening.

"Take it easy," Fray says in a soothing tone. "I thought it was something like that. Did you know earlier?"

Giving into Fray's powerful stare and apparent sincerity, Brad answers, "Since I was ten years old."

"That's good. I hate people who just all of sudden say they're gay. That's such bullshit. When you're gay you just know! You might deny it but you're always that way. I come here so that I can relax and have fun. I'm a faggot, Brad, and you are one too." Brad flinches, turning away from Fray's pointed stare. "I'm here I'm allowed to be free from what the world outside those door wants—no—expects to see. If you can't even be comfortable here then I know something's wrong. Do you understand what I'm saying?" Fray asks with a thoughtful smile.

"Yes . . . Not entirely. I can't be the way some of these people are," Brad says as he gestures with his hand. "I can't swish around or talk one way or another or . . ." Again Brad finds himself cut off, this time feeling a short sensation of anger about the interruption.

"Damn it, it's not about swishing around and wearing flaming clothes or anything like that. It's about accepting yourself and being comfortable. It's a tough world out there, Brad. We live in a heartless world. Yes, this place can be cruel too but we all share something special. It forces us all together . . .

. . . "What do I do? He's so sure of himself and of me. I don't want to let him down." Brad thinks to himself. "Damn it, didn't you hear a word of what he was saying? Don't let yourself down. Relax." Brad gives into the meaning of Fray's words. For the rest of the night he tells himself not to worry. "Take it slow," he thinks and starts moving to the music. They dance.

Through this story, Carl pictured how his surrogate Brad was helped to gain insight and self-confidence in his identity. Carl was clearly more comfortable at this point, because he allowed himself to share this story with his new professor and his new classmates.

A little later that spring, Carl went even further in opening himself to others. In a play written for the same creative writing class, he used his real name as well as the real names of his friends and members of his family. In the play, (as the narrator) Carl talked about how he arranged for a journal he had kept "involving some of my experiences in trying to get a taste of my [gay] subculture" to be left on his desk, "knowing that if the 'right' person walked in, my 'secret' would at last be revealed." That person was his mother and, as he had planned, she found and read the journal. The next morning, he said, "I remember sitting in the living room, wondering why mom avoided me when I tried to kiss her hello. Perhaps I have bad morning breath, I thought." The following day, Carl described how his mother "grabbed" and "spoke and cried at the same time":

> Come here and sit. I want to talk to you. I want you to know that I still love you and I don't want you to leave the house. You have to understand this some things parents do not wish for their children. You also have to understand that we can not tell your father. He would get angry and throw you out of the house.

Carl told his mother that it had been hard carrying "these thoughts" since he was 11 years old. He reluctantly accepted his mother's idea that he would not tell his father about his homosexuality "only because I know what he'll do to you and to me. . . . Once I'm gone, if he ever asks, I'm going to tell him the truth." Carl then tells all his sisters about his sexual orientation, and although they are accepting of his life, they warn him: "But we want you to understand how our parents are feeling. They're from a different country, a different background, all this is new to them."

At the end of the play, Carl, the narrator, analyzes his reactions to his decision to inform his family:

And so that's how it went with my family. . . . That weekend that my journal was discovered was a major one for me. The reactions of my family fell neatly into the molds I had worked out. I sometimes wish that the revelation had happened under different circumstances but I know that wishes never really come true. There really isn't that much more to rant and rave about. I still get worked up about the situation every once in a while Anyone who sees me on a day to day basis knows that. I still worry about what some of my friends will think should I ever come to them. . . . Well I'm drained. I have classes in the morning and then work. I don't expect to be worrying about this for another two weeks or so, but then who can really predict when their depressing moods set in? I certainly can't, not anymore. Okay. I've babbled enough. I'm going to sleep. [End of play]

Carl's ability to share his homosexuality with his family was a true turning point for him. He had been helped by the acceptance of his friends, colleagues, classmates, and professors, all of whom seem to have supported him. Getting the message to his family seemed to be the overcoming of the final hurdle that would now allow him to become a public advocate for the needs of others as well as himself.

A year later, in the spring of 1993, Carl wrote a paper for a psychology course in which he described how his own sense of identity and community had changed since he had started in the college in the fall of 1989. In the paper, titled "Homophobia: Why, How, and Who?," he described how his perceptions of gay individuals changed over time. A section of the paper titled, "Who is homophobic?," is presented here:

Unfortunately, because everyone has a little bit of prejudice within them, it is simply a matter of degree.

I have been guilty of being homophobic. Back in 1989, I was on my way to work and I happened by Central Park where the Gay Pride Parade participants were gathering. At that point in time, I was still struggling with my sexual orientation. I was put off, almost scared of the men in drag, the very masculine women, the leather crowd, the pierced bodies of some of the participants and all the "oddities" of the parade. My mind wasn't able to deal with the shock of it all. I was scared that I would turn into one of them, never realizing that there were people within the gay community who weren't like that, that if nothing else, our community was about diversity and that everyone had to be accepted. Just as I wanted to be accepted by my straight friends, I would have to be willing to accept gay people who were different from me.

As he explained in the play he wrote the year previously, other gay men helped him overcome his prejudices and accept the diversity within the homosexual community.

Carl summed up his feelings about himself in an interview in the late spring of 1993. When asked whether any big changes had occurred in his life during the past year, he said: "I'm being more open about being gay. It made relationships stronger. I had a nagging doubt about whether people would react negatively, but they haven't. Everyone at work [at The New York Times] knows. I talk about it a lot at work. People ask me questions because

I'm more accessible." In commenting on ways that he felt he was a different person from the person he was when he started City College, Carl said, "I'm a bit more stable—my job, my whole attitude about being gay." Carl's growing acceptance of his sexual orientation brought about a steadiness in his life. Once confident about his personal identity, he could focus his energies on his academic and work lives, both of which brought him praise and satisfaction.

The statements of Delores, Audrey, Chandra, and Carl over their college years illustrate how their experiences both in the academic setting and the real-world environment increased their sensitivity to how gender and sexual orientation were perceived. Rather than being daunted by any negative stereotypes or criticisms, they were strengthened in their determination to improve the way others of their backgrounds were portrayed. Being able to write about these topics in their classes provided them with opportunities to explore, analyze, define, and assert their personal identities. Through these reflections on their lives, they were able to bring their convictions into harmonious conjunction with their academic studies. They became increasingly active as proponents of social change.

Pressure to Conform to Majority Standards

Pressure to conform to traditional standards is most commonly applied to women. But in this study, the women students' pride in their identity as strong women allowed them to shrug off any concerns that their behaviors were not appropriate for women. Some of the men in the study examined how expectations about male behaviors needed to be reconsidered.

In the fall of his fourth year at the college and his second year as a communications major, Donald wrote a paper on the following topic: "How do I relate to the images and language being given to me in advertisements?" Selecting an ad for a hair cream directed to African-American men, Donald analyzed the message being sent to potential consumers of the product. He seemed aware of the cautions that Langstraat (1995) offered in her analysis of how the "self" is portrayed in popular magazines. Langstraat pointed out that "fashion magazines promote normative and regulatory ideas of gender roles [and] reinforce heterosexist norms of identity" (p. 7). She saw a contradiction between fashion being presented as oppressive and as emancipatory, and encouraged her students to be aware of these contradictions as they examined the "relationship between images and consumerism, advertising and class image, and gender and race representations in clothing styles" (p. 7). Donald, in particular, was sensitive to how personal identity was tied up with what the larger society regarded as normative behavior:

The first ad I will analyze is the "S-Curl" product by Luster's. The headline for the ad reads, "S-Curls the Way for Styles Today." The shot shows a handsome black man who is well shaven and semi-professionally dressed. His hair is shy and wavy signifying he recently used the product. Behind him is a beautiful woman, looking seductively into the camera. The [message] being given is, if you use S-Curls you too can look suave and sophisticated. It will complement your appearance, and add a beautiful woman at your side.

This ad is very inviting because most men want to be handsome professionals with beautiful companions. But what this ad is telling me is, I must change my appearance to meet this criteria. My hair must be wavy, and if its curly or even tangled, it's not appropriate. At this point I see my self acceptance being weighed. I see my self-esteem and pride being demoted. I ask myself, am I meeting the norms of society?

Society has told us, you are beautiful if you look like this. And to achieve this level you must discard your natural order, our culture. When the black male goes and makes these changes he is unconsciously denying himself and his heritage. Many people would say that is only hair. That bit of hair is only the start; the process of change will continue, If I change my appearance, I will be more socially accepted. But the question still lies on acceptance by whom; the Black or European society.

In his analysis of the advertisement, Donald saw the larger issue of the majority culture demanding conformity to its mores. His awareness of the insidious nature of the message is particularly notable since at that time he was planning to participate in the world of communication, possibly through direct advertising. He was being taught in his courses to learn to manipulate potential buyers through "pitches" that could appeal to individuals' sense of social standing. The larger question for him remains: With what level of integrity will he design his own ads? It does not seem likely that Donald would have compromised his integrity or his social values if he had had an opportunity to work in the field of communication.

It is not surprising that Ricardo is an individual who would not let majority views influence his actions (as long as he was not harming others). Using the metaphor of a colorful umbrella in a paper he wrote for a psychology course in the fall of his fifth year at the college, Ricardo asserted his confidence in himself as a complex, autonomous person:

In the last month as the winter waned away and spring began to entice in its spell an interesting event kept repeating itself every time I used my colorful bright umbrella. I received from fellow students, friends and acquaintances a very similar comment, they all asked if I took my wife's umbrella. I gave the same answer to all of them and that was that it was indeed my umbrella. That is not your umbrella! or they said, That is a woman's umbrella, not a man's umbrella! I was shock by their response to my colorful umbrella and I decide to give it some thought.

I began to question what made my umbrella men or a woman umbrella? So began a little search for some ideas about what they thought? I began with a young female student who said, those colors are not man colors they are woman colors. She was referring to the bright yellow, greens, blues and red colors over a white background on my umbrella. I ask her why I couldn't have those colors on my umbrella at that moment a fellow student (who happens to be gay) told me, those bright colors are saying to the world, look I'm here and I'm gay! I answered that I like my umbrella because those colors make me feel good in a cloudy/gray rainy day. It was to no avail. They all have a prejudice against my poor little umbrella. Besides my gay friend told me those colors were tacky and that even him, a gay man, would not dare been seen with such a thing. That caught my attention because I thought that I fitted a schema that they have (gay people wear colorful things), but now it happens that my umbrella is not fashionable. An interesting discovery. . . .

I wondered what causes this reaction on people of different ages, background and ethnic groups? I think that they all have suffered the same social/cultural influence. That influence may have come from television, magazines or from a need to belong/to be part of a group. A social influence that dictates the way men and women are different. Different because, by my umbrella example, they all think that a bright lively colorful umbrella is a women umbrella. The men's umbrella must be of one solid color like blue, black or brown. It clearly seems to me that they all conform to the social norm, in this case that is the color of the umbrella. I also think that in a way they all wanted me to throw away my umbrella and comply to a non-written society rule. As I am writing this I realize that to a great extent they are obedient to that rule. I have turn back into memory lane and they all have in their possession solid color umbrellas during those same rainy days. . . .

In conclusion, I think that in general and based on my umbrella experience these particular group of people have a prejudice attitude against my umbrella. I believe that they are not aware that they are conforming and are compliant to a non-written society rule, the color of a men and women umbrella (that makes it a Cultural truism). At the same time as I looked back in my memory they have shown me that they are obedient to those rules because they all had solid color umbrellas during rainy days. I like my umbrella. It is bright when its gray and cloudy and makes me feel happy and warm for that reason I will use my tacky (for some), non-fashionable (for others), non-conforming colorful umbrella for as long as I can. I guess that makes me the non-conforming, non-compliant, non-obedient citizen of the group!

Not threatened by the views of those who critiqued his individuality, Ricardo not only asserted his right to be a nonconformist in dress but also indirectly to be a nonconformist in his actions if this was warranted. In these papers, both Donald and Ricardo rejected the dictates of society that attempted to determine how one should look and dress. Confident in their own gender identity, they saw no need to rearrange themselves to satisfy someone else's perception of how they should look or behave. Cultural stereotypes repulsed them as they rejected the dictates of society that demanded conformity.

Opportunities for the Future

The roles for women in the future particularly attracted the attention of the students. Recognizing both generational changes and the need to change stereotyped views of femininity, Linda and Delores addressed these issues in their writing. Linda indicated her awareness of the differences in generational opportunities for women, particularly African-American women, in a paper she wrote for her English 1 class:

> During my mother's generation in the 1950's, black women were given menial jobs such as secretarial, clerical and housekeeping. Unlike today, where black women can excel in high level positions such as Chief Executive, departmental Managers and Corporate Executives.
>
> In conclusion, I am very fortunate to have the opportunity to advance in high marketed jobs today. Whereas my mother was not privileged to do so during her generation. I feel that the experiences I am going through now in my generation, are much better than the experiences my mother went through in her generation.

As stated earlier, over the years of her college experience, Linda found herself able first to plan to be a nurse, then to work in psychology, and finally to apply to graduate school. She was well aware that these options were not available to her mother since her mother only finished high school, and opportunities for African-American women were scarce when she was a young woman.

Delores examined how the cultural pressures on women could be so strong that they could be prevented from accomplishing their potential. In a women's psychology course in the fall of 1993, she wrote a paper titled "Society is making me ill . . . ?" The paper dealt with the stress put on women to "be very thin and even a bit underweight." Delores discussed the causes of anorexia nervosa and bulimia as eating disorders caused by these pressures. In the conclusion to her paper, she stated her own views on this problem:

> By reviewing part of the literature on women's eating patterns, we have seen some of the many factors affecting the psychology of women that would lead them to have disordered eating habits, depression, anxiety, etc. One can conclude that if women are becoming sick in the attempt to fulfill the beauty standards of society, and if achieving in professions where the presence of men dominates, it comes to mind that [it] is time for us women to set our own standards for beauty, and begin to define ourselves in terms of academic and professional achievement in our own settings. I agree with Silverstein and Perlick's conclusion in that it is not the increase opportunity for women that is making them depressed, Anorexic or anxious, it is the decrease in prestige of homemaking, and at the same time the elevated significance place upon nondomestic achievement for women and the still existent walls women confront and that limit them from being successful.

Like Chandra, Delores believed that women needed to become active in changing the perceptions of the society about what is valued. As a professional person, she would surely try to help women to "define themselves" in the future according to their own preferences, without suffering from the demands of the external society.

Clearly the students have become not only more secure in their gender identities and their sexual orientation over the college years, but they have become advocates for change that will erase the negatively charged stereotypes they see applied to women, men, homosexuals, and members of racial and ethnic minorities. Because most of these students belonged to more than one of these categories, it is not surprising that they came to assert their identities in complex terms, as Delores does when she identifies herself as a Black Latino Woman. Their writing is not limited to the reflexive, but becomes extensive and analytical as they resist the attempts to typecast them into narrowly defined categories. They have been strengthened by role models in their lives, from parents (particularly mothers) to grandparents, colleagues at work, fellow students, and professors. With the support of family members and friends, they have been able to move from considerations of stereotyping on individuals like themselves to the effects on the larger society.

CLASS

The relationship between socioeconomic class and academic success is most strikingly reflected in the need students have for outside work while they are attending college. The working situation for the students in this study who began their college experience in 1989 was worse than the economic situation that Lavin and Hyllegard (1996) described for the students who enrolled at City University of New York in the 1970s under the open admissions program. In the early 1970s there was no tuition cost and federal assistance programs provided more support than in the late 1980s. Even with free tuition and federal support, the open-admissions students of the 1970s had economic difficulties that affected their academic performance:

> Even though CUNY was a tuition-free university when open admissions began, many students worked at full-time jobs during their college years, presumably to pay living expenses and to help their families. In the four-year colleges, open-admissions students more often held such jobs than regular students, but ethnicity also made a difference: minority students worked full-time more frequently than whites. . . . Overall, across the university, about 30 percent of minority students and 13 percent of whites worked full-time. Students who did so could be expected to find that work took time away from study time, perhaps diminishing their chances for academic success. Moreover, full-time work could force students to attend college on a part-time basis, thus extending the time they need to earn a degree. (Lavin & Hyllegard, p. 37)

Although Lavin and Hyllegard focused on the potential problems of full-time work, part-time work, especially when students were holding down two or three jobs simultaneously or working and doing an internship at the same time, had similar disruptive effects.

For example, in her fourth year at the college, Joan was working at Radio City Music Hall while simultaneously doing a part-time internship, 3 days a week at a health center. She told me, "The most significant thing that happened to me in the past year was that I was able to pull off working at Radio City Music Hall, working at the clinic in my internship, and doing my school work without going crazy. I can handle these things because I have nothing else. This is the only thing I have to look forward to." She said that she had lost weight that semester, "not intentionally." She found it hard to get enough sleep because she was so busy. She got home at 1:30 a.m. and had to be up at 6 a.m. to go to class. Sleeping and eating had become problems for her. Working experiences like these were not uncommon in the student population I studied. Students with such drive and dedication have earned respect and admiration, but their perseverance should not been seen as rationales for providing inadequate financial support to their peers. Why should students from poor socioeconomic backgrounds have to sacrifice their health as well as their personal lives to fulfill their academic goals?

Another sharp difference between the cohorts studied by Lavin and Hyllegard (1996) in the 1970s and 1980s is in the immigrant status of the population of City University of New York. In the 1970s cohort immigrant students "constituted a negligible proportion," whereas in the 1980 cohort, they constituted 15% of the students at CUNY (p. 219). In my initial study group, 25 of the 53 students were born outside the continental United States, including 3 born in Puerto Rico; thus, 47% of this cohort were immigrants when they began their college studies, more than three times the number even in 1980. Of the 9 students who are most closely followed in this study, 3 were born outside the continental United States: Ricardo (Puerto Rico), Delores (Dominican Republic), and Jacob (Korea, but reared in Australia). Although born in the United States, Carl was strongly affected by the Ecuadorian cultural influence of his family.

In considering how issues of social class affected the students' academic experiences, I considered their relationships with friends, family, and community, the transition of moving from a less complex society to a more complex one, and the effects of having to work while attending college.

Relationships With Friends, Family, and Community

It would be too easy to think of the students in this study as a monolithic group. It is true that all but Audrey came from minority racial groups, and it is true that all of them had to work while they were in college to meet their financial obligations. But they were not monolithic in their attitudes toward others in their communities who were not pursuing a higher education: friends, acquaintances, even family members.

At the end of the students' third semester at the college, December 1990, I asked them several questions that would help me understand their relationships with those in their communities. In particular, I asked them whether their ties with their friends and family had changed since they had started college. I received a surprisingly wide range of answers to these questions.

Three of the students said that there was essentially no change in their relationships with others. Audrey said that initially her family had been worried that she would not go to college; now they were happy that she was a student again. She said she lived on the East Side in Manhattan where there were "some Jews, mostly WASPs, and all Whites except for the maids." In such a setting, her being a student didn't affect her relationship with others. (She seemed to have no connection to the minority workers in her area.)

Jacob lived in a section of Brooklyn where there were not many Asians, "mostly Germans and Hispanics." He said that the groups "get along." Being a college student in that setting did not affect his life, he said, because he was "mostly a private person."

Ricardo was the most thoughtful in responding to this question when he told me that the ethnically and racially diverse groups where he lived in Bushwick, Brooklyn, "got along." He said he had no difficulties in his relationships with others because he was a college student, "but," he added, "I can analyze better how others are living in oppression. I don't tell them that." Aware of the disparities between his own potential for improving his life compared to the circumstances of others, Ricardo expressed concern for those who might not have the possibilities he had worked so hard to have: "I am worried that other people won't have the opportunity I have now because they won't be able to afford it. The quality of basic education that people in this city are receiving is diminishing. My friends who are teaching say that students lack ability or teachers don't have equipment or are not related to students' backgrounds." Ricardo's fears that even more limited opportunities would exist for those who followed after him have been realized even at City University of New York where decreased support for remedial courses has been instituted and where economic difficulties for students have increased. The paradox is that as students are less prepared by the public schools, the colleges are demanding better preparation, as if *saying* that students should have a better education in the elementary and secondary schools actually brings those changes into being.

Like Ricardo, Donald wanted better opportunities for others. Living in Kings County with a population of Hispanics, Blacks, and Jews, Donald said that there were no problems among those in the community. He tried to encourage those young people who were "hanging out" to go to school, but he said that they "ignored him." This attempt is typical of Donald's efforts to help others through his participation in church work.

Because they had to work so many hours, some of the students recognized that their ties with their family and friends were being weakened. Chandra said that she felt she was "neglecting" her family. She had moved out of the apartment where she had lived with her mother, as the area became more drug infested, and moved in with her sister. Where she was now living in the South Bronx, in a community of Hispanics and Blacks, she felt she was in a supportive environment where "people are protective of each other because it's such a bad community." She said the people living in her apartment building wanted her to finish college. Chandra had had a brief flirtation with success before she started at the college, but she had found the experience disconcertingly unsatisfying. While still a high school student at the School for Performing Arts, Chandra was offered a part in a television series. She described her experience in a paper for the English 2 course her first semester at the college:

> About ten days later, I received a phone call from the head casting director. She told me "Knightwatch" was going to be filmed in Canada and my transportation was all set. A limousine picked me up at my doorstep and took me to the airport. After my flight, another limousine took me to my hotel where I received the royal treatment. I had cable television, a king size bed and practically everything one could imagine. It was the best ten days of my life. Although I had it all, I still felt an emptiness. I always thought that as long as I was successful, I would be happy but success is nothing if you don't have anyone to share it with. My way of thinking changed after this experience because I was on the other side. I was a success. I knew what it felt like and what it meant.

Chandra's experience with success sensitized her to the emptiness she felt since no one else seemed to care about what had happened to her or had a stake in her experience. As has been mentioned earlier, she later became aware that her identity as a proud African-American woman didn't really emerge until she had been in the college for a while. She probably felt isolated in high school, treated, as she described herself, as a "wanna be White girl."

Joan received emotional support from her mother, but she felt that her sisters had gotten lazy, wanting her to do things for them such as shop or pay bills. She said they treated her like a "machine." In the Bronx, where she lived in a predominately Hispanic and Black community, she said people got along pretty well. "They have more respect for me and leave me alone. They don't pester me to do things," she added, an apparent contrast with the demands being made on her by some of her family members. Her living conditions were clearly difficult. She told me in an interview in her fourth year at the college that because the elevator in her building broke down frequently, and she lived on the 15th floor, she was unable to invite friends over. She said, "I've been surviving without friends so far, and I guess I'll continue to do so." And in a paper she wrote in her first semester at college, she almost resignedly described the day-to-day living conditions she endured: "The cause of this electrical shortage was an electrical storm which was so strong that it knocked out all of the electrical power on my line. In project housing, it takes much longer to get things fixed." Six years later, after her graduation and her work experience, she told me she would finally be moving her mother and herself out of the projects.

Delores reported that she did not have time for friends because of her school and work commitments. (The increasing burdens she carried in both areas are detailed later in this chapter.) She said that in the Bronx area where she lived, there were mostly Puerto Ricans, with some Dominicans, but not many Blacks. She said the Hispanic groups went to church together and had pretty good relationships. She didn't have time for social relationships, and, at the time, she was hardly even seeing her boyfriend.

Both Linda and Carl indicated that they had somewhat more negative experiences in their home communities. Linda said that she "didn't bother" with the people she used to "hang out with" when she was in high school. She said, rather disdainfully, "They want to marry or take low paying jobs," clearly two steps that Linda was not interested in at this point in her life. She said that in the apartment building where she lived in Brooklyn, there were West Indians, Hispanics, Jews, and Blacks. She said that they had good relationships with one another. "But," she added, "the people in my building have no life. They sit around and receive public assistance. They tell me that I act stuck-up because I don't hang out with them. The boys in the building give me problems because I don't want to date them. They don't harass me, though," she said, "because they say I'm dull." Although some might take that as an insult, Linda seemed to thrive on such a characterization, since she did not want to identify with people who believed her interests were uninteresting to them.

Although she was very critical of those in her community who had no formal education or higher aspirations, Linda was much more empathetic toward members of her family. In a paper she wrote for a psychology course in the spring of 1993, Linda interviewed female relatives for a study on whether age was "a vital contributing factor in our impressions or rather the way in which we judge [people] as individuals":

> Easter Day was a perfect time to gather as many participants as possible. I had to scan out what age group I wanted to explore. My twenty, thirty or forty year old relatives. I decided to go with the twenty-something group. So now I was set. I had my age group consisting of all African-American females which are dominate in my family. Next, I got my studies out and shuffled them up a bit. I then pulled each of them aside, when I felt they weren't busy and I gave them each a questionnaire and asked them kindly to read the instructions and fill out the paper.
>
> Of course, I had some cousins who thought that I asked them in a foreign tongue. No matter how often I told them what to do, they always came back saying, WHAT? So, slowly, as if I was talking to pre-school children. Again, I told them what to do. Finally, they figured out how to do it. While many of them filled out the form, I watched with fascination their facial expressions while they completed the questionnaire. They seemed to be so absorbed with the project that I had to beg them to eat! I was quite proud at how my participants were excited and wanted to become very involved with my project. I had had one cousin who I didn't want to participate in the research. Simply because she just didn't understand it. It took her an hour just to read the case study. She couldn't understand the study no matter how many times I explained it to

her. I just didn't have the time to constantly go over the study. I gave it to someone else to complete.

What is interesting about this description of her research population is the relatively unjudgmental language she used to describe her relatives. Although she complained of the slowness, like "preschool children" of some and the impossibility of one cousin "to understand the study no matter how many times I explained it to her," Linda provides no information on the educational or professional levels of her relatives. It may be that her growing knowledge of the field of psychology made her sympathetic to the backgrounds of her cousins and understanding enough of their likely limited educational backgrounds to focus her attention on her pride "at how my participants were excited and wanted to become very involved with my project." She seemed unaware that it was her academic language that appeared to be foreign to her relatives.

As described earlier, Carl had already distanced himself from his family. So it is not too surprising that he also had "grown further apart from old friends." He said he didn't have much interest in socializing and he had made a few new friends at work, more than at the college. Where he lived in Manhattan, on the Upper West Side near 105th Street, the community consisted primarily of people of Spanish background—Ecuadorians, Dominicans, Puerto Ricans—and some "Yuppie Caucasian groups" and a "decent percentage of Blacks." He said that the groups got along. He "looked down at the teen age hoodlums," but said that they "didn't bother" him. So his social life increasingly consisted of his friends at work and his friends in the gay community.

Transition to a More Complex Setting

Just as Ricardo gave a report of the changes he felt after he left Puerto Rico, and Audrey told of her move from a small town in Iowa, so Delores, in a paper for her English 2 class her first semester at the college, described the changes that occurred in her life when she moved from the Dominican Republic to New York at the age of 14:

Blanco al medu Fenanares, Dominican Republic. Everything is quiet, only the little birds singing in the trees. In the river the water in its way runs to the sea. Men in the farms taking care of the cows, the children coming to school. The mothers in the kitchen preparing dinner. And the girls helping the mothers with little ones. This is a typical scene of my home country town. The little house one for each family. I use to live near the river. My room had a window that had a view to the patio. I lived with my grandmother since my parents went to Puerto Rico. There in this place you live so well your life goes easier. People like each other, help each other. Everybody is friendly. Now that I live here in New York my feeling about that place I use to live where you don't worry about that you would get hurt if you are in the street, that the

winter is not so cold, the summer not so hot. I always will remember that place with
love. For me this experience was an important one in my life. My residence in this
little country town was of much good for the formation of my personality. Here I learn
that you respect the older people. I learn to love the nature, the flowers, the birds. I
learn to eat what was good for my health. But the most important thing I learn from
this experience was that everybody is equal, that I must love the others as I love myself.
That the person is the [one] who counts, not what the person has.

Delores' values were clearly established in these formative years of her life,
just as Ricardo's and Audrey's had been. Not as strongly as Ricardo, but in
her own quiet way, Delores became an activist as she increasingly valued
her identity as a Black Latina woman.

Effect of Work on the Academic Experience

A book-length treatise could be presented on the effect of work on the
academic experience for these high-risk students at an urban college. I cite
several "stories" that encapsulate these effects by presenting the students'
narratives.

Delores' experiences over the years of her college education reveal the
complexity of juggling studying, working, and commuting, while simultaneously striving to sustain the high goals one has set. Her life was further
complicated by the fact that she lived and worked in different places during
her first few years at the college. She lived during the week in the Bronx, a
necessity to establish her New York state residency and qualify for in-state
tuition, while she worked on weekends in her mother's restaurant in New
Jersey. She told me in the fall of her second year that she was working 30
hours a week in her mother's cafeteria in New Jersey on Fridays, Saturdays,
and Sundays. She found that this was causing her to rush through her
schoolwork.

By the next semester, the spring of 1991, she had two different jobs, one
at the college and the other at a woman's clothing store in Manhattan. She
worked 4 hours a week in the computer lab at the college and about 22 hours
a week at Lerner's. She worked 6 hours each on Fridays, Saturdays, and
Sundays and 2 hours each on Mondays and Wednesdays. She had time free
on Tuesdays and Thursdays to do school work because she had only one
class each of those days. She said that she did not have much personal time,
but she was used to that. Her boyfriend at the time was also busy, so "it works
out okay" for them. (Although these 26 hours of work each week might not
qualify as "full time" according to the discussions of Lavin and Hyllegard,
1996, they did fill up every hour that Delores was not attending class or
preparing for her courses.) Later that semester, Delores told me "everything
is a mess." Her mother still had the restaurant in New Jersey, but the family
was living in the Bronx. The commute was hard on everyone. She was

working at the restaurant a few hours a week while working at her other job 15 hours a week. This was added to her school work. Over the coming summer, she expected to work in her mother's restaurant. She got her driver's license and she now had a little car of her own that she was driving to New Jersey.

By the fall of the next semester, Delores was back to working Friday afternoon and all day Saturday and Sunday at her mother's restaurant in New Jersey. She was still living in the Bronx during the week and staying at her mother's apartment in New Jersey on the weekends. She also was working in the library at the college on weekday nights. She said that sometimes these responsibilities interfered with her doing her school work.

At the end of that fall semester, Delores' life became even more complicated. She told me that having to work had affected her college experience. She sometimes had to leave classes to go directly to work without having time to do her school work. Her mother had given up her house in the Bronx and rented a house in New Jersey. When Delores had to take the bus and train from New Jersey to New York, it took her 75 minutes. During the week, she stayed in the library until 8 or 9 p.m. trying to finish her school work. She was so tired when she got home that she felt exhausted.

On January 27, 1993, I ran into Delores in the hallway of the North Academic Center at the City College. I had not been able to be in touch with her during the previous semester because her phone was disconnected, and I did not have her correct current address (a common problem in carrying out this study). She told me that her mother was selling her restaurant in New Jersey because of ill health. Instead of working there on weekends, Delores was now working in a medical office on Mondays, Wednesdays, and Fridays, for 6 hours each of those days. She was still living in New Jersey and commuting to the college in Manhattan.

In the fall of 1993, her fifth year at the college, when she started to take graduate courses in the combined BA/MA in psychology program to which she had been admitted, Delores told me that she was planning to leave her job in the doctor's office, where she had been working from 18 to 20 hours a week since the beginning of the previous October. She said that it had been too hard to do that and her school work. Her mother would support her by doing sewing work at home.

At that same interview, Delores gave me a portrait of her composing process that can be seen to have been affected by the requirement to support herself during her college years. When asked to describe her school writing from the time she first received an assignment until she handed in the finished paper, Delores said:

> If [the paper] has to do with something I read, I'll choose things I want to discuss and make an outline. I start the task at home at a desk in a little studio off the bedroom. I do an outline by hand. First, I bring material from the library home. I write the draft

of the paper by hand. I come to school to use the computer. I have to wait for one to be free, sometimes 15–20 minutes when the room is crowded. I put the draft into the computer. Maybe this takes 3 days. I save the work and for m%okjob if I'm working on a long paper. [She told me that she sometimes had time to do schoolwork at her job in the doctor's office.] I print the paper out as I'm working [presumably in the doctor's office or in the computer center at the college]. I make changes on the draft and make changes on the computer and then print it out again. I really have to start early.

Because her time is so fragmented by her working hours and her commuting hours, Delores has learned how to handle her tasks "in parts" and to plan her time very carefully and very far ahead.

At the end of that semester, Delores said that she had had to leave her job because of school. She had financial problems, but her mother was helping her. She had moved to an apartment in the Bronx that she was sharing with a girlfriend. She visited her family in New Jersey over the weekends. She had bought a computer for herself.

As this story reveals, Delores' determination to persist and succeed enabled her to overcome the many financial, logistical, and personal problems that she encountered. Although she often told me that she was exhausted from all these efforts, her commitment to a better life for herself never diminished. I regret that I have been unable to reach her since she graduated, so I do not know what she is doing now.

I had said earlier that Joan's persistence had been one of the dominating factors in her personality that caused her to continue at the college despite all her personal and family problems. An excellent example of this persistence is revealed in a paper she wrote in her first semester at the college. After describing Booker T. Washington's tenacious efforts to gain admission to Hampton Institute, she gave an account of her own efforts at finding a job.

Job hunting takes lots of patience. I was out of work for 4 months. I had no type of income coming in. I had applied almost everywhere trying to find a job. I had no luck but I didn't give up. Until one day I had an interview with someone from Martin Luther King Health Center. I was determined to get that job. But later they told me there weren't any openings. They told me to call in everyday to check. I did this for an additional 2 months. Finally they informed me that they had a position open for switchboard operators. I filled the position. Booker T. Washington's ambition has inspired me. This is proven by the above written assignment that I've just written.

It is easy to picture Joan calling the office at the health center every day. She needed this job and she needed to persist. Her tenaciousness was evident in every aspect of her life, where she was determined to succeed at her college studies and not follow the paths of most of her brothers and sisters.

A year later, Joan told me that her life had changed since she had started college in that she was always rushing—she felt she was burning herself out.

The semesters seemed so short with more work than could be handled. She was always cramming, no matter how much she tried to plan ahead. She was tired from the demands placed on her from school, work, and family. Hopefully, all of this would pay off for her. She was always told by her family to go to college, but she was too tired now to be happy. (As described earlier in this chapter, Joan's work requirements and her internships continued to induce fatigue in her throughout her college years.)

Chandra was another student who struggled with having enough money to continue at the college. She told me that the spring semester of 1992 had been a hard one. She had been working at two jobs, for 20 hours, and she had taken five classes. She said:

> I could rarely find time to read and write the papers the way I wanted to. I can't cut down on the number of hours I'm working. I may have to take out more loans, so I can finish next year. I want to do quality work, but juggling two jobs and school becomes confusing—what do I do today? My first concern is how to get money to continue next semester. I have to pay off this year's loan and I may need to take another loan for the $500 tuition increase.

She told me that while the tuition was going up at the college, the money she was being paid for her jobs was not changing. This was a sadly common refrain, as the tuition at all the campuses of City University of New York were increased over the years that the students in my study were attending City College.

Although I have cited this example before, Ricardo's experience bears repeating here, as it encapsulates the feelings and frustrations of many of his classmates. After 2½ years in the college, Ricardo felt the oppression of his economic situation weighing on him. When asked whether his commitment to his academic studies had changed over his years at the college, he said,

> It's diminishing. It's more and more frustrating to stay in college and survive. I'm very committed to keep my academic standards, but cut backs have depressed me [in college aid, in rising tuition costs]. I could get "Cs" with no effort, because grades don't mean anything to others. But I will try not to diminish the quality of my work. I've been on the honor roll for three years, but if I can't pay the rent and eat, who cares about grades? Twenty to 25% of the students in the Communications program didn't register because they think they won't have the money. The economy is bad, financial aid is worse, tuition is higher, the faculty can't pay attention to so many students—there are 30 students instead of 15 in the production classes.

During a period of serious financial hardship, Ricardo made the decision to drop courses, when he had to increase his working hours, rather than perform poorly in the classes. He rejected the advice given to him by friends: "I came to the realization that some people close to me told me to just finish and not worry about grades, but that's not the reason I'm here. I want to keep my average up, so I dropped classes instead of just getting through."

When asked whether any big changes had occurred in his life during the previous semester, Ricardo replied with a resigned voice, "I got older. I'm learning to be patient."

It would be possible to understand if sheer fatigue, economic pressures, and frustration at being unable to do the best work possible were to undermine the commitment of the students in this study to complete their academic responsibilities honorably and with pride. But they did not falter—they made adjustments where necessary. They tried their best not to compromise their academic standards. Instead of just giving them credit for their success, the society should mobilize itself to improve the conditions under which such dedicated individuals can aspire to higher levels of personal and professional lives. Certainly better preparation at the precollege years is highly desirable, but in its absence in urban areas like New York City, the colleges should be set up so as to foster opportunities for students who earnestly wish to make up for their poor previous educational environments. Smaller classes in initial years, programs like the enrichment program tried out at City College, and more—not less—financial support for the students and public higher education could diminish the gap between the truly rich and the truly poor in our urban centers.

IDEOLOGY

In a discussion on the relationship between ideology and rhetoric, Berlin (1988) described the three rhetorical approaches most commonly found in the college classroom: the rhetorics of cognitive psychology, of expressionism, and of social–epistemic:

> Each of these rhetorics occupies a distinct position in its relation to ideology. From the perspective offered here, the rhetoric of cognitive psychology refuses the ideological question altogether, claiming for itself the transcendent neutrality of science. This rhetoric is nonetheless easily preempted by a particular ideological position now in ascendancy because it encourages discursive practices that are compatible with dominant economic, social, and political formations. Expressionistic rhetoric, on the other hand, has always openly admitted its ideological predilections, opposing itself in no uncertain terms to the scientism of current-traditional rhetoric and the ideology it encourages. This rhetoric is, however, open to appropriation by the very forces it opposes in contradiction to its best intentions. Social–epistemic rhetoric is an alternative that is self-consciously aware of its ideological stand, making the very question of ideology the center of classroom activities, and in doing so providing itself a defense again preemption and a strategy for self-criticism and self-correction. (p. 478)

(Although the rhetorical approach of cognitive psychology now calls itself a "social cognitive theory of writing," for the most part, it frequently neglects issues of race, gender, and class, even though lip service is sometimes paid to the significance of these aspects of students' lives.)

Berlin's defense of a social–epistemic rhetoric is one of many positions critiqued by Hairston (1992) in her article, "Diversity, Ideology, and Teaching." Hairston argued that in particular the freshman composition course should not focus on political or ideological issues:

> We have no business getting into areas where we may have passion or conviction, but no scholarly base from which to operate. When classes focus on complex issues such as racial discrimination, economic injustices, and inequities of class and gender, they should be taught by qualified faculty who have the depth of information and historical competence that such critical social issues warrant. Our society's deep and tangled cultural conflicts can neither be explained nor resolved by simplistic ideological formulas. (p. 186)

Hairston's article raised a firestorm of critical responses which were published in *College Composition and Communication* in 1993. Trimbur (1993), for example, complained: "Finally, what I find most troublesome about Maxine's line of reasoning is that she doesn't trust her students' ability to handle the social and cultural differences that organize the realities of contemporary America. The implicit message is that they can share their differences, but they shouldn't have to engage in the rhetorical act of negotiation" (p. 249). Wood (1993) cited Giroux's belief [*Border Crossings*, Routledge, 1990] that teachers need "to consider how knowledge is understood within the contexts of the experiences students bring to our classes" and to "be self-critical ourselves and learn from the forms of knowledge produced as they come from the class, from our students, from the community, and from their texts" (p. 57, cited in Wood, p. 250).

Hairston's argument focuses on whether ideological positions should be the appropriate areas for consideration in freshman writing courses. The implication is that such issues should only be considered when "experts" in each domain are available to provide direct instruction. But to limit students' considerations of aspects of their lives to only the areas that come to their attention through the eyes of "experts" is to close off and devalue the unique perspectives the students can bring to bear on the wide range of topics to which a college education is intended to expose students. The value of a liberal education is reduced, if not lost, if students are not challenged and encouraged to bring their knowledge to bear on the "received knowledge" of all the subjects they are studying.

If a primary goal of a college education is to foster analysis and synthesis, the best way to achieve this is through encouraging questioning of the status quo. It is difficult to argue that reflection and questioning should be put off until experts can deliver the accepted versions of their academic fields to students, the "banking concept of education" so derided by Freire (1970/1993). Certainly knowledge and expertise are to be valued, but this knowledge should be used to open areas for examination, not close them off. There seems to be no reason why freshmen should not have these opportunities at the beginning of their education as an indicator to them that their insights and expertise will be valued as contributions not only to the accumulation of knowledge but to its revision.

Lavin and Hyllegard (1996) reported on a number of studies that suggest that political and social values become more liberal as a result of a college education. They noted that college graduates "come to be more accepting of individual diversity and able to think in nonstereotypic ways about others who are culturally and ethnically different from them" (p. 177). They also note that college graduates develop greater "participation in civic and political activities and exhibit increased commitment to the protection of civil rights and liberties" (p. 177). If students have not been encouraged to analyze both the strengths and limitations of the assumptions behind the value system of their society, they will not be prepared to challenge existing beliefs or argue for change. They need to recognize the opportunity to "reposition" themselves, as Min-Zhan Lu (1992) proposed (p. 910).

Many of the examples previously cited in this chapter could easily have been placed in this section on ideology. Ideology clearly reflects students' perceptions about how race and ethnicity, gender and sexual orientation, and class affect the values and beliefs of the larger society. I present in this section, then, the writing of only two students, Carl and Ricardo, to illustrate further how students became more aware of their responsibilities to examine the values of the dominant culture and effect strategies to bring about change.

Carl's passage in his search for a confident identity has already been presented. Papers and an article he wrote for *The New York Times* between 1991 and 1993 demonstrate his eagerness to explain why changes in social attitudes toward homosexuals are needed. His growing willingness to take public stands through his college writing, through publication in the most respected newspaper in New York City, and through his participation in the Gay and Lesbian March on Washington in the spring of 1993 provide evidence that he saw the rights of homosexuals as an ideological issue.

In a final paper for a speech course in the fall of 1991, Carl argued the following thesis: "I believe that homosexuals should not be banned from the military." He dealt with several substantive points: "(1) Homosexuals are not different then heterosexuals; 2) Homosexuals are more open to blackmail; 3) Homosexuals create disorder, disunity, problems with morale and are incompatible with military service; and 4) Battle for equal rights is being fought outside courts." Supporting Point 1 and arguing against Points 2 and 3, Carl concluded his paper as follows:

I strongly feel that the ban against homosexuals should be dropped. There has never been a concrete reason for their banishment, at least, never a reason that can be proven true. The right to serve in the military is one that every citizen has. Whether they chose to exercise that right is up to them. It should not be taken away from anyone. The policy stems from one of prejudice and discrimination. Is this America? It is not too late to change.

Although Carl wrote on many topics for his many classes, it is clear that when given an open topic or a creative writing opportunity, he frequently selected one related to his homosexuality. This willingness to openly discuss issues related to his sexual orientation demonstrates his maturity and acceptance of his identity.

In his years of working at *The New York Times*, Carl had many different responsibilities, mainly managing support services for writers, but also occasionally doing rewrites of pieces that were telephoned in or summarizing pieces for news capsules. (By the fall of 1993, Carl had accepted a full-time supervisory position at the *Times*, delaying the completion of his degree in communications until he could take the credits in his major that he needed through evening courses. In this position, he was in charge of 90 people who worked on news desks or who did research. He also answered inquiries from the public or did research for reporters.) The one feature article that he produced, in the spring of 1992, was about the Out of the Closet Thrift Shop in Manhattan. This store had been opened "by four friends who saw it as a way to raise money for dozens of AIDS organizations desperate for funding. The store donates all of its profits to AIDS groups."

In the article, Carl described the range of customers who came to the store and their varied reasons for shopping there. One customer who owned a flower shop in the neighborhood said, "We've found a number of containers for our flowers here. We prefer lots of stuff from the 40's and 50's. And here, when you buy, you feel like you're doing something, helping a cause." The store's workers, who are volunteers, expressed similar views. A retired museum worker who helped out on Saturdays, said: "AIDS is the concern of everyone. I wanted to do something for AIDS and the homeless. I work at a shelter. I'm also a New Yorker. I'm convinced that this is a great town and I want to help make it better."

Carl's own ideas about the importance and value of the store were summarized in the final words by the store's manager: "Mr. Maloney said he was proud that the store had brought together many different kinds of people, not only those affected by AIDS. 'I think it's great that so many communities have come together in the alchemy of the store,' he said." These, too, were clearly Carl's feelings as he took advantage of his connections at the *Times* to publicize this effort to provide assistance to people with AIDS. The article, with its byline, was also another assertion of his public identity.

In a psychology paper on homophobia in the spring of 1993, Carl devoted one section to concerns related to multicultural education:

> The recently proposed "Children of the Rainbow" curriculum [for New York City public school students] can attest to [prejudice against the actions of a few who taint a group such as gay individuals]. A curriculum developed to encourage racial respect and understanding came under fire by a small community group in Queens for being "homosexual propaganda." The propaganda? Three pages out of more than 400 which suggested that teachers instruct that gay and lesbian people are human too.
>
> In the maelstrom of propaganda, parents felt their kids were going to be taught about "gay sex." All the children were going to be taught was that gay and lesbian people exist, it's not a bad thing to be gay. Some parents didn't see it that way. They thought their kids would be corrupted by such words. Corrupted? Not likely. Accepting? Possibly. Not bothered? Most definitely.
>
> Parents underestimate their kids. Given a chance, they'd most likely forget the curriculum if it had managed to make it into the classroom. They would not have been swayed over to the "homosexual lifestyle" but it would have been a learning experience.

Because Carl recognized how learning experiences could increase tolerance for difference, he was disturbed by the view that knowing something about homosexuality would automatically corrupt young people. He was perhaps not sensitive enough about the term "corrupting" being applied to the gay community, but he recognized the dangers that ignorance could foster.

In April 1993, Carl attended the "March for Gay, Lesbian, Bisexual and Transgender Rights" in Washington, DC, his most overt and public acknowledgment of his homosexual identity. In a paper that he wrote for his journalism class that semester, Carl described some newspaper coverage of the march, and then he provided his own analysis of the significance of the event:

> The march on Washington showed America the diversity of the Gay, Lesbian, and Bisexual community. The participants, in all shapes, sizes and colors, were individuals who represent all walks of life. And no matter what the count of the marchers was, 300,000 or 1.1 million, the impact remained the same: America saw us as human beings, real people, individuals, rather than strange, unusual or dangerous people who ought to be shunned. Despite the differences among us, all of the speeches that afternoon echoed the same theme: unity, perseverance, and the need to combat ignorance about homosexuality relentlessly. We want people to know who we are; indeed, this goal is imperative. We will not step back into the closets that confined us.

Carl's clear identification with the marchers is apparent through his use of words like "us" and "we" that indicate his oneness with the marchers and the causes they represent. Through his acceptance of his own identity, Carl more and more publicly asserted his pride in his own singularity. Opportunities to write about his beliefs strengthened his commitment to make the larger society examine what he considered their unfounded prejudices.

In an interview in the fall of 1990, his second year at the college, Ricardo similarly evaluated the role of writing in helping him assess the ideas he encountered in his courses. He said: "Writing makes me able to question readings and analyze them in more depth. I can have a dissenting opinion. I bring evidence to bear [on the topic] from essays and then I read different opinions and I come to my own conclusions. My professors like that. Writing gives me more time to think and reflect." In his writing, Ricardo had initially presented himself in a confrontational style, but as he gained more experience in using analysis he was able to offer more cogent and reasoned arguments that would be convincing to this instructors. It is significant that he perceived that his instructors valued independent thinking.

In a paper for a U.S. society course in the spring of 1992, his third year at the college, Ricardo wrote a paper about the life of people in Concord before and after the Revolutionary War. First, he provided factual information about the divisions among the colonists in their attitudes toward independence, and then he turned to the difficulties experienced by particular groups:

> The Women's role in pre-revolutionary society was a very oppressed one. Women did not have the right to vote. Nor could they make contracts or serve as witnesses in court. Abuse against women was tolerated by society and even encouraged since they didn't have legal recourse. They were not allowed to get an education and become professionals and were taxed without representation. In family matters the woman was totally subordinated to the husband. Her role was basically one of bearing and rearing children. They were bound to follow and obey their husband. If a woman was convicted of adultery, it was considered a crime against the husband's property and he could sue for damages. While on the contrary, a man could never be found guilty of the same because it was solely a woman's crime.
>
> For the poor the struggle was different. They were an unwelcome guest in town and they were reminded of it in their visits as soon as they arrived by the constable who told them to get out of town. In many instances they were physically expelled from town [only] to receive the same treatment at the new town [when] they arrived. They did not have the right to vote and were not represented in the decision making process.
>
> For the slaves their struggle was for freedom. They told [the] General Court that they were willing to fight for independence but that they also wanted their independence. They were not given weapons because the colonist were afraid that they may rebel. In some instances they had to flee from their slave holders to escape punishment for the simple act of defending themselves against abuse. . . .
>
> In conclusion I think this was a very interesting insight of colonial society. The war for independence was led by the elite socio-political governing class of colonial society. They controlled the recently formed militia, the commanding officers were from the elite class while the common people were the rank and file soldiers. Before the war they were already in control of decision making process by serving as Selectman. Before the war only the elite class held these positions and after the war the great majority of them were replaced by their sons.
>
> The woman's only gain was that they began practicing birth control after the war.
>
> For the slaves it didn't change much. After the war many bought their freedom or were set free, but most stayed with their ex-masters as they did not achieved financial

independence. Their freedom not only meant cold and hunger, but it also meant being subjected to abuse and violence from the whites.

The poor didn't gain much either. They were still an unwelcome guest in town. The ones that settled in town were segregated from the elite colonial class. This practice of class segregation was exemplified during the reception of the Marquis of Lafayette in 1824. Only the rich and the politicians were allowed close to Lafayette, the poor were not allowed near him and when they pressed against the dividing barriers to get a closer look, they were push back by the soldiers.

Ricardo's focus on the effects of the War of Independence on women, the poor, and slaves reflect his dedication to improving the prospects of those deemed most helpless in the social stratification of the larger society. From the discouraging tone of his analysis, it can be seen that he saw the problems of members of the groups he had discussed as ongoing problems, and that he was committed to seeing that positive changes needed to be made.

CONCLUSION

In the section on ideology and in the previous sections of this chapter, the excerpts from student writing relate the facts of the students' lives and backgrounds to the attitudes and values of the society around them. As they acquired analytical skills, they could apply their "old knowledge" to the new knowledge their college courses were exposing them to. Thus, Ricardo and Chandra could see how stereotyping of minorities and women in films and television must be changed. Donald could use his awareness that minorities had been discouraged from applying to respected colleges; he could try to urge others in his community to overcome such obstacles. Ricardo could protest the injustice of being stereotyped as a "typical Puerto Rican thief." Carl could become active in the fight for respectability for homosexuals. Donald and Ricardo could argue against the demands of a society-based definition of masculinity. Delores could assert the strength of being a Black Latino woman and through her example of determination and hard work build respect for others of her background. Seeing the differences in generational opportunities, especially for minority women, Linda and Joan could help strengthen appreciation for African-American women who came from economically poor backgrounds but demonstrate the potential for success if they are given reasonable opportunities. Audrey could model the choices that women have today, whether they come from small towns or urban centers.

Should we think of race, gender, class, and ideology only as "topics" that students write about during their college years, or should we probe more deeply and ask ourselves what the *effects* of these factors have been on the student's academic lives? How have these factors sensitized them to the justices and injustices of the society in which they are living? How can they productively bring about the changes that will improve the lives of others of their background as well as the larger society? I hope that the excerpts in this chapter from the students' writings will begin to answer these questions. Their writings reveal that they are capable of looking at the problems they must face in the society as members of minority groups in focused ways that can change the quality of their lives. They have developed analytical styles that lead them first to the questioning of existing assumptions and then to the recognition that they must be active participants in bringing about the changes they see are needed in the larger society.

If we deny students the opportunity to bring their world knowledge and experience to the fields they are studying, we will be denying not only them but the entire society the opportunity to change in directions that will benefit all. If, for example, New York City and other urban areas do not make it possible for their young people to get an education and improve their lives in the ways that Lavin and Hyllegard (1996) described, who will suffer? Not just will the individuals, but the entire community will as well. As Lavin and Hyllegard pointed out, increasing educational attainment and narrowing ethnic inequalities are not current priorities in the nation's agenda (p. 240). But the consequences to the cities and the country are dire if they do not soon take precedence.

4

Writing Demands in Relation to Composition Instruction

COMPOSITION INSTRUCTION

The effects of composition instruction are most frequently examined in terms of the accomplishments of students over a single semester. Because of the longitudinal nature of this study, it is possible to follow students through several levels of instruction within the composition curriculum and beyond into their upper level courses. Since I have partial data for students other than the 9 students whose work has been examined in previous chapters, I am able to present findings from a somewhat larger sample of the original population. For the composition sequence, my data includes papers from 4 students who completed the two levels of basic writing, English 1 and English 2, 2 students who completed both basic level courses and the freshman composition course, and 8 students who completed the second level of basic writing and the freshman composition course. (Brief demographic backgrounds are provided for the "new" students.)

Although I have observation reports of a large number of courses, classroom observations did not officially begin until the second year of the study. What this means in relation to composition instruction is that I do not have many reports of composition classrooms, because most of the students completed their composition courses during the first year of the study. In addition to my own years of composition teaching, I have observed many writing classes, first at Indiana University where I was director of basic writing and then director of composition, and then at City College where as part of a union-required observation requirement, I assisted by observing and evaluating adjunct and regular faculty for 10 years. During these years, composition instruction changed markedly, the movement from "product to process" became institutionalized everywhere, and collaborative learning became an integral part of instruction. I cannot report on how the instructors of my students used these approaches except by inferences drawn from the texts the students produced. Where revisions of papers were invited, clearly "process" instruction was involved. Necessarily, then, my discussion of composition instruction is primarily text-based, although, as will be seen,

114

instructor comments on papers were often revealing of instructional peda-gogies.

COMPOSITION PEDAGOGY

As in this study, Haswell (1991) also called attention to the fact that writing processes do not proceed in a neat, linear manner: "For the writing teacher, recursion means that the new techniques or understandings of writing will be learned only by active comparison with the old. *Learning is as much a revision of old practices as a trial of new ones.* The pedagogy, it must be emphasized, refutes the standard idea that writing skill proceeds step-wise and that to rise to a new step, the student must have one foot securely on a solid lower step. . . . *Generative advance in writing proceeds not only by acquiring new frames but also by breaking old frames*" (p. 144).

One of the serious limitations of single-semester instruction in composi-tion sequences, especially through a series of "basic writing" courses to a "regular" freshman composition course, is that each instructor sees only a small, isolated step of the student's progress. Goals within each course are frequently measured in terms of improved sentence structure or control over grammatical features rather than seeing the progression as a combination of growing strength in handling both content and form. Instructors need to recognize that students must develop proficiency incrementally in both areas simultaneously and that both areas need to be stressed in subsequent courses over subsequent semesters. When instructors focus on both content and form and see improvement in both areas, they can feel more secure in moving students on to the next level where they will continue to work on these aspects of the writing process. Programs like the 1-year enrichment program at City College, started in 1993, where students stay with the same instructor over the entire year, represent another model to serve the needs of students better than would a semester-by-semester sequence because they provide more time for students to work simultaneously on the many facets of their writing that require attention.

In his examination of the papers written by sophomores and juniors in the advanced composition class, Haswell (1991) expressed concern that the instructors of these courses will note the absence of the traditional markers of writing competency (e.g., failure to provide a title, isolation of the introduction, absence of examples, etc.) while at the same time neglecting the students' shift toward a more learned vocabulary, different forms of logical organization and syntax. Increased skills in spelling and punctuation may be rewarded, whereas red marks indicate displeasure on the part of the instructors (p. 59). Haswell feared that these responses would lead the instructors of the advanced composition course to decide that the "ad-vanced" course should essentially be a repetition of the "beginning course"

(p. 59). Such an attitude may lead to the belief that skills have deteriorated. Haswell saw a potential harmful consequence of this perception: "[T]he legend of decline may end in a remarkable confined or blind circularity, recycling older students from advanced courses back into basic courses by means of some 'rising junior' competency examination" (p. 60). Such examinations frequently send the negative message that surface features of writing are the most important indicator of writing competence. (The effects of institutional testing are examined in more detail in chapter 5.)

In opposition to this frame of decline, Haswell (1991) posited a frame of growth: "It assumes that a second course will be different from the first and that the second course will be in sequence to the first, changed just as the students are changed to meet and abet that growth" (p. 61). But, as I pointed out in chapter 2, Haswell was cautious about the underlying assumptions of this frame of growth and realized that questions must be posed and examined: "Is the change adopted by the students a change in the right direction? Up to this point, I have avoided words implying that the natural development of students is necessarily a change for the better, words such as *advancement, progress, improvement.* Growth may not be unlearning or deterioration yet may still be warped, or misguiding, the students mislearning" (Haswell, 1991, pp. 61–62). It is also likely that growth will not be linear, as many factors may influence the responses of students to specific tasks at specific times in their lives.

A series of papers written by Delores, from her start in the English 2 basic writing class to work written for graduate courses in her combined BA/MA program in psychology illustrate how development in content and form are fostered over the full time-period of academic study. (All excerpts from the papers are presented exactly as written.) In the English 2 course, Delores' work manifested the second-language interference patterns that caused her to be placed at that level. She concluded her paper on Maya Angelou's autobiography, *I Know Why the Caged Bird Sings,* as follows:

> By examining M. Angelous behavior in each one of the situation in which she was involved, can be describe by the experiences that made M. Angelous more independent and courageous individual as she grew older. As the time passed, she became a less dependent person from those people who supported her in her child-hood years. Her persistence in getting the first job the control of the situation when lost in the junkyard, made her a more mature and therefore independent individual.

Sentence-level and punctuation problems abound in this paper. But it is equally clear that Delores has understood the significance of Angelou's experiences and has begun the process of analysis. My comments on the paper responded to both aspects of her writing: "You provide good evidence and tell the importance of that evidence. Unfortunately, the sentence-level problems make it hard to give you a better grade." She received a "C–" on the paper.

In the next semester, when Delores was enrolled in the freshman composition course, her new instructor's end comments on her papers responded
to the content, but markings all over the paper made corrections in style
and form. Delores' paper was about the disintegration of the American
family. In her conclusion, she wrote:

> In summary, I would like to say that even though the women's liberation movement
> has brought many changes in the role of the american women, the real women can
> take care of the family, and at the same time be able to help her husband or their
> family. The liberation of women not only has shown the american women that she
> can go out and take care of businesses, it also show the american women that she can
> be a good wife, a good worker, and the most important a real mother if she wants to
> be so. I think the if women try to be the three above mentioned there is still hope for
> the traditional family.

From a content perspective, it is clear that Delores had her own mother's
struggles in mind, as she defended the capabilities of women to take on these
demanding and difficult roles. Her instructor's interlinear changes respond
to wordiness (as in the opening of the summary paragraph), to vagueness in
some of the assertions (as she marks the phrase "help her husband or their
family" as vague and then adds the word "financially" after this phrase), to
diction (as she replaces the phrase "can go out and take care of businesses"
with the word "achieve" followed by "what?"), and to completion of a
thought (as she adds the phrase "to survive all the changes" to the last
sentence of the paragraph). In her final comments, the instructor was both
encouraging and specific in her recommendations for future papers: "Too
much is repetitive. You need to take one idea and look at it from *different*
and *many* perspectives, points of view. But this first essay is a *good* start. You
have organized well, your ideas are clear and, of course, valid." Delores
received a "C" on this paper. Delores was given an opportunity to rewrite
this paper. In the conclusion to the revised version, she was much more
succinct in her observations:

> In conclusion, the status of women today have changed greatly in the United States
> over the years. Women's roles as well as women's attitudes toward work, family, and
> their education have changed their status. The lives of women have become far more
> easier than it was previous decades. Many of these changes can become noticed in
> the work they do and in their new perspectives toward life. I think that it is up to
> women to continue making positives changes, which are good for the society and
> women themselves.

Delores' instructor is pleased with the changes and comments: "Rewrite is
much, much better; clearer, and more detailed." Delores received a "B–" on
this revision.

Through her two semesters of composition instruction, Delores' writing
received the attention it needed both in terms of content and form. These

experiences began to prepare her, then, for the writing demands of the upper level courses she would take, both in core courses such as world humanities courses, in the psychology courses she would take in her major area, in the paper she would develop as part of the special Lehman College project (that was preliminary to her master's thesis), and in her graduate courses in psychology. She would need additional time to work further on the problems of repetition and sentence structure over the ensuing years, with these problems fading and then re-emerging as she confronted different tasks.

In one of the first psychology courses Delores took, during the fall of her second year, she wrote a paper on the relationship between cognition and aging. The continuing problem she was having with repetition of ideas is illustrated in one of the paragraphs in this paper:

> This loss of speed and cautiousness is a phenomenon basic to mental events and one intimately involve to cognitive abilities. The time to respond an aging person takes to is related to how precise the answer will be. Researchers have study the concept of "accuracy vs. speed" the idea that a older person take more time in responding than younger person in order to answer accurately. An instance of this is the case of an older person taking more time in responding to a statement that requieres to think abstractly and precise than a younger person.

In giving Delores a "C–" on this paper, her instructor called attention to the problems in the paper, while encouraging her to perform better:

> My reactions are mixed. The topic is a very important one and you cover a number of the important aspects. Unfortunately, your writing is often poor. It tends to be disjointed and many times you repeat basic points that you have already made rather than deepening or clarifying the discussion. And there are many places where the writing is awkward and unclear. Also there are many spelling and/or typing errors. So what could have been quite a good paper is hampered by poor writing.

Delores took these kinds of admonitions to heart and she worked on overcoming these problems.

In the spring of her second year at the college, Delores took the first level world humanities course, a part of the college's core curriculum. In a paper on Dante's *Inferno*, she wrote:

> A fact that can be pointed is that Dante felt a higher degree of sympathy and respect for people who were famous on earth. He felt compassion for people who were related to him through the arts, poetry writers, writers like Virgil or even political figures. Dante probably felt empathy for most of the artists because he had many things in common with them. These people at some point in their lives were famous, felt similar emotions about their art. These people at some point influenced the lives of many people by making them more enjoyable with the different pieces of art they created. Like Dante these people were masters in their fields. For example, he felt sympathy and respect for Ser Brunetto Latino, a writer and friend of Dante who helped him in his development as a writer. In hell Brunetto Latino is being punished for being a sodomite, which is the crime against nature.

As a marginal comment to this paragraph, Delores' instructor wrote, "Good—but you should look at the evidence." In his final comment, her instructor prodded her to think more about the significance of the work. He wrote, "You need more of a sense of why being sympathetic to sinners is a problem—after all it seems to go against god's justice. Is Dante questioning the divine plan when he's moved by sinners? Even more problematic is showing respect to them. Also you need to consider his encounters more thoroughly—figure out what moves him and how it is related to the sin each suffers for what you have here is too speculative; you need to collect more material to base your conclusions on." Delores received a "B+" on this paper. It is clear that her instructor's request that she examine evidence more clearly in coming to conclusions is important advice for Delores to receive at this point in her academic experience. The sentence-level problems found in her earlier writings are significantly reduced, although they continue to remain a permanent feature of her papers, reflecting the difficulty of entirely eliminating second-language interference patterns in writing.

By the fall of her fourth year at the college, Delores had been accepted into the Project in Bronx Studies at Lehman College of the City University of New York. As a participant in that program, she was required to undertake original research under the supervision of a mentor. Delores' project, "Skin Color and Its Impact on Latino Self-Concept," became the preliminary study for her master's thesis. After doing some initial research, Delores described some anticipated findings in the proposal for her Bronx Studies paper:

> Puerto Ricans and Dominicans who were born in the United States, and those who by virtue of naturalization share citizenship with the dominant group, may be prompt to adapt assimilationist attitudes. Also, Puerto Ricans and Dominicans may realize that by forming part of the dominant group, they will better their opportunities to climb the economic ladder. DeAnda (1984) asserts that minorities who are close in appearance to the majority culture, especially individuals who are anonymous participants. For example, as customers in a department store, they will be treated as members of the dominant culture.
>
> Puerto Ricans and Dominicans who follow the pattern of integration are the ones retaining their hispanic identity and at the same time adapting the norms and value of the dominant culture. Puerto Ricans and Dominicans following this pattern of acculturation prefer a bicultural style, depending on whether the individual is interacting with their ethnic or with the dominant group (Berry, 1979; Mendoza, 1989). This pattern is show when Puerto Ricans and Dominicans chose to be bilingual: they learn English and maintain Spanish as their native language. They may speak spanish with members of their group, while they will shift to English interacting with Anglos.
>
> So far, the literature suggests that skin color correlates with the patterns of acculturation Latinos may follow in the United States. Skin color also seems to be influencing the way Latinos are perceived by other and also the way Latinos perceive themselves. Latinos who share the features of Anglos are perceived as members of the dominant group and may be accepted as part of the dominant group. The opposite is true for latinos who do not share the same features with the dominant group . . .

In responding to this proposal, Delores' mentor cautioned her, "To do the research project you will need to select 1 or 2 of the many questions and relationships you've mentioned." Although there are still some sentence-level problems, they can be seen to be very minor in comparison with the growth in Delores' conceptual and analytical abilities. By originating this study, Delores demonstrates her ability to draw from her academic studies and identify an issue pertaining to her own culture and identity that motivates her to a deep commitment to an intellectual enterprise. Still an undergraduate, she provides evidence through her work and her accomplishments that patience is required to ascertain how much growth can be achieved over time, especially for those students labeled "basic" or "remedial" when they enter the academic environment.

At the end of that academic year, in the spring of 1993, Delores was ready to present the findings of her study, first in her final project paper, and then in an oral symposium conducted by the Project in Bronx Studies at Lehman College on April 30, 1993. I was honored by Delores to be given one of her invitations and I went to hear her give her presentation. In the final paper, she summarized the findings of her study:

> Although weak, there is a significant relationship between self-esteem and skin color of the sixty-four students. This finding gives some rationale to the my hypothesis that in the populations of Dominicans and Puerto Ricans, the relationship is probably not zero. This means these two variables (self-esteem and skin color) are some what related.
>
> One explanation for this significant relationship between self-esteem and skin color could lied in the fact that when I compared the two groups (Dominicans and Puerto Ricans) in how worthy they valued the perceived self, Puerto Rican seems to value themselves significantly higher than Dominicans.
>
> The results could be explained in the sense that Puerto Ricans are, in the average, lighter-skinned than Dominicans and as such, when asked to rate themselves in a continuum of color from 1 to 10, they rated themselves significantly lighter than Dominicans. It gives rationale to the hypothesis that the lighter one is the better the one feels about one self, the higher the self-esteem.
>
> Another explanation for the finding that Puerto Ricans valued themselves higher than Dominicans, could be the fact that Puerto Ricans are lighter therefore, they feel more attached to the Anglo Americans for the virtue that they share a similar physical traits with the dominant group. It is important to notice that although the correlation between skin color and self-esteem was significant, I must say that it only accounts for 9% of the total variance. This is that the variable of skin color is only related to self-esteem for this population, 9% of the time.

Delores went on to discuss the other factors that could account for the other 91% of the variables—length of time in the United States with Puerto Ricans being in the country an average of almost 19 years, whereas Dominicans were there only almost 9 years, the relationship of length of time in the country to acculturation and economic status, and the fact that Puerto Ricans are entitled to certain services as members of a Commonwealth of the United States that Dominicans are not entitled to. Delores was able to see the complexity of the issue she was studying and was unwilling to come up with a facile analysis. Her years of study in the field of psychology prepared her to analyze and synthesize data honestly, not allowing herself to overemphasize those aspects of her study that would have favored her initial hypothesis. She had become a true researcher.

In one of her final research papers in a graduate course in the spring of 1994, Delores wrote a paper titled "Subjects' attitude toward psychology as a function of volunteering or refusing." Again, she was unwilling to accept simplistic explanations of the results of her study. In the discussion section of her paper, she wrote:

> The present study investigated students attitude toward psychology as a function of volunteering or refusing to participate in a psychology experiment. The data failed to confirm the hypothesis that students who volunteer to be subjects in a psychology experiment view the field of psychology more positive than students refusing to volunteer. No significant difference was found between volunteers and refusals in their attitude toward psychology. It is possible that students in the refusal group were not really refusing to volunteer. They declined because they had other activities at the moment they had to attend to. They wanted to do, but other outside stressors (e.g., having a class in the next few minutes, going to class) were preventing them from doing so. Thus willingness to volunteer or refusing might be a function of outside stressors versus inside desirability. Future studies might look at the relationship between less stressful environment and willingness to volunteer (e.g., a park, a student lounge).
>
> The data also illustrates the problem of subject bias. Subjects react to a request to volunteer for an experiment as a function of the personalities mediated by outside factors. . . . It is possible that in the present experiment, students were turn on or off when they were told the nature of the experiment. Fact that the experiment was related to math affected their willingness. It is possible that students who are apprehensive about their abilities in math declined more readily than those feeling competent about. Thus it is possible that feelings of insecurity and incompetence affects subjects' willingness to volunteer.
>
> It is also possible that the experimenters were biased when choosing the subjects. In the same manner that the subjects would decline or accept to volunteer, experimenters also had the choice to approach or not a certain subject . . .
>
> In conclusion, results of our study failed to confirm our hypothesis. It might have been due to the poor design of the experiment. The attitude scale used to measure attitude toward psychology was a poor measure only containing five items. It is hard to really measure attitude with such a small scale. Future studies might include more items.

It is clear that in this study, as in the one on skin color and self-esteem, Delores was open to critiquing her own work and looking for possible explanations for her findings. This search was not directed toward finding an excuse for failure to support the hypothesis of the study but toward the redesign of the study so future studies could produce more valid and reliable findings.

As this survey of Delores' writing over all her college years reveals, she never fully mastered all the grammatical conventions of edited English. But it is equally clear that these deviations in sentence form are far less central to her development as a writer than is the conceptual and analytic growth and maturity that her writing conveys. If an argument still needs to be made in favor of basic writing students' deserving the opportunity to demonstrate their capabilities over time, Delores is one of my prime candidates to support this view. In my last interview with her in December 1994, she told me she was applying to PhD programs in psychology, but she did not expect to hear from any of the schools until late the following semester.

Onore (1989) noted the danger of assuming that improvement in writing will follow a linear model of growth (p. 233). She pointed out how increasing cognitive challenge can be expected to affect aspects of writing style: "[I]t seems unlikely that students will improve their writing if we simultaneously demand new insights and new text options" (p. 234). She said that when writing is taught as a process, then instructors should expect "textual performances that show both occasional gains and frequent losses" (p. 234).

In working with their middle school students in the Webster Groves, IL, study, Krater et al. (1995) confronted a problem all too familiar to teachers of basic writing courses at the college level: "When an inexperienced writer faces several constraints—distant audience, formal tone, essay mode—reducing the range can be comforting. An essay map provides structure for kids to hold on to as they grapple with the new task. So we do teach the five-paragraph essay" (p. 130). The motivation for doing this closely resembles the motivation of instructors at the college level who are preparing their students for required institutional testing: "Hoping to improve [the students] performance on the annual writing assessment, Sandy tried teaching the eighth graders the five paragraph formula. She was so pleased with the results, and with the new confidence of her weakest writers, that most of the middle school teachers followed suit. We have observed that most target students like the security of the formula essay" (p. 130). Of course they recognized the danger that their students would get "hooked" on a formula and apply it rigidly whether or not it was the appropriate form for a particular paper, and to minimize the risk of this happening, they stressed that students should consider options when choosing a particular form for a particular message (p. 131). Unfortunately, once learned, the pattern of the five-paragraph theme becomes a dependable crutch for students, one they may continue to use throughout their college years.

Krater et al. (1995) were also disappointed to find that more than two thirds of their students equated revising with correcting mechanics (p. 403). Like other teachers at all levels of instruction, they encouraged their colleagues "to stress substantive revision even more" (p. 403). Chiseri-Strater suggested that it is the revision process itself that leads to learning through writing. Teachers' comments are the keys to the choices students make as they contemplate revising papers. If the overwhelming responses have been to sentence-level features, these are the "corrections" that will be made. Only when instructors pose questions that require students to probe more deeply into their ideas will further analysis or interpretation be seen as the priority for revision. In the middle of these levels of response is the familiar request for more information or evidence to support the writers' points. These, too, are demands for substantive thinking.

EFFECT OF TEACHER'S COMMENTS

Among the many problems that second-language and second-dialect speakers confront in their writing courses is the frequent failure of instructors to address the content of student writing, instead focusing on structural and grammatical problems and conflating form with intellectual ability. Using as a base their extensive analysis of a sample of the 21,000 teacher-marked student essays they collected, Connors and Lunsford (1993) established categories for describing the types of responses teachers gave. Although their discussion focused on a statistical breakdown of the features found in the 3,000 papers they examined, examples of the teachers' responses in the various categories are helpful in relating their study to my much smaller one. The advantage in my study is that my readings of papers written over time by individual students can give better insight into what Phelps (1989) called "the writer's developing cognitive, linguistic, and social capacities as they bear on writing activities" (p. 53).

I have papers of two students who enrolled in the entire composition sequence in place when this study began, English 1, English 2, and English 110, the freshman composition course. Stanley is an African American who graduated from Automotive High School in New York City. In several interviews, he told me that he "liked to work with his hands," which he called "creative work" and that he had been pushed into going to college by his mother, a beautician, who wanted him to have the opportunities she had not had. He had financial problems and family problems, causing him to take several leaves of absence. He finally had to drop all his classes in the spring of 1992, including his second attempt to take the English 110 class he was enrolled in on Saturdays, because he was working 40 hours a week. In the English 1 course, Stanley wrote of an experience at the 1989 New York Auto Show when he was a senior at the Automotive High School. He was selected "to discuss how the industry should or could cooperate with city schools by helping to donate equipment, so students can properly learn the trade." His presentation resulted in an interview by Pete Hamill of *The New York Post* who wrote an article which included a description of Stanley's presentation: "He asked in clear language for more space at school, for better technical facilities, a greater chance to work with the auto industry in learning new systems. He didn't whine or threaten. He didn't say that the alternative was crack. This was some kid" (Hamill, 1989). I encouraged Stanley to expand the information he was presenting in his papers and tell why the evidence he presented was important. In a revision of a paper comparing his experiences as a commuting college student with the experiences of those who are able to live on campus, Stanley wrote:

> My mother always has some type of suggestion whenever I do something, like when I get dressed, she would suggest something else like a sweater or switch shirts or pants. I don't feel like I have any freedom because I can't do something or go somewhere on my own, without the assistance of 'mommy dearest.' I do appreciate her help, but sometimes I would like to have just a little time to myself.

Although this excerpt was clearly not a deep analytical response to his conditions of living at home, it reflected an understanding that he should begin to look for implications of events he describes. In a conclusion to a paper on Toni Morrison's *The Bluest Eye*, Stanley wrote: "In a way, I think that Tony [sic] Morrison was trying to say that people should be contented with what they have because, asking for a little bit more could lead to a lot of unhappiness." My end comment on the paper attempted to prod Stanley to go beyond his conclusion: "Don't you think she is saying that people should have pride in themselves and not try to be someone else?" In each case, my comments were intended to encourage Stanley to reexamine his own ideas from a broader perspective.

In his English 2 class, Stanley found his papers marked mainly for stylistic features, with comments such as "wordy," "avoid passive voice," "well-written sentences," "diction—wordy and awkward." On one paper, the instructor asked for "some more concrete detail" and "some pertinent information." In this paper, Stanley wrote about his experience working in an ice cream parlor. Although the instructor requested more details, he never prodded Stanley to think about the significance of the experience he was describing. In this paper, Stanley related how he resented having to go to work after his classes:

> Every afternoon after my classes are over, I feel so relieved and happy that I could just take a nice long nap. Another day of classes has been completed for me and I'm ready to get on the train and head home, but then I realize that I can't because I have to go to work. On the way there, I try to think of so many reasons and excuses to tell my boss why I wouldn't be able to come in, but I end up going anyway.

The narrative goes on to relate the details of Stanley's working day, but never examines the issue of the effect of work on schooling, on morale, on fatigue, or any of the other consequences that might have been explored. Stanley is not a bad writer here, but the sense of lost opportunity is very strong.

Stanley attempted English 110 twice. The first time, in the spring of 1991, he withdrew from all his courses because he needed money and he had to work full time. I have a few journal entries and a short story he wrote in that course. In an interview at the end of that semester, he told me that he had been assigned to write a three-generation family narrative. He said that it would have been difficult for him to write that because his family "was not close." He also said that it was easier for him to write papers that used different sources from books and reports, thus supporting the view that some students prefer not to write about personal topics. The few journal entries—really free writings—do not attempt any analysis of the topics addressed. The short story describes how a cat climbs a tree, eats a bird, and is then killed when a lumberjack cuts down the tree. Stanley's attempts at a "moral," perhaps the point of the assignment, are weak: "The moral of the story is not to judge a book by its cover; no matter how well you plan things, things don't always go according to plan." These brief descriptions of Stanley's travels through his English courses suggest that opportunities have been lost; here was a student who could have been encouraged to develop his analytic powers, but who was not galvanized to do so.

Linda's experiences through the three levels of composition were more stimulating and moved her in more productive directions than Stanley had been led. In the English 1 course, my comments on Linda's papers were divided between issues of content and form. When Linda attempted statements of analysis, I tried to encourage her. When she compared her experiences of living at home with students who live on campus, she wrote about the difficulties her family had in understanding the demands of her college life: "They don't realize there are other priorities in our life [other than playing games or baking cookies] we have to take care of in order to succeed." My marginal comment was: "Good point. Develop it further with specific examples." So-called final drafts were still open to revision, and Linda was told to revise this version further which she did. Linda wrote an analysis of one of the characters, Cholly, in Toni Morrison's *The Bluest Eye*:

> Cholly decided to leave and look for his father. His father spurned him and told him to go away. These experiences led Cholly to believe he was unwanted and unloved. Cholly was made to feel that he was a burden to everyone.
>
> When Cholly became a grown man he met and married Pauline Williams. Afterwards Cholly became a father. He did not know how to handle that kind of responsibility. Cholly did not know how to raise children. His childhood denied him the privilege of experiencing the joy of being raised by parents. This denial contributed towards Cholly's behavior of his own children.

My final comment on the paper was: "Good discussion of his background and his behavior." I regret that I did not comment on Linda's perceptive discussion of the link between the two. What can be seen here is that at the

English 1 level, students like Linda have the capacity to apply analytical frameworks to the works they are studying.

In the English 2 class, the teacher was primarily interested in stylistic features of writing, and Linda's papers were full of interlinear word and phrase substitutions, such as "obviously" for "therefore"; replacement and addition of words that changed meanings such as "a conversation would have taken place" replaced by "a conversation probably would have developed"; and the addition of words that carried meaning not placed there by the student, such as "unfortunately" or "really" as an intensifier. Comments at the ends of papers were of the generic type: "pretty good" and "not bad." This type of comment does not help the student understand any specific ways to improve her writing. Linda's attempts at analysis were responded to negatively, with the instructor rewriting statements that she felt were poorly expressed or thought through. Linda wrote in one paper about the danger of handguns and someone she knew who had played Russian Roulette with friends. In the following excerpt, the teacher's comments are interpolated in brackets:

> Whoever [whenever someone] answer[ed] the question wrong [he] had to put the gun to his head and pull the trigger. The man answered the question wrong He pulled the trigger and was killed instantly. [Finally one man made a mistake and when he pulled the trigger he was killed instantly.] The others were arrested and charged [as] with accessories to a murder. Dangerous games like this could lead many people to be killed or jailed [Dangerous games like this couldn't happen if guns were not so easily available]. (This last change was accompanied by the marginal comment "too obvious to mention!").

The instructor's rewordings certainly clarified Linda's meanings, but the disparaging tone of the corrections had to be discouraging to her.

In the English 110 class, Linda found more challenging comments addressed to her. In a paper on the issue of women choosing to remain childless, Linda wrote:

> I want to talk about a topic which is not talked about often—childless women. Believe me, there are women out [there] who do not want children just as much as women who do. Childless women aren't as equally respected as their maternal counterparts. They are considered selfish women who are not doing their duty.

Linda's instructor wrote in the margin of the paper: "You need a more definite thesis. What do you believe about this? What's your argument?" Such comments prodded Linda to think analytically about how to formulate a thesis so that it could be argued effectively. The teacher's final comments encouraged Linda to reflect more fully and deeply about her ideas: "Good points. I think that if you had used more specific examples of prejudice against childless women and analyzed these prejudicial attitudes (e.g., their origins and underlying assumptions) your essay would have been stronger."

How much more useful these comments are than those that end with the kind of phrase that the comment here uses only as a takeoff point, "Good points." In a later paper on Frederick Douglass' autobiography, the instructor continued to promote an analytic stance by questioning, at the end of the paper, "Why was literacy so important to Douglass?" The more that Linda was confronted by the "why" question, the more she was encouraged to probe topics thoughtfully. Thus, as Linda progressed through the composition sequence, she was alternately encouraged, discouraged, and encouraged to risk taking analytic stances. Fortunately, she became more willing to take such risks and look beyond surface meanings to deeper interpretations.

Connors and Lunsford found that 77% of the papers in their study contained global or rhetorical comments, while 23% did not. Seventy-five percent of the papers were graded. Sixty-four percent of the papers had initial or terminal comments and, of those, 16% had initial comments and 84% had terminal comments. Of the global comments, nine percent were essentially positive, 23% were essentially negative, 42% began positively and turned negative, and 11% began negatively and ended on a positive note (p. 207). That the largest percentage of these comments should begin in a positive way and then turn negative is not surprising, as the all too familiar "but" in teacher's comments is found as part of a wide practice.

Another kind of taxonomy for looking at teacher responses to student writing was outlined by Warnock (1989). Drawing on Burke's writings, Warnock outlined a category system based on schools of criticism. The major categories she identified were (a) text-centered (e.g., "Lacks complexity" or "Is this appropriate?" or "Out of what conditions might this have arisen?"), (b) author-centered (e.g., "What do you mean?" or "I think I get your point, but I'm not sure" or "Write in your own voice"), (c) reader-centered (e.g., "I don't get it" or "Have you considered this?" or "In my view . . ."), (d) subject-centered (e.g., "Wrong" or "Right" or "Undeveloped"), and (e) context-centered (e.g., "What are the assumptions?" or "What is missing?") (pp. 68–69).

Straub (1996) was critical of the dualistic frameworks that have been set up to look at responses to student writing: "directive or facilitative, authoritative or collaborative, teacher-based or student-based. One is encouraging and good, the other critical and bad" (p. 224). Flynn (1989) proposed a perspective from which to examine teachers' comments on student papers, masculine or feminine styles of response. Flynn noted that "males tend to objectify, to detach themselves from the experiences they are observing or the individuals with whom they are communicating. Females, in contrast, tend to empathize with others and to interact with them more readily than do males" (p. 51). Flynn noted that her findings were complemented by those of Bleich (1986) in which "he found that males tend to focus on literary narratives as objects constructed by an author whereas females tend to participate in the experience evoked in the text" (p. 53). Against these dichotomies, Straub argued that there is a great variety of ways in which teachers can legitimately respond in relation to teaching styles, classroom goals, and the needs of individual students. Straub concluded his article with the recognition that even if one style of response is not necessarily as good as another that "surely there are better and worse ways to respond—and even wrong ways to respond" (p. 247):

> At one extreme, some comments are overly harsh or disrespectful, and usurp control over student writing, making sweeping editorial changes and dictating what should be said or how it should be presented from top to bottom. At the other extreme, some teacher comments are so minimal and generic that they become detached and offer no help, no real response. Both extremes ought to be avoided. Students must be allowed to develop their own ideas and encouraged to take responsibility for their writing; they must be allowed to make their own writing decisions and learn to make better choices. Comments that recognize the integrity of the student as a learning writer and that look to engage him in substantive revision are better than those that do not. (pp. 247–248)

Although the papers collected in my study were almost always final drafts, I can attempt to look at teacher comments that were directed at changes in subsequent papers, particularly in the composition courses. A few students did provide me with successive drafts for papers they wrote for composition or upper level courses.

In addition to the kinds of potential comments cited above, there are two other common forms all too frequently found on student papers, the generic comments (briefly mentioned by Straub) that are not text-specific and that could be interchanged from one text to another and the comment presented to justify a grade. All of these are considered in examining the responses to the student writing from my sample.

Following Bizzell's (1986) call to consider students' world views as one responds to their writing, Anson (1989) elaborated on the factors that need to be understood better:

> Large gaps exist in our understanding of the relationships between the developing of writing abilities and the "ways of knowing" that are part of students' intellectual, cognitive, and social backgrounds. What sorts of world views, particularly views of knowledge, do students bring into academia? How are these views related to their abilities as writers? What beliefs about learning do we convey through our responses to student writing, and in what ways do these encourage (or inhibit) the further development of literacy? (p. 333)

Anson was also interested in "the relationship between students' ways of analyzing the world, as expressed in their essays, and the views of knowledge, learning, and writing implied in teachers' responses to these essays" (p. 333).

CONTENT AND FORM

Zamel (1995) was sensitive to the importance of teachers responding to the meaning of student writing first before pointing out sentence-level or structural problems. In commenting on a response she received from a composition teacher to a survey she conducted with teachers of non-native speakers of English, Zamel lauded the instructor who "does not despair over the presence of second language errors, over the short essays, the 'sweeping generalizations,' the empty introduction, the 'wild assertions.' Instead, this instructor seems to persist in his attempts to focus the student on content issues, to respond to the student seriously, to push him to consider the connections between what he was saying and the assigned reading, to take greater risks, which he succeeds in doing 'by the fourth essay'" (p. 508). In particular, Zamel suggested that the composition instructor has asked the student to "trust" him that serious engagement with the course material is desired and that the instructor understands that "it takes time to acquire new approaches to written work" (p. 509). An art history instructor responded to the same survey with a markedly different response. Zamel pointed out that this instructor assumed that "language and knowledge are separate entities [and] that language must be in place and fixed" in order to do course work (p. 509). Furthermore, this latter instructor believed that "language use is determined by a knowledge of parts of speech or grammatical terminology" (p. 509). As Zamel pointed out, this type of "failure" is often blamed on composition instructors who have not fulfilled their "gatekeeping" function (p. 509).

Connors and Lunsford (1993) also found that many teachers did not use their comments on student writing to engage content issues:

> Teachers seemed unwilling to engage powerfully with content-based student assertions or to pass anything except "professional" judgments on the student writing they were examining. Only 24% of the comments made any move toward arguing or refuting any content points made in the paper, and many of these "refutations" were actually formal comments on weak argumentative strategies. In some way, then, teachers seem conditioned *not* to engage with student writing in personal or polemical ways. What we found, then, in short, was that most teachers in this sample give evidence of reading student papers in ways antithetical to the reading strategies currently being explored by many critical theorists. (pp. 214–215)

The examination of student writing over several semesters, with comments from a range of instructors, can reveal the kind of message that is sent to student writers about the value the academic institution places on meaning.

One of the students who was placed in my English 2 section, Marielle, found herself in diametrically different settings in her two attempts to complete the English composition requirement. Marielle's mother was Latino and her father African American. She wrote movingly in her papers about her unwillingness to be labeled after her mother's parents refused to acknowledge the family relationship. Marielle wrote: "My . . . grandmother told my mother, in front of me, she did not want my mother to tell anyone that she or we were related to her in any way. When I asked, 'why,' she looked me right in my eyes and told me that my being black was something she would always be ashamed [of]." Additional complications ensued for her with her Latino heritage as people expected her to speak Spanish because she had a Latino-sounding last name "and became upset when I could not." Marielle solved her identity issue by asserting, "When people ask me who am I, I tell them American."

In her writing in the English 2 course, it was clear that Marielle had difficulty with developing her ideas fully, but she did not evidence serious sentence-level problems. In writing successive drafts of papers, she sometimes omitted critical information in her final draft that had appeared in an earlier draft. For example, in comparing her experience with that of an anthropologist in her first field trip setting, Marielle wrote that she was "considered an exotic sight" and attracted attention when she attended a church service. She wrote simply, "I did not expect my clothing to make or attract any attention." In an earlier draft of the paper, she had described her clothing and explained why she attracted this attention: "During the Mass I was trying to figure out what it was that I had done wrong. Later I noticed that all the women were wearing dresses or skirts. Now I know I was wearing pants. I was the only woman wearing pants. I felt very embarrassed because I was trying my best not to get noticed and now I find myself the talk of the church." In my comment on her paper, I urged her to take the details from her drafts and use them as necessary in her final paper.

In a paper on Maya Angelou's *I Know Why the Caged Bird Sings*, for her English 2 class, Marielle identified with Angelou's pride in being Black, but she did not provide pertinent examples from Angelou's experiences to support her argument. Her writing was not unlike that commonly found in developing writers, and I had no problem in passing her from the course with a "C." She passed the required WAT at the end of that semester.

In the next semester, Marielle enrolled in the freshman composition course. There is not a single substantive comment written by her instructor on the three papers I have from that course. One paper has a minus sign at the end, one a "D," and the third an "F." (She received a "D" on the paper described earlier where she discussed the issue of personal identity.) Spelling and grammatical problems are marked on all papers. On two of the papers, the rhetorical comment "thesis" is written at the top. Although the individual grammatical features are corrected on the papers, there is no indication that the student needs to identify patterns to work with. In a practice exam paper apparently in preparation for the department-wide essay examination at the end of English 110, the instructor wrote only a single word, "shallow." With such discouraging messages being sent to her, it is no surprise that

Marielle failed the composition course. What is even more discouraging to see is the complete failure of the instructor to provide any guidance for the student to improve her writing.

In direct contrast to this experience, Marielle's instructor in her next attempt to complete the composition requirement focused her attention on helping her improve her ability to convey her meaning in her writing. When Marielle wrote about a small park located on the campus where she went when she "needed a place to get away or study," her instructor wrote as an end comment:

> [Marielle]—This essay has more substance than [your last one]. But it has less purpose. Why are you writing about the park? Does it have some special meaning for you or for other people? Does it symbolize something about City College? Can we consider it a symbol of some larger aspect of City College? Does it serve an important function here? Is it particularly beautiful? Why are you writing about the park?

As this extensive comment reveals, the focus for this instructor was not only meaning but also the effort to move the student further toward analysis. When Marielle revised the paper, the instructor again commented fully on the rewrite, pointing out improvements in descriptive and figurative language as well as improved development of specific points. For this paper, the instructor began by marking individual lines with a check-mark where grammatical or spelling problems existed, and she added a section in her final comments asking Marielle to proofread much more carefully.

A later paper in the course continued the instructor's focus on meaning and form as closely intertwined. Marielle wrote a paper about a Vietnamese woman and her son who immigrated to the United States after a difficult period in a relocation camp. Despite many hardships, the woman succeeded in improving her life. The instructor commented that Marielle had presented good information, but the "depiction of these women's lives almost seems too easy. It is cliché that people come here to succeed. More complications would make this sound more believable." At the same time, the instructor alerted Marielle to the fact that her sentence-level problems had to be addressed more seriously: "The proofreading that was not done really mars my experience of reading your paper. The errors jump out and grab me. They distract me from my reading of your meaning." Such a comment is likely to have a much more serious effect on a student than the placement of a minus sign or an "F" at the end of a paper. Here, the instructor is asking the student to take responsibility for improving both the form and content of her papers for her readers so that they can better understand and appreciate her meaning.

Rose (1985a) argued against separating the teaching of language skills from teaching about the importance of content. He noted that teaching only mechanical and grammatical skills prevents teachers from exploring what the students know and have experienced. Such a separation has led to the denigration of the teaching of writing (p. 348). Connors and Lunsford (1993) also pointed out that there is "a pervasive tendency to isolate problems and errors individually and 'correct' them, without any corresponding attempt to analyze error patterns in any larger way" (p. 217). Such a set of markings is overwhelming to students who perceive that they have thirty problems rather than three or four patterns of features that need to be worked with.

It should not be surprising that the papers of students who were placed into the English 1 section, which I taught, should contain comments almost evenly balanced between content and form. The writing of students placed at this level on the basis of their performance on the WAT manifested many sentence-level problems. What this meant for instructors was that they needed to stress meaning *and its expression* to students, while simultaneously helping them to recognize the features of their writing that they needed to work on. When instructors failed to keep these issues in focus for the students, they did them a disservice. Commenting on content alone was not an adequate response to student writing either at the English 1 or English 2 level.

The most blatant example of the problem with ignoring form and writing only generic comments ostensibly related to content on student writing came from a set of papers written by a student who began in English 1 (which she passed with a "C") and who then continued on to English 2, which she failed. Yvonne had completed all her education through high school in Puerto Rico, where she had only one class in English. (She transferred to a technical college after her first year.) In her writing in the English 1 course, I commented on the content of her papers and also pointed out *patterns* of sentence-level problems she was having difficulty with. In one paper, I noted that she needed to work on sentence fragments, telling her that "almost all of these should be joined to the sentence before" and she should "check that all verbs are consistently in the same tense." On another paper, I pointed out that she still needed to work on sentence fragments and I also urged her to check subject–verb agreement and possessive forms. By the end of the semester, she seemed more in control of these sentence-level features and it was possible for her to pass the course. In an interview in March 1990, the middle of the next semester when she was enrolled in English 2, she told me that she was "doing well" in the course. It is easy to see how she got this impression by looking at copies of the papers she wrote. Virtually every paper had "good" written in marginal comments and every paper had "very good" as an end comment. Occasionally, a verb form was corrected on a paper, but no directions were given for continued attention to sentence-level problems except for one paper that had as an end comment, "Notice where I have added commas or endings." So, it was with some shock that Yvonne found herself not passing the English 2 course. She had failed the WAT which was then required for completion of that course. Although I will argue that over-attention to grammatical features on institutional tests is not justified, especially for second-language and second-dialect speakers, in this case it is clear that her instructor did not fulfill his responsibility to her because he did not attempt to assist her in the development of the language patterns she needed to control in her formal writing.

In looking over the papers that Yvonne wrote in her English 1 and 2 classes, I was startled to see that she had "recycled" some of her English 1 papers into her English 2 class. She took several papers that she had written the previous semester and presented them as formal papers or journal entries in the English 2 course, carefully copying any corrections I had made on the earlier papers. Since instructors rarely see papers that are turned in for subsequent courses, this discovery made me wonder how common this practice is. (I laughed at myself when I saw that I had made a mistake in one of my corrections, writing "belief" where the proper word was "believe," and then seeing that Yvonne dutifully copied my correction into her journal entry in the English 2 class.)

Another student, Georgio, who was more successful in English 1 and English 2, also failed to receive sufficient direction in his English 2 course. Georgio was born and educated in New York City. His mother had come from the Dominican Republic and his first language was Spanish. He was initially undecided on a major, then chose political science, graduating in the spring of 1995. My comments on his English 1 papers urged him to reread the materials on which some of the essays were based to analyze them more fully, to develop more points in his writings, and to be more specific with the evidence he was presenting. My major focus was to encourage him to look more seriously at the implications of what he was reading. For example, Georgio concluded a paper on The Bluest Eye by Toni Morrison by writing, "The purpose of the comparison is that the author Toni Morrison wants the reader to see the lifestyle of a black person compared to [a] white [person]." My end comment was: "I wonder if the comparison is deeper than that—between a person of any race who has a loving family and a person of any race who does not." Perhaps Straub would see that comment as too directive, but my intention was to ask Georgio to explore the conditions portrayed in the novel as having a broader perspective than the one he had proposed.

In interviews the following semester, Georgio told me that he had turned in three or four papers to his English 2 instructor, but she had "corrected" only one, marking the other papers with only a check or a check-plus. No grammatical features had been marked. He told me, "Nobody participates—the class is boring—I'm not learning anything new." By contrast, the next fall he said that he "learned how to write a very good essay" in his freshman composition course and he passed the English Proficiency Test (required for graduation) the semester after finishing the composition course. Georgio came to see me for interviews through the spring of 1991, the end of his second year at the college, but he did not provide me with copies of his papers after his first semester.

Flower (1994) has noted the potential negative effect that peer pressure can place on students. "'Acting white,' which can generate enormous peer pressure and rejection, is, unfortunately associated with school achievement, including specifics like using Standard English, speaking in class, doing work on time. Students who enter high school as high achievers sometimes negotiate this dilemma by keeping a low profile and what Fordham calls a strategy of 'racelessness'—a behavior that entails genuine costs and that becomes increasingly difficult for males to maintain" (p. 34). In an interview in the spring of 1993, the end of her fourth year at the college, Linda told me how she had been affected by a peer pressure experience she had had in high school: "I speak out more, but at times I'm afraid to speak out. In high school, I had a bad experience. When I raised my hand, I was ridiculed because I always spoke out. I have a fear of being ridiculed, even if I know the answer. Maybe I'm off track. I recite now more than I used to. My teachers used to have to pull it out of me. Students tease me when I answer all the questions." According to a report in *The New York Times* on August 7, 1996 by Mary B. W. Tabor, peer pressure is still exerting a negative influence on the performance of some high school students. The article described the findings of a book by Lawrence Steinberg, a psychology professor at Temple University, *Beyond the Classroom: Why School Reform Has Failed and What Parents Need to Do.* According to the article, "peer groups act as cement shoes . . . [N]early 20 percent [of the students] said they did not try as hard as they could in [high] school because of worries about what their friends might think" (p. A12). The book also argued that parental attitudes toward school performance are crucial, but they can be overshadowed by peer-group attitudes (p. A12).

INTELLECTUAL ABILITY
AND GRAMMATICAL STRUCTURES

Another important insight in Zamel's (1995) discussion is that the composition instructor recognizes that it is inappropriate "to draw conclusions about intellectual ability on the basis of surface features of language" (p. 509). Such an understanding might have mitigated many of the problems that students in my study had when they were evaluated on the writing assessment tests required by the college. All too often, surface features appeared to be conflated with intelligence, as the examples of Ricardo's many attempts to pass the WAT, cited in chapter 1, attest to. This view considers language to be a skill that can be taught separately from meaning "and that must be in place in order to undertake intellectual work" (Zamel,

1995, p. 510). (The effects of second-language and second-dialect patterns on passing institutional tests are considered in chapter 5.)

Ackerman (1993) pointed out that there is an illusion that the university and the culture at large is homogeneous, and that those who use literacy standards advocated by Bloom (1987) and Hirsch (1988) "ignore the diversity of American colleges and universities" (p. 338). Since no remedial writing classes were offered at Washington State University at the time of Haswell's study (1991), the impromptu samples from the freshmen, sopho-mores, and juniors included papers that might have been written by students assigned to basic writing courses at other institutions of higher learning (accounting perhaps for the features he found in what he called "the bottom nine"). Haswell selected the nine essays receiving the lowest rating on his holistic scale, noting that "the teacher-raters tended to agree most on these bottom nine, although there was significant disagreement on the ratings of the top nine" (p. 269). A possible explanation for the agreement on the bottom nine essays is posited by Haswell: "They have all the classic signs of writing called 'incompetent.' They are halt with mechanical errors, quirky in paragraphing, and backward in production, averaging 196 words com-pared with 364 for higher rated student essays. They are scant of title and topic sentence and introduction and supportive elaboration and other reader amenities. Perhaps remedial writing is easy for evaluators to catego-rize because it bears, or bares, its earmarks flagrantly, on the surface" (p. 269). But Haswell is suspicious of these judgments, noting that "when we look under the surface, the picture changes, in some ways dramatically. The most dramatic is top-level logical organization" (p. 269). Here is further evidence that attention to surface features overwhelms judgment in assess-ment and seems to preclude analysis of rhetorical features and content-fea-tures that might lead to recognition and valuing of strengths such as found by Hull and Rose (1989) in their study of underprepared writers. It also points out the weakness of basing assessments on single impromptu pieces of writing (an issue taken up in chapter 5 on institutional testing). Ques-tioning the many studies that argue that basic writers lag in cognitive maturity (Bradford, 1983; Lees, 1983; Lunsford, 1979; Stotsky, 1986), Haswell asserted that assessments need to look "beneath the surface of error and ineptitude with more care at the way . . . essays are organized" (p. 270).

Flower (1994) argued that:

> correctness and control of privileged conventions have lost some of their status as definers of literacy or as ends in themselves. They are instead recognized as valuable tools and skills that let writers function in certain contexts (like school), even as they serve to bar the door of entry to students who are less prepared. Such skills are important, sometimes dramatically, critically important, *but not because of their inherent value as a necessary building block or tool for thinking* [italics added]. They are important in part because certain groups of people, like teachers, administrators, employers, and readers make them so. In this discussion, *students are no longer defined in terms of*

intellectual, cultural, or informational deficits [italics added]. . . . However, novices are not blank slates, but learners who bring a great deal of cultural capital and literate experience with them (that may both help and hinder learning in school)." (p. 19)

A number of researchers argued against cognitive deficit models. Rose (1983) wrote: "Our students are not cognitively 'deficient' in the clinical sense of the term; if they were, they wouldn't be able to make the progress they do. Our students are not deficient; they are raw. Our job, then, is to create carefully thought-out, appropriate, undemeaning pedagogies that introduce them to the conventions of academic inquiry" (p. 127). Kogen (1986), too, was critical about the belief that basic writers do not have the ability to conceptualize or reason abstractly. She said, "I would like to step back from such categorical assumptions of inability and inadequacy. It is all too easy to conclude that those who do not do, or do not wish to do, what they seem to be able to do are deficient and underdeveloped. But, more important, such assumptions about reasoning and its role in discourse are not borne out by experience" (p. 25).

Martinez and Martinez (1987) also argued against the too-simple idea that basic writing characteristics should be equated with cognitive deficiencies:

> Certainly, the study of cognitive strategies underlying the composition processes has much to offer the writing teacher, but we must avoid the temptation to play psychologist, to diagnose and measure and provide therapy for deficiencies that are apparent rather than real. To state the obvious, our students are basic writers because they have problems writing. If we focus, then, on finding solutions to their writing problems rather than attempting to rework their mental structures or even revise their world views, our chances for success should improve—much as using an eggbeater rather than a rolling pin to beat eggs improves the result. (p. 11)

It is noteworthy that Martinez and Martinez understand that the educational experience should improve students' abilities to express their world views more clearly, as Bizzell (1986) argued, rather than to alter them.

Eduardo is a Black male, born in Guyana, who originally enrolled at City College in the mechanical engineering program. Although he passed the composition and core courses without major difficulty, he had problems with the science and math courses, taking, for example, the required chemistry course four times. He withdrew the first two times, earned a "D" the third time, and finally received a "B" on the fourth try. He had similar difficulties with the mathematics courses. Like many other prospective engineering students at City College, Eduardo had to begin his studies with a long series of remedial math courses, because he had not studied the required areas in high school. This long time delay before he could enroll in the higher level courses naturally became a discouraging factor for him. By the time he changed majors, Eduardo was in his sixth year at the college. He decided to become a physical education teacher in the public schools, and he was successful both in the education courses and the physical education courses. In the fall of 1995, he was still enrolled in the college, having completed 106 credits with a cumulative grade point average of 2.71.

Placed in the English 1 level because of sentence-level problems on the WAT, Eduardo quickly demonstrated thoughtful perspectives in his writing. In the English 1 course, he wrote a paper on Toni Morrison's *The Bluest Eye*. In this paper, Eduardo contrasted the ideal family depicted in many children's book, Dick, Jane, Mother, and Father (described by Morrison in the introduction to the book) with the family of Pecola, the main character of the novel:

> Dick, Jane, Mother, and father were used in the novel by Toni Morrison to potray the tipical story book family. A family that is united and happy. Pecola's family on the other hand, is the opposite to this story book family. Her family is not always united and surely not happy.
>
> In the typical story book family, the father plays with Jane. Mother play with jane. Jane is very happy and beautiful. Pecola does not feel that way. People hardly talk to her. She also thinks that see [she] is very ugly. In the story, if a girl wanted to get a boy upset, all she would have to say is "John loves Pecola." The boy would get upset because Pecola is not so good looking. Her brother runs away. Most of the time her father is drunk. This we do not see in the story book family.
>
> The comparison between these two families showed exactly how the story book world is not all alike for many people. They could only wish for a life as such, in turn feeling very sorry for themselves.

Although this paper is not a fully developed analysis of the novel's major theme, it demonstrates the beginning of a reflective stance that Eduardo was able to develop more fully in later courses. I have only papers from Eduardo's first 1½ years at the college, but a paper he wrote in a political science course the fall of his second year (1990), reveals an ability to take a more critical stance toward materials he encountered. In a paper on voter participation, Eduardo assessed the effects of individuals who decided not to vote in elections:

> At the moment, there are two major dominant political parties in the United States. The Democratic party and the Republican party. I never knew that involuntary nonvoting had an effect on one of these parties while the other is almost not affected at all. Nonvoting has tend to take set on the class system in America. People with limited education, political information and the poor tend not to vote, thus affecting the Democratic party. The Republican party remains unaffected because they are structured on the upper class of the american society.

In his comment on the paper, the instructor noted that the articles the students have read "suggest that non-voters would vote much as voters do. So you may exaggerate this point." Eduardo may have brought his life experience to bear on his analysis, while his instructor attempted to move him toward a more objective stance.

Students like Eduardo benefited from comments on their writing that helped them integrate their experiences with the academic materials they were encountering, while not ignoring misreadings that could lead to faulty conclusions.

WRITING IN UPPER LEVEL COURSES

The importance of teacher support becomes crucial as students encounter writing assignments across the disciplines (Penrose, 1993; Walvoord & McCarthy, 1990). They must not only "learn the forms and conventions of writing in each of the disciplines they encounter, they must also recognize the types of learning that are expected in each of them" (Penrose, 1993, p. 57). Some examples of upper level writing are examined in this chapter, particularly as they relate to students' attempts to apply composition instruction to discipline-based demands. Other examples of upper level writing are presented in chapter 7 with the reports of case studies. In chapter 3, many examples were provided of students responding to topics that allowed them to integrate their worldviews with the academic tasks they were encountering. But it is important to point out that students also learned to respond to traditional academic tasks, demonstrating increasing ability to handle complex analyses of literary works as well as materials in other humanities and social science areas.

Students who received constructive comments on their papers as they enrolled in upper division courses benefited from the reinforcement of what they had learned in their writing courses. Sonia is a White student who went to elementary and middle schools in Connecticut, junior high in New Jersey, and high school in Florida. She started at the English 2 level. Her original major was education, but she switched to biology in her second year with hopes of becoming a physician. Although she had some difficulty with the math and science courses, she persisted, retaking courses when necessary to earn "Bs" or "Cs." When her mother moved to Ohio at the end of her third year, Sonia transferred to Lake Erie College. She graduated in the spring of 1995 with a degree in biology. Sonia kept in touch with me by mail after she left the college. She wrote that she had applied to a College of Osteopathy, but was denied admission. She enrolled in a nursing program at the University of Akron in the fall of 1995.

Sonia's writing in the English 2 course was virtually error-free and my comments on her paper were directed toward encouraging her to provide adequate information to support her points and to analyze and interpret the materials more fully. She received an "A" in the English 2 course. In the freshman composition course, her instructor's comments were mainly rhetorical (e.g. "a good clear introduction") or addressed the syntax of her sentences. Comments on content were generic. In a paper on "The Origins of Family Life," an end comment that typified others read: "A good rewrite. However, you still need to concentrate a bit on sentence structure. Rewrite those [sentences] marked 'Syn'—See me if you wish. You have organized well. Your thesis is clear. Good!" Sonia's paper received a "B." Other papers had initial comments that were similarly generic in relation to content: "Well done. Well expressed. Clear," or "Good" or "Excellent." Despite these comments, Sonia received a "C" in the course and was not provided with any direction on how to improve her writing.

The next semester, Sonia enrolled in a world humanities course. In a paper about *Shekuntala*, Sonia received substantive criticism from her instructor: "The significance of the ring is not that it will identify Shekuntala but that the King will regain his memory of her when he sees it. The bad-tempered sage had cast a spell on her that only the ring can undo. Good. B+." This serious response to Sonia's possible misinterpretation of part of the text assures her that her paper has had a serious and thoughtful reading. She received a "B" in this course. The following semester, Sonia enrolled in the second level of the world humanities sequence. She concluded a paper on *The Underground Man* by writing: "The underground man will never truly be a friend to anybody. It's hard to decide if the underground man would be better off alone. He can't even be a friend to himself because he hates everything he does or the way he acts." Her instructor wrote: "Very good. Very clear and interesting with a very concrete and well-illustrated analysis of the Underground man's character. Good writing throughout! A–." She also received supportive comments, albeit generic ones, on a paper she wrote on Kafka's *Metamorphosis*: "Very good. Very well written! A." She received an "A" in this course.

The next fall, Sonia enrolled in the third level of the world civilization sequence and chose a course in Asian History. Rather than writing extensive end comments, her instructor used marginal comments to respond to her ideas. He questioned some of her ideas as "over generalizations" such as the statement, "In tradition Chinese families valued sons more than daughters because they were considered useless." When Sonia presented a discussion of Confucianism as dividing people into classes on the basis of intellectual capacity, her instructor wrote in the margin: "This seems more Hindu than Chinese." Although the paper was ungraded, she received a "C" in the course. What can be seen here is that in these upper level courses, Sonia's ideas are taken seriously and responded to thoughtfully. With the exception of her freshman composition course, content was the basis for engagement with the writing, thus reinforcing the point that writing is a purposeful and meaningful activity.

Linda, who started at the English 1 level, also demonstrated her growing ability to use analysis in her writings. In her English composition course, in her third semester at the college, she wrote about the exploitation of athletes "by universities, managers and media." She began her paper by discussing university athletics:

> Athletes of today are exploited by the universities. Coaches from respectable schools recruit young inner city and rural men on a scholarship to play at their schools and recieve a free education. These men consider this an opportunity for them to attend college and a chance to play in professional sports. The sad fact is that majority of these men excel in their sports and not in academics. This will result in them being suspended from the teams and forced to attend their classes full time. The problem with this is that some of these players cannot read or write on a collegiate level. There is really no help given to them by their coaches or the professors. The overall fact is that these teachers don't have the time to teach these men and the coaches only want them back on his team. Problems like this can cause these men to drop out, lose their scholarship and dreams.

Although this discussion could hardly be characterized as profound, it does illustrate that Linda is looking at the implications of the material she is considering.

While still a nursing major, in the spring of 1991, her second year at the college, Linda wrote a paper on "Nursing Salaries." She considered how the profession of nursing had acquired greater respect and status over the years, but income of nurses was directly affected by the relationship between the supply and demand of individuals to fill these roles: "Overall, if the shortage has its advantages, its been on the salaries. The main thing here is that many hospitals will become self-satisfied once the shortage eases. Many people will forget about rewarding good nursing; then enrollments will drop again and the shortage cycle will start all over again." That same semester, in a women's studies course, Linda wrote about the way women were perceived in the society. One issue she raised concerned how women interact with men in conversations:

> Certainly another final rule in man's view of women is to never include her in conversations. The rule is that women, as children, should be seen and not heard. Women should be used as a conversational piece. Meaning, that she sits or stands and listen to what the man has to argue. She, on the other hand, has only one requirement of her. That is to nod in agreement wherever necessary. Even if a woman can take on the verbal challenge of a man, she's viewed as a "smart ass" who's only talking from [the top?] of her head silly female nonsense. The "pass it on code" among men is to avoid or prohibit women's talk as much as possible or one will be there all night!

Linda's sarcasm was clearly intended and illustrates her growing ability to develop a rhetorical style to convey her meaning.

In the second level of the world humanities course, which she took in the spring of her fourth year at the college, Linda responded to essay examination questions on the readings in the course. In discussing Kafka's *Metamorphosis*, she listed five factors in the story that affected Gregor's behavior and then discussed each one:

> In *The Metamorphosis*, Gregor was a man who was eventually destroyed by his society. Gregor came from a time when the old regime of the children providing for their family was battling with the new regime of "youth independence." Gregor could no longer gain control of his life and surroundings anymore. Therefore his *sanity* was destroyed because he could no longer cope with the harshness of reality. *Love lost* was also a contributing factor in his demise because the people, his parents, he thought would be there for him. They were no longer there at the vital point where he needed them most. His deterioration lead to *power* being instilled in Grete and the father. In Grete since Gregor wasn't central focus. Grete started influencing her family that it was time to dispose of Gregor because he was a burden. The father sought his power through his uniform because during that time Eastern Europeans held high regards for uniforms.
>
> *Independence* came in once Gregor had died and Grete was determined to lead a life of her own. Never to fall into the fatal mistake her brother made. *Rejection* from his family made Gregor death even quicker.

Over time, then, it can be seen that Linda moved from literal readings to more analytical interpretations, preserving her world view experience, but not letting it prevent her from assuming the academic stance required by particular tasks.

CONCLUSION

Composition instruction cannot be seen in a vacuum. Perhaps that is the greatest lesson that can be learned from examining student writing over an extended period of time. Composition instruction is an important first step in assisting students to formulate their ideas and learn how to express them clearly. But composition instructors should not believe that they are the final influence, or perhaps even the most important influence, in the development of writing abilities. Their role is a crucial one, to get students started in understanding what the goals of writing should be: the ability to develop a purpose for writing, the ability to formulate ideas clearly and succinctly, the ability to develop and defend the most crucial points in the argument, the ability to analyze evidence, the ability to synthesize ideas, the ability to influence an audience, and the ability to express their points clearly. Once students can recognize these goals, they will understand that it will take time, effort, and commitment to be able to carry them out. But the period of a college education does provide the time to practice these activities and to master these processes. Starting out in the right direction is one crucial step. Working on all these aspects of writing in each composition course and in each upper level course is essential to reinforce the understanding that all of these aspects of writing are needed to produce a paper that will be meaningful to its writer and to its audience.

5

Institutional Testing

The WAT, the successful completion of which is required of all students at all campuses of City University of New York (including City College) before they can begin their 60th credit, is not unlike writing tests at many other colleges and universities across the United States. When the test is used as a placement exam, students are given 50 minutes to respond to one of two impromptu prompts that are provided to them at the time of the exam. The papers are rated on a 6-point scale, with each paper receiving two readings. (The conditions described in this chapter were those that prevailed during the testing of the students in my study. In 1995, serious discussions were taking place throughout the City University of New York on the modification of the testing procedures.)

Students whose papers are rated from 2 to 5 (combined ratings of 1, 2, or 3 by two raters) are placed into English 1; students whose papers are rated from 6 to 7 (combined ratings of 3 or 4) are placed into English 2; students whose papers receive a combined rating of 8 or above (4 or more from each rater) are placed into English 110, the freshman composition course. Each of the 6 points on the scale represents evaluation of both content and form. (The entire scale is presented in Appendix B.) The important dividing line for students comes between scale points 3 and 4: An assessment of 3 by a rater virtually guarantees placement in a basic writing class while an assessment of 4 places the student in the freshman composition course. The criteria for these two scale points are as follows:

3—The essay provides a response to the topic but generally has no overall pattern of organization. Ideas are often repeated or underdeveloped, although occasionally a paragraph within the essay does have some structure. The writer uses informal language occasionally and records conversational speech when appropriate written prose is needed. Vocabulary often is limited. The writer generally does not signal relationships within and between paragraphs. Syntax is often rudimentary and lacking in variety. The essay has recurrent grammatical problems, or because of an extremely narrow range of syntactical choices, only occasional grammatical problems appear. The writer does not demonstrate a firm understanding of the boundaries of the sentence. The writer occasionally misspells common words of the language.

4—The essay shows a basic understanding of the demands of essay organization, although there might be occasional digressions. The development of ideas is sometimes incomplete or rudimentary, but a basic logical structure can be discerned.

142

Vocabulary generally is appropriate for the essay topic but at times is oversimplified. Sentences reflect a sufficient command of standard written English to ensure reasonable clarity of expression. Common forms of agreement and grammatical inflection are usually, although not always, correct. The writer generally demonstrates through punctuation an understanding of the boundaries of the sentence. The writer spells common words, except perhaps so-called "demons" with a reasonable degree of accuracy. (The City University of New York Freshman Skills Assessment Program: Writing Skills Assessment Test Evaluation Scale)

As can be seen from these scale points, some attention is paid to organization, content, vocabulary, syntax, grammar, and spelling at each level, and all items appear to have equal weighting. There is scant attention to the quality of the ideas being expressed and no concern with the writer's purpose in responding to the test question.

The test questions are based on an agree–disagree format, requiring that students take a "side" in discussing the question they have selected from the two choices made available at each test sitting. Typical statements that students were asked to "agree or disagree" with include the following:

Young people today should wait to get married and have children until they complete their education, begin their careers, and develop their identities.

Students who are late for a class more than three times should be expelled from the class.

Students who have to work their way through college should not have to do as much school work as students who do not work.

Fishman (1984) argued that this format can be disabling to those "who don't want to take a reductive position on a topic but haven't practiced how to avoid this in an impromptu situation" (cited in Soliday, 1996, p. 90). During the semester when this study was initiated, students in the English 2 class retook the WAT at the end of the semester, a requirement to successfully complete the course. Readers for the exams were the instructors of other sections of English 2 that semester. Students who failed the test at that time had to retake it again (and again as Ricardo's experience demonstrated) in large hall settings where the retests were offered. It was at this point that the WAT became the equivalent to a "rising junior" exam as its passing became the entree to courses beyond the 60th credit.

A second test, the Writing Proficiency Test is required of all students at City College before they can graduate. This test includes an option for responding to questions based on a reading distributed some weeks before the test, but the Proficiency Test is still a timed examination carried out in a large lecture hall. Both these tests are required of all students, including, of course, second-language and second-dialect speakers. It is not unexpected that students with these language backgrounds fail these institutional tests at a higher rate than native speakers of English. One of the major difficulties is that the readers of these examinations are not knowledgeable about language development and thus expect a level of language expertise beyond the students' developmental abilities at the time of testing. Zamel (1995) pointed out that faculty [and other readers, who are often less well-trained] need "to look below the surface of student texts for evidence of proficiency, promoting a kind of reading that benefits not just ESL students but all students" (p. 518).

IMPROMPTU WRITING

In 1996, White addressed the complexity in considering the appropriateness of using impromptu writing in institutional testing situations. He pointed out that in a single-sitting impromptu essay testing situation, students do not have the opportunity to demonstrate what skills they have learned or to show their overall ability in writing (p. 30). He made the important distinction between using such impromptu writing for placement purposes and for other purposes, such as a "rising junior" examination (or a graduation requirement test like a Proficiency Test). White believed that a great deal of information was not needed for placement purposes because the tests need only distinguish "between those who are likely to do passing work in freshman writing courses and those who need additional instruction before they have much chance of doing well" (p. 33). He was much more critical of the use of such tests when they have been used to admit students to junior level courses or for graduation (p. 34).

At City College, during the early years of my study, 1989 to 1992, the WAT was used both as a placement test and an exit exam for English 2. After 1992, the WAT was no longer used as an exit test from English 2 (with most instructors starting to use portfolios for the evaluation of all writing courses), but the college continued to require students to pass it before they could enroll in courses beyond the 60th credit, thus retaining the WAT in the role played by "rising junior" examinations at many other colleges and universities. Because the new director of composition was concerned with the inappropriateness of the backgrounds of the readers, especially of the retests, she initiated a policy of allowing students to appeal the scores. Readers from the composition faculty then undertook the task of rereading and rescoring these examinations. With their knowledge of language development and their attention to content issues, the readers recognized that many students who had received failing scores because of a set of linguistic features that were still in development were deserving of passing scores. These rereadings were obviously a highly inefficient way of rescoring such exams, and the director of composition moved to institute a training program for new readers she would select who would be more cognizant of the appropriate bases for scoring them.

White (1996) was also concerned that even under the best conditions, when test developers do provide clear and stimulating topics, still "it is only one question (on rare occasions two) and therefore restricts the multifold domain of writing to narrow categories. The standardized test conditions strip natural context from the writing, allow no collaboration or preparation, and disallow more than token revision" (p. 36). In their attempt to design a better placement test at the University of Washington, Haswell and Wyche-Smith (1994) described the limitations they perceived under traditional impromptu testing conditions: "The primary [indictment] is that holistic scoring is product centered. It compares one student's writing sample, *as a product*, to an ideal performance, as described in the rubric of subskills" (p. 228). This emphasis on subskills is apparent in the WAT scoring guide, where content is only one of the six criteria for assessment, and did not function as the major criteria in the rating sessions that I participated in during the years when English faculty (overwhelmingly teachers of literature) read the exams for placement purposes.

Haswell and Wyche-Smith (1994) worked closely with their departmental and institutional colleagues to design a placement test. (At the time of their writing, they were still working on the junior level exam.) The placement exam needed to distinguish among three groups of writers: basic writers, regular freshman composition students, and composition students who would concurrently take a 1-credit pass/fail tutorial course to provide extra instructional support at the campus writing center (p. 224). Although they never provided a specific example of the type of question they designed for their placement test, Haswell and Wyche-Smith discussed several aspects of the testing environment they worked on: They decided to write "rhetorical tasks that were fairly sophisticated" (p. 230); they handed out the prompt sheets 15 minutes before the bluebooks were distributed so "students would be almost forced to compose themselves and comprehend the task beforehand" (p. 231); they took "special pains to write clear directions" (p. 231); and they trained their readers to be familiar with "the ways timed writing impacts prior knowledge, test apprehension, cultural background, personality type, and composing habit" (p. 233) to reduce the readers' expectations that they should expect to find a finished product. Improving the conditions under which impromptu writing must occur (considering factors such as time constraints during summer orientation and registration periods and fiscal constraints) is clearly desirable, and although Haswell and Wyche-Smith reduced some of the objections to testing through impromptu conditions, they did not eliminate them, as all designers of such tests have become increasingly aware.

Chandra's experience in taking the placement test exemplified the difficulties with timed, impromptu writing. In an effort to produce her best work, she wrote a two-page rough draft (which she labeled "scrap") before beginning her final version. As time apparently ran out for her, she was only able to complete 1¼ pages of her final draft, leaving her ideas uncompleted. The readers, who, of course, could easily see from the test booklet what had happened, and who could have referred back to her rough draft to see the completion of her ideas, were unmoved. She received ratings of 3 and 4 from the first two readers, and the third reader, who was needed to reconcile her placement, scored her exam with a 3, thus relegating her to the English 2 section that I taught. An illustration from her final draft reveals that she had no serious writing problems:

> I definitely agree that society emphasizes success in sports, education, and work to much. Success is something we learned is extremely important from an early age. When you think of everything in a win lose situation, you lose sight of the important rewarding issues, such as how you reached success.
> I've never enjoyed playing sports because I am not very good at it. Whatever the sport, whatever team I was on, I always recieved negativity from the rest of my teamates. I was considered a foul up. Instead of being commended for my efforts to try to play the sport to the best of my ability, I was always being put down. Coaches always put the best teamates in the game, stressing the need for success. Of course no one wants to lose, but think how fun the game is for players like myself. Sports are games. Games are made for fun. Should a person be taken from a game because they are not a good player?

Although this excerpt manifests some spelling and minor grammatical errors, the writing is clearly of a level that could function successfully in a freshman composition course. That Chandra was penalized by the time constraints for trying to produce a rough draft before a final draft seems an incredible irony in a field in which revision is so highly valued.

Another student who received mixed scores on her placement test, a 4 from the first rater, a 3 from the second, and a 3 from the third decisive rater, was Judith, a student of Puerto Rican background who was born in the United States. She attended elementary, middle, and junior high schools in New York City, but she received her high school education in Puerto Rico. She was placed into the English 2 level on the basis of her scores on the WAT. Judith transferred to Borough of Manhattan Community College, nearer to her home, in the fall of 1990. In the placement exam, Judith responded to a question about whether students who are late to class more than three times should be expelled from the class. In her reply, she noted specific steps an individual should take to avoid lateness:

> To avoid inconvenience and lateness to class everyone should do the following the night before: check the car for gas, oil and enough air in the wheels, if you have children you should double check with the baby sitter, iron your clothes, and put all that is needed on the table by your keys, so you won't end up looking for them either. The alarm should be set a half hour before the usual so all can be done calmly. If you'll be traveling by bus or train it is wise to leave with at least 45 to 30 minutes of anticapation. These are everyday problems to us.

Although I would not want to argue that this is a profound response to the question, the writing does not demonstrate many serious difficulties that would exclude her from the freshman writing course. At least one of the raters believed the paper to be sufficiently competent to allow Judith to enter the regular freshman course. By the end of that semester, Judith not only passed the retest of the WAT, but she received scores of 4 and 5 from the two raters. Writing on the topic of whether young people should wait to get married and have children until they complete their education, Judith concluded her essay examination as follows: "Marriage is a beautiful sacrament, but it should only be preformed when ready. An education and career prepare us for the great challenges in life. It helps us to become stronger for the greater responsibilities of life, and I can say that the greatest and hardest obligation in life is to properly take care of a family." I would love to take credit for the improvement in Judith's writing, but the truth is that she was already capable of thoughtful ideas when she wrote her placement test paper. The vagaries of impromptu, timed writing combined with the lack of appropriate training by the raters at the time these placement tests were evaluated to produce harsh placements that penalized students and delayed their opportunities to enroll in the required courses of the college.

Juan is one of the few students in my study population who was already enrolled in the college when the study began in the fall of 1989. Juan had taken the WAT for the first time in August of 1988. Receiving a total score of 5, he was placed into an English 1 section. On this original placement exam, he wrote on the topic of whether being late to class should result in expulsion from the course. His response was short and full of syntactical problems: "My thoughts about the lateness problem is as or greater than the teachers. I feel this so because of the fact that the teacher already have and education, But like myself and others we just don't have it to the fullest extant and so the interruptions just prolong it even more." Juan failed the English 1 course and took it over in the spring of 1989 and earned a "B." He enrolled in my English 2 class in the fall of 1989. Taking the WAT again at the end of that semester, he received a split rating from the readers, with the first reader giving his paper a 3, the second a 4, and the final deciding rater giving a 3. Since passing the WAT was then a requirement to pass English 2, he failed the course. In that exam, he had responded to the question about marriage, education, and children. A section of his response reads as follows: "Young people are frustrated when they find that working so many hours in order to pay for rent and necessity. Which is still not enough to pay for their expenses because they have a child to support as well. Some young people return to school in order to better their life, but end up leaving school because it is to much work to handle. Young people may even take out their frustration on the child or the spouse which would lead into child abuse or a devorse." Juan demonstrates here that he can draw implications from the evidence he is presenting. Although there are still some sentence-level problems, it is difficult to see why his paper could not have received a passing grade so he could go on to the freshman composition course. Juan enrolled in English 2 again the following semester and once again failed the course because he failed the WAT. On his third try, in the fall of the 1990, he received a total of 8 on the WAT and passed the English 2 course with a "B." On this test, he responded to a question about whether the New York Transit System (the MTA) should shut down the subways between 1 a.m. and 5 a.m. in order to avoid the need to raise fares. In the introduction to his response, he wrote: "Each year millions of people ride the MTA system for various reasons, either for work, school or simply to get from one place to another. The MTA is the main mode of transportation that the city has, therefore, it is a necessity to all. In order for the MTA not to lose more of its riders, it must not increase the fare, but find other means to raise money instead." It is difficult to see how this response level differs substantially from the one given to the original English 2 exit exam, but because of his failing score, Juan was delayed a year in being allowed to enroll in the English composition class. (He passed English 110 the following semester with an "A.") Although he had hoped to become an electrical engineer, Juan performed very poorly on both the remedial and required mathematics courses, and he dropped out of the college after the fall of his fourth year, having passed only 37 credits with a grade point average of 1.58.

White's (1996) criticism of using a test like the WAT as a rising junior or graduation requirement focused on the differences that should be inherent in such a test at a higher level as compared to a placement test:

> When we look at what those tests are attempting to discover, the *inappropriateness* of a brief impromptu essay (by itself) for that purpose becomes obvious. Among other matters, advanced or graduating students should be able to use sources intelligently to support—not substitute for—their own ideas, discover and revise complex arguments, show some depth of understanding of a topic, and understand the discourse community of a particular field. It is unlikely that a short impromptu essay test can provide us with much useful information about such matters. (p. 34).

By these criteria, it is clearly inappropriate to use the WAT as a rising junior exam (as a prerequisite to enrolling beyond the 60th credit) while officially at City University of New York, it is touted as only a "minimum proficiency" test.

The Proficiency Test does not fare much better, as it is also an impromptu writing test. The only positive feature of the Proficiency Test that can be cited is the option that students have to write on a topic related to a reading distributed earlier to them, but even this feature falls far short of the rigorous demonstration White called for. Unlike many of the responses to the WAT questions, the students' views on the issues raised in the Proficiency Test questions were almost always presented from an objective stance, with little personal experience supporting their perspectives. This was true regardless of whether the students responded to "cold" questions or to questions based on previously supplied readings.

Georgio, who had started at the English 1 level, took and passed the Proficiency Test in the spring of 1991, his second year at the college. (Students were permitted to take the Proficiency Test any time after they successfully completed the English composition course.) In his reply to a question on whether funds supplied by New York City for the St. Patrick's Day parade should be diverted to meet the needs of the homeless, Georgio wrote:

> The most important problem New York City is always facing is the problem of the poor people. There are people that have financial responsibilities such as paying rent, supporting their sons or daughter, and supporting themselves that they cannot afford. The government will help by giving them public assistance, but its just not enough. When they look for a job, they get turned down because of their status. New York City should make special programs that will help the poor people get jobs such as, a computer training course, a bank teller course, and an office training course. These special programs will help people because they will have the skills that it takes to get a good job.
>
> In conclusion, New York City is a big city with a large population. It has to take care of its residence the best way possible without spending money on useless thing like the parade. With the cost of the parade, N.Y.C. can do a lot of better things for its citizens.

As pointed out in chapter 4, Georgio told me that he had received very good composition instruction in his English composition course, allowing him to make strong progress through the required writing courses and institutional tests.

Another student who took the Proficiency Test the semester after completing the English composition course was Audrey, who had placed directly into the English 110 course. In the spring of 1990, Audrey selected a topic based on a reading about how Donald Trump's recent marital problems "represent the most significant public event to American society in recent years." Audrey's rejection of the attention paid to Trump's problems is scathing:

> America doesn't seem to know what to do with itself since the world started to free up. We are too busy worrying about fools like Donald Trump, and have forgotten to ask ourselves what we can do for our country rather than what our country can do for us. A vanishing pride in America is infesting the air at Donald's New York City, or should I say Japan's New York City. Since the story repeats itself, the wise man would get out of America now before he or she wakes up to nothing but the smelly old shoes of Drexel Burnham and Donald Trump, and others. I suppose if there is a heaven, Martin Luther King and John F. Kennedy are saying to themselves "And I died for this?"

As is clear from Audrey's response, although the writing is based on a reading provided to the students from New York Magazine, "Trump the Soap," the conditions of the examination still do not provide opportunities for students to probe sources deeply or to show sophisticated understanding of a topic, as White (1996) had called for.

Delores delayed taking the Proficiency Examination until the spring of 1992, her third year at the college. She chose to write about a topic based on a reading dealing with the relationship between the commission of crimes and the media's coverage of criminal acts. Perhaps as a result of her studies in psychology, she took a carefully worded stance toward this issue:

> Unfortunately the media is a part of our lives that cannot be denied; our lives and ways of thinking are influenced by the media. It does not only influence our ways of thinking, but also our behavior as a whole. The same way the media influences us to buy a certain product, in the same way, frequent crime reportings could have an effect in our society. Crime reporting should be more subdued and downplayed from the media.
>
> Children's minds are prompt to imagination and fantasy; therefore their minds could be influenced by too much media crime reportings. A child growing up in an environment where all he/she hears is talking about crime, he or she will actually think that crime is a part of life and might even want to practice some things they hear and see . . .

Although critical of the media reporting on crime, for the most part, Delores couched her criticism in carefully chosen words such as "could have an effect," "should be more subdued," and "could be influenced." Her training in reporting the results of psychology experiments sensitized her to the need to use qualifying language. But, again, the source reading itself did not provide adequate information to allow her to demonstrate her ability to use such materials to support her ideas, nor did the constrained time period offer her the opportunity to show her depth of understanding of a topic. Understandably, because the constraints on the testing situation were so confining, no such demands were made for passing the test.

Jacob, who probably could have passed the Proficiency Test immediately after completing the freshman writing course, delayed taking the test until the spring of his fifth year, the semester he was graduating. It is likely that his postponement of taking the test was just a matter of his suddenly realizing that it was one more requirement for graduation that he needed to fulfill. He chose a topic that had greater potential for bringing in personal experiences than most of the other possible topics on the Proficiency Test, a discussion on the ramifications of being the first-born in a family. In his response, he alternated between discussing the topic from an objective stance and a personal point of view. The first two paragraphs of his paper illustrate these shifting perspectives:

Some say, there is nothing as special as the first born. I guess one might draw an analogy with a first love or a first impression, and any other "firsts" into virgin territory. Such exposures are said to leave an impression more readily, and once made tends to linger on long after others have come and gone. This may be true for children also, but no matter how breathless was the reception of the first born, by the time of the second child there must inexorably be a shift of affection—or at least attention.

One might discard this point by saying that both children get their share of demonstrative love, only at different times. However, there is a crucial difference: one child experienced someone taking his or her place as the center of the parents' lives and the other suffered no such abrupt change. In my own family of 4, I am the youngest. Everyone has, to different degrees, suffered through this hurt of sibling jealousy, except me. As the youngest child, I was the recipient of effusive care and attention, well past the normal age for such treatment. Of course this may also be a double edged sword, for one needs that certain detachment from one's parents in order to mature as an adult. However, how one responds to this situation, I believe, is largely due to the individual. Some might welcome the benefits and eschew the pitfalls, while others might fall right in.

As this excerpt indicates, Jacob could switch easily from identifying an issue to selecting evidence, here from his own experience, to support his views. But, once again, although the topic has the potential for serious discussion of many issues in relation to birth order, the student was not provided either with the time or the materials to demonstrate the abilities of complex reasoning and handling of source materials that White believed such an examination should offer.

The Proficiency Test, as offered at City College during the years of my study, gave students the opportunity to demonstrate that they could organize their writing, provide some evidence to support their views, and draw conclusions. But it seriously failed to provide students with the opportunity to prove that their college years had taught them the more substantial characteristics that writing could demonstrate, the ability to analyze and synthesize and the ability to discover new insights. Under timed, impromptu testing conditions, it is not possible to demand the level of writing competence that should be expected from college graduates. Thus, the importance of writing effectively is demeaned by the formats of institutional testing.

SECOND-DIALECT AND SECOND-LANGUAGE ISSUES

In the early 1970s, researchers were interested in quantifying the frequency of nonstandard uses of linguistic features such as the past-tense marker (-ed) and the third-person–singular present-tense verb form (-s or -es). But rather than counting discrete "errors," they were searching for linguistic patterns that had some basis in historical backgrounds of language development in what were then considered nonstandard dialects of English. My own disser-

tation research (Sternglass, 1974) centered on such questions. Studying
Black and White students in basic writing classes at a university and a
community college in Pittsburgh, I compared frequency of nonstandard
forms in linguistic feature patterns in these groups and correlated the results
with language history background, race, gender, and socioeconomic factors.
My study revealed that with the exception of one feature, the invariant "be,"
students in both groups produced the same nonstandard features in their
writing, with the Black population producing them at a higher rate of
frequency than the White population. The important point of that study
for the purposes of this study is that *patterns* of linguistic features were
examined rather than discrete examples of usage. In reading WAT papers
for placement or exit purposes, readers at City College who were unfamiliar
with linguistic research tended to focus on the number of individual items
that were not in standard form rather than the number of patterns that the
student did not yet control. For example, 4 -*ed* endings missing out of a total
of 10 past-tense verbs in a paper constitute one problem, not four. Furthermore, it should indicate to the reader that this is a feature that the student
does not yet control automatically; it is not a feature that the student does
not know. Such a student needs to be taught to do more careful proofreading, but, under timed, impromptu conditions, the student rarely has the
opportunity to go back over the writing for editing purposes. Thus, students
who do not control these features automatically are harshly penalized in the
timed testing environment. Although meaning is generally conveyed without difficulty to readers, writers are generally given little credit for their ideas
as surface features frequently dominate placement decisions.

Haswell (1991) pointed out that the teachers tend to notice "misinfor-
mation first, thought second" (p. 193). Priority is assigned to these surface
errors and has a powerful effect on the "teacher's appreciation of other
rhetorical matters" (p. 193). "Measures of error—usually misspellings—usually end up among the top three predictors of quality judgments by teachers
of student writing, along with vocabulary and essay length" (p. 193). This
interpretation strongly supports the way placement and competency exams
have been evaluated at The City College and I feel certain at many other
institutions where similar testing mechanisms are in place.

As early as 1981, White and Thomas (1981) compared the performance
of minority groups of students on usage tests and essay tests. For both Black
students and ESL students, they found that there was an important difference between the pattern of score distributions on usage tests and essay
tests. Both second-dialect and second-language interference seemed to
have contributed to more negative evaluations on the usage tests than on
the evaluation of the students' writing (p. 281). Such differences can be
readily understood, because both second-dialect and second-language students benefit most strongly from opportunities to revise and edit their
writing, opportunities not available on usage tests or timed writing tests.

Corder (1981) made a "distinction between *mistakes* and *errors*" (p. 10, cited in Haswell, 1991, p. 195). According to Corder, mistakes are due to performance factors or chance circumstances. They are stumbles in haste or distraction, slips of the pen, memory faults, misunderstandings of the assignment, applications in good faith of bad teacher advice. Errors are due to what Corder usefully called "transitional competence" (Corder, 1981, p. 10, cited in Haswell, 1991, p. 195). They are "re-creations," generated as all novel expressions are by developing writers, through restructuring and transference (Corder, 1981, p. 93, cited in Haswell, 1991, p. 195). "[Errors] arise not out of incompetence but positively out of the writer's current knowledge or concept of language. The competence happens be transitional because it is still moving toward social, pragmatic standards. Mistakes, then, tend to be unsystematic, errors systematic" (Haswell, 1991, pp. 195–196). The errors found in the writing of second-dialect and second-language speakers need to be interpreted knowledgeably as markers in a developing language system and as parts of language patterns, not as lists of discrete mistakes.

Joan took the WAT on August 5, 1989 and scored a 6 and therefore was assigned to the English 2 level. It is difficult to understand why she was placed in a basic writing section. Her paper was organized in a very traditional way: an introduction, two paragraphs of development, and a conclusion. The best guess for the reason for failure is that there were a few grammatical errors (e.g., a comma placed after the word "but" instead of before it, a missed possessive apostrophe, the confusion of "loose" with "lose," and the use of "took" instead of "taken" as a past participle). (The absence of the possessive marker and the past participle forms could be seen as "systematic errors," features indicating transitional competence and second-dialect interference, while the punctuation and word confusion were what Corder called "mistakes.") Missed by the readers were Joan's thoughtful points on the topic. Writing on the topic of whether students who are late to class more than three times should be expelled from the course, Joan noted that the students became disadvantaged when they were late because "most lessons given by teachers or college professors are started out with an aim which sometimes revolves around the lesson itself. By the student being late, he is or she is totally lost because they have missed the whole meaning of the lesson which could be the beginning of the end for the student." Although the idea is not stated as clearly as it might have been, Joan was successful in identifying an important reason why students should be prompt in their attendance. Her point was one that was not made in other student responses to this question.

At the end of the English 2 course, Joan took the WAT again and passed it. The test asked students to agree or disagree with the proposition that the MTA should shut down the subways between 1 a.m. and 5 a.m. instead of raising fares. Joan's points of development included overcrowding of buses and subways, problems of the homeless sleeping on the subways, and crime. For each point of development, she provided a personal experience. Because her writing did not include grammatical problems, she passed the WAT. Of the Skills Assessment Tests she had to take in reading, writing, and mathematics, the writing test proved to be the least difficult hurdle.

James is a Black West Indian, born in St. Vincent. His first language was English and he had been in the United States for 8 years when he took the WAT as a placement test in the spring of 1988. His intended major was electrical engineering, but he had difficulty with the math courses, starting at the lowest level of basic math courses and failing them repeatedly. He dropped out of the college and returned sporadically. In the fall term of 1995, he was enrolled for 12 credits, attempting to fulfill the core course requirements. In his previous two semesters at the college, he had received better grades in courses in economics, political science, history, and philosophy.

In the initial placement test in 1988, James' paper received an unusual set of scores, a score of 1 from one rater and a score of 3 from the other. This total of 4 automatically assigned him to an English 1 section. The response reflects the dilemma confronted by the raters:

> In a math class, students are busy trying to understand the problem which the teacher is explaining to them and in walk a late student. Everyone is disturb and the problem the teacher is explaining seem more confusing to the student. This is not the first time the class had been disturb and the problem the teacher is explaining seem more confusing to the student. This is not the first time the class has been disturb by late students. The teacher is agitated and the students concentration is broken. Should we allowed the class to be constantly interrupted by late student? If students are going to be late for class more than three time, they should be expelled from the course. . . .
>
> Lateness to class shows us students who does not care about an education and education itself. Late student just want to get by without making any self-sacrifice. If the students who comes to class was motivated and interesting in the class, they will be willing to make sacrifices. Lateness shows student lack of interest.
>
> Students should be expelled from a class if they are late three time or more. They [unfinished]

This paper illustrates several of the language patterns that James does not yet control: noun singular and plural forms, past-tense forms of regular verbs, and subject–verb agreement, all features of the Vernacular Black English dialect. Yet, for each of these patterns, there are instances where he handles them correctly, even hypercorrecting some verb forms, indicating that he "knows" the proper forms, but he does not produce them automatically, and in a timed setting, he has no opportunity to carry out editing or proofreading activities. Also, if the rater is counting the number of discrete "errors" rather than looking at patterns, the paper will be seen as a weak response requiring high levels of remedial instruction.

James did not enroll in the college following his initial placement writing test. He entered instead in the fall of 1989, took the WAT again, and received, again, a total score of 4, this time a score of 2 from each rater. In his second attempt at the placement test, he happened to receive one of the same questions as the initial set of questions he had been given in 1988, and he chose to respond to the same question. His response revealed the same language patterns as his initial attempt, not surprising since he had received no instruction in the interim period. In the introduction he wrote: "Every school have a lateness problem. But it is not up to the school to judge the students so rashly. There are always reason why a student is late. Even though the reason may not be exceptable by the school. A student should not be expell from school if they are late three or more time because it is unfair and an inappropriate rule." In this excerpt, as in the earlier one, James' writing again contains features of Vernacular Black English, this time subject–verb agreement, noun singular and plural forms, and past-participle endings.

James passed the English 1 course at the end of 1989. He took the WAT again in May 1990, but failed the test and thus the English 2 course he had been enrolled in. Although his exam paper still contained some evidence of second-dialect features, they occurred infrequently and need not have been the deciding factor in his evaluation. Choosing the topic of whether sex education should be provided in the schools, James wrote:

> Sex had been a taboo subject since this country was born. Anyone who spoke about sex were considered disgraceful in the eye's of our society. Today, our society is very permiscuous, and sex is discus more openly. Sex education should be taught in schools because there are more information available on sexual diseases and birth control that our parents do not know about . . .
>
> Millions of teenagers are pregnant every year because they lack birth control knowledge. I was surprised when a friend of mine got pregnant this year. She told that it was a mistake because she did not know what to do in order to prevent herself from getting pregnant. Now, she is thinking about getting an abortion . . .

The number and frequency of sentence-level problems ought not to have prevented this student from enrolling in the freshman composition course. In the fall of 1990, James enrolled in English 2 and passed the course, after successfully passing the WAT on his third attempt.

Second-language users may have more difficulty in conveying their meanings to readers than second-dialect writers. As Fox (1994) pointed out:

> Words or concepts can be untranslatable, equivalent verb tenses can be nonexistent or have different usage, linguistic elements can be completely absent (such as the articles "a," "an," and "the," which are absent in Chinese, Korean, Japanese, Hindi, Russian, and many other languages). . . . Because truly mastering a language is so difficult, the idea that students who write confusing papers have "language problems" may be validated by instructors who give extensive feedback on surface errors or even

suggest that the student have an editor before submitting papers for comments on content, for mechanical details are easier to spot than the cultural differences in organization, forms of evidence, and approach to knowledge. (p. 78)

The issues Fox describes are severely exacerbated in the testing environment, where the lack of knowledge of language-development and rhetorical strategies hinders readers, and the impossibility of revising or reshaping the text adds additional pressure to the second-language student who already feels threatened by the demands of the testing situation.

Some features in second-language development can only be acquired over time. To expect a student to master all the particulars of tense, subject–verb agreement, and use of plurals, for example, before allowing them to enroll in courses in their major area is to seriously delay their academic progress. Manuel is from Colombia and he arrived in the United States in 1982. He entered the college in the fall of 1986. Seven years later, in the spring of 1993, he received a bachelor's degree in electrical engineering, a testimony to his dedication and perseverance. Manuel was enrolled in English as a Second Language (ESL) classes for 2 years. In his first attempt to pass the WAT, in the winter of 1988, when he was taking the highest level ESL course in writing, he received a score of 3 from each of the raters; thus, he failed the exam. Had he passed the WAT at that time, he would have been permitted to enroll in the freshman composition course. (In the semester that he failed the WAT, he passed courses in philosophy, speech, and world humanities.)

In this first attempt, he responded to a question about whether individuals should be allowed to play music at a high volume. His paper contained some features of second-language interference that he did not yet control automatically, but the content revealed his thoughtfulness about the topic:

> Sometimes teenagers with their modern customs can be so annoying. This is the case of turning up the volumes very high their portable radios at the beach or in parks. The fact of playing music at a decent volumes can be relaxing but when teenagers "pop-up the volumes," they are contributing to noise pollution and are violating somebody else's rights.
>
> A few years ago, city representatives came up with a law to reduce noise pollutions. For example, there are certain places in the city like Lexington and 59th Street in which no unnecessary horn blowing is allowed . . .
>
> Every human being needs quietness and peace to function as a normal person. I think we have the right to relax even if we are in areas like the beach or parks. That's why we must keep public places clear of noise pollution. If teenagers want to listen to their music so loud, force them to use a walkman.

In the summer of 1989, Manuel enrolled in an English 2 section. (Students who had had extensive work in the ESL program were sometimes allowed to enroll in the second level of basic writing in the English department if it was felt that such a change in instruction was appropriate.) Manuel made two attempts to pass the WAT that summer, and he was successful on the second attempt, thus allowing him to enroll in the freshman composition section I taught in the fall of 1989. In his successful WAT paper, Manuel wrote on the topic of whether or not alcohol and tobacco should be made illegal like marijuana and cocaine:

> Recently, the State of New York has made many addictive drugs illegal. Illegal drugs like marijuana and cocaine are very harmful to anyone's health. Alcohol and tobacco are also dangerous to a person's health. Therefore, the government should make alcohol and tobacco illegal, too.
> Making tobacco illegal will be the most beautiful thing that the government should do because many people are harming themselves by smoking cigarettes. Tobacco is an addictive drug like marijuana and cocaine. Tobacco contains nicotine which anyone addicts to it. Like marijuana, nicotine is very harmful to the lungs and the throath because both can cause cancer and lung disease. In order to save many lives the government should make tobacco illigal. By the passing the law people will be force to stop smoking and will have tobacco free enviroment . . .

Aside from a few spelling errors and one incorrect verb form, Manuel demonstrated that he could produce the forms required for formal writing.

COMPARISON OF TIMED AND PREPARED WRITING

Haswell (1991) found 36 to 38 "total blunders" per 1,000 words in his *timed writing* of freshmen to junior students, whereas Connors and Lunsford (1988) found 23 per 1,000 for *out-of-class writing* (italics added, Haswell, 1991, p. 198). Notably, neither study breaks down the items called "blunders" into language patterns. Haswell (1991) found that "especially in impromptu writing, more attention on correctness mean[t] less attention elsewhere, just as, quid pro quo, more concentration elsewhere may mean more mistakes" (p. 204). Schumacher, Klare, Cronin, and Moses (1984) reported that older students thought more about content, planning, support, ideas, and other nonformal factors (cited in Haswell, 1991, p. 204). Haswell concluded that holding ground with mechanics meant that students could gain ground elsewhere. Clearly, prepared writing offers better opportunities to control mechanical features than does timed writing, especially in testing situations.

Gleason (1997), a professor at City College and former director of the English composition program, wrote about issues beyond language development that affect second-language students' ability to pass required institutional tests:

> Among the criticisms of this test [the WAT] are the following: the questions require cultural knowledge that students may not possess, the time limit imposes restrictions on the possibility of revision—which is a primary focus of writing classes—and it

discriminates unfairly against second language speakers. Most problematic is the fact that the WAT actually screens for a number of variables—not all predictive of successful college writing: speed in producing a first draft, cultural knowledge, mastery of standardized forms of written English, test-taking ability, handwriting, spelling, and ultimately—culture, class, and ethnicity. It is also a fact that many students who repeatedly fail the WAT fare rather well in their college courses . . .

Gleason's last assertion rings soundly when Ricardo's experiences at the college are examined.

In my analysis of the data collected over 6 years, I was rarely interested in undertaking quantitative analyses, seeing the study as mainly descriptive and ethnographic. But when I contrasted Ricardo's strong success in his academic courses with his difficulties in passing the required institutional writing tests, I decided to explore whether there were significant differences in the numbers of surface errors he produced in prepared writing and writing under testing conditions. I examined papers he wrote for his courses during the same semesters that he was trying to pass the WAT for two features, the percentage of times the -ed marker was absent on past-tense verbs and the number of fragments and run-on sentences produced in each writing. Table 5.1 indicates the findings.

As the data in Table 5.1 indicate, there were far fewer absent past-tense markers in Ricardo's out-of-class writing than in the impromptu, timed writing conditions of the WAT, even though the papers were sometimes longer than the two- to three-page average length of the WAT exams. Run-on sentences and fragments occurred more frequently in the prepared papers, but the number declined over time. These data are not presented to make the argument that students should be evaluated solely on the basis of grammatical proficiency, but to demonstrate that revision opportunities

TABLE 5.1

Comparison of Surface Features in Testing and Out-of-Class Conditions

Semester	Absence of -ed Endings		Fragments and + Run-Ons	
Fall 1989	WAT = 50%	Eng. 2 = 24%	WAT = 1	Eng. 2 = 5 (2.75 pages)
Spring 1990	WAT = 17%	Com. 101 = 6%	WAT = 1	Com. 101 = 3 (6.5 pages)
Fall 1990	WAT = 50%	World Civ. 102 = 4%	WAT = 3	WC 101 = 3 (2.33 pages)
Fall 1991	WAT = 0%	U.S. Soc. 101 = 11%	WAT = 0	USS 101 = 3 (5 pages)
Spring 1992	WAT = 75%	Com. 401 = 44%	WAT = 2	Com. 401 = 0 (2 pages)
Fall 1992	WAT = 0%	Com. 395 = 14%	WAT = 2	Com. 395 = 0 (2 pages)

allow students to proofread for grammatical features that have not yet become automatic in their writing.

In terms of content, an even stronger argument can be made that out-of-class writing offers students the opportunity to rethink and reformulate their ideas. The weakness of pure quantitative analysis becomes evident when examples from the papers written for the WAT exams and the upper level courses in the same semester are examined.

In the fall of 1990, for the WAT exam, Ricardo wrote on the topic of whether homework requirements should be reduced for students who had to work at outside jobs. In his response, Ricardo pointed out the necessity of an academic degree being credible: "I don't believe that by diminishing the require homework is going to solve the problem. On the contrary it will created a double standard in the educational system that will affect in a very negative way the validity of our degrees." As this short excerpt reveals, Ricardo does not yet control the past-tense marker of regular verbs, but his use of a hypercorrected form, *created*, indicates that he is attempting to monitor this construction, but under timed, impromptu conditions he is unable to focus on such a structure. Instead, as in all his writings, content is paramount for Ricardo and he is anxious to demonstrate his academic credibility. Sadly, in this setting, the thoughtfulness of the content is undervalued.

That same semester, Ricardo wrote a prepared paper for his world civilizations course. He described a political system that had started in Puerto Rico in 1509: "The *encomienda* system was the beginning of a lengthy process of exploitation to which the native people of the Americas are still subjugated to. In 1992, some people are going to celebrate what they call the 'discovery of the new world.' For others, like me, it would be a moment of mourning and remembrance [of] the massacre of my people by the Spaniards." Not only does Ricardo's paper demonstrate his powers of analysis and reflection here, but it also reveals his control of "standard" academic sentence structure and grammatical competence.

Two years later, in the spring of 1992, Ricardo was still struggling with passing the WAT. In Table 5.1, inappropriate forms of the past-tense marker appeared in 75% of the cases. But a close look at the examination paper itself reveals that there were only four occurrences in which past-tense forms were called for, and three of those four involved a single verb, the word "look." In each instance of that verb, Ricardo failed to mark it with the proper -ed ending, thus accounting for the high percentage of verb form errors. The paper responded to the issue of whether sex education should be taught in the schools. One of Ricardo's paragraphs read as follows:

Many of our school teachers are look with respect by our kids. There is a line of communication already in place. Teachers are look as a treat. Some are look as friends and many as confidants. As a teacher, I discuss many subjects with my students.

> Sometimes they even tell me that they never discuss about these subjects with their parents. My students like to show how intelligent they are, and most important they like to be given the opportunity to express their opinions. Something that in many of their households is not allowed. Some parents do not have either the skills or the time to listen and talk to their kids. That's were the role of the teacher becomes fundamental in communicating the right information to our youngsters.

Assuredly, the paragraph contains one sentence fragment and an occasional idiomatic lapse. These few problems within a sensitive construct should not be sufficient to penalize such a student by requiring him to take and re-take and re-take this stressful test.

Also, in the spring of 1992, Ricardo wrote a paper for his Communications 401 course on the issue of stereotyping. In that paper, Ricardo reflected on how a movie made by Spike Lee reinforced stereotypical perspectives:

> A stereotype is defined in the book as "a fixed mental image of a group that is frequently applied to all its members." Starting from this point Spike Lee, already has the responsibility of not using stereotypes that will perpetuated the preconceived ideas that his audience may already have. By portraying most of his characters upon these stereotypes he reinforces and perpetuated those ideas which in turns, robs whole ethnic groups of their dignity and humanity.

This paper is hardly error-free. It contains, for example, a hypercorrected verb form and comma errors. But the grammatical problems do not undercut the expression of his meaning nor the thoughtful analysis that is included.

CONCLUSION

In chapter 4, I argued that writing instruction needed to be thought of from a long-term perspective and that issues of content and form should be pursued at every level, both in composition courses and in content-level courses. Many of the examples cited in this chapter reflect the sentence-level features that gave difficulty to the students in my study, particularly when they were confronted with demands for timed, impromptu writing in testing conditions. These language features ought not to be ignored, but they should be seen as part of the students' larger developing language competence. Content, especially in testing situations, needs to be weighted and valued at a higher level so that students' intellectual abilities can be recognized, fostered, and rewarded. Students' progress over time in the academic setting demonstrates that sustained practice with challenging writing tasks will help them develop their abilities to express their increasingly complex ideas in appropriate forms.

By using timed, impromptu writing tests as the sole determiner of students' placement into writing courses, the institution ignores issues of language development well-known to professionals in the field of composition. In an urban academic setting, students deserve respect for their serious attempts at mastering the conventions of written English. Their entire intellectual competence should be the basis for the assessment that is made of their ability; where needed, intensive instructions in the niceties of language form can be provided in supplementary workshops or through tutoring at a writing center. But students should not have their academic progress stifled by the appearance of language features in their writing that they demonstrate they know but do not yet control automatically. Institutional testing should be an indicator of the type of help that students need at a particular time, not a hindrance to their advancement.

6

Instructional Settings

RELATIONSHIP BETWEEN
INSTRUCTIONAL SETTINGS AND WRITING

Noting that there are significant differences between the contexts of individual classrooms and more widespread institutional practices, Ackerman (1993) advocated a closer examination of these institutional contexts:

> The institutional contexts in which write-to-learn activities are embedded have not been fully explored or explicated—either the context of the classroom or the larger context of cross-curricular or process-centered institutional agendas. To state this more positively, if we advocate and model writing and learning, we might also attempt to characterize the institutional contexts and philosophies that support our successful teaching strategies and anticipate ones that do not. The stock we have placed in autonomous classroom behaviors may result somewhat from another sense of autonomy—in theories of writing and learning that promote individual acts of discovery and expression. (p. 346)

Through observations of a wide range of courses in different disciplines and at different levels, it becomes possible to characterize the larger institutional context of learning environments. Then it is possible to examine the writing produced in a range of disciplines to determine whether the appropriate learning environment has been presented.

In arguing that ethnomethodological research can incorporate both cognitive and social views of composing, Brandt (1992) cited analysis of instructional settings as one aspect of composition studies that can benefit from this perspective:

> For instance, in classroom research, the habit of automatically seeing "teachers" and "students" and "classroom organization" must be problematized. That a researcher can take such categories so easily for granted, that these categories are so directly 'scenic' to anyone entering a school, only speaks to how widely sanctioned and understood are the roles of teachers and students and classroom life in general, how well embedded and routinized they are in normal life. Yet an ethnomethodological vision requires inquiry into how any instance of classroom life actually gets accomplished on a day-to-day, minute-to-minute basis by the participants on the scene. (p. 346)

Through investigation of patterns of classroom practices and then descriptions within each pattern of what actually happens for teachers and students in specific classrooms, it is possible to examine how writing functions within such patterns to foster learning.

CLASSROOM FORMATS

Seventy-four classroom observations in 20 disciplines were made over the 6 years of the study. Summary data on these observations is presented here to provide a context for the following discussion. The disciplines and numbers of observations are presented in Table 6.1.

TABLE 6.1

Classroom Observations Across Disciplines

Discipline	Number of Observations	Percentage of Observations
Psychology	23	31%
Communications	14	19%
Physics	8	11%
Nursing	4	3%
Art	2	3%
Chemistry	2	3%
Economics	2	3%
Electrical engineering	2	3%
English	2	3%
History	2	3%
Mathematics	2	3%
Secondary education	2	3%
Sociology	2	3%
Anthropology	1	1%
Biology	1	1%
Black studies	1	1%
Health education	1	1%
Philosophy	1	1%
Speech	1	1%
World humanities	1	1%

The uneven distribution of the observations is accounted for by an early decision I made that I would concentrate on the disciplines in which the students who remained in the study chose to major. Four of the students who continued, Linda, Joan, Delores, and Chandra, majored in psychology. Three, Ricardo, Carl, and Donald, chose communications as their major field. Jacob became a physics student, and Audrey concentrated in economics. The observations of the classes revealed the following formats as shown in Table 6.2.

It is not surprising that many of the introductory courses in physics, psychology, chemistry, biology, economics, and mathematics were primarily in the lecture format. Class sizes in these courses ranged from 30 to 300. The larger lecture classes, in physics, chemistry, and biology almost always had discussion sections and laboratory hours. In addition, several instructors arranged for voluntary tutorials to be available to students. These courses assessed student work through quizzes and exams. Only one physics professor included essay questions in his examinations. One upper level English class observation for writing in the sciences recorded an instructor lecturing on grammar to the students.

The largest percentage of classes combined lecture with discussion. Discussions were generated by questions from the professor to the class or from students to the professor. In psychology courses, students were most frequently assessed through a combination of quizzes, exams, and final papers. In communications courses, students frequently had quizzes and exams, with writing assignments focusing on projects and portfolios in such courses as advertising, journalism, screenwriting, and public relations.

TABLE 6.2

Classroom Formats

Format	Number of Classes	Percentage of Classes
Primarily lecture, few questions	17	23%
Lecture and discussion	34	46%
Primarily discussion	4	5%
Review for exam or return exam[a]	8	11%
Oral reports	5	7%
Collaborative learning	1	1%
Miscellaneous: film, individual painting, workshop, in-class quiz	5	7%

[a]The number of reviews or returns of exams may have been exaggerated by the timing of the observations, usually around the middle of the semester.

The ethics course required analytic writing on the ethical circumstances of a current issue. Requirements for papers were specifically detailed in many of the syllabi of the courses provided by the instructors.

Observing the lecture–recitation format used in the art history course of one of her case study students at the University of New Hampshire, Chiseri-Strater (1991) noted that the students became an "appreciative but nonparticipating audience" (p. 146), involved in a passive form of learning. She contrasted this format with a later class meeting in the same course where the instructor "turned her classroom over to her students, engaging them as novice art-critics, . . . [becoming] involved learners, even taking risks in their responses" (pp. 146–147). Chiseri-Strater argued that if learning is accepted as a process rather than a mere transmission of knowledge, students will be better prepared "for the critical thinking they will later use in writing for the discipline and presumably in all their courses" (p. 147). In many cases in my study, the lecture–discussion format did not lead to passive behavior by the students. Students became active in developing questions for discussion, providing examples from their own experiences to support theories and principles being presented, and working with their professor to understand difficult concepts and problems. This is not to say, of course, that there were no observations of instructors' trying to encourage their students to participate in discussions but the students' remaining passive and unengaged.

The purposes of class discussion may be seen quite differently from the instructor's and the student's perspectives. One of the students interviewed by Belenky et al. (1986) described the purpose of class discussion as she interpreted it: "It helps to see if the students are doing the reading. There's not much else to grade on" (p. 108). In their analysis of this response, Belenky et al. pointed out that the student sees the purpose of discussion being an opportunity to provide data for evaluation. They further comment that this helps them understand why the student they interviewed rarely spoke in class (p. 108).

The categories of "discussion" and "oral reports" could easily have been combined because discussion was frequently generated from reports, informal or formal, that students gave on projects they were working on or experiences they were having in professional roles. For example, students in secondary education classes who were student teaching shared their experiences with one another. In an economics class, students described ongoing research projects. Reports of advertising approaches were commented on both by students and instructors in a communications class. In an English composition class, discussion centered on a reading with which students were engaged. In speech classes, students had to provide both oral and written responses to assignments. Oral reports were almost always the prelude to long research papers due at the end of the semester.

As mentioned earlier, in eight classes instructors were either preparing students for examinations or returning examination papers. These classes were always a combination of lecture and discussion with the instructor reviewing material and answering questions or explaining the required responses to test questions and responding to inquiries for further explanation. The exams were almost always multiple-choice or short answer formats, but students frequently were also given some combination of short and long essay assignments.

Dickson (1995) maintained that "novice writers trust teachers only when they give explicit directions for passing tests or when they create very concrete guides to passing a course. This plethora of factual information and concrete rules lulls the novice students into believing that knowledge is reducible to fact" (p. 12). The likely truth of this assertion supports the approach Geisler (1994) described as existing in middle and high schools where students are tested on recall of facts. Although some students may wish to perpetuate this approach to learning in the college years, most instructors desire to move students away from this passive learning, with demands for analytic and evaluative writing becoming the appropriate mechanism. As mentioned earlier, many students in my study preferred writing papers to taking examinations, believing they could then better present their understanding of course material. Dickson pointed out that novice writers may distrust their instructors and "hesitate to venture out and offer their own opinions because they are on unfamiliar ground" (p. 12). Although this may be one reason for students to be reluctant to offer their own opinions, another may be the implied punishment if the student disagrees with the instructor's views as examples of Ricardo's and Jacob's writing and interviews presented in earlier chapters attest to.

The one example of collaborative learning that was observed occurred in a psychology class. Students were working in small groups in preparation for a group paper they were writing. Each student was responsible for one aspect of the topic. The professor walked around the classroom, meeting with each group, answering questions and making suggestions. The students planned to meet again outside of class time.

This set of observations does not reveal anything surprising to college instructors who may have led classes in these different formats under different circumstances. But it does reveal how flexible students have to be as they encounter this range of instructional approaches with their differing emphases and methods of evaluation. Examples of how students interacted with and responded to these learning environments illustrate how central the instructional setting can be in fostering (or not fostering) the kind of learning college students are expected to achieve.

VARIATION IN WRITING OVER TIME
WITHIN DISCIPLINE TYPES

In their call for research areas that need further examination, Walvoord and McCarthy (1990) recognized that the fullest picture of student writing can be obtained through looking at writing that has occurred over time in multiple settings: "How much variation in roles does a single student exhibit among all his/her classes? Does the text-processor role represent a stage in some students' development? How are roles related to other elements such as the students' and teachers' past experiences, the classroom dynamics, gender, culture, or the students' anxiety, motivation, or other characteristics?" (pp. 232–233). Walvoord and McCarthy defined *text processing* as the approach in which "the student focuses centrally on processing texts in some way (summarizing, synthesizing, reviewing, commenting) rather than on addressing the issues and solving the problems outlined in the assignment" (p. 9). An analysis of writing over time, particularly in different courses within a discipline, can begin to address these questions.

An advantage of ethnographic research in a longitudinal study is that materials are available from different perspectives over time to examine the work done by students. Papers written in courses in which observational reports were collected are supplemented by the students' own comments about their experiences in the course collected through the interviews carried out twice each semester.

In three consecutive semesters, Joan took psychology courses for which I have observational reports, papers, and interview material. In the first of these courses, psychology of infancy and childhood, the fall of 1991, her fifth semester at the college, Joan talked about the course both at the beginning and the end of the semester. She said that the theories of Locke, Rousseau, and Freud were useful in helping her to understand small children and stages of development. She also commented, "You learn about yourself as well." She felt that the courses that were most helpful to her were those that required writing. By the end of the semester, Joan had clearly sought out a more intense relationship with her psychology professor. She told me that she had discussed outside assignments with her professor who told her how well she was doing and what she needed to do to continue to do well. Joan felt encouraged by this support. She went to ask her how she could develop a better paper and then went on to have further conversations with her. Joan was told that her papers "lacked certain things" and that she had to do better proofreading. (This was the semester that Joan was working long hours, for example, from 7 a.m. to 5 p.m. the day before our interview.) She told me that she was now working harder in her major, psychology.

The class meeting that was observed was the only one in which collaborative learning took place. For the first 15 minutes of the class, a spokesperson from each group reported on the group's project. A discussion of problems and progress in group work ensued. Then the groups began to work on their projects, helping each others as problems arose. The professor walked around to the groups, listened, made suggestions, and offered alternatives. She emphasized that the paper the groups were working on was not just to give a written statement about what they had read but to communicate with others and to transmit ideas. The students made plans to meet outside of class and they discussed presentation styles for their upcoming report to the class.

For a homework assignment, students were directed to "Take an example of a child that is crying. What would Locke say to the mother of the child? What would Rousseau say to the mother of the child?" Joan set up an example where a mother was in the kitchen cooking dinner. The child wants to participate in the food preparation, but the mother refuses to let her help. The child "starts to cry non-stop." When the child realizes that she is being ignored, she starts to throw a tantrum. The mother "is fed up" so she goes to Locke and Rousseau for help.

> Rousseau: This child is a curious human being. Let this child explore her curiosities in an environment that is similar to this one, but safe. The child will not only stop crying, but she will also, as she grows older, find her own identity and know what she wants out of life in the future. If her experiences are limited, the child will not be as well rounded.
>
> Locke: This child is one who needs more of a backbone structure. Talk to the child, let her know that this is not what a child 2 yrs. old is supposed to be doing. Give her some toys of her own appropriate for a child her age and make sure she understands that this could get her into trouble, that getting into mischief is unaccepted. Show her how to play with her toys in a correct manner.

Her teacher commented that her thinking was "brief, but thoughtful."

In a longer paper for this course, Joan wrote a "Case Observation Explanation" of a 2½-year toddler named Stephanie. In her introduction, Joan wrote she would "compare [Stephanie's] behavior actions to Piaget's cognitive and developmental theories." In some cases, Joan was able to apply Piaget's theories cogently to Stephanie's observed behavior, while at other times she drew conclusions without providing the essential connections between theory and observation. For example, Joan noted that Stephanie entered the classroom and quickly climbed up on a chair. Joan analyzed this activity as Stephanie "mastering the task of developing a schema or scheme. This is a set of movements used to perform a task." The professor commented "OK" in the margin. But when Joan went on to write, "Piaget uses the example of a baby sucking its finger," the comment was "How compared?" In other words, the request was for a more explicit connection to be made between the two examples that were being cited and how they were related theoretically.

In later sections of the paper, Joan was more successful in presenting the relationship between theory and observation. She presented Piaget's theory of object permanence by which a child in the preoperational thought stage will find an object placed at point 1, "but if you place an object under the blanket at point 2, the child will proceed to reveal the object at point 1." "When the professor placed a small horse under the blanket at point 1, Stephanie revealed the horse. When the horse was placed at point 2, Stephanie immediately looked for the horse at point 1 where she did not recover it. This proved Piaget's object permanence theory to be true." The instructor commented, "Very good" in the margin.

Similarly, Joan recognized Stephanie's behavior in relation to pictures in a book as a sign of her developmental stage. She wrote:

> Although I believe that Stephanie is smart, I observed that when she was asked would she like to swim in the water with the dolphins, she responded yes and began to pull off her clothing to swim in the water with the dolphins. She even went as far as to sit on top of the book, indicating that she was swimming in the water with the dolphins. When she did this, I was led to believe that Stephanie has not reached the level where she can tell the difference between reality and fantasy. She is quite young yet, however, the distinction between reality and fantasy will come with age.

Her professor wrote in the margin, "Good! Animism." thus giving Joan the appropriate psychological term she needed to describe the behavior she had observed. The overall comments on the paper responded both to the form and the content: "Your writing could use more practice. Most insights are very good—you did not cover an entire theory. Your thinking is rather scientific and systematic." She received a "B+" on the paper.

As can be seen from the intersection of the interview comments, the classroom format, and the writing assignments and responses, this psychology course provided an encouraging and facilitating environment in which Joan could learn. Her anxiety was reduced and she felt comfortable asking for and receiving help. Her commitment to the field of psychology was enhanced as she felt she was not only learning psychological concepts and how to apply them, but she was also learning about herself.

The next semester, Joan enrolled in a course in abnormal psychology. She told me in an interview about a third of the way through the semester that this was the most difficult course she was now taking. She said, "The professor is complex. It's more like a philosophy class. The professor doesn't lecture from the book; he gives his own lecture and we have to read the textbook and other books on our own. We can ask questions during the lecture. He tells us, 'Don't give opinions or say I feel—but base your answers on facts.'" Joan tells me that she feels these directions eliminate her ability to elaborate on the subject. What she seems to mean is that the professor discourages the students from bringing in their own experiences when they write about assigned topics. They are to focus strictly on the information being provided in the lectures and readings. Joan follows these directions in the writing she does for the course, providing analyses but no insights gained from her own world knowledge. At the end of the semester, she tells me, "This has been one of the better semesters for me. The professors have been 'more giving.' They work more closely with you. They're more involved with the student—more on a personal level outside of class."

In the class observation a week later, the professor began by discussing the upcoming midterm exam that would be a multiple choice test with no essay questions. He then wrote an outline on the blackboard of what would be presented during that class period. The professor then proceeded to lecture for the next 15 minutes, trying occasionally to involve the students in his presentation. One student asked a question during this time period. For the next 15 minutes, in a very darkened room where it was impossible to take notes, the professor showed slides. He spoke about the slides very rapidly in a rather monotonous tone. In the last 15 minutes of the class, he became more animated and discussed issues relating to drug abuse. The environment of the classroom itself was dispiriting—there was disturbing noise from the next classroom where television was being played and the air in the room was very close and stuffy, contributing to a sense of fatigue. (This seems an appropriate place to mention that the North Academic Center building at City College, comprising one city avenue and three city blocks, was a truly "sick building." With windows that did not open, and with most classrooms and offices having no windows at all, the building depended on an inadequate heating and air-conditioning system. Most classes in the humanities, social sciences, and education were held in this building.) Evaluation in the course was based on two examinations and a "writing assignment in which you will review and analyze pertinent articles in the field of abnormal psychology." The writing assignment counted for one third of the final grade.

Explicit directions for the term paper, as indicated in the course syllabus, were as follows:

> (a) Find five articles that are pertinent to the field of abnormal psychology in *The New York Times, Newsday, Wall Street Journal* (but not *The Daily News, N.Y. Post* or other trash paper), or weekly publications such as *Newsweek, Time Magazine* or *U.S. News and World Report*. It can be a news article, column, opposite the editorial page (op-ed) piece, letter to the editor, a business section article, say, on the marketing of a new drug to treat mental illness, or even an obituary. The publication date of the article(s) must be between *January 1, 1992 and May 14, 1992*. Of course, the more creative you are in selecting articles the better your grade will be.

Students were instructed (b) to turn in photocopies of the articles and to respond to the following points:

(c) Review the article's relevant points in your own words. (d) Why did you choose this article? Describe its relevance to the subject of abnormal psychology. What theory or theories (found in your text or heard in lecture) does it relate to? In what way (how)? (e) If the article specifically reports research findings, describe the type of study that was done. Review the strengths and weaknesses of the research design chosen by the investigators. Would you do the study in the same way? What would you add or subtract? Can you think of an alternative explanation for the experimental results? (f) Remember, what you "feel" about the article (story) is of no concern in this course (do not even think of starting or ending your report with "I feel that . . ." Your conclusion(s) should relate to the *facts* of the article and how the article relates to abnormal (behavior) psychology

The paper was to be between 5 and 10 pages long. Students were instructed to "make sure all grammar, spelling and typos are corrected before handing in the paper. . . . If the paper has an abundance of grammar, spelling (or typos) errors it will be returned to you unread (as if the paper had never been turned in)." Such specific instructions provided importance guidance to students. The clear emphasis was on analysis and elimination of personal opinion.

Not surprisingly, papers responding to this assignment contained what Belenky et al. (1986) called "received knowledge," relying on authority to support the points being made. Joan selected five articles for analyses: the first dealt with a physician who inseminated his patients with his own sperm; the second was about the slaying of a Bronx youth; the third concerned a sex-assault case; the fourth dealt with a parolee accused of five murders; and the last was about cutbacks in medical care.

In her discussion of the first case, Joan diagnosed the doctor's condition as narcissistic personality disorder. She defined this condition as "an individual having a superiority complex about his/herself. These individuals believe that they are so perfect that he or she has no thoughts or consideration of others. These individuals suffer from low self-esteem and may go through great lengths to demonstrate their self-worth by making themselves the center of attention." In her analysis of the diagnosis, Joan cited authorities from her textbook and outside readings. As part of her discussion, Joan noted that "there are six areas of functioning to be central to narcissistic personality disorder that I agree with, one is that he or she is always ready to shift values to gain favor. Dr. ＿＿＿＿ demonstrates this by changing his story saying that there were no unanimous sperm donors available." Her instructor noted in the margin, "Excellent observation." Her rationale for selecting this article was that "it drew my attention because of the seriousness of the crimes committed as well as the observation of the individuals manipulation of others." It is clear that in her consideration of this case Joan has carefully relied on outside authorities to support her diagnosis and evaluation. Her reasons for considering this topic remain objective.

In her analysis of the fourth case, where a paroled repeat offender is accused of five murders, Joan characterized his condition as suffering from antisocial personality disorder. She defined this as "a disorder where individuals cause harm to others by violating the rights of others through aggressive, anti-social behavior without remorse or sympathy to anyone." She characterized such behavior as follows: "Anti-social persons are said to also suffer from low self-esteem, come from broken families and also show no grief for their actions. Serial killers, and rapists fall into this category of being anti-social individuals. These individuals usually display withdrawn behavior casually but when they engage in vicious acts such as homicide or rape, this can become an act on *impulse*." Empathy with the families appears to be the reason Joan chose this article, although she did not use this term: "I can't really go on to tell you how overwhelmed I am by such acts being committed. I chose this article because when I read about how the families of the victims grieved, it made me angry as well as eager to tell about it; my heart goes out to them." Joan comes close to phrasing her response in terms of personal feelings, as students had been admonished not to do, but by placing the emphasis on the families' reactions, she reduced her vulnerability to this charge.

Joan received an "A" on this paper with her professor commenting: "First rate." At the end of the paper, he responded to her final comment that she hoped the reader "found this research report interesting." He wrote: "Needless to say, I do. Terrific job. This is an interesting neatly written paper."

Here it can be seen that Joan thrived by carefully following the specific instructions set out by her instructor. Although in her first interview she said she felt constrained by not being able to bring her own experiences into her analyses of the material she was studying, she demonstrated through her final paper that she had found a way to involve herself in her analyses without violating the professor's dictums. She did not introduce her "feelings" about the cases she was studying, but she permitted herself to identify with the feelings of those involved in the cases.

The next semester Joan enrolled in a course on social psychology. At the beginning of the semester, she told me that this was her easiest course so far. She said, "It's common sense. Ideas are easier to grasp. I have to write two essays." At this point in her college experience, she was seeing clearly the value that writing had for her: "I forget most of what I read, but if I have to write it, it's part of a recording. When you write, it's recording what goes on. It sticks with me. I can remember what I wrote and how I wrote it." Although these comments center on writing as a way of remembering, they reflect a learning style that she had begun to appreciate, particularly as her visual disability made reading much more problematic for her. By the end of that semester, she had become an acute listener of her professors' lectures and language. She told me that she had learned to use transition words more. "I learned it from my professors," she said. "Professors love it when students mimic them. My psychology professor used 'moreover, in that.' I used the terms he did. I also apply it to papers in other courses—all professors like that." When asked what had been the most interesting thing that happened to her during that semester, she said, "meeting Professor _____, my psychology professor. I learned a lot from her—things you can use in everyday life. She also brings in outside materials to read. For example, people in a group are more likely to conform than a person who is alone. The larger the group, the heavier the influence. You need at least two dissenters to support each other." As these comments reveal, Joan was becoming a careful observer of her academic experience, making the transition between being a passive learner and an active one.

For the first 30 minutes of the class meeting that was observed, the professor returned the multiple-choice part of the midterm examination. She responded to questions that students had and raised questions herself. The students were attentive and asked about how essays written for the course were evaluated. She said that in the essays she had been concerned with the content, the way the answer had been written, and how the students expressed themselves. She told them that if the grammar in the paper had been terrible, they would have to see her in her office. She explained that the essay had a diagnostic value so people could see if they needed help. Evaluation in the course was based on two multiple-choice examinations and two essay examinations. For the last 15 minutes of the class, the professor lectured on aggression, writing key words on the blackboard. Students paid attention but did not ask any questions.

In one of the essay examinations, Joan carefully defined the term she was about to discuss.

> Misogyny is conveniently defined as a hatred for women which goes back to classical Athens. There are 3 components of misogyny. These are power, sexuality, and inferiority. *Power* is totally based on the suppression of women to prevent them from obtaining power. These men believed that women were sexually dangerous, in that women's genitallia could actually destroy 20 men in one day. Moreover women could use their sexuality to ruin men occupationally as well. The last component of mysogyny is inferiority. Men felt that women were inferior to men. In Scandinavia, the amount of education was determined by the men in this country because of the fear of power which comes into play again. These men believe that education would give a woman power which causes disobedience in women.

In the balance of the essay examination, Joan cited examples from different cultures and religions where misogyny was practiced. Joan received an "A" on this paper, and her professor commented, "Good work. It is solid. It is literate." It can be seen that Joan took seriously the admonition that content and writing would both be valued in the essays required in the course. It is also notable that she incorporated the term "moreover" carefully into her response, indicating not only that she wanted to please her professor but that she understood the usefulness of such transitions in writing.

As can be seen, there were similarities and differences in these instructional settings and in Joan's responses to them. In all three courses, analyses were required with little opportunity for bringing in personal values or beliefs. In each case, to use Walvoord and McCarthy's (1990) characterization, the professors demanded that the students "address the issues and solve the problems outlined in the assignment." In the first course, psychology of infancy and childhood, Joan developed a personal rapport with her instructor that gave her support and encouragement. The instructional setting was open and informal, engaging students in collaborative work with each other and with their professor. The writing that grew out of this course was no less demanding with students learning to apply psychological concepts to case studies. In the abnormal psychology course, students were left much more on their own to integrate material from the textbook with the material presented in the lectures for course examinations. Although students were expected to know the materials presented in the lectures, the physical conditions of the classroom sometimes interfered with their ability to take adequate notes or even to hear the professor's words clearly. On the other hand, very specific guidelines for writing the final paper facilitated students' approaches to writing the assigned paper. Students were fruitfully guided to consider the relevant aspects of the materials they were analyzing, and they were provided with clear organizational patterns for presenting their findings. In the social psychology class, Joan found herself becoming more conscious of academic ways of presenting information, and she used this knowledge to improve her own methods of writing. She was told explicitly that content and expression were both going to be evaluated when her papers were read. In all the courses, students were expected to read thoughtfully, bring analytic perspectives to bear in their writing, and to relate theory to particular data or cases. Clearly, the students were being appropriately prepared to function in the discipline of psychology and Joan learned how to take advantage of these settings and approaches to improve her ability to become a professional person.

In his third and fourth years at the college, while he was working at *The New York Times*, Carl enrolled in three communications classes. He received "A's" in two of the courses and dropped one of them. Interview comments, observation reports, and papers written in all these classes reflect the differing approaches he took in these classes. The first of these courses was in mass media communication. In an interview at the beginning of the semester, Carl told me that he had almost completed the core course requirements of the college. He said, "I like the communication class a lot—I'm finally within my major. It's a general introductory course and it seems easy." At the end of the semester, he reiterated that he had taken one course in his major and "was satisfied so far."

The course provided a general introduction to the field of mass communication with the first half of the semester examining history and trends in newspapers, radio, and film. In the second half of the semester, law and ethics in relation to mass communication were studied. At the class meeting observed, the professor led an active discussion on what the media had reported on during the previous weekend. The professor advised the students that a guest lecturer would be coming to the next class and that they should read the appropriate section in the textbook so they would be prepared with questions. The next topic that was raised dealt with the differences between advertising and journalism. Throughout the discussions, the instructor wrote student responses on the blackboard and encouraged students to participate. The students listened to each other respectfully and discussed the issues among themselves as well as with the teacher. Both the instructor and the students offered appropriate examples to illustrate the ideas. The instructor was careful to ask for sources and evidence to support the students' views and she made certain that each point was clearly understood. The class environment was comfortable and collaborative. Students were required to write occasional two-page papers and take three quizzes, a midterm, and a final.

For one of the short papers in the course, Carl reviewed the presentation given by a guest lecturer who was a senior correspondent at a local radio station. The correspondent described how he was initially hired in a low-level job "during the peak of the racial unrest that gripped the nation." He went on to indicate that there was, at that time, only one Black reporter on a national radio network and only one Black news director that he knew of. Carl was somewhat skeptical of the implications of this. He wrote: "Though I can see the point to having more minorities as news directors, I don't think a black radio news reporter would be able to make much of a difference in reporting short news briefs when compared to a white reporter." Although the statistics cited by the reporter might suggest discrimination to some, Carl seemed oblivious of this possible implication. This is surprising considering his great sensitivity to discrimination against homosexuals, as evidenced by his writing in other courses.

Another assignment was to compare the coverage of a news story in different print media, with particular attention to be paid to the page the story was on, its length, what facts were different in the coverages, and whether facts were left out. Carl chose to examine "the double unrelated deaths of a police officer and a fire fighter" in the editions of three Saturday newspapers. Fuller coverage of the police officer's death had been reported in the Friday editions, so on Saturday, the two deaths were handled differently by the newspapers. Carl noted that one paper (*Newsday*) gave the fullest coverage on Saturday, with pictures of both men on the front page, and continuing separate stories on inside pages. *The New York Times* combined coverage of the stories, starting their report on the lower half of page one and continuing inside. *The Post* referred to the firefighter's death at the bottom of page 1, leading to an inside story on the firefighter as well as a short article on the individual accused of killing the police officer. Carl's attention was drawn to the different ways the newspapers covered the lives of the men who had died:

> Newsday did a superb job on giving both the firefighter and the police officer a full story that told of their demise as well as the funeral, and some of the life. The Times had more an after effects type story. Their article, though it did touch upon the events leading up to their demise, did nothing to flesh out our knowledge of these men who lost their lives in protecting the city. The Post carried the shortest article with no real care for the actual persons involved or much of anything else.

Carl's analysis illustrates his compassion for others, but his writing reflects some insensitivity to discrimination or stereotyping of racial minorities.

In another paper for this course, Carl stated that the assignment was "Should reporters take sides on the issues they are covering?" His professor noted on the paper that she "thought the question was: Should reporters take public stands on the issues they cover?" In his analysis of *The New York Times* reporter's coverage of the rape victim in the West Palm Beach Kennedy case, Carl noted that the reporter was "missing both conscience and objectivity in an April 1991 article." Carl wrote, "The way the article was written, it was as if Ms. Brown [Bowman] was on trial, that she was the one who committed a crime. Her past history should have remained just that—in her past. [The reporter] seemed too eager—too aggressive in his coverage. It was as if he took it upon himself to decide her guilt or her innocence. The poor woman never had a chance." Carl's instructor commented on this section of the paper: "[The reporter] didn't actually take a public stand. He skewed his story through the selection of facts." Through her comment, she was reiterating the nature of the assignment she had given rather than Carl's interpretation of the task. Carl's discussion continued with interviews of newly hired reporters at *The New York Times*, asking them whether they believed that "taking sides on an issue is wrong." One reporter noted that "if reporters want to make their opinions known, they can become columnists." Another said, "People will always have a twinge of doubt on the facts the reporter presented." His professor responded favorably to these insights, commenting at the end of the paper, "This is an important point and a good one to end on."

In these papers, then, Carl had been provided with opportunities to respond to different issues that confront professionals in the world of communications. For the most part, he displayed sensitivity to issues like objectivity and empathy in an instructional environment where students felt free to express their opinions, but knew they had to support their views with appropriate evidence.

The next semester, Carl enrolled in a journalism class. At the beginning of the semester, he told me that the concepts in the course were familiar to him from a high school class and from his work at *The New York Times*. He also told me that the emphasis was on reporting "being objective and fair." "It's a moral-minded class," he said. He noted that he was learning journalistic techniques. By the end of the semester, he told me that he had dropped the course because it conflicted with his working hours. He had completed a news story before he dropped the class, and he had sold a version of it to the metropolitan desk of the *Times*. Since I have a class observation report and papers he wrote for the course, I have decided to include it here to demonstrate what the demands of this type of course are.

The syllabus for the course described frequent writing assignments and two quizzes over the semester. Students were required to write a 500- to 700-word term paper in which they were to "identify and *analyze* an important clash (argument or struggle) today between government (or some other entity) and press over freedom of the press." Further specific instructions including the requirement for outside research were provided as well as the handing-in of a 100-word memorandum to be given to the instructor about a month before the paper was due. The memo had to describe the topic and receive the approval of the instructor.

In the class session that was observed, students were reading aloud the leads they had written for newspaper articles. The professor and the students participated actively in the discussion, making suggestions and pointing out strengths and weaknesses. When the papers were returned to the students, there were many suggestions written on them.

The writings I have from Carl's work in this course all discuss "Out of the Closet," the thrift store run by the Gay Men's Health Crisis, the proceeds of which go to AIDS research. The leads Carl wrote for the class that was observed reveal a rarely shown sense of humor:

> Both owner and objects alike come from 'out of the closet' and thus the upper east side "Out of the Closet" thrift store and foundation inc. are aptly named.
>
> Out of the Closet, an upper east side thrift store, is aptly named: Both the owner and throw away knick knacks it sells have spent many years in the closet.

Carl also chose to write about the store for his final paper, and he prepared the required memorandum to describe his project. He noted that he "would like to do a story on the first thrift store, or the growing number of thrift stores in the city, whose proceeds go to AIDS research." He wrote that he had located the first of these stores to be founded and identified the issues he would pursue: "If I focus on the first store, I can pursue the story in terms of the people who shop there: Are they victims of AIDS? Their friends? Do they know that the proceeds go to AIDS research? I can also look at the owners of the store: Have they had any problems in running the store? How much business does the store do? Are they supported by any outside sources?" Carl's instructor commented: "What will be the 'news' focus, as opposed to a profile of the store?" Since Carl did not complete this paper for the journalism course, he felt free to abandon any necessity to provide a news focus, rewriting it as a feature article which was later published in *The New York Times*. The tone of the article is set by its introduction, one that is very different from the "news lead" that he had written earlier: "From an 18th-century Samurai longbow to an antique elephant headdress to the hats of Gypsy Rose Lee, The Out Of The Closet Thrift Shop offers more than just exotic items. The store, founded by gay men, offers its customers a chance to participate in the fight against AIDS." As is apparent from this opening, Carl understood well the necessity of attracting his reader's attention through unusual details, before he could introduce the more serious aspect of his feature article.

The journalism class reinforced the importance of objectivity and fairness in news reporting that Carl had studied in the mass media course the semester before. In his writing in the journalism class, he demonstrated that he could produce "catchy" headlines that would attract the attention of readers. He began to see that news stories had to be differentiated from feature stories. As in the papers for his creative writing courses, he demonstrated an artful ability to write a feature story acceptable to one of the most widely respected newspapers in the country.

A year later, Carl enrolled in an introduction to public relations course. When telling me about his experiences in many of his classes, Carl was frequently critical of the abilities of his fellow students. His comments about the public relations course are typical. He told me toward the end of the semester that he did not feel that he had needed any additional preparation in high school that would have helped him academically. "No," he said, "other people needed more work in writing. In my public relations class, some are unable to grasp the basic idea of writing a press release. On the last day of class, the professor is still explaining how to do it." The next semester he noted that he had initially found the public relations course frustrating. "It seems the first two weeks of every class are lessons on how to write," he said.

The class session that was observed was held in a room that was too warm with distracting noise coming from the hallway. Although the professor spoke loudly and clearly, the warmth and strain of listening made everyone lethargic. The professor read the best two papers that had been handed in for the previous class. After a student read his paper aloud, the professor asked, "Why is this a press release?" No one responded to her question. The professor began to lecture, writing ideas on the blackboard, explaining difficult words, and illustrating ideas with examples. A few students contributed ideas to the discussion, but most seemed to be waiting to be fed with information. When a student asked whether the observer was a guest lecturer, the professor introduced her to the class and commented, "I hope you are not observing me!" This was one of only two cases in the 74 observations where the professor acknowledged being self-conscious about the observation. In addition to the press releases students wrote over the semester, they were required to write a midterm project paper and to take an in-class final examination.

For one of his press releases, Carl wrote about McDonald's changing its logo. The headline read: "From 'Golden Arches' to the 'End of the Rainbow' McDonald's Changes Logo." The press release went on:

> The Golden Arches that for years graced the top of McDonald's nationwide were retired today in favor of a new rainbow logo.
> "These are changing times we live in—" Carlos Briceno, spokesperson for the McDonald's corporation said. "And McDonald's is changing with them. The rainbow logo symbolizes what this company is all about: renewal, multi-culturalism, and caring about the environment. The rainbow logo will lead us into the 21st century."
> This is the first time McDonald's has changed its logo since it was founded back in 1955.

Carl's originality shone clearly from this innovative and socially conscious presentation. There is no indication that McDonald's is following this suggestion.

For his mid-term project paper, Carl followed up on this proposal, providing research and analysis supporting the change in McDonald's logo. The paper is a memorandum from the C.E.O. of McDonald's, laying out its larger goals and discussing areas of attention the company will explore, based on an extensive nationwide survey that "had a high return rate, perhaps due to the $5.00 book of McDonald's coupons that was attached." The overview states that the company will focus on "the environment and spreading multiculturalism" that the new rainbow logo will incorporate. Among the issues raised in the survey was a suggestion that McDonald's should provide child play areas not only in suburban locations, but also in urban locations. The response of the company to this suggestion was entirely pragmatic as outlined in the memorandum:

> The play areas for kids is not as big an issue as we initially thought. We are going to try and add play areas to a few urban area restaurants. Some parents questioned thought any small play area was "good enough" and that anything too extensive would give them "trouble" in getting their kids out. "Sometimes I just have time to run in, get the kids dinner, and run out again. If I have time to let them play, I do, but most of the time I don't so if the playground was made even more interesting, I may end up losing the battle to them," a Ms. Mercy Van Black from Levittown, PA said. Besides, we do not want people hanging out at the restaurants all day, as we have seen in a couple of branch stores. Average stay should not run longer than half an hour.

In this ironic justification for not extending the playgrounds, Carl demonstrates his awareness of how grounds can be provided for pragmatic company decisions.

Toward the end of that semester, Carl wrote an analysis of the coverage of the March for Gay, Lesbian, Bisexual and Transgender rights that had occurred a few days earlier on April 25, 1993. In his analysis, Carl cited coverage from *The New York Times* and then appended his own response to the issues raised:

> The march was about a lot of issues and the New York Times, in their front page analysis of the march, questioned its focus. "What did the marchers today want most? Overturning the ban on homosexuals in the military? More financing for the fight against AIDS? Equal civil rights for homosexuals? Gay marriages? Eliminating laws against sodomy?"
>
> It would be impossible to speak for the entire gay community but I think the march was about all those issues and more importantly, about being recognized as human beings and being proud of who we are.
>
> Being recognized, being counted was very important and march organizers made sure that everyone was approached to sign an "attendance sheet" of sorts. Everyone who did received a sticker saying "I was counted."

Through the use of "we," Carl not only aligns himself with the group under consideration, but he also insists on their being accorded respect and dignity. He is not only comfortable with his identity, he is proud of it.

Through his writings in the public relations course, Carl continues to assert that recognition must be accorded to those who have failed to receive it from the larger society. The field of public relations provides openings to influence public opinion and mold it in directions that individuals and corporations support. Carl wishes to move McDonald's to a more socially responsible position on issues such as the environment and multiculturalism, just as he wishes to move the larger society toward respect for homosexual identity.

Through these three communications courses, Carl grew in his understanding of the need for media sources to be fair and objective. He also came to understand their power in influencing public opinion, and he began to see that he could use his social consciousness to urge changes in community attitudes toward issues of importance to individuals, groups, and larger organizational entities. He became sensitive to the differences between objective reporting, feature writing, and public relations writing, all providing opportunities to sway public opinion. Although each demanded a different approach, each was also obligated to fairness, honesty, and integrity in communication.

As Joan and Carl progressed through the psychology and communications courses, they were continually required to provide objective analyses of the materials and issues they were confronting. Not surprisingly, personal values and world views were downplayed more in the field of psychology where practitioners need to retain objectivity, particularly when they might have to interact with troubled individuals. But the field of communication also held high standards of objectivity for its participants, especially as this field recognized its power of persuasion through its opportunities in the public media. Neither Joan nor Carl were likely to lose the moral values they held strongly, but through these upper level courses they increasingly learned the importance of honestly portraying the complex issues they were confronting. Rather than being changed themselves, they were able to change the ways in which they presented their views to others so that they could be seen as more credible sources of information.

VARIATION OVER TIME
IN WRITING IN DIFFERENT DISCIPLINES

Another way to investigate the impact of instructional settings on student writing is to examine the work of students as they encounter the demands of different disciplines. The reports on the work of the two students detailed in this section center on their experiences when they changed majors.

Linda had come to City College with a deep commitment to her nursing major. Despite difficulties in the math and science courses, she continued to pursue nursing until the spring of her fourth year at the college. Although she had expressed reservations about the program in interviews during her third year, it was only in February 1993 that she actually declared a change in majors to psychology. In addition to her dissatisfaction with how the students were treated by the nursing faculty, Linda found that a new policy had gone into effect that semester. The nursing department would no longer guarantee admission to the program to all students who wanted to enter. Her weak grades in some of the prerequisite courses might have diminished her chances of being accepted into the program. She told me in a sad tone, "I wonder if all that blood, sweat, and tears was a waste. There's no one there to help you. They need to get it together—the faculty. There isn't any support from the faculty to the students. If you're with me, I want to achieve more, but if you're not, I feel alone."

Her discouragement with the nursing program was countered by her positive experiences with the faculty in psychology. She told me at the same interview in February 1993 that "certain professors [in the psychology department] can be your mentors. We can do research with the professors some time—I'd like to do it some time." She went on to say that she was interacting more with the psychology teacher she had that semester. "She is nice, cheerful, young. I feel better about the faculty in psychology than in nursing. I know many of the professors from earlier psychology courses. I only knew one person in the nursing faculty." So, by the time Linda decided to change her major, she had taken two psychology courses, and she already felt more comfortable with the faculty than she had in the nursing program.

Initially, Linda had been enthusiastic about the nursing program. In the spring of 1991, she took her first "real" nursing course, "Nursing as a Profession." She told me that it was the easiest course she was taking that semester, "not as difficult as [she] had expected." She said that "starting on the major makes it more exciting." In the same interview, she noted that she had taken a psychology course the semester before and that "the professor was serious about the writing requirements—very strict— and helpful to me." The professor encouraged her and allowed Linda to rewrite a paper after the course ended. This kind of experience influenced the decision she would make to change majors two years later. By the end of that semester, Linda had revised her judgment that the nursing course was an easy one. She told me, "I have to work harder. As I get deeper into the course, I have to study harder. There is a lot of deep thinking, especially about ethics. Things are complicated—there's not a right way." She also reflected on the role that writing was playing in her academic experiences: "Writing helps teachers discover more of a person—how mature a student is and what the student is learning. I consider I progressed. I like the writing and the progress I'm making. Teachers like the points I make. I come up with new ideas and teachers like that." Linda's attraction to writing and her evident satisfaction with her progress would later find better outlets in a social science field like psychology than in a more scientifically, clinically oriented field like nursing. The clinical work in psychology allowed for more interpretive interactions than the medical aspects so critical to nursing.

The observation of the nursing course took place near the end of the semester. In the class meeting, the students were reminded that their group presentations would begin the following week. The professor introduced the lecture and wrote an overview of the topics to be discussed on the blackboard. Students were active in responding to questions, drawing individual charts, and discussing a woman's health survey made available through the student health services. Students were told that if they wished to respond to the survey, the professor would turn their questionnaires in. The discussion of the survey focused on its format as a particular type of research. The professor then distributed copies of an article on how nurses can help patients recover more quickly. She discussed the article in terms of its research design and helped students design an experiment. She asked students to write out the hypothesis that generated the research. After the class was over, the professor told my research assistant that she had found that the students "don't like to write. They have trouble reading and writing. I give them take home essays on the final." She also described the course as introductory, in which students were exposed to the ethics, practice, and theory of nursing. They were expected to learn to read nursing journals critically. Students were assigned to carry out individual nurse interviews and then combine the information gathered with other members of their small group to produce a group report, which they would write as a formal paper and give as a presentation to the class. In addition, each student had to write an individual paper investigating a problem that had been cited in the initial nurse interview. A midterm short-answer examination accounted for 30% of the grade, the final for 30%, the group paper and presentation for 20%, and the individual paper for the final 20%.

Linda's group paper dealt with the issue of nursing shortages. Because the paper was written by five students, it is difficult to assess the extent of Linda's contribution. The paper summarized the interviews of the 12 nurses carried out by the group, mentioning such factors as "nurse burn out" brought about by increasing work loads and the frequent demand that nurses work double shifts or overtime. Suggestions made by the nurses to overcome these problems included "shift flexibility, continuing education, tuition free reimbursements, on site low cost child care facilities, and major medical and dental coverages." Such changes, they argued, "would improve employees' morale and decrease staff turnover." The conclusion to the paper reflects the analytical stance taken toward the issues raised: "The concept of nursing shortage entails much more than just a lack of staff. It incorporates patient care or lack thereof, staff retention, nurse burnout, the definition of nursing roles, education, and interstaff conflicts. Unless many of these suggested solutions are put into practice, the many problems plaguing the nursing profession will continue and may even worsen, having a profound effect on direct patient care." The quality of the writing in the group paper, especially in its ability to draw implications from the evidence, seems somewhat more advanced than the papers Linda had produced individually to that point in her academic courses.

Linda's individual final paper dealt with nursing salaries. She presented information relating nursing salaries to perceived shortages, particularly in specific geographic areas. She drew one strong implication from the evidence she presented: "Overall, if the shortage has its advantages, its been on the salaries. The main thing here is that many hospitals will become self-satisfied once the shortage eases. Many people will forget about rewarding good nursing, then enrollments will drop again and the shortage cycle will start all over again." Linda's professor encouraged her to think more deeply about the problem. She commented at the end of the paper: "How can we get society to value nursing? A common explanation is that nursing is women's work and therefore is low paying."

Linda's initial experience in a nursing course was a positive one. She came to see the profession more broadly and was encouraged to reflect on the field as a profession and on her personal involvement in it. But other experiences in the program and related required courses served to discourage her commitment and move her toward the field of psychology where she felt more welcomed and more comfortable.

In the fall of 1992, before she changed her major, Linda had enrolled in a course on the psychology of women, offered jointly through the psychology department and the department of women's studies. One of the papers assigned was to be an interview with the oldest woman in the family, describing how she was raised and came to identify herself as a woman. Linda chose to write about her mother. In an interview at the end of that semester, Linda told me that she was frustrated with the nursing department. "It's unorganized," she said. "They're not helping the pre-clinical students or the clinical students. They should be talking to the students and helping them, but they're not doing that." She said that the students had been having meetings about the lack of support and how low the passing rate was on the nursing boards. She even believed that some students were cheating in the science courses, paying other people to take their exams. She said that when such students got into the clinical courses, they were unable to do the work. With a passing rate of only about 33% on the state licensing boards, it becomes understandable why the program, a year later, restricted the admission of students who had not performed well in the pre-requisite courses. At the same time, Linda was enjoying writing in her courses including the psychology course on women's studies. She said, "Writing helps me understand things. I feel more free—it's a way of escaping."

At the class observation in the psychology of women course, the professor was somewhat defensive about the observer's presence. She asked the students whether they had any objection to her being there, and told them, "If you don't want her, take her out. Anyway, you can talk about her after she's left." The observer remained but, as in all other observations, did not participate in any way in the class discussion. The students sat in a circle. The professor asked the students to comment on a paper that had just been read by a student, and when no one volunteered an answer, she said, "Don't embarrass me in front of our guest." Eventually, the professor explained what she wanted the students to understand from the paper. This lack of participation by the students continued almost to the end of the class session when the professor introduced the topic of different languages being used by men and women. The students "became alive" and an active discussion ensued. Students took two quizzes plus a final examination in the course and were required to write three papers, including the interview, and give an oral report on their final paper.

In the interview paper on her mother, Linda set the tone of the paper with her introduction: "I want to take you down a path of a woman's life who is very special to me. Her name is ____, my mother, my friend." Linda's closeness to her mother has been cited earlier, but in this paper Linda revealed some of the dynamism in her mother that would not be apparent if one looked only at her age, her education, or her occupations. She described her mother's attitude toward schooling:

> [My mother] was never a person who liked school very much. Of course, she
> completed kindergarten to high school because her mother nearly kicked her butt

blind just to get through those years! Even though she was no scholar, she did, however, loved to read. The things she loved to read were Ebony, Jet, her childhood Ted & Sally books and her collection of Lil 'Abner, Superman and Archie comic books. [She] was also considered honorary induction into the Twilight Zone!!! The reason I say this is because she was one who hardly paid attention to any thing that was happening around her. She didn't like television very much, couldn't stand newspapers nor listening to the radio. Her mother dubbed her the damn idiot of the family.

Although this sounds like a severe indictment of her mother's abilities, Linda was quick to draw out what she perceived to be her mother's strengths. Her mother loved running and participated in track events, winning many plaques. Linda recounted that her mother and her friend "missed the Olympics by one-tenth of a second in the relay races." During track season, her mother became a counselor to track students, earning money for her "school clothes and other miscellaneous goods." Linda noted tellingly, "She was satisfied with the amount she earned." In light of Linda's own previous writings about nursing salaries and her growing sense of independence as a woman, it is noteworthy that she recognized that her mother had no awareness of the inequitable treatment of women when she was growing up.

Linda then described her mother's marriage. "Overall, it was a good marriage. [She] had her daughter [Linda] before her marriage and two years later her second child." When her husband joined the service and went overseas, Linda's mother "spent most of her time with women friends" and they spent their time at the bingo club at the base. Linda reported: "The happiest times in [her] life was traveling with husband. Her greatest achievement were her awards from track and her recognition for excellent work in daycare on the base." So, although Linda depicted her mother as doing nothing but playing bingo on the base, she apparently did spend time there taking care of young children and she was proud of being recognized for this service.

Linda skipped over many years of her mother's life in this report, telling nothing of her parents' eventual separation. She wrote that her mother "is satisfied with what she's done with her life" although she "admits that she wish that she could've done more." Her mother is especially happy "that her children are getting an higher education and didn't stray away, such as using drugs or getting impregnated early or becoming a high school dropout." Linda's mother is apparently pleased that her daughters will have greater opportunities than she had. Linda concluded her paper by saying that "My mother is my best friend and confidant. She's a true gem and a fabulous woman and I thank god every day for her being here (even though she doesn't know it!). It was a treat doing this report!"

In the interview I had with Linda, she told me that the assignment to interview the oldest woman in the family was to consider how she was raised, how she identified herself as a woman, and how her beliefs were instilled. Linda's narrative account did not include much analysis of her mother's experiences and her professor's comments at the end of the paper reflected this lack: "You have an interesting writing style—via report. This is your analysis of the sex role factors in your mother's life experiences?" The question obviously implies the failure to provide the required analysis. At this point in her academic career, Linda found the field of psychology hospitable to her energetic writing, even as she came to realize that it would have to take a more analytical turn to satisfy the demands of her instructors.

In the spring of 1994, now a declared psychology major, Linda enrolled in the most demanding course in the program for her, experimental psychology. She had managed to pass the statistics course with a "D," and she would now be required to use these formulas in her analysis of the experiments. Linda said that she had understood "statistics at the end, but I got a 'D' because of the difficulty of the final. I feel I understand it and can use it in Experimental Psychology this semester." In our interview about five weeks after the semester had begun, Linda told me that the course in experimental psychology was her most difficult one. She was learning that there were specific guidelines for writing up research and she had to follow them. Her professor was teaching the students the format, and he expected them to improve with each report. Students had to produce ten reports over the semester, and the grades on the highest four would be counted. An adjunct instructor, who assisted in the laboratory hours for the course, read the reports, graded them, and advised the students. Linda felt that her professor was "good and cool and laid back."

At the end of the semester, Linda described her approach to writing the experimental reports: "When you sit down, you actually think about what you did in the experiment, look over the notes, write the paper in one or more drafts. If confident, one draft. If not confident, more than one draft. I got 70's on the papers. I was weak in the results, sometimes in the introduction. Descriptions were easier, but calculations were harder—out of range by a few points. I may have made mistakes in the calculations. The math part has been the hardest, but I'll be able to handle it for the courses." Linda passed this course with a "C."

In the classroom observation, the professor's lecture covered several experimental procedures. He was careful to clarify terms, explain the way raw data should be used, and make students sensitive to ethical aspects of experimentation. Students responded actively to questions, raised questions, and took careful notes during the lecture. Evaluation in the course was based on the four highest scores on the ten laboratory reports and a final examination.

Linda's grades on the laboratory reports improved steadily over the semester, from a 35 on her first report to a 77 on the last one. The adjunct instructor made many specific suggestions and corrections on Linda's early reports, urging her to present her results more clearly. Linda also had problems including extraneous materials in her reports, and she was told to "only mention things that are necessary for replication." The instructor rewrote large sections of Linda's early reports, and on the second report she wrote, "Please see me. I have some constructive comments to give you." Receiving this help, Linda's reports began to improve and her grades increased first to 65 on the next two reports to 70 on the two following. Even though the reports were improving, Linda was still being advised that she needed to expand the discussion and results sections of her papers. For example, in a report on how the behavior of a rat was conditioned, extinguished, and reconditioned, Linda produced the following discussion section. Her instructor's comments are interpolated in brackets to represent where they appeared on her paper.

> The rat successfully learned how to be conditioned [explain how it responded], reconditioned, and extinction. It was quite surprising that the loud noise of the lever pressing didn't startle the rat too badly [why, expand]. The rat could have started off at a much faster pace [you do not know; only tell what was observed] but it kept grooming itself, sniffing its environment and lounging at the water bottle. Beside these distractions, the rat performed very well [why; explain].

As can be seen from the instructor's comments and suggestions, Linda still needed to be much more explicit in her descriptions and to provide an analytic frame to her discussion.

In a subsequent laboratory report on whether individuals were more likely to detect a feature (color in this case) that was present or absent, Linda was able to produce a more acceptable discussion section:

> The Feature Positive Experiment does work [appears to work as predicted]. In the first part of the experiment in which subjects had to detect the feature positive, the subjects were eventually able to identify the stimulus after a certain amount of trials. In the second part of the test, subjects didn't seem to be able to detect the (fn) [note: feature negative]. Why was it easier to detect something present than something missing?
>
> There are three possible reasons to this question. First, humans are programmed to know what's in our environment at that moment. Secondly, something added to the environment receives attention, and lastly, unless you are functionally involved with something, you may not know it's missing.

The instructor put two check marks after Linda's conclusion, indicating her satisfaction with the discussion section.

Linda's progress in this course, although certainly not exemplary, at least rose to a satisfactory level. Her writing became more precise and focused, and she demonstrated an ability to handle the quantitative aspects of the experiments. The clarity of her professor's explanations in the lectures with questions invited and responded to assisted her greatly as did the detailed suggestions of the adjunct instructor. Linda was clearly receiving the support and attention she needed to succeed in the field of psychology, the kind of support that she felt was lacking in the nursing program. In the discipline of psychology, she found herself able to work in areas close enough to her original goal of helping others to sustain her personal and professional commitments.

In earlier chapters, Ricardo's decision to change directions from communications to medicine was presented. Although he eventually completed the requirements for the communications degree, in his last two years, he delayed taking the final courses in that area to enroll in courses in mathematics, biology, chemistry, and health education. The different demands in these disciplines drew somewhat different responses from Ricardo, although unsurprisingly he retained the same sense of integrity and seriousness of purpose in every course he enrolled in. I have interview data, observations, and papers or reports from two communications classes and one health education class. I have interview data about the biology and chemistry classes, an observation report of the biology class, and a laboratory report from the chemistry class. I decided to combine these materials into a discussion of his classes in the physical sciences because the demands of both courses seem similar.

Ricardo enrolled in the ethics and values in communication course in the spring of 1992. Although papers from this course have been cited in previous chapters, I try to place them into the instructional context more fully here. Ricardo was immediately enthusiastic about this class. He told me that before the ethics class, he "never thought about these issues to this degree of self-examination." "I analyze complex issues by seeing more than one opinion," he said. "To get to a conclusion, I have to have all the information available. It's a very difficult class—a good challenge. I have to select and define a problem, write how the problem affects the final issue, break it apart, write down the details, what I think and others think, and how it affects people." The next fall, he told me that the most valuable thing he had learned in the previous semester was from the ethics class. "I learned how to analyze a situation from different points of view, from a broad range of views, how to focus to one decision taking the best from all positions. I also learned diplomacy."

The class observation began with the professor discussing a film she had seen. She asked the students to comment on what ethical rules had been violated. The students were very active in responding to her questions. Next two students gave a presentation about a case where a reporter had to decide whether to break his promise to keep an informant's name secret. After these two students gave their opinions, the class was invited to join the discussion. The professor helped the students to stay on the topic and to find a solution. The professor then began a lecture on ethics and rules a journalist should follow. When students asked her how she would resolve a dilemma, she turned the question back to them for further discussion. At the end of the class meeting, the students packed their books away and applauded the professor! Grades in the course were based on student attendance, participation, completion of reading and research assignments, group presentations, quizzes, three one-page papers, and a final paper.

In his final paper for the course, Ricardo considered the ethical position of NBC in relation to the privacy rights of Patricia Bowman who accused William Kennedy Smith of rape. Ricardo concluded that NBC's competitive position with other media did "not justify the outrageous intrusion on a victim's right to privacy. . . . It is not the network's right to further victimize a rape survivor by invoking their First Amendment Rights and their Freedom of the Press. . . . For the few victims that potentially would be willing to go through a biased legal system in search of justice, they are going to be thinking or will outright refuse to denounce such a violent crime for fear of being victimized for a second time. But this time the perpetrator will be the news media."

In her response to the paper, his instructor prodded Ricardo to delve more deeply into some of the issues he discussed, while praising his analysis of the situation:

> [Ricardo]: How did the media, NBC/the NYT [*New York Times*] justify themselves? What, aside from ratings was their journalistic stance. That the "other guy" did it (i.e. the tabloids) so we just follow through? or was there more? Also, are we creating a double standard. Should the names of the males involved in these cases be printed prior to a verdict? After all, a rape charge on a male has significant long term ramification on his name/privacy, even when found innocent. Overall: good paper, good sources, well written. Writing and analytical skills are improving. "A"

Ricardo flourished best in environments like this where he could develop a moral position he believed in and support it with evidence, knowing that he would receive supportive and helpful comments that could further hone his analytical skills and sharpen his sensitivity to fairness.

The next semester, Ricardo was enrolled in a broadcasting seminar cosponsored by the City University of New York and CBS-TV. The course was coordinated by a City College communications professor. The class met in an elegant conference room at CBS.

Broadcast law was the topic under discussion at the class that was observed. A guest lecturer from the network spoke on the issue, and the students were very critical of some of the points he raised. The following semester, Ricardo told me that he and other students had had a confrontation with the CBS lawyer at that class. When the students were critical of the lawyer's statements that the network included public service announcements that were required by the law, the speaker accused the students of being communists. Ricardo had learned over the years to use more tempered language in his academic writing, so his papers for the course were not directly confrontational. Short, 200-word papers were required every week. The papers were graded, but no comments were provided.

On a final take-home examination, Ricardo responded to a question about the individual he believed "played a significant important role in the development of CBS." He was to say "what that role was and why it was significant." Ricardo chose Edward R. Murrow to write about. After recounting the trust that Murrow achieved from his reporting during World War II, Ricardo went on to discuss the various documentary series Murrow developed. It is not surprising that Ricardo focused on Murrow's integrity:

> Ed Murrow was a person of high moral and ethical principles. Those principles drove him to do a piece on his show "See It Now" about a blacklisted Air Force Reserve. He was pressured to stop producing the show. He even confronted the dilemma of the U.S. Air Force declining to tell their side of the story. At the end he decided to do the show, because he felt that being silent was allowing one side to veto over broadcasting. Ed Murrow showed his courage by taking a stance and doing a show about Senator Joseph McCarthy and his Senate investigations. He felt that the Senator work was a cancer eating away the base of society. It was a great piece of journalistic investigation. In conclusion he was the person that helped make CBS News the best news organization of its time. He was a true believer of the need for the broadcasting industry to become a tool for the education and enlightening of society, to a point of taking on his own network. Ed Murrow brought credibility, honesty and respect not only to the new medium but to CBS as well.

It is an easy leap of the imagination to believe that Ricardo would have modeled his behavior after Murrow's if he had chosen to stay in the field of communications.

From his experiences in these two communications classes, Ricardo demonstrated clearly how his sensitivity to ethical issues had been stimulated. His decision to change direction and prepare himself to enter a physician assistant program can be seen as both idealistic and pragmatic. He had had an early interest in becoming a physician, but his limited educational background in Puerto Rico denied him the opportunity to prepare himself academically for that profession. In addition, his lack of adequate financial resources toward the end of his undergraduate years made it impossible for him to consider assuming the debt that would be required to enroll in medical school. He also had had a specific experience that had influenced his decision to enter the medical field. He told me that he had cut a finger off, but through plastic surgery, the finger had been reattached. That "made me decide to go into the medical field." he said. "I wanted to do something where I could make a contribution." His idealism to serve his community remained, and the development of physician assistant programs allowed him to reignite his childhood dream of participating in the field of medicine. When he realized that "there was a bad market in film and photography," he decided to prepare himself academically for the field to which he had initially aspired.

In the fall of 1992, the beginning of his fourth year at the college, Ricardo enrolled in and then withdrew from courses in mathematics and biology. He told me at the end of that semester that he had decided to drop these classes "instead of just getting through" because he wanted to do well and keep his average high. His heavy work load that semester denied him the necessary hours for academic preparation. He said, "I got older. I am learning to be patient."

The following semester, Ricardo enrolled in a chemistry course and a mathematics course as part of his academic schedule. He told me that he started out "weak" in the math course, but later did well, earning an "A." He had similar problems with the chemistry course, receiving an "F" at midterm, but then passing the course with a "C." During that semester, he was working full time 3 days a week and part time 1 day a week.

In the fall of 1993, Ricardo enrolled in a biology class, an organic chemistry class, and a mathematics class. He earned an "A" in both biology and chemistry, and he dropped the mathematics class. He said that the requirements of the science courses had been very "rigorous and demanding." After he received low grades on the first exams in these courses, he decided to drop the math course. After that, his "grades went way up in the other courses." He joined study groups in both science classes, and he felt that they helped him greatly. Ricardo said that he was keeping notes from his science classes that explain medical terms in laymen terms. By the end of that semester he had had an interview with the physician assistant program to which he was later admitted.

There were more than 100 students in the biology lecture class that was observed that semester. During the lecture, the professor frequently wrote on the blackboard to illustrate the cell structure he was speaking about. He drew examples from real life and asked questions, but because of the speed of the lecture, students did not respond and the professor had to answer his own questions. As the class proceeded, the professor slowed down the rate of the lecture and students were better able to respond to his questions. Students took notes throughout the class session. Students had a lab with this class as they did with the chemistry class. Ricardo told me that he liked the subject of biology and that it was "one of his strongest fields." He said that his chemistry professor explained things "over and over again," but that he did not speak clearly, making it difficult for Ricardo to understand. To compensate for that, Ricardo studied from his textbook and did the homework carefully. He said that in both the biology and chemistry classes he did reviews of everything. He took a different notebook to each class, putting all information in each notebook "in an organized manner." He would "write–listen–analyze–write–and then read and try to make sense of what [he] had written." "I do this," he said, "even if I don't have to write papers." His advanced level of study skills made it possible for him to perform strongly in these areas.

The lab report from the chemistry course is a technical description of several experiments in which three theories are presented along with the properties of the chemicals that will be used. The three experiments are detailed with careful attention to the procedures to be followed. The results are not given in the copy of the report I have, perhaps the first pages that Ricardo prepared. What is clear from the data I do have is the careful specificity of the procedures that were required to be followed.

Although Ricardo initially had difficulty with these science courses, he demonstrated that he could adjust to the demands being made on him so that he could achieve the level of performance he valued. He concentrated all his attention and drew on all the skills he had acquired over the previous three years to succeed at a level that would make him a strong candidate for the program he wanted to enter. Motivation, talent, and endurance combined to make him successful.

In the spring of 1994, Ricardo enrolled in a health education course titled "Health Concerns for Teachers and Health Professionals." At the beginning of the semester, Ricardo told me that this was his easiest course so far in the semester. He said, "It's an interactive class between the students and the teacher, discussing issues like the use of drugs in the community." He also told me, "The professor is good." Although the class that was observed was basically in a lecture format, on the topic of drugs and tranquilizers, students frequently asked questions and were active in providing examples from personal knowledge of use of tranquilizers. The students were comfortable and relaxed in this environment. They took notes throughout the class period. Students were required to keep a class journal, prepare a group visitation report on a visit to a rehabilitation center, and prepare a term project paper.

Ricardo started out his journal by commenting on the effectiveness of the professor having the students get together in small groups so that they could start to know each other better. "It's a good beginning for this class," he wrote. The journal format was to divide the page in half. On the left side, students were to complete one of the following sentences: "I have learned that; I never knew that; I realize that; I know that; I have discovered that." On the right side of the page, they were to "indicate that which touched your personal value system, what touched you personally. Indicate how it affected you and how you felt as a result." The instructor noted on the syllabus that "the content of the entries will be not be evaluated; however, the thoughtfulness will be evaluated. A careful and thoughtful journal will raise the final grade 5 points."

A set of journal entries for two consecutive days gives a sense of the flavor of Ricardo's journal:

> Statement: Today we started discussion of child abuse. I know the definition of child abuse since I had dealt with it before. We discussed how it got manifested and how to look deeper for those signs. I realize how much an education is needed to open people's eyes and ears in order to help our children.

Comment: I didn't know that this class will be the equivalent of the 2 hour training on drug and alcohol and child abuse training. I know first hand what child abuse is like. I hope that becoming aware and educated about it, I can help others and minimize harm and suffering to a young child.

* * *

Statement: Today we continued the discussion on child abuse. I wasn't aware of the statistic of 1 of every 5 females may be abuse sexually in their life. That is a difficult issue to deal with. Child abuse accusations are very serious business, not only for the accuser but also for the defendant. Is interesting that emotional abuse not only takes place with children. Many adults reflect that same behavior that they suffered during childhood. We see people mistreating others emotionally. I just wonder, "were they abused as children?"

Comment: I believe that any child that raises such accusation must be listen to. For many adults is easier to look the other way and not become involve. I just hope that many more people could get active in the education and prevention of this crime. Child abuse is a cycle that must be broken. It will repeat itself throughout generations if it's not broken. We must try actively to break it.

Through the readings, lectures, and discussions, as well as his own life experiences, Ricardo is able to bring a mature perspective to serious societal problems and reinforce his commitment to help others.

The final paper for the Health Concerns course consisted of a series of terms that were to be defined. Prepared out-of-class, Ricardo's definition of AIDS can be seen as particularly poignant, because he had told me in an interview that his brother-in-law, who had contracted AIDS through an unprotected heterosexual experience, was living with him and his wife. A sample of Ricardo's definitions include:

AIDS: The result of the infection by the HIV virus to the body. HIV debilitates the immune system, specifically the T cells, this gives opportunistic diseases an opening to attack the body. At the beginning AIDS was affecting mostly gay men and drug addicts, but it is now becoming a serious threat to the heterosexual population. A person can become infected by unprotected sex, sharing needles and blood transfusion (blood not screened for virus).

Emotional maltreatment: Defined as emotional neglect on children less than 18 yrs. of age and whose parents, legal guardians or caretakers creates a state of substantially diminished psychological or intellectual functioning. It includes a failure to thrive and development of self-destructive behavior. Lack of proper clothes, food and education also create emotional neglect.

Notable for their academic tone, Ricardo illustrates in these responses the growth in his ability to assimilate information, analyze it, and present it effectively to an audience. His professor gave him a 95 on the final paper and wrote: "Excellent—Thank you for being an important member of the class." There is little doubt that in this supportive environment, Ricardo was an active participant in the class discussions.

Two important things were happening to Ricardo as he fulfilled the science requirements for eligibility to apply to a physician assistant program. He was learning basic information in the core sciences and he was exposed to a fuller intellectual perspective on the medical and social implications of the conditions he might encounter in treating patients in the future. He already had the social conscience to make him responsive to the needs of those he would be able to help; now he was beginning to acquire the knowledge that would make him a competent professional.

As Ricardo moved from his communications major to his commitment to the physician assistant program, he carried with him the ethical values that had been reinforced over his college years. Every experience Ricardo has had has enriched his desire and his ability to help others.

Linda and Ricardo moved in different directions when they changed their majors, but neither significantly changed their orientation to their life goals—helping others. Linda's experience in the nursing program had not been a positive one; she had not received the encouragement, assistance or personal support that she needed to make it possible for her to succeed in that field. By choosing psychology as a major, she moved into an environment that was more productive for her and still allowed her to retain her personal objectives. Although Ricardo's move to a new field was a more radical change, he retained his strengthened value system and redirected it to a field where he would be able to see more tangible evidence of his efforts. He had felt supported in both disciplines, and practicality combined with idealism to move him in the new direction.

CONCLUSION

With these complementary perspectives of student perceptions, instructor perceptions and comments on student papers, classroom observations, course syllabi and examinations, and student papers, the complexity of assessing the role of instructional settings becomes evident. To what extent are student–instructor relationships central to a hospitable learning environment? What is the role of types of tasks chosen by instructors both for writing assignments and examination evaluations? How supportive is the instructional setting itself? To what extent can students be made to feel that they are genuinely contributing to the learning environment and how important is that? These questions cannot be definitively answered, even in a longitudinal study of this type. However, insights from these multiple perspectives into learning environments can lead instructors to construct a combination of factors that will facilitate learning for their students, engage their curiosity, and spur them on to the desire to make contributions to the discipline itself.

The degree of empathy and support between an instructor and an individual student can play a crucial role in the student's ability to succeed in a discipline or even to be motivated to continue in that discipline. Linda's experiences are the most dramatic example of a student being discouraged about a field that she had had her heart set on for as long as she could remember. Although it is true that her academic performance in the prerequisites for the nursing program was not strong, she had been sufficiently motivated to retake courses to improve her performance. The absence of a viable support system in the nursing program made her reconsider her occupational goals. Although she was able to remain in a "helping profession" by switching to the more supportive environment in the psychology department, there is no doubt that she was deeply disappointed by her failure to be able to pursue her initial dream. Encouragement was also essential to Joan, who found support within her psychology classes even as she struggled to fulfill the demands in the field. Carl's apparent arrogance and disdain for the qualifications of his fellow students were tempered by the demands in his communications courses to always provide sources and evidence in such courses as mass media. The more rigorous the demands, the greater was Carl's respect for his instructor. Ricardo thrived in classes like the ethics course in which he learned how to better justify the socially conscious positions he so deeply felt. He had learned over his years at the college how to take good notes, analyze materials, reread, and rethink important ideas and concepts. These skills stood him in good stead as he encountered the lecture classes in the physical sciences, since he recognized that he did not immediately need to fully understand the material presented.

As these examples reflect, over the years, students came to understand that supportive teaching facilitated learning. They also learned to compensate for difficulties that arose by using the coping strategies they had developed. Most courses in the college evaluated students through a combination of quizzes, examinations, and papers. Quizzes and examinations were almost always of the short-answer type consisting of multiple-choice questions, definitions, and matching terms. Occasionally, questions required very short sentence responses. Papers in upper level courses prodded students to analyze materials and to link examples with theories. Many professors supplied very explicit guidelines for the papers as typified by the requirements in Joan's abnormal psychology class. There was a demand for justification for positions taken on issues, with students required increasingly to provide documentation and evidence to support their views. Narratives were increasingly discouraged unless they were accompanied by analytical discussions. Although most of the examples cited in this chapter focus on objectivity in writing, other pieces of student writing gathered in this study—as for instance those presented in chapter 3 that reflect student views on issues such as racism, ethnicity, gender, and ideology—demonstrate that students did not lose their social consciousness or their world views over the years, but they learned ways to strengthen their presentations. Instructional settings that promoted analysis and synthesis allowed them to become stronger advocates for issues that were important to them.

The physical conditions of classrooms at the City College were generally dispiriting and frequently interfered with students' ability to process information comfortably. Most of the classrooms in the largest building on campus, the North Academic Center, had no windows and were often too warm or too cold. Some classrooms were oddly shaped, with the poor acoustics interfering with the ability to hear either lectures or discussions. Other buildings on the campus were not quite so inhospitable, with a range of newer and older, frequently remodeled, classrooms and lecture halls providing at least minimally acceptable learning environments.

Student contributions to classroom discussions were almost always highly valued. As students gained more expertise in their major discipline areas, greater demands were made on them to integrate earlier learned knowledge with the new topics under consideration. The students were also expected to produce writing that was cogent, soundly argued with good evidence and analysis, and in correct grammatical form. The writing of papers provided students with the opportunity to demonstrate what they had learned and how they could apply newly learned insights to issues in their fields.

In all, the instructional settings at the college provided support and encouragement for students, especially as they became more proficient in their major areas. No longer anonymous, they began to develop professional relationships with their instructors who frequently served as strong role models and mentors for them.

7

Case Studies

In presenting case studies of four students in this chapter, it becomes necessary to include material that has been cited in previous chapters. The attempt here is to examine the students' entire experiences chronologically, bringing together interview data, student writing, instructional experiences, and testing requirements to construct a full picture of the students' development over their college years. It should be clearly understood that these will be academic portraits, fleshed out by life experiences that have been shared with me over the years, but there is no attempt to produce a personal biography nor a psychological analysis. Students were asked questions that related to their academic performance as well as about factors in their lives that affected that performance. The extent to which they wished to share personal experiences was left entirely up to them; no prodding or follow-up questions were asked that would have made the students uncomfortable. Even within such restrictions, students were remarkably candid at times about their life histories and experiences, even when these experiences were painful. A recurrent question in my interviews over the years was, "What seems to be the most significant thing that happened to you this semester (or this year)?" Students sometimes asked me whether I meant their personal lives or their schooling, and I always answered, "Whatever you think was significant." This question frequently triggered the recounting of life experiences they felt comfortable sharing.

Research in the narrative study of lives provides helpful insights for examining the information students shared with me. Rosenthal (1993) pointed out that "each interview is a product of the mutual interaction between speaker and listener. Narrators do not simply reproduce prefabricated stories regardless of the interactional situation, but rather create their own stories within the social process of mutual orientation according to their definition of the interview situation" (p. 64). Thus, the kinds of questions I asked the students focused their attention on the interests I had selected as the major areas for consideration. Rosenthal went on to note that analysis of the responses must take "into account such aspects as the range of possibilities open to the subject in a certain situation, the selection made, the possibilities ignored, and the consequences of the decisions" (p. 66). Over time, however, it is possible to see how information shared at a later date can affect decisions that were made at an earlier time. In studies of biographical interviews, Rosenthal differentiated between what she called *narrations,* the transmission of former experiences, and *argumentation,* the representation of the perspective of the present. Thus, student accounts of experiences, present and past, can be seen as a recording of the experiences themselves, while evaluative accounts of earlier experiences from a present perspective constitute analyses. In the case study presentations that follow in this chapter, I briefly summarize the background history of the students, then present a chronological ordering of their experiences, with their reflections as they arose over the time of the study.

Another researcher of narrative life stories, Widdershoven (1993) believed that an individual's personal identity "is the result of a hermeneutic relation between experience and story, in which experience elicits the story, and the story articulates and thereby modifies experience" (p. 9). The telling of stories becomes an interpretive act:

> From a hermeneutic point of view, stories are based on life, and life is expressed, articulated, manifested and modified in stories. Stories make explicit the meaning that is implicit in life as it is lived. In stories we aim to make clear and intelligible what life is about. Thus stories are interpretations of life in which the meaning of life is spelled out, in very much the same way as the meaning of a text is spelled out in a literary interpretation. In telling stories we try to make sense of life, like we try to make sense of a text when we interpret it. (p. 9)

The life stories shared by the students in this study thus consist of their interpretations of their life experiences. These interpretations may be presented to excuse or justify certain actions or to account for decisions that affected their academic or personal lives. To reiterate, although this study does not attempt to reconstruct all the salient factors in students' lives, whatever experiences were shared contribute to fuller insights into the reasons why students made certain choices or performed in certain ways under particular academic situations.

Reinharz (1984) proposed another way of describing the relationship between researchers and their informants. Reinharz coined the phrase *temporary affiliation* to describe her group's modification of the participant–observation method. "This term, Reinharz thinks, better captures the 'human mutuality' that should characterize the relationship between researchers and their informants. The researchers act as 'short-term partners' who give the informants a chance to be heard and provide feedback to them. For a brief period, researcher and subject meet on common turf, each truly 'being with the other'" (Belenky et al., 1986, p. 225). Although Reinharz characterized the term *temporary affiliation* as applying to short-term relationships, I believe that it applies equally well to the extended relationship I had with my students as I believe we sustained a "being with the other" connection over the 6 years of the study. Otherwise, it is difficult to explain why individual students chose to continue sharing their experiences with me for such a long time. Nevertheless, even the extended time frame of this study must be seen as a temporary affiliation. (For some students, however, the relationship extended beyond the completion of the study, with Linda, for example writing to me in the fall of 1995 asking me to send a letter of recommendation for her for her application to graduate school, and Ricardo writing to me in November 1996 to tell me that he had completed the physician assistant program successfully.)

EXAMPLES OF PREVIOUS CASE STUDY RESEARCH

Other researchers have incorporated background knowledge of students' lives in their analysis of their academic work. In their case study of Tanya, a 19-year-old community college student, Hull and Rose (1989) examined in detail her response to a summary writing task based on a reading titled, "Handling the Difficult Patient." Although "Tanya's summary is the kind of writing that feeds everyone's worries about the consequences of illiteracy and the failure of our schools" (p. 147), after interviews with her, the researchers identified two intentions in the student's writing: She wanted to display and convey knowledge, and wanted her teachers to know that she was not the kind of student who would copy (i.e., plagiarize). They also came to recognize that the most important factor in the construction of Tanya's summary was her decision "to choose details, not because they were important to the original text, but because they were important to her, and their placement, therefore, had more of a personal than a textual relevance" (p. 149). Hull and Rose accounted for this phenomenon, also found in other samples of Tanya's writing, to an "assertion of her own self-worth in relation to a life and school history that left her feeling that she was not worth very much" (p. 150). Because they knew details of Tanya's personal life (being kicked out of five schools, being on the outs with her mother and an overbearing stepfather, living on her own in a drug-infested apartment complex, and being pulled by a legion of boyfriends), Hull and Rose were prepared to interpret Tanya's response to the summary writing task as one that allowed her to "hold on for dear life to the idea that she can be a nurse, and that she can succeed" (p. 150). Rather than using these factors to explain away the problems in Tanya's writings, because they understood the source of some of her difficulties, Hull and Rose were able to recommend pedagogical strategies that they believed would foster writing development for Tanya, for example, to temporarily suspend concern about error and pursue "her impulse to don the written language of another" (p. 151) and to build over time ability to handle certain sentence and discourse patterns. This brief discussion of the case study of Tanya just starts to hint at the richness of analysis possible when full contextual factors of individual's lives are factored into analysis of writing strategies and products.

Chiseri-Strater (1991) followed two case study students at the University of New Hampshire through a common upper level prose writing course and separate art history and political science courses. Wanting to see the students' academic experiences from a fuller, more contextualized perspective, Chiseri-Strater tried to establish a broader bond with them. Describing her relationship with Anna, the art history major, she notes: "With me, she shares her academic life, many parts of her personal life, understands my project, and cooperates in handing over any scraps of literacy information that might make my task easier—from an exam paper to an art poster she's helped with. There are no stated boundaries, no unmentionable territories, in my exploration of her thinking" (p. 34). Although I applaud this effort to place Anna's academic responses within her fuller life structure, I do believe it is somewhat naive to believe that there are "no unmentionable territories" in the relationship between a student and a researcher. The students in my study have frequently shared intimate experiences in their lives, but there have also been times when they acknowledged that there were personal matters of some importance to them that they were reluctant to share. Such privacy, of course, is entitled to full respect.

Anna finds the art history course environment initially more restrictive than the prose writing course had been. Without collaborative support or opportunities to revise, she is dissatisfied with her writing on the midterm exam, sensing "the tension in her academic life between fields that require distance, detachment, and objectivity [represented by her art history courses] and those that welcome intimacy, engagement, and subjectivity" [represented by her prose writing course]" (p. 56). In their reexamination of Perry's (1968) and Gilligan's (1982) studies, Belenky et al. (1986) developed coding categories "designed to capture the ways in which women construe their experience of themselves as developing beings and experience their learning environments" (p. 16). One of their categories contrasted the experiences of collaborative and solitary learning. They wondered whether learning was being treated as cooperative or competitive (p. 17). Anna had flourished in the collaborative environment but had much more difficulty adjusting to the solitary setting. Only with the final project paper in the art history course, where she could incorporate some of her personal value structure, did Anna begin to demonstrate some of the strengths in her writing that had developed in the prose writing class. This analysis suggests that it is not using personal experience that leads to more reflective thought but rather the opportunity to incorporate ideas and perspectives that have been significant in the individual's life.

Ackerman (1993) provided a different analysis of why students like Anna may have had problems in her art history class that she did not have in the prose writing course. He suggested that classes that offer opportunities for expressive writing, ungraded writing assignments, group work, and peer-response techniques may contrast too sharply with instruction in logic, conventions, and evidence associated with discipline-specific genres. But, as was demonstrated in earlier chapters of this book, bringing personal experiences and world views to bear on the analysis of concepts in a range of disciplines has the potential to add to or change the perspective through which "accepted knowledge" is different fields is treated.

CASE STUDY INFORMATION RELATED TO WOMEN'S WAYS OF KNOWING

In terms of the ways that women and men resolve serious moral dilemmas, Belenky et al. (1986) contended that men "evoke the metaphor of 'blind justice' and rely on abstract laws and universal principles to adjudicate disputes and conflicts between conflicting claims impersonally, impartially and fairly (p. 8). In contrast, women operate within a morality of responsibility and care and

> argue for an understanding of the context for moral choice, claiming that the needs of individuals cannot always be deduced from general rules and principles and that moral choice must also be determined inductively from the particular experiences each participant brings to the situation. They point out that dialogue and exchange of views allow each individual to be understood in his or her own terms. They believe that mutual understanding is most likely to lead to a creative consensus about how everyone's needs may be met in resolving disputes. (p. 8)

Belenky et al. (1986) grouped women's perspectives on knowing into five major epistemological categories:

> *silence*, a position in which women experience themselves as mindless and voiceless and subject to the whim of external authority [These women have little awareness of their intellectual capacity];
> *received knowledge*, a perspective from which women conceive of themselves as capable of receiving, even reproducing, knowledge from the all-knowing external authorities but not capable of creating knowledge on their own [other voices and external truths prevail];
> *subjective knowledge*, a perspective from which truth and knowledge are conceived of as personal, private, and subjectively known or intuited [but without a public voice or public authority];
> *procedural knowledge*, a position in which women are invested in learning and applying objective procedures for obtaining and communicating knowledge [but still adhering to sex-role stereotypes or second-rung status as a woman with a man's mind, but a woman nevertheless]; and
> *constructed knowledge*, a position in which women view all knowledge as contextual, experience themselves as creators of knowledge, and value both subjective and objective strategies for knowing [showing a high tolerance for internal contradiction

and ambiguity, abandoning completely the either/or thinking so common in the other positions. (pp. 15, 134–137)

At the stage of procedural knowledge, Belenky et al. (1986) drew a distinction between separate and connected knowing. With an orientation toward impersonal rules, the separate knower asks questions like "What standards are being used to evaluate my analysis of this poem? What techniques can I use to analyze it?" (p. 101). With an orientation toward relationships, the connected knower asks, "What is this poet saying to me?" (p. 101). Connected knowers shift from the facts of other people's lives to their ways of thinking, still focusing though on the form rather than the content of knowledge. Separate knowers use formal instruction to adopt a different way of looking, learning how to view a discipline in the way its practitioners do. "Both learn to get out from behind their own eyes and use a different lens, in one case the lens of a discipline, and in the other the lens of another person" (p. 115).

Of the four students whose experiences are being described in this chapter, the three who started in basic writing courses, Linda, Ricardo, and Joan, demonstrated the importance of having set their own standards and their own goals for themselves. The student whose success would more certainly have been predicted by his previous life experiences, Jacob, was the least satisfied of the group. He had given ownership of his life to his family, particularly his mother, who placed no value on his writing talents and prodded him into career areas that he publicly disdained.

ACADEMIC AND SOCIAL PREPARATION
FOR COLLEGE WORK

Not surprisingly, the students placed into the English 1 and English 2 classes had been less prepared academically than the student described here who placed directly into the freshman composition course. The three students placed into the basic writing courses had varying levels of difficulty with reading, writing, and mathematics. The two African-American women were native speakers of English and the Latino male student was a native speaker of Spanish. The Korean student had been urged by his mother to speak only English when the family emigrated to Australia and, as a result, to his regret now, he is unable to speak Korean.

What can be gleaned from this review of the experiences of under-prepared students who enter a large urban university? First, they all became quickly aware of the limitations their previous education placed on them. Ricardo even wrote in a paper in his English 2 class that "I strongly feel that I needed to start in a more basic English class." Although the readers of his placement paper probably recognized his intellectual ability in placing him in the second level of basic writing, Ricardo felt anxious about his "grammatical problems." Linda had admired her junior high school teacher who challenged her, but she disdained the time spent in creative writing in high school which was not rigorous enough for her. Joan believed that she had been adequately prepared for her college writing demands until she faced the reality of her assignments. And even Jacob, who excelled in his early years of the college, came to recognize that hard work would be required to successfully meet the demands of his upper level courses. It is very telling that when he received a "B" in an architecture-related course, his response was to change majors. Without immediate recognition of his "brilliance," he found it difficult to accept any evaluation but the highest.

It is also important to consider why three of these four students changed majors during their college years, thus prolonging the amount of time it would take for them to complete their studies. Linda, who was described in an earlier article (Sternglass, 1993), had been deeply committed to her nursing major, but her poor background in mathematics made her required chemistry courses extremely difficult for her. As her grade point average in mathematics and science courses weakened, and she was no longer guaranteed entree into the nursing program, her disillusionment with the program and the faculty bubbled over. In switching to psychology as a major, she saw herself continuing in a "helping profession." As a nursing major she had been denied the opportunity to take courses in nursing itself until she fulfilled the core and basic science requirements of the college. Thus delay in participating in her major also contributed to her disillusionment. In the psychology program, after taking only a few core courses, she was permitted to enroll in any of the other psychology courses she was interested in. This opportunity, combined with the reinforcing support of the psychology faculty, was of critical importance to her. Ricardo, who had studied photography in the vocational school his father sent him to, enrolled in a communications program because he had some background in this field and he felt it would be compatible with bringing about political change. But a declining job market caused him to reassert a permutation of his earliest dream, to be involved in the medical profession. And Jacob, who cared not what his major would be since it could not be creative writing, shifted from architecture to social science (which he quickly left because he told me he did not like to work so much with people) to physics, an abstract field not requiring much human contact. Adding these changes to the time that it took students to complete their remedial studies meant a college period of from five to six years. In addition, three of the students, Ricardo, Linda and Joan, worked at outside jobs and the latter two also had time-consuming internships. These students did not experience the stereotypical four-year, fun-filled lives that college students are often pictured as having.

CASE STUDIES OF HOW THE WRITING
PROCESS CHANGES OVER TIME

Among the many advantages that longitudinal research has over shorter-term projects is that it can provide the data that allows analysis of change over time. In the fall of 1993, I collected a writing history from the students in my study, adapting a questionnaire developed by Cleary (1991). Their responses give insight into Hull and Rose's question: "What happens when the student sits down to write" (p. 144)? Using this picture of the student's behavior in the fifth year of the study, it becomes possible to go back to earlier descriptions the students have provided to examine the changes that have taken place.

Linda

Linda, an African-American student originally placed in English 1, received her elementary and middle school education on an airforce base in Germany and her high school education in New York City at a school that sent approximately 30% of its students on to college. Her parents separated when she was 12, and she has lived with her mother and sister since that time. An aunt and cousin, who were "mean drunks," were frequent visitors to her home where they left the family "in disarray." Linda was a dedicated nursing major until her fourth year in the college when she became disenchanted with the program and the faculty. Her difficulties with math courses and chemistry left her uncertain of her official acceptance into the program. Feeling that the faculty had not taken any interest in her or attempted to provide her with support, she changed her major to psychology, in which she felt welcomed and was provided with assistance.

Linda had difficulty both with writing and math. In giving me a writing profile in the fall of 1993, she told me that her high school should have helped her to become a better writer before she entered college. In junior high school she had had a very strict teacher who required that all papers follow a specific format: introduction, body, conclusion. Although other students considered this teacher "cruel," Linda respected her for her toughness. "The teacher was serious about writing and she was doing it for us, not just for herself," she said. This teacher had high standards for the students and Linda appreciated this. But in high school, although she loved creative writing assignments, she felt that the teachers did not care about the students.

By the end of her first semester, Linda said that the most important thing that had happened to her was the she was learning to be an independent thinker. She told me she realized she would need to have good skills in writing and to speak efficiently. She added, "I'm aware that I have to learn more about improving my critical thinking skills. First of all, the semesters go by very fast. It was very confusing; then it became easier to adjust to this campus. Some of the classes were very stimulating and caught my attention. I say it was a very good experience." She had passed all her classes and had earned a "B" in the first remedial math course as well as in English 1.

In her writing in the English 1 course, I encouraged her to provide more specific information and, in an assigned comparison paper, to provide a comparison between her own experience and the one she had been reading about. In her paper, she wrote: "Parents nag kids to let them know they care and love you. My mother nags me because she claims I have a lot to learn. She wants me to notice her, by her constantly nagging, she's letting me know 'look kid, I [am] here and don't you forget it either.'" In addition to comments on the sentence-structure problems, I wrote in the margin: "You need to explain this more fully and provide a specific example. You also need to compare it with Bellitto's experience [the college student they had been reading about].

In her second semester, Linda said that "reading helps me understand what to do, in developing ideas about what to write. It gives me a lot of energy. I could go on writing for a long time because I like to do it." She told me that in high school her teachers had not pushed her. They had read her papers, but they had not provided much instruction. The math teacher had paid more attention to gifted students and did not help those who needed assistance. Linda noted that "writing helps teachers discover more about a person—how mature the student is and what the student is learning." She was beginning to come up with new ideas in her papers and her teachers "liked that." Like other students who started in basic level courses, Linda preferred courses in which she could write papers to those that evaluated students on the basis of short answer or multiple choice tests. Linda had come to the point in her learning when she recognized that writing provided her with opportunities to come to more complex understandings and to display those understandings to her professors. Short answer exams, often tricky in nature, did not provide her with the right set of circumstances to reflect on ideas.

In her English 2 class which she completed with a "B," she wrote occasional practice exams for the Writing Assessment Test she would have to take at the end of the semester. On one such practice exam on the topic of whether there should be random drug testing in the workplace, as part of her response, Linda wrote:

A majority of people are against this type of testing. They think it is a violation of their rights and privacy. This should not be a problem. The testing should be done confidentially and with respect for the individual. There should be an open discussion between employer and employees on the importance and safety reasons for drug testing. People who use drugs on the job, should be aware not only are they putting themselves in danger and their job on the line. They are also jeopardizing other people lives who trusts them and uses their services.

Her instructor commented on the punctuation and other grammatical problems, but she also advised Linda to provide an example before she ended her paper. She commented that the paper was "a pretty good start," and that she needed to "notice the subject–verb errors and possessive forms."

In the actual test-writing, Linda chose a topic in which she was to agree or disagree with the proposition that too much money was being spent on the space program. Her introduction gives the flavor of her response: "Today, there is an excessive amount of money being spent on space programs. It should be spent on more important issues such as the educational system and the health care system. This, therefore, is why we need to stop wasting money on outer space." As this introduction reveals, Linda has learned the "format" of introduction, two or three paragraphs of development, and conclusion that will lead her to successful completion of the writing test. Furthermore, she is careful throughout the paper to edit for subject–verb agreement. Not surprisingly, her paper easily passes.

That same semester, Linda felt uncertain about what her psychology professor wanted in the assigned papers. Linda was told that she didn't quite use concepts the way the instructor wanted. She said that she understood "better what to do next." She was taking an introductory psychology course that was offered as a "bridge" section, available to students in basic skills classes. In a paper applying psychological concepts to the case of a female medical student who was turned away after seeking to assist in surgery, Linda wrote as part of her analysis: "In the *Reference Group,* Dr. Harmon turned to his collegues for ideas and projects. Dr. Harmon uses them because they are prominent powerful figures who he can depend on to help him solve problems that are associated with the job. Reference groups are people who we have close contacts with on a daily basis." The instructor's comment on this section of the paper read: "Link to prejudice and this incident." In commenting on the paper overall, he wrote: "Nice job. Your story was quite crisply told. You grasp of the concepts is okay, but could be firmer. Ask questions. 13 of 15." Through this evaluation, Linda was both encouraged and challenged. She received a "B" in the course. On Belenky et al.'s (1986) category system, Linda was at the stage of received knowledge, reproducing information but not yet linking it to the issue under consideration, as her professor's comment urged her to do.

At the end of the semester, Linda told me that "the most significant thing that happened to me during the past year was getting out of remedial courses and now taking harder courses like psychology. I find them more challenging." She also said, "I need to clear my mind and get serious—think about what the teacher wants." In her writing, she said, she was going back to revise, especially introductions and endings. "I write a draft, see something that doesn't sound right, have to change the phrasing to make it clear." She said she preferred writing to talking for that reason. At the end of that semester, she recognized that she had not had opinions before, but now she was taking positions on issues and she liked that. Although Linda was successful in the humanities and social sciences courses she took that semester, she failed the second level of remedial math.

On a personal level, the biggest change that had occurred in her life that year was that she was receiving "more attention from guys than before. I'm not dating anyone," she said. "School work comes first. I went to an all-girl's high school and I didn't date then."

As her comments on her first year's experiences reveal, Linda began to see the usefulness of writing as a tool in pursuing the more rigorous demands of college work. She had always enjoyed writing, but now her responses to assignments had to be both more substantive and more formally correct. She had not yet developed an analytic perspective.

At the beginning of her second year at the college, the fall of 1990, Linda reiterated her recognition of the important role writing played in her academic progress: "The most important thing I learned in my courses last year was that writing makes or breaks you. I learned to take time. I enjoy writing. I like to free write so I don't have to pay attention to grammar, can edit later. I'm doing freewriting in my English composition course now." She added that in the psychology course she was taking that semester, she had finished a paper. She said, "The more I wrote, the more I understood what I was writing about. I could tell what I felt about the reading and what I knew and understood. Writing makes it flow more easily."

In courses like chemistry where she had to memorize many details or courses like world humanities where she had to read complex books, the work did not come easily to her. As her courses became more difficult, she began to seek out tutoring, especially for the chemistry course. The fall semester of her second year had been especially difficult for Linda: She was depressed over the death of a favorite cousin who had died on Linda's birthday. This event had interfered with her work for a time, but by the end of the semester she said she was able to concentrate better. Linda had separated herself from the "people she used to hang out with." She said she didn't bother with them now "because they want to marry or take low-paying jobs." She lived in an ethnically mixed community in Brooklyn—West Indians, Hispanics, Jews, Blacks—and she had good relationships with these people, but her former friends thought that she "acts like [she is] stuck up." The "boys" in the building gave her problems because she did not want to date them, but at the same time, they didn't harass her because they said she was "dull." Linda took this as a compliment. She had only made one close friend at the college.

In the English composition course, Linda wrote a paper about her vocation, nursing. She first described how she used to visit the military hospital in Germany where her father worked when she was a young child, and then she recounted her experiences in high school in New York where she took prenursing classes, receiving a nursing scholarship when she graduated. In the conclusion to her paper, Linda emphasized her dedication to a nursing career:

> My vocation may not let me have the opportunity to off the latest fashion or go primping around in heels in big offices. It's not glamorous nor does it have an extensive list of clienteles. My vocation is an unsung hero. Meaning, it never received the recognition it rightfully deserves. The truth is, I love nursing. It's tough, demanding and rewarding. It's frowned upon at scoffed at. In the end, there will always be someone who would need the hands of a skilled healer. The hands of a professional nurse.

Linda's instructor respects the content of Linda's essay, but recognizes that the writing needs to be improved. She comments on the paper, "Good work, but you need to watch out for sentence fragments. Come to my office for a conference, to discuss this."

Linda earned a "B" in the English composition course and a "B" in the psychology course. Her difficulties continued in the required science area, and she received a "D" in the chemistry course, which she would then have to retake.

Linda's recognition that the teachers were looking for more than she had been initially prepared to do continued into the next semester. "When I was told I had to do a research paper, I was nervous," she said. In the spring of 1991, Linda told me that she had not been taught to do research in high school. She said, "Students didn't learn how to develop points or write longer thesis papers." At the beginning of the semester, she felt that her first nursing course was "not as difficult as she expected," but by the end of the semester she realized that as she "got deeper into the course, I have to study harder. . . . There's a lot of deep thinking especially about ethics."

During the spring semester of 1991, there was a student takeover of college buildings by students protesting tuition increases that lasted from April 8 to May 1. Most classes were canceled for 3½ weeks, a week of spring break followed by the student takeover. Linda said that this shut-down affected her by not giving her enough time to study all the things that needed to be studied. Although the semester was lengthened, some courses she took omitted chapters from textbooks that would otherwise have been covered. Linda said that this had happened in her world civilization course, her sociology course, and her nursing course. In the classroom observation of the nursing course, carried out near the end of the semester, after the student takeover had ended, the class discussion focused on an article dealing with how nurses can help patients recover more quickly. The professor emphasized how the study was designed and helped students learn to design an experiment. After the class was over, she told my research assistant that the students "don't like to write. They have trouble reading and writing." In the course, students were required to interview a nurse, work in small groups with other students to combine the interviews to produce a group report, which they would write as a formal paper and present orally to the class.

Each student also had to write an individual paper on an issue that had emerged from the initial interview with the nurse. The professor's lack of confidence in the students' abilities may have contributed to Linda's later disillusionment with the nursing program.

In her individual paper for the course, Linda wrote on the topic of nursing salaries. Her instructor commented both on the content of Linda's writing and her presentation style. The instructor's comments are indicated in brackets in the following excerpt from the introduction to the paper: "How much higher can salaries go? This was a question asked in the American Journal of Nursing [author, date]. The biggest salary breakthrough came from the New York State Nursing Association. [NYSNA doesn't have the power to raise pays]. They had raised the pay [?] for experienced nurses to record levels. . . ." Through these comments, the professor was indicating to Linda that she needed to be more careful about her factual assertions, and that she needed to document more precisely her sources of information. Later in the paper, Linda raises the issue of how nursing shortages affect the increase and decrease in nursing salaries. The instructor's final comment supports Linda's discussion of this problem: "An interesting problem—that is, how to ensure adequate salaries when there is no nursing shortage." Linda received an 85 on this paper and a "B" in the course. She also passed the remedial math course she had failed a year earlier with a grade of "C." She was doing well in the core course requirements, receiving a "B" in a sociology course and an "A" in a world civilization course.

By the end of her second year, Linda was performing well in the humanities and social science courses she was taking, receiving "As" and "Bs" in all these courses except the world humanities course for which she received a "C." On the other hand, she had received a "D" in the required chemistry course, had initially failed the second level of remedial math, passing the course on her second try with a "C." Although at the end of this second year, Linda evidenced no outward discouragement with the nursing program, her difficulties with the science and math courses would continue in later years.

By the fall of 1991, Linda's third year at the college, she noted that writing made her more interested in the topic she was writing about and that research made her more involved and better informed. She said, "When you know more about what you want to write about, the something extra you've learned, you can keep in your brain." The theme of being "more interested" in a topic when she had to write a research paper was one that echoed through her interviews for several years. Outlines and free writing, when she was stuck, were helpful writing strategies for her. She reported that her college skills (reading) classes had not been helpful to her, but the basic writing courses (English 1 and English 2) had "pushed her to write and think." She was retaking the chemistry course, which she told me was still her "most difficult course," but this time she was able to pass with a "C."

During the previous summer, she had passed the introductory biology course with a "B." Her easiest course that semester was her women's studies course in which she was learning about "people in society and how they interact." She said there were discussions about "why the culture is male-dominated." "It's not a radical course," she added. "We look at both sides of issues."

In a paper for the women's studies course, Linda provided a number of examples illustrating how society "never encouraged women to succeed in life." She cited psychologists' views (such as Freud), the depiction of women in fairy tales as helpless or competitive with each other, the adage that "women should be seen and not heard," and the sexual exploitation of women in advertising. She concluded her paper as follows:

> I, overall, have shown just a microcosm of women's problems from assorted viewpoints. Women have suffered so much in this world of ours. Unfortunately, women's cries go unanswered. As human beings, we should teach our society to understand the plight of women's hardships just as we thoroughly study the plights of others. People should be taught about women and their struggle to cope in a rampantly sexist society. Showing people daily experiences of what women go through will not only open their eyes but it will give them a better sense of understanding the women who incorporate their lives. Today, nothing could be more vital for a woman and also a man. Once we establish a basis of equilibrium between the sexes, the better the future will start to hold for them.

Linda's instructor commented, "A good start. But you really don't give enough attention to the kinds of evidence that support your very important insights. B–." Here again, Linda receives both the support and critique she needs to improve her writing. It is evident that she is writing from a perspective of "subjective knowledge," where the "truth" is personally known, but her professor wants to move her toward "procedural knowledge," where she will be able to apply objective approaches to this knowledge. She received a "B" in this course, a "B" in anthropology, and a "C" in a world civilization course.

Although she had been successful in passing the chemistry course that semester, she told me that she felt she "had slacked off after going to summer school." She said, at the end of the semester, that she thought she would do well in her courses, but she didn't "feel right" about how she had done that semester. She believed that the break between semesters would help her.

In the spring of 1992, Linda was having problems with her philosophy course. She thought that everything was over the students' heads and she was disadvantaged by having only exams with true–false, multiple choice, and essay questions, instead of having the opportunity to write papers. She failed the course and took it over the following semester. She said that she needed to put more time into the course, because "it's too deep for me. Every time I leave that class, my brain hurts." Part of her problem with the philosophy course was related to her difficulty with the second-level chemistry course she was taking that same semester. At the end of the semester, she told me that the most important thing she had learned during the past year was not "to get too wrapped up in one course, the chemistry course." She said, "It's crazy—spending so much time on chemistry that I'm neglecting philosophy." She did succeed in passing the chemistry course with a "C." She said that she realized "how dedicated I am to my major. They changed the curriculum in chemistry. When I first took it, I felt I didn't fit it, but now I do. I fit in better with the lab and the lecture, and maybe the professor makes me feel better. I have more confidence in my ability." She was expecting to start taking clinical courses the next semester since she had now successfully completed the chemistry course. She said that when she had to research something, she got more interested in it. "Even after the paper is handed in, I still feel involved," she said.

Her personal life had changed during the semester. She had a new boyfriend who wanted them to have a serious relationship. She had met him about a year earlier. He wanted to marry her in the Catholic Church, but she didn't want to be in a rush. Her schoolwork still had the priority, and she told him everything depended on her work. (Although she never told me specifically that this relationship broke up, when I spoke with her in November 1996, she was still single.)

That semester, then, Linda passed the chemistry and nursing courses with "C's," the women's studies course with a "B," and she failed the philosophy course.

In the following summer, she took an advanced biology course which she passed with a "C," and she passed the English Proficiency Test. In her paper, she wrote about discovering the value of taking liberal arts courses while pursuing a nursing major. After describing a world civilizations course in which she learned about customs in a number of different cultures, she recognized the point of learning about these customs even if she did not agree with them. She wrote:

> Many of us was stunned and reacted very negatively to this procedure [clitoridectomy]. The professor was very angry and said something that I embedded deeply in my mind. "You may not concur with the traditions of many cultures. The one thing, however, that you must do is that you should respect it and therefore not pass judgment based upon your beliefs." For the first time in my life, I had actually listened to my professor and took his saying to heart. By this saying I began to soon understand how my world history lessons played a major role in my nursing career.

Linda's paper included appropriate support for her assertions, and it evidenced very few sentence-level problems. She passed this writing test on her first attempt.

By the end of her third year at the college, Linda's writing had started to mature. She was being prodded to be more analytic, and she was becoming more adept at providing evidence to support her views.

In the fall of 1992, her fourth year at the college, Linda was enrolled in an advanced biology (anatomy) class, the second attempt to complete the philosophy requirement, a psychology/women's studies course, and an anthropology/women's studies course. In retaking the philosophy course, Linda said that her new instructor was breaking the concepts down more clearly and that was helpful to her. She passed the course with a "C." At the beginning of the semester, she told me that in the biology course, "the professor is tough. He wants us to know a lot, memorize things. He's treating us like medical students." She said that she had to learn concepts, but she did not feel that they were too difficult. This was also the semester that Linda first expressed her disillusionment with the nursing program to me. She said that the students had started to meet about the lack of support from the faculty and the low passing rate the graduates had on the nursing licensing exams. She made other accusations about students cheating in a variety of way that troubled her deeply. Although she was now passing her chemistry courses with "C's" and the philosophy course with a "C," she failed the second-level biology/anatomy course that semester. This difficulty clearly added to her reassessment of her future plans.

Even though the observation report of her psychology/women's studies course did not reveal an entirely comfortable environment for the students, Linda did respond well to the topics in the course on the psychology of women. She wrote a paper about her mother, a rather loving indictment of her mother's limitations and an expression of admiration for her strengths. She concluded her paper as follows:

> I enjoyed talking with my mother about her childhood. Sometimes she gets so carried away that I wind up leaving her in the kitchen by herself! My mother can talk a blue streak up a cow's back! But seriously, it was fun. Even though my mother never received a Bachelor's or a Master's Degree, doesn't mean that she's stupid. I feel I learned more valuable information from her than all my professors combined. My mother is my best friend and confidant. She's a true gem and a fabulous woman and I thank god every day for her being here (even though she doesn't know it!) It was a treat doing this report!

Her instructor commented on her "interesting style," but also encouraged her to be more analytical in her writing. At the end of this semester, she passed the psychology/women's studies course with a "B," received a "C" in the philosophy course, failed the biology course, and had an Incomplete in the anthropology/women's studies course. (She later completed this course with a "B.")

By the spring of 1993, the second semester of her fourth year at the college, Linda had changed her major to psychology. She never told me explicitly that failing the biology course had been a factor, but when this difficulty was combined with her previously stated dissatisfactions with the nursing program and the new, harsher restrictions on admission, it became evident that an alternative major would be better for her. She still felt that she would be working in a service profession, and she was particularly interested in assisting elderly or disabled individuals. Since she had previously taken two psychology courses and had earned "Bs" in both, she felt more confident about her future and she was able to interact more with her new professors. She said, "I'm more involved with my major. . . . I feel like I'm doing something associated with my major instead of waiting and waiting as I did in nursing." Writing was also becoming easier for her, she said. In her social psychology course, she was interviewing people for a paper she was writing. "I would have been scared as a freshman, but I'm a little more daring now. I would have considered ten people too many to ask questions to when I was a freshman. Papers 8–10 pages seem like nothing now, but as a freshman, I would have been afraid. It would have seemed like 100." She also said that research no longer intimidated her. In an interview she told me, "Writing helps me research material more—to understand it better. When I'm writing, I'm learning more about [the topic]. I may do more research because I want to know more about it, partly for the class and partly for me—to expand the mind. It doesn't hurt."

In a writing profile that semester, Linda, who had said she was "nervous" when given an assignment to write a research paper in her first and second semesters at the college, could now provide a confident description of her process:

I look at what the professor wants. I go to the library to get the feel of the topic. I research little by little. I have a little notebook, gather all the data, look it over carefully. Sometimes it's difficult when you have a lot of data and you don't know where to begin. I gather all my research, prepare an outline, look over the research again. I start to write a rough draft in my notebook, check it over, talk with the professor if I'm stuck or confused. I work at the dining room table at home. There are papers all over the table, papers, pen, typewriter, big dictionary, mug. I write drafts in longhand first, sometimes draft after draft, looking it over until everything looks great. Then I type it as finished work. If I'm in school doing research, I like to be in a tiny cubicle in the library. I don't like to be near people while I am working. I've learned to be creative in my writing. Before I write, I'll look at the professor who has read 5,000 boring papers and perhaps I'll do something different. For example, I might start a paper with a story related to the topic. Teachers say "Good reading." My mother helps me by encouraging me. She reads my papers—sometimes the ideas go over her head—but she loves to read my papers.

This is hardly the voice of the frightened underprepared freshman who started out in the lowest level of basic writing. This kind of growth may have been unimaginable to those who would have selected an easy label to characterize Linda when she began her first semester at the college in the lowest level basic writing course.

Proof of her growing analytic focus and her increasing ability to express herself more cogently can be found in her writing of examinations and papers during that spring semester of her fourth year. In the second level world humanities course, Linda responded to an examination question by relating naturalism to some of the readings in the course. Her instructor's comments are interpolated in brackets.

> In *The Dollhouse*, one could find naturalism being presented. Take the case of Nora Torvald. Her father was considered a man of loose morals. Nora was also considered a woman of loose morals, due to the fact that she performed an illegal act, forgery. Plus, she also walked out on her husband, a idea Victorian women *never* set forth to do. [Good]
> Also, Dr. Rank's father was a womanizer, therefore, Dr. Rank suffers from the "spoils" of his father's unnatural deeds. Genetic inheritance is what one calls this.
> In *The Metamorphosis*, the movement displayed here would also be called Naturalism. Not so much that its didactic. In so much, that determinism comes to play a big role here. No one seems to be escalating to any sort of higher status. One only seems to remain a slave of their class and eventually die in that very same class. Case in point, where is Gregor in the end? [Great]

From these excerpts, it can be seen that Linda is able to utilize knowledge from her study of psychology and apply concepts analytically to the literary works under investigation. Her academic vocabulary has grown and improves the precision with which she can interpret the readings.

In a social psychology course Linda took that same semester, she designed her first psychology experiment and then reflected on the potential findings on a midterm examination. In this experiment, Linda imagined herself to be a teacher who would treat male and female students differently. For example, the men would be required to sit in the front of the classroom, while the women sat in the back. "I will start assigning more work for the women and less for the men," she wrote. "Attendance will be mandatory for the women, but not for the men." These and other requirements were designed to disadvantage the women. Linda's analysis of the effects of this treatment read as follows:

> Reaction wise, I expect the whole class being in a state of shock. Eventually, the realization will set in. The men, of course, will be happy. The women, however, will be angry, upset and most likely, rebellious. The men will participate more, show up to almost every class, their attitudes would be positive and they would most likely score higher on exams and hand in higher quality reports. Women, on the other hand, will participate less in discussions, become frequently absent from class, score low [on] exams, hand in poor quality reports and possess a negative attitude. [Good!]
> These reactions will basically be similar to the third graders in the film we viewed. I think that with college students they will react to this experiment much more passionately than the elementary children. It would be fascinating to see because college students are so intense and so very outspoken. [True!] So, just the first day of class, the instructor will have to be fully prepare. One will have to perform this vast task slowly so there won't be any violent outbursts. Overall, it should be interesting. [I agree!]

The professor's overall comment on this section of the exam was that it was "excellent." On this exam, Linda's cumulative grade suffered from the fact that on the multiple-choice section, she only scored 40 out of a possible 60. On the two essay questions, she scored 18 out of 20 on the first (the design of the experiment just cited) and 16 out of 20 on the second. Thus, her total score was 74 and she received a "B–" on the exam.

In an interview that same semester, Linda recalled that she had had bad experiences in high school when she recited in classes. "I speak out more now, but at times I'm still afraid to speak out. In high school, when I raised my hand, I was ridiculed because I always spoke out. I have a fear of being ridiculed even if I know the answer. I recite more now than I used to. My teachers used to have to pull it out of me. Students tease me when I answer all the questions." This response to her active participation, both in high school and college classes, is troubling because it implies that there is a pressure in the academic environment, especially in settings where many students may be having serious difficulties, not to succeed. For someone like Linda to have developed the self-confidence to participate actively in her classroom discussions is a significant accomplishment, suggesting that her belief in herself has grown so that she can ignore or at least tolerate the "teasing" of others. This reaction is understandable in relation to Linda's early comment that she knew she had to differentiate herself from others in her community who "have no life."

At an interview the next semester, Linda said that the social psychology course had taught her how to do real research. "I really learned how to put all the stuff I learned to use. I'm really learning to think—how to use data." The Science of Behavior course she was taking this next semester was "pulling a lot of things together for her." This was the point at which Linda recognized that research enabled her to know more about a topic not only for a class, but also for herself. The statistics course she was required to take was "really tough in the beginning," but she had had "great improvement" and expected to pass the course. She did pass with a "D," but she told me that she received that grade because of the difficulty of the final and she understood the concepts well enough to handle the work in the experimental psychology course the next semester.

By the fall of 1993, Linda was writing her papers on a computer. She would write a first draft, look it over, see her "mistakes," backtrack, and fix them. She was also able to add ideas, a characteristic of writing on the computer that helped her. She had learned to move paragraphs, and add and delete ideas as she worked on computers that were available in the library. She said, "I'm surprised that I could juggle 17 credits. My determination made it possible. If I take something on, I finish it." This tenaciousness, like Joan's, is critical to the ability of students who start in remedial classes to sustain their commitment over the 5- or 6-year period needed to complete a degree. Linda was also planning to work for a year or two and then go back to school.

She said she "didn't want to delay going back to school." And in a letter to me in the fall of 1995, asking me to write a letter of recommendation, she indicated she was indeed applying to graduate school, hoping to start after her first year of work.

That fall, her fifth year at the college, Linda took two psychology courses, two world arts courses (core requirements), a world civilization course, and a physical education course, for 17 credits. She said that the most important thing she was learning this semester was to network. "I tried to do this in nursing, but I failed miserably. The faculty is there for me in psychology," she reported. "I talked to psychology majors about which courses to take and which not to take. That made a big difference," she added. To help herself in the difficult statistics course she was taking that semester, Linda asked a classmate for assistance. (Delores, another student in this study, was the one who helped Linda.) Together, Linda said, they went over old exams and equations, step-by-step. "It really helped," she told me. Linda had difficulty with the final exam in the course, but she passed with a "D."

The class observation that semester was for Linda's other psychology course, science of behavior. Linda had told me that this course "wasn't being taught by the book." "My professor is teaching us research. He does dream research and he wants us to pick a topic related to sleep such as the effect of snoring on sleep or dreams in sleep." The professor begins the class by reading an article from *The New York Times*, explaining the meaning of difficult vocabulary words and providing interesting examples to illustrate his points. Students listened attentively, and some took notes. Students felt comfortable to ask questions and to risk answers to questions when they were not certain they were correct. The professor corrected student errors as the discussion continued. The emphasis in the discussion was on experimental methodology.

In her paper for the course, Linda wrote what she called a "Sleep Log Paper." She had problems with this paper both in describing the methodology of the study and in presenting her results in an acceptable form. She received a "C" on the paper and a "B" in the course. As part of her introduction, she wrote in the informal style she felt would interest her professor: "Since our need for sleep is routine like eating and elimination, did you ever take the time to think about how well you know your sleep patterns? Can you guess how long it takes you to fall asleep or the number of times you woke up due to nature's calling or a nightmare that you refuse to go back to? Just as I thought! You don't know and neither did other people when they were confronted with the same questions." Beside this section of the paper, her professor wrote, "Casual but good." Thus Linda was reinforced in this style of writing, although it was not acceptable in the more formal sections of the paper.

For her world arts courses, Linda wrote art, dance, music, and theater reviews. In the theater review, for example, she assessed the staging, the costumes, the lighting, the music, and the acting. She only commented briefly on the content or theme of the play. She received an "A" in one of the world arts courses and a "B" in the other.

Linda took the experimental psychology course the next semester and passed with a "C." She learned how to write papers following the strict format she was instructed to use. In her other courses (political science, world humanities, speech and a second psychology course), she found that once she wrote an outline for a paper, "my ideas flow easily." She said she constructed an outline for each paper and filled it in.

The observation of the experimental psychology class revealed that the professor explained experimental practices in great detail, clarifying new terms for the students. He encouraged students to respond to his questions and to raise their own questions when they were uncertain about his explanations. He emphasized the importance of using raw data correctly and discussed ethical aspects of experimental research. Students were engaged by the lecture and felt comfortable as they took notes and raised questions. Requirements for the course included carrying out 10 experiments and writing up the results. The four highest scores on these reports were counted in the course evaluation along with a final examination. An adjunct instructor served as the laboratory assistant, and she provided extensive notes on the students' reports, and she met with them in conferences.

Linda's grades on the experimental reports gradually improved over the semester, ranging from 35 on the first report to 77 on the last. In her early reports, Linda did not know how to describe an experimental procedure. For example, in the "Procedure" section on an experiment on "mental influence on coin tossing," Linda's writing was covered with interpolations from the laboratory assistant:

I [no I's, we's, you's] found a clean, flat and smooth surface for the experiment to be conducted on. Next, I took out my notebook and created six columns. Three were titled "Willed Outcomes" and the other three were titled "Actual Outcomes." With both columns, I numbered them each from one to one hundred. That's why there is three columns. [This entire section is crossed out, and the lab assistant wrote, "I don't think this is necessary for replication."] They are there to accommodate the numbers. There should be a total of two hundred columns. I started off with the "Willed Outcomes" by writing my expected outcome and then flipped the coin. In the "Actual Outcome" column, I would report the actual result of the coin. The overall tally of flips was two hundred.

In place of this discussion of the procedure, the lab assistant proposed an alternative description:

The subject flipped a coin on a clean, flat and smooth surface for the experiment. During the first 100 trials, the subject "willed" the outcomes by . . .
All trial outcomes were recorded by the subject. . .

Through these comments, the lab assistant was providing Linda with the formal format appropriate for describing experimental procedures. The lab assistant also prodded Linda to provide more precise quantitative data before drawing conclusions about the experiment.

In a later report on an experiment involving size discrimination, Linda's procedure section was presented better, although there were still some problems involving clarity:

> Using a method of constant stimuli, subjects were asked to judge if comparison stimuli was greater than or less than a standard [excellent!!]. The stimuli was set up in a 225 cell matrix (15 rows & 15 columns) with the asterisk measuring 4 wide by 3 high. They were separated by 31 mm. The asterisks appeared on the screen for 2.5 seconds. The subjects had to make judgements about the asterisk time. [Each of these sentences was accompanied by a check mark placed by the lab assistant.]
>
> The subject had to choose whether the stimulus on the left, standard stimulus, or the stimulus on the right, comparison stimulus, was larger. The prompt on the screen gave instructions on how to choose the answer. (1) was for the stimulus on the left of the screen as being larger or (2) for the stimulus on the right. The standard stimulus always appeared first on the screen. Each subject initiated each trial by depressing the space bar. Each test involved 55 trials and 22 comparison stimuli at a constant of 60 and 120. [To this point in the paragraph, several statements had been marked with a check, but at the end of this sentence, the lab instructor wrote, "unclear. Be a little clearer about the two conditions (60 and 120) each containing 66 trials."] The order of the comparison was randomized in order to make the two conditions counterbalanced. [More details about the comparison stimuli]

Linda's gradual improvement in presenting experimental studies allowed her to complete the course successfully. The support of the classroom lectures and the detailed assistance of the laboratory instructor were crucial to her success in this course.

In her other psychology class, Linda wrote a term paper on transvestites. In this paper, Linda demonstrated her growing awareness of the complexity in controversial social issues. After describing the plight of women who fled their countries through cross-dressing as males to attempt to find better lives, Linda considered the different reasons why men and women chose to alter their appearance:

> There was also some differences as to why each gender cross-dressed. The women who cross-dressed were poor and lower class while the men came from a higher class background. The women cross-dressed as a mean to escape their restricted lives as women. the men cross-dressed as a form of sexual gratification and as a release from societal's views of masculinity as being ideal in their noble class setting. regardless of one's sexuality, cross-dressing cut all boundaries.

In this paper, Linda demonstrated that her accumulated knowledge in the field of psychology was making her much more aware of the intricacy of describing human actions. Her ability to see such complexities contributed to the analytic turn in her writing. Through her analysis, Linda had reached Belenky et al.'s (1986) stage of "constructed knowledge," wherein the writer is able to view all knowledge as contextual and experience herself as a creator of knowledge.

A reading journal was required for students in the world humanities course that Linda was taking simultaneously. The readings were from a wide range of cultures, but Linda reacted most strongly to one about African Americans. A journal entry asked for a response to Toni Morrison's *The Bluest Eye.* Linda wrote: "This story hits close to home in many ways. I haven't suffered any of the pains that the characters did, but *I know a lot of people who have.* Living in the American South, you come across a lot of people who endure the same *pain* and heartaches *of poverty, incest, family conflict and self hatred.* It's amazing when one sits down and read a book which talks to you exactly about the struggles you know all too well." Although Linda never spoke about being discriminated against herself, and only rarely about personal experiences with family or friends in troubling lives, it is clear that she was aware of the kinds of difficulties Morrison described through personal knowledge. Her only personal observation to me about such difficulties in her own family came when she described an aunt and cousin who were "mean drunks" and who disrupted Linda's family household.

Now, at the end of her fifth year at the college and officially classified as a senior, although she had one more year to complete before graduation, Linda wrote an expressive journal entry at the end of the semester in her world humanities course:

> Finally, it's the end of the term.
>
> I am so happy, I could scream. I'm happy that I'm completing all of my term's work. Handling sixteen credits, including a demanding psychology class which requires 11 short experimental papers is very demanding. Juggling reading ten books on top of assigned chapters of other texts is something of an experience that I can't even explain.
>
> The main reason, however, that I am determined to go through with this because I am a senior. Yes, folks, I am finally going to get the hell out of here regardless of what I have to do to reach that incredible goal. I've worked too long and too hard to let it go to waste and I am not about to. This semester has been hectic, but I have been through much worse. I do want to do a lot of things this summer that I didn't have a chance to do in previous summers. But for now, I would just concentrate on passing my classes and going on with my life. I think that I deserve a break today!

Her instructor drew a "smiley face" on Linda's journal and wrote, "Enjoy your well-deserved break!" Linda received a "B" in this world humanities course as well as "B's" in political science and the other psychology course she took. She earned an "A" in the speech course and passed the experimental psychology course with a "C."

So, at the end of this fifth year, Linda could look back proudly on her accomplishments to this point. She had survived the rigors of the most difficult aspects of the psychology program, the statistics and experimental psychology courses, and she was performing well in her other classes. Her analytic powers had improved, and she could increasingly demonstrate to her professors that she was a worthy student.

In the fall of 1994, she recounted how she had come to understand "how I will never escape writing. I wrote 15 papers in the last semester." "When I write something," she added, "I read [the material] more. I become more involved. I think about it more. I try to develop it more. Writing helps bring out my own ideas about what I'm writing about. I understand [the material] better. Ideas start flowing. That happens to me a lot." At this next-to-last semester in Linda's 6-year journey, writing had become an essential tool for her as well as a source of pride and delight. She only had to write one paper that semester, for an astronomy course, but it served double duty for her as the adjunct instructor in her humanities course told students to turn in a paper written for another course. (The decision of her instructor to make such an assignment deserves nothing but contempt.) Ironically, she received a "C" in the astronomy course and a "B" in the humanities course. At that point, her future plans after graduation had crystallized, working for an agency for a year and then applying to a master's program in social work. Her eventual goal was to work with the elderly.

Linda's paper for the astronomy course was primarily a recitation of facts, recounting the characteristics of Neptune. A paragraph from her paper illustrates the dry tone:

> Scientists are speculating that perhaps the temperature of Neptune is caused by materials that are separating, within the planet, into layers. A similar reaction, like this, occurred on Saturn. Heavier materials sink to the center while heat is generating. Towards the planet's warm ocean, at the bottom, there is very high-pressure which causes molecules to break up into atoms. One of the various substances, Methane, which dissolves in the water, consists of hydrogen and carbon atoms.

As this section of the paper illustrates, Linda has learned to produce certain required types of academic writing. The style is far from the more casual one she prefers, but she has understood the importance of selecting the approach called for in a particular assignment. The inappropriateness of having a paper like this serve double duty in a humanities course is self-evident.

Like Ricardo, in her last semester of the college, Linda needed only one course to graduate, but she took a full program to ensure receiving her financial aid benefits. She needed to fulfill her foreign language require-ment. In addition to the required course in Spanish, she took an anthropol-ogy course, a psychology course, and a sociology course. She passed the Spanish course, received a "B" in the anthropology course, and "A's" in the psychology and sociology courses.

The classroom observation for that semester was of the anthropology course titled "Witchcraft, Religion, and Magic." The first 35 minutes of the class were spent in viewing a film on the divided roles of men and women on a small Greek island. In the discussion that followed, the professor emphasized cultural differences and tried to make the students aware of their egocentrism. A few students participated actively in the discussion. Evaluation in the course consisted of two quizzes and one 10- to 15-page paper or several short assignment papers.

Unfortunately, I do not have copies of any of the papers that Linda wrote in her final semester. Linda's practice had been to give me copies of papers from the previous semester when I met with her the following semester. As this was her last term at the college, her papers had not yet been returned to her, and I do not know whether she ever received any of them back from these last semester courses. Thus, I have only one limited sample of her writing from her last year at the college, the rather stilted paper for the astronomy course. Nevertheless, as papers from her courses in the latter years of her academic work attest, she had indeed matured both in content and style in her writing.

Linda has differentiated herself from the others in her community. She wrote to me in September 1995, telling me that she was "working part time at a drug abuse service agency, giving referrals to drug addicts and/or parents or spouses who want to help loved ones get off the drug." She asked me to write a letter of recommendation for her to the Graduate School of Social Work at one of the New York City private universities. When I spoke to Linda on the telephone in November 1996, she told me that she had been working full time since February in the drug-abuse center doing administrative work, arranging for family medical leave and orientation of new employees. She was planning to stay on full time at the drug abuse center, but she had been admitted to a graduate program in guidance and counseling that she was planning to enter on a part-time basis in the fall of 1997. She expected the program to take her more than 2 years to complete, and then she wanted to work in a public, private, or parochial high school as a guidance counselor. Never losing her orientation to work in helping others, Linda had channeled her interests to different types of assistance.

When she began her college studies, Linda quickly became aware of her limitations in critical writing and mathematics. Even so, she recognized that writing papers gave her a better opportunity to demonstrate her knowledge than short-answer examinations. She learned in her first year of composition studies that the structured format of introduction, development, and conclusion would lead her to success in required college examinations, but she chafed at such restrictions, searching for more original ways to interest her professor-readers in her papers. Sometimes, such strategies were successful, but, in other instances, professors were more demanding of content-based, evidence-based, analytical writing.

At the end of her second year at the college, Linda was still nervous about writing long research papers. She felt that her high school English courses had not prepared her for this depth of writing. Nevertheless, she found herself more successful in the humanities and social science classes than in the sciences and mathematics. Although retaking her chemistry course in her third year required her to neglect other courses, Linda remained committed to her nursing major. Her writing had become more analytic, and she had come to understand the importance of providing evidence to support her views. Her women's studies course had bolstered her sense of her personal identity.

Despite her dedication to the field of nursing, after failing a required biology course in the first semester of her fourth year, Linda was forced to confront her academic weaknesses in mathematics and sciences. When the nursing program tightened its eligibility requirements at just the time that Linda was becoming disillusioned with the faculty and the program, she decided to change her major to psychology, an area in which she felt she could be more successful and in which she would receive the support she needed. She had become more confident about her writing, and she had developed a workable strategy for handling long and complex research papers. As she continued in her psychology courses, she found herself able to adapt concepts from that field to the analysis of literary works in world humanities courses. In psychology courses, she learned to design, carry out, and analyze the results of original studies. Writing on the computer gave her the flexibility she needed to revise her papers. Although she struggled with the statistics and experimental psychology courses, she was able to complete both and thus fulfill the requirements in the psychology program.

Here, then, is a detailed picture of a student who started at the lowest level of basic writing, "nervous" about writing research papers, but subsequently found that writing provided her with the best outlet to demonstrate her knowledge and learning. Research became an energizing tool for her as she probed more deeply into the field of psychology, no longer wanting to learn just to demonstrate her ability to her professor but wanting to increase her knowledge for her own sake. Such students may be labeled "underprepared" with some justification when they begin their college experience, but no label portrays the dedication and persistence within the individual that accounts for the success achieved both in an academic and a personal sense.

Ricardo

A quintessential outsider who came to realize the importance of becoming an insider was Ricardo, a Latino student placed in English 2, who had emigrated from Puerto Rico after he had completed his elementary and secondary education. Ricardo had had most of his early education in Spanish. In middle school, he had done a little writing in English "but not much effort was put into it." Although he had aspirations to become a physician, after his parents divorced, and he lived with his father, he was sent to a vocational school to study photography, where he did little writing. At the age of 16, he enrolled in a community college in Puerto Rico, but, not motivated and using drugs, he was not successful there. He had wanted to go into a premed program, but he was refused admission because he had had no chemistry in the vocational high school.

Since he had some expertise in photography from his schooling in Puerto Rico and work in New York City, Ricardo enrolled at City College as a communications major, believing he could combine his skills with a socially activist profession. When the job market in communications declined, he turned again to his initial ambition, to become a physician, but this, too, was thwarted because of the huge financial obligations required. He eventually enrolled in a physician assistant program. But even that process was not simple for him. In a homework assignment paper he wrote in his last semester at the college, he noted that his application to the Harlem Hospital physician assistant program had been turned down because "the school (CCNY) did not provide them with a transcript of my records!" He was accepted then into the program at Bronx-Lebanon Hospital. In a telephone conversation I had with him in September 1995, Ricardo told me that he was finishing his classroom training and starting the clinical work. He had received a scholarship for his 2 years of schooling, and, in return, he would owe 1½ years service for each year to the state. He was planning to work in a community group or clinic. The pride of accomplishment in his voice was strong. Ricardo wrote to me in October 1996 to tell me that he had completed the physician assistant program. In his note, he said, "Thank you for believing that I could do it." He would be pleased, I know, to see this book as a testament to the conviction that students like him with initial weak academic backgrounds have the potential to succeed as he has.

A political and social activist, Ricardo staunchly defended his views even when he feared retaliation for taking controversial positions. This activist stance had started in his high school days. In an autobiographical paper in his first semester at the college, Ricardo wrote: "In my last year of high school, I got involved with the school paper. I was the dissident of the paper, and I was censored and barred from writing articles that will talk about the unsanitary conditions in the school. I was very upset about been silenced. My attitude and respect for authority after this incident was negligible." The consistency of his commitment to social justice had started early in his life.

Ricardo's many attempts to pass the required WAT were presented in detail in chapter 1. It is worthwhile to consider here why this student who was consistently earning "A's" and "B's" in both the required core courses and the courses in his communications major had to retake this test so many times. Instead of recognizing the maturity and complexity of his ideas, attention was directed toward his difficulties with grammatical features, even thought it is well known that second-language users develop these skills over time. In fact, he graduated with a 3.55 grade point average.

Writing was always an important means of presentation for Ricardo, and he used it consistently as a basis for learning. He had already come to understand when he was a student in Puerto Rico that if he wrote notes out after reading a chapter of material that he would understand the material better. He began to use this strategy again as soon as he entered the college. "In this way," he said, "I use writing and my brain." In the English 2 course, his early writing strategies were to read and analyze the topic, make an outline, and then write "responses" to the parts of the outline. In writing a paper comparing his experiences as a photographer in Korea with those of an anthropologist on her first trip to Africa, Ricardo's outline set forth the structure of his paper:

Comparison Paper

E. S. Bowen Paragraph	Model Paragraph
Traveling as an Anthropologist	Traveling as a Photographer
First day on the field	First job overseas
Language difference	Language difference
Conscious of being watched	Conscious of being watched
Learning about the natives	Learning about the natives

Although he developed these ideas in his paper, sentence-level problems plagued Ricardo throughout that first semester. What is evident is that Ricardo knew certain structures, such as past tense verb forms, but they were not yet automatic for him, and his proofreading skills were not adequate to allow him to catch all the errors. Here is a sample from his comparison paper:

> As we traveled to different continents outside our western world Ms. Bowen went to Africa and I went to North Korea. We can appreciate the different experiences that we both had about the trip. We can sense that Ms. Bowen was not prepare to the kind of attention that she was receiving from the natives. You as a traveler must be prepare not only to observe but to be observe as well. We have been lucky enough to be part of a small group of Westerners that have able to travel to those land.

Instructors of composition courses will have no difficulty identifying the grammatical weaknesses: verb tense forms, dependent clause comma omitted, absence of noun plurals, addressing reader as "you." My responses to Ricardo's paper that semester were both substantive and form-oriented. In addition to commenting on the content, I advised him to concentrate on a few specific grammatical problems such as verb tenses and sentence fragments and to try to memorize some idiomatic uses of prepositions. In addition to the classroom work, I recommended that he go to the Writing Center for additional work on sentence-level problems.

Ricardo's social agenda was clearly in place by the time he began his academic work at City College. The conclusion to an autobiographical paper he wrote in the English 2 class revealed his personal and political orientation:

> It hasn't been easy to start all over again. I'm giving it the best I got. The financial responsibilities and the cost of living in New York are obstacles that are making it very difficult. I plan to get my degree in Film & Video. I want to be able to use my art to educate people, an prepare them to fight against the injustices and the prejudices that bear all over us. You don't need weapons to create awareness. You need books to eliminate ignorance We can only do it, if we have the education.

As Ricardo's later writings reveal, his belief that education is the means to fight against injustice and prejudice continued throughout his college years. My substantive comment on his paper read as follows: "This is a very insightful paper. Your strength and determination will be the factors that make your success possible." I have never wavered from that view.

The freshman composition course he took in his second semester was his most difficult course and he felt he needed more time for writing and thinking. (He eventually earned a "B" in the course after having received a "C" in English 2 the previous semester.) In the freshman composition course taught by a professor in the English Department, he was permitted to use a research paper he was preparing for a Communications course on the media as a final paper for the writing course. In that paper on U.S. media, Ricardo wrote, in the confrontational style he said he later abandoned:

> The U.S. media has been promoted as an objective, balanced, and unbiased medium. But on the contrary their role has been one of propaganda and disinformation. It has worked as a catalyst in controlling the American public mind. An example of this was the recent press coverage of the invasion of Panama.
>
> The news that we received, in New York, through the press and networks TV stations was geared to maintain a passive audience and was blatantly defending the interest of the U.S. government. The media did not fulfill it's mission of providing all the elements from which the audience could form an unbiased opinion.

After detailing the news coverage, Ricardo pointed out how the media consistently portrayed "the suffering of the U.S. soldiers and the anxiety of their families," while neglecting to focus on "the suffering of the thousands of people [in Panama] who became homeless or of those who had lost their loved ones. It clearly demonstrated the power of the media in suppressing information from the public." (His strong feelings on this topic became clear when City College proposed to give General Colin Powell, who had been President Bush's chairman of the Joint Chiefs of Staff and who had graduated from City College in 1938, an honorary degree at its spring commencement in 1990. Ricardo was part of an activist Latino group that threatened to picket and disrupt the graduation ceremonies. General Powell did not attend the commencement but received the degree later in a private ceremony. The following semester, Ricardo told me that he had been granted amnesty for participating in the sit-ins that had been held over tuition increases at the end of the spring term.) Ricardo received an "A" in the Communications course and a "B" in the English course.

Ricardo was opening himself up to learning, he told me in the spring of 1990. "I learn from everything and make my own judgments. When in conflict with teachers, some avoid and some allow students to make their points. I learned to listen better," he said at the end of the semester. "I absorb information first and analyze it later. I missed things before." This was a strategy Ricardo mentioned several times over the years. He had learned to take notes, even when he was uncertain about the significance of the material at the moment, and then examine them critically at a later time. He was also very aware of how language features in his writing affected the acceptance of his ideas. He acknowledged that "one of my biggest drawbacks is that I can't transmit what I'm thinking in writing. Correctness of form is the problem, grammar errors, not vocabulary." Although many of his instructors, over the years, urged him to edit more carefully for sentence-level problems, on the whole, they did not discount the value and credibility of his ideas. He had also learned that some professors were more tolerant than others of dissenting views.

The comments of one of his professors, on a paper he wrote for a communications course at the end of his first year, typify the encouragement he received for the quality of his ideas and the admonishment he received on the form of his writing. In the following excerpt from a review of the film, *Full Metal Jacket*, the professor's comments are interpolated in brackets:

> This is a movie that deals with the atrocities of war, in this case the Vietnam war. Not only of the inhumanity of man against man, but the transformation of the mind's of the young recruits from a healthy one to an ill [choose a better word] one, the one of a killer [not a sentence, rephrase].
>
> The movie recounts the events from the moment private Joker entered the basic training grounds of the U.S. marines in Paradise Island, North Carolina. The plot evolves around their basic training. The content is how their mind's were being transformed by that training [good].

As can be seen here, the professor clearly appreciated Ricardo's ability to phrase the theme of the film in a clear analytic statement, while he wanted him to be aware that formal expression was required. This point was reinforced by the professor's final comment on the paper, "Watch your sentences—make them complete."

At the end of his first year, then, Ricardo had been strongly reinforced in his view that education was the key element in having a successful life. He had risked his academic standing by participating in student activities that spoke to his sense of social and economic injustice. He had acquired specific learning tools, listen first, analyze later, that would allow him to succeed in complex academic settings. He already understood how far he could go in expressing his dissenting opinions, and although he never abandoned his principles, he was learning to avoid unnecessary confrontations.

In the fall of 1990, the beginning of his second year at the college, Ricardo said that the most important thing he had learned the year before was "how to question authority and back up your position with sustained evidence." Writing had made him able to question readings and analyze them in more depth. If he had a dissenting opinion, he could read differing opinions and then come to his own conclusion. He would write out answers to questions at the beginnings of chapters in his textbooks and then go back and make any necessary corrections after he read the material. He took notes in all his classes, reviewed them daily on the subway ride to the college, and wrote analyses of the notes that he would use to review for exams or for writing assignments. When given a writing assignment, he would read the question, write down possible ways to answer it, search for appropriate evidence, consider a possible conclusion, and then begin to write the drafts of the paper. "Writing makes you analyze and think," he said at the end of his second year. "It gives me an opportunity to communicate better, to express ideas. Writing helps—it certainly does."

During that fall semester of his second year, Ricardo wrote a paper for his world civilization course in which he explained how the Spaniards enslaved the native Taino Indians in Puerto Rico beginning in 1509. His instructor provided comments at the end of the paper that helped Ricardo realize that he could become a more effective writer by using evidence to support his views. The instructor recommended a book for Ricardo to read and then commented both on the book and Ricardo's paper: "You will observe that a genuinely critical approach with an explicit and committed set of values is in fact more powerful in exposing relations of exploitation and subjugation when it *enlightens* rather than *preaches* on social relations." Ricardo took this kind of advice seriously. He received a "B+" on the paper and an "A" in the course.

In the world arts course he was taking that same semester, Ricardo provided an analysis of the film *Paul's Case* in an examination essay. He included an analysis of Paul's character, the film techniques, and the settings. The ending of his paper read:

> The use of settings is extremely important. They show the positiveness of Paul's reaction such as when he was at the Plaza Hotel or at the Opera house. They also

show the negativeness in Paul life as when he was at school and also when he was at his home.

In summary, Paul's Case is the story of a young man who made a choice. A choice that if he wasn't able to live in luxury and glamour life was not worth to live. This an excellent film.

Ricardo received a 99% on this exam and a "B" in the course.

The next semester, the spring term of his second year, Ricardo enrolled in two communications courses, a required philosophy course, and the second level of world arts. Although he felt that the philosophy course was his most difficult one that semester, Ricardo declared that his "instructor is good, but I don't understand the ideas." "The instructor is using logic to answer questions. I'll go to see him for help." He added that the instructor encouraged disagreement and discussion. Clearly Ricardo felt comfortable in this environment to seek help. He received a "C" in the philosophy course. He also told me at the beginning of that semester that the most valuable thing he had learned the previous semester was "a lot of history I didn't know." He said his studies made him "understand what's going on in the world now and repercussions, the shape and politics of different countries and their differences." When asked about the role of writing, he said, "It makes you analyze and think. I want to write better—have the opportunity to communicate better, to express ideas. Writing helps—it certainly does."

For one of his communication courses, Ricardo wrote an extensive discussion of neorealism and its expression in films. Toward the end of this paper, in a section titled "Movements," he wrote about neorealism in the film, "Open City," as presented by Rossellini:

A film shoot during the german occupation of Italy in WW II is about the heroic resistance of the Italian people against Fascism. In this film the main characters are a priest who was a collaborator of the resistance movement, a devote communist who the germans were searching for. In it Rossellini stereotyped the german oppressor represent by major Bergman and by Ingrid one of his soldiers (they were both gay). This is the weakness of the film because it made the characters unbelievable and flat. This film have all the traces of the Neorealistic movement, but it also have non Neorealistic traces such as the use of music and special effects lighting.

Again, it can be seen that Ricardo's critical apparatus was in full force, but the sentence-level problems in writing remained.

At the end of his second year, Ricardo's analytic skills were sharper, but his writing still contained the kinds of sentence-level problems that composition teachers despair over. Nevertheless, as second-language interference patterns continued to characterize his writing, his overall educational experience strengthened him and made him a more astute observer of the world around him. He was becoming a more knowledgeable critic and, therefore, a more powerful one.

Now more aware of the need to support his controversial ideas, Ricardo told me in the fall of 1991, his third year at the college, that he listened to the agenda that his professors announced and then wrote practice questions related to that agenda. In his comments, he would note whether he agreed or disagreed with what the professor had said. If he disagreed with the professor, he would communicate his views to the professor in papers, in class discussions, or after class. Sometimes the professor would be open to his critiques, sometimes not. Just as Linda had become disenchanted with the nursing program, Ricardo found himself critical of the conditions in his major department. Discouraged by the poor technical equipment available, the facilities in general, and the departure or impending departure of some of the faculty he respected, Ricardo initially decided to speed up his schooling so he could graduate early. He later slowed down and delayed his graduation to take the science and math courses he needed to apply to the physician assistant program so that he would remain eligible for financial aid.

At the end of that semester, he told me that it was becoming more and more frustrating to stay in college and survive. "I am very concerned to keep my academic standards, but cut backs [at the college] have depressed me. I could get Cs with no effort because grades don't mean anything to others, but I do not want to diminish the quality of my own work. I have been on the honor roll for three years. But if I can't pay the rent and eat, who cares about grades? Financial aid has become worse, tuition has risen, and faculty can't pay as much attention to students as classes get bigger." During that semester, Ricardo had been working from 20 to 25 hours per week. He said he could use "extra time" to do his school work, but he was already having problems "with rent money this month."

Of course, he did not lower his standards, but he was clearly hamstrung by these complications in his life. Diminishing support for public higher education, especially prevalent in New York State and New York City, was discouraging those who had already sacrificed so much and were willing to sacrifice as much as they could, but even such committed students had limitations on what was manageable.

During this term, Ricardo was writing avidly for his communications courses. Not surprisingly, the themes of his works had strong social agendas. He prepared a script for a television public service announcement for one of his communications courses. He stated the problem to be presented in a short, initial summarizing statement: "The idea of the ad is to have a young man, that by his involvement with drugs looses possible great opportunities of love, family and education." He has his main character tell of his downfall from a successful life and concludes by having him say, "I have loss my Friends, my Family and even my Future. 'Don't let this happen to you.' Please look at me, Don't try Drugs. Please don't do Drugs, Don't become one of me." The most striking original line of this announcement is the last, and knowing of Ricardo's past involvement with drugs when he was a college student in Puerto Rico, the genuineness of his appeal is evident. His own life stands as a model of what can be accomplished by an individual who started out with much less than the character he portrays in the announcement.

In the same semester, Ricardo was writing an original screenplay for another communications course. He wrote seven drafts of this screenplay, and in the last version made several substantive changes. The screenplay was about a young man originally called Bob, changed to Diego in the last version, who encounters a brutal confrontation between pickets ("mothers with their children, elderly folks with their nurse aids at their side, students, and many other working poor people that are marching in protest of Govt. budget cuts") and a "white man" who yells at the marchers, "Fuck you Commies, this is Amerikka. If you don't like it, go back to your fucking hole." The violence escalates and the agitators turn out to be undercover police who rush in and beat the protesters with sticks. In the earlier versions, "Bob," a lawyer, remained an observer, but he was so distressed by the violence that he considered leaving New York City. He decided to remain although no specific reason for his decision was given. Ricardo's instructor gave him some suggestions for revision after the third draft: "The Demonstration/Beating has to have a deep impact on Bob's life. He has to be different as a result. What are other options than packing [his clothes] and making coffee. Stretch your imagination." The instructor also noted, "Please be mindful of grammar and sentence structure."

By the seventh and last version, "Diego" no longer remained an observer. He attempts to calm down the agitators/undercover police who have covered their police shields, but he is attacked by the police as they begin hitting everyone in the crowd. One of them shouts, "Let's kill all the Spicks and the Niggers!" Diego finally escapes from the crowd, his "face and clothes are stain with blood." As he heads for the subway station, he encounters "his friend and fellow lawyer Julia." After telling Julia what has happened, Diego is told by Julia "that there is something you may be able to do to help others." She tells him about a secret proposal to close down all city shelters that a group of lawyers are fighting. She warns him, "Please understand that you don't have to get involve if you don't want to. I know that it could be very dangerous to your career." The scene ends with Diego agreeing to attend a meeting that night at the Center for Constitutional Rights and inviting Julia to dinner after the meeting.

In this last version, then, Ricardo has not only presented the problem of injustice that he is so deeply concerned about, but he has presented a way for his protagonist to use his skills to work toward bringing about social change. He is very cognizant of racial antipathies and attempts to expose their virulence in this screenplay. Righting social injustice is the same motivation that later impels Ricardo to work in the medical field in poorer communities in New York City.

Ricardo's views on racial injustice were also expressed in a paper he wrote about Frederick Douglass' autobiography in a course on United States society that semester. Not surprisingly, one of the issues Ricardo was most concerned about was the effect of a lack of education for the slaves:

> Other forms of control was the law of non-education on the slaves. They [the slave holders] wanted to prevent the development of the slaves learning abilities of reading and writing. The purpose of such an act was to suppress any possible contact with the growing anti-slavery movement and to maintain a total and absolute control over a very ignorant population. Douglass tells us how the Slave holders whipped those slaves who were found with books. He also mentioned how they were stoned by the whites when they were found to be holding a Sabbath school.

In comments to me in later years, Ricardo reflected on how ignorance made people he knew unaware of the unfairness of the social and economic deprivation they were experiencing. Such empathy is clearly visible in this passage about the plight of the slaves Douglass described.

In the spring semester of 1992, Ricardo was enrolled for 17 credits while working at least 24 hours a week to support himself and his wife, with whom he had recently reconciled after a period of separation. The ethics course in the communication program was making him think about issues he had never examined before. He felt he had learned that "to get to a conclusion, you have to analyze complex issues by seeing more than one opinion. It's necessary to have all the information available." For him, this was a difficult and challenging course from which he was learning how to select and define a problem, identify how the problem affects the larger issue, break the problem apart, write down details about what he thinks and what others think, and how the problem and its solution will affect people.

This approach was modeled in the classroom discussions. An observation report of this class in March 1992 noted that the professor avoided giving the students answers to the ethical questions under consideration. Rather, she turned the students' questions back to them for further reflection. At the end of this class session, as the students were packing their books away, they spontaneously applauded their instructor.

An exam paper he wrote for the Ethics course illustrates the learning that was taking place for Ricardo. He wrote on the topic, "Should hate speech be tolerated?" He presented his position in his opening statement: "I do not believe that hate speech should be tolerated in any society." He went on, "Hate speech as I define it is the denigration of any ethnic group by the use of words or statements to cause harm to them, causing harm to those groups by using stereotypes as a way to denigrate or strip them of their humanity." In developing his argument, Ricardo cited controversial work of two professors at City College whose views on racial issues had received national attention. He wrote:

> An example or I should say a couple of examples I should say are the two professors here at City College. Dr. Leonard Jeffreys [sic] and Dr. Levin. They have both used stereotypes to carry or convey their messages or ideas. Dr. Levin claims to have found that Blacks, Women and minorities are less intelligent than whites. This is a pure manipulation of facts. He doesn't take into consideration the lack of educational opportunities to minorities or the way scolastic test are set up. It has being proven that those test are bias against minority groups. Why then he should be allow to perpetuated those stereotypical ideas. What about the harm that those stereotypes will cause to minorities?

His instructor comments on this section of his paper, noting: "If Levin believes what he says is TRUTH—How can society tell him not to speak? If Jeffries believes what he says is TRUTH, How can we ask him not to speak?" By prodding Ricardo to look at his position from an alternative perspective, his professor was assisting his learning "to analyze complex issues by seeing more than one opinion." In this exam paper, Ricardo demonstrated that he understood argumentative structure well enough that he had to present another position than his on the issue. He cited the arguments about first amendment protection and that "the market will demonstrate that what people like Dr. Jeffrys and Dr. Levin say will be corrected if there is no interference by government or society in bringing laws to restrict such speeches." He follows this discussion with his counter arguments, in part by noting his own willingness to restrict his freedom of speech if this could prevent harm to others.

In his final paper for the ethics course, Ricardo addressed the issue, "Was it ethical for the NBC network to identify the rape victim in the William Kennedy Smith trial?" After reviewing extensively the arguments for and against the television network and, subsequently, newspapers identifying the victim, Ricardo concluded with his position on the issue. An excerpt from his conclusion reads:

> They are not easy answers to very difficult ethical questions. This is one of them. But, as I weigh the reasons presented by those involved I feel compel to reject the "Libertarian Theory" and respect the right to privacy of Ms. Patricia Bowman. It is clear that a major news organization like NBC, has to be preoccupied with ratings. The pressures on a news organization to achieve higher ratings and maintain their competitive edge is being lived by those news organizations in a daily basis. It does not justify the outrageous intrusion on a victim's right to privacy. It is the victim's right to come forward to denounce the crime. It is not the network's right to further victimize a rape survivor by invoking their First Amendment Rights and their Freedom of the Press. The long-term harmful consequences of this action are greater than the reward.

In this peroration, Ricardo demonstrates that the Ethics course has provided him with the tools he needs to argue the issues that trouble him. He received an "A" in the course.

Not only did Ricardo's analytic skills strengthen further during his third year, but he complicated his thinking in several ways. He recognized that his views would be received more credibly if he provided appropriate evidence to support them; he learned that the ethical dimensions of issues are as significant as the substantive ones; and he recognized that social activism can be carried out through participation in community and professional groups. Despite the continuing financial strain in his life, Ricardo did not lose his commitment to do the best work possible.

In the fall of 1992, Ricardo ran out of money and had to work as many hours as he could. He dropped three of his five classes, including the science and math courses. He made a conscious decision to drop courses instead of just getting through so he could keep his average up. He earned "A's" in the two communications courses in which he remained while working. (By the end of the semester, he was working 3 full days a week.) He felt that writing helped him "to use the brain twice, once to have to think to write and then to have to read while [he's] writing." He also said that writing helped him to remember and analyze things better.

One of the communications courses Ricardo was taking was a broadcasting seminar at the CBS-TV headquarters in New York City. Ricardo was disappointed in this seminar, feeling that the lecturers provided by the network were unenthusiastic and only fulfilling an obligation. Similarly, he was critical of the students in the seminar, noting that they remained primarily "passive" during the classroom sessions. In the particular class session that was observed, however, the students were actively critical of the network's lawyer who spoke on the topic of broadcast law. The next semester, Ricardo told me that the students had had a confrontation with this speaker, arguing that the station was only carrying the minimum number of required public service announcements. The lecturer then accused the students of being communists. Having learned that abrasive language would not accomplish his goals, Ricardo tempered his language in his writing for the course.

In a paper for the broadcasting seminar on the topic, "What is the situation of the CBS Corporation today?" Ricardo took an objective perspective in his discussion of the strengths and weaknesses of the network. An excerpt from the end of his paper reflects this stance:

> As the CBS Corporation announced a reduction on the payment that the affiliates received from carrying its programming a rebellion started to brew. This resulted in the decision by some CBS affiliates of purchasing programming from syndicates, instead of carrying CBS produced programs. An example of this is the recent decision by WJBK TV from Detroit to stop carrying "CBS This Morning." To contain the damage of this unpopular decision, CBS announced a plan to give more time to its affiliates for local newscast within its programming. Another weakness is the decrease in local radio advertising that dropped 11% as a result of the current recessionary economic conditions throughout the nation.

In conclusion CBS Corporation is in a strong condition in the broadcasting industry. They are some problems that need immediate attention such as the rebellion of the affiliates, but they are nothing that could create any major destabilization for the corporation if they are properly taken care off. After achieving a major victory with the Approval of the Cable Bill by the U.S. Congress and undertaking a major re-structuring, CBS Corporation is positioning itself to move forward as a strong competitor in a fast changing and aggressive broadcasting industry.

Ricardo received an "A+" on this paper, and his instructor commented, "Well informed paper." Although Ricardo had claimed earlier in his academic experience that vocabulary was not a problem in his writing, it is clear here that he had now acquired the more extensive academic language needed to express his ideas. By the end of the spring semester, he said the biggest change that had occurred to him was, "I got older. I'm learning to be patient." He had also finally passed the dreaded WAT.

Working 20 hours per week the following semester, the spring of 1993, he was taking the chemistry and math courses he would need to apply to the physician assistant program. Although he started poorly in the chemistry course, with an "F" at midterm, by the time he learned enough math to understand the chemistry, he started to do better. He completed the course with a "C" and earned "As" in all his other courses. He had been given credit for the introductory biology course he had taken as a college student in Puerto Rico. Ricardo found himself using the same strategies that had worked for him before in mastering the new field of chemistry. He took notes on the lectures and the assigned readings. He wrote down where he was confused and went back to the book to check the information until he felt he understood it. He made his own study guide to prepare for exams and did the problems in the study guide the professor provided.

Ricardo wrote many papers for his world humanities course that semester. He said, "I know how to organize things. I know what the professor is looking for and I present information in a way that I can support arguments. I organize ideas—my ideas toward the statement or topic for the paper." One in-class writing assignment asked students to respond to the question, "Is Don Quixote crazy/insane? Why?" Ricardo's response revealed both his serious thinking about the literary work, and how his own experiences affected his interpretation:

I have been asking myself the same question. I'm not sure if I can call him crazy. He was an Idealist/a dreamer. He wanted to pursue a dream (being useful to others) and that is how he [illegible word] into reading books of chivalry.

How come people that deviate from what is called society normal behavior are called crazy/insane. Don Quixote lived a very sedentary life before his adventure. He may had at some point being in a better economical position. What happened before the story began that changed his life? Is there more background information that we don't have?

> Coming back to the issue of his sanity. Sometimes when there is a goal to achieve there is nothing else that seems real. It becomes an obsession (not a Calvin Kline). I think that he wasn't crazy. He was living a dream, a dream that on his mind he made it real.

As this in-class paper revealed, Ricardo's analytic powers were strong, but the assignment did not provide any opportunity for him to do sentence-level editing.

In a prepared paper on the relationship between Sancho Panza and Don Quixote, Ricardo emphasized the friendship between the two men. In his conclusion, he wrote:

> One of the most important things that I enjoyed was the real friendship and love that evolved between the two of them. After so many misfortunes (and they were too many), Sancho was still on the side of his friend. Yes, there was an offer of some material reward (an island), but the hardships that they both suffered was too much to take in exchange. When in Chapter XV they decided to separate (Sancho was sent out in an errant), they cried! Every time that Don Quixote had a misadventure Sancho ran to his side. That's true friendship.

Although, as this excerpt indicates, there are still minor sentence-level and spelling problems in Ricardo's writing, he demonstrates that his editing skills have improved when he has time to rework his papers.

In another paper about a Chinese poet who lived in the 800s, Ricardo related the insights of the poet to current environmental and political concerns. In the conclusion to his paper, he summarized his response to the poem:

> To conclude, I want to tell you that this poem reminds me a lot about time past. How when I was fishing I was always careful not to abuse my surroundings. How today I stop to listen to those conversation of my "barrio" characters and learn things from them. Is amazing how Lu Kuei-meng saw the cycles of life and how he was able to accept and live with them. How he was wise enough to recognize wisdom in his neighbor the fisherman.

His instructor admired this paper and commented, "A beautiful thought and beautifully expressed." He received an "A" in this world humanities course, the only one he had to take since he had been given transfer credit for a humanities course he took in the college in Puerto Rico.

At the end of that semester, when I asked Ricardo in what ways he thought he was a different person from the person he was when he started at the City College, he said that he used to be angry, but now he was agitated. The difference for him what that he now could see what a problem was and what could be done about it. Instead of acting quickly, he could now act in a calmer, more mature way. He said, "What am I going to do—be angry all my life? No. I'm much more intelligent than I was four years go. I get annoyed by people who are ignorant if they had an opportunity to do better." Despite all the really serious obstacles in his life, Ricardo had fought successfully for his achievements.

Delayed by financial problems during this fourth year, Ricardo never considered compromising the quality of his work. He had not lost any of his energy in responding to issues of social responsibility, as exemplified by his confrontation in the broadcasting seminar course, but he had developed a clear understanding that his views had to be tempered by solid evidence in his writing. Not only had he gotten older, he had also become wiser.

Taking advanced chemistry and biology courses the following semester, for the first time Ricardo joined study groups. He felt that these groups helped him considerably and he earned "A's" in both courses, the only courses he was taking after he dropped a math course which he took the following semester and earned an "A" in. The observation of the advanced biology course revealed that the instructor, who started off lecturing at a brisk rate, gradually came to realize that the students were failing to respond to his questions. After about 30 minutes, he slowed down the pace of his lecture, allowing students to catch up. As Ricardo had told me earlier, he had learned how to take notes rapidly, understanding that he could go over them again later and analyze them. This study technique doubtless helped him succeed in this difficult course.

This was the semester, the fall of 1993, that Ricardo gave me his writing profile. In the course of this interview, he shared personal experiences that had influenced his life. He had told me earlier that his father had forced him to go to a vocational school "so he wouldn't have to support me," but this was the first time he related the degree of his father's cruelty. Ricardo said that his mother had almost cut his father's arm off when his father refused to take Ricardo's sister to a hospital to be treated for a heart murmur. After his mother left his father, she became a nurse and was able to support herself. Having been exposed to heartless treatment as he was growing up, Ricardo can be further admired for his commitment to assist less fortunate others. He developed empathy, not cynicism.

His approach to preparing papers had evolved to embrace the "writing process" model well known to composition teachers. He read the assignment and required outside readings. He then selected a main idea "to emphasize or criticize." He sought out information to support his idea, and then he started to write drafts, "a lot of drafts." He tried to put all the information into the first draft, including the supporting evidence for the points he was making. By the third draft, he was "looking at the grammar and syntax." He sometimes asked his wife, who was then working on a combined BA/MA in social work, to read his drafts, and he found her suggestions helpful. He ignored the advice of a friend who wanted him to change his point of view in a paper he was writing. Ricardo was fully aware that he had developed a style "that was not as confrontational" as it used to be. He wanted to "present ideas in a more subtle way." He said that his work was now "better received" as his words were "more carefully chosen." He had benefited from the suggestion of a professor who told him that his words were "too political," and who suggested he "should find different ways of saying things." "That's working better," Ricardo added. He had not written any papers that semester, because he was taking only science courses.

During Ricardo's last semester in the college, while fulfilling the final communications requirements, and health education and math courses he needed for the physician assistant program, he realized that he had learned to write in many different styles over the years. In the film classes, although the format was frequently chronological, he knew that the development of characters required description and analysis. In our last interview at the college, in May 1994, just before he graduated, he told me: "Writing is everything when you're in school. You have to be able to express yourself in ways that others can understand you." By this, I think he meant that he had truly come to understand that in order to support his views he would have to provide convincing evidence to those who might be skeptical or critical of his perspective.

Ricardo also took a psychology course his last semester in the college. In a paper, he compared the hysteria of "Anna O.," a famous patient of Breuer's who influenced Freud's work, with the condition of contemporary women. After discussing the inhibitions imposed on women of Anna O.'s time and comparing them with the apparent freedom of today's women, Ricardo concluded his paper by writing:

> To conclude in my opinion "hysteria" was a non-verbal way of crying out for help. It was the psychological escape used by the unconscious of many women in the 1880's to seek out some help and/or find relief of the oppression and restrictions imposed by their societies. Unfortunately the medical profession was not ready and willing to take their cases seriously until the case of Anna O and the innovative treatment of Dr. Breuer's.

Even Traub (1994), who denigrated the value of remedial education at City College as being too costly and producing too little true intellectual development, would find it difficult to criticize the complex reasoning skills that Ricardo had achieved.

Ricardo took two courses in the Health Education Department that semester, one in stress management and the other in health concerns. For his stress management class, Ricardo had to keep a time management journal. Students had been encouraged to schedule a break each day for some relaxation, which Ricardo usually filled with listening to music. A typical schedule of a day in which he had classes and was not working read as follows:

7:30 a.m.	up and shower
8:00	breakfast
8:30	travel to college
9:25	class
10:45	class
12:00 p.m.	lunch and review one of class papers
2–4	class
4–5:30	travel home
6:00	relax, music
7:00	shower
7:15	cook dinner
8–9	pay bills
10:00	dinner
11 p.m.–2 a.m.	study

The schedule varied, with some days recording time for library research, writing papers, or attending meetings at the college. Ricardo tried to say "good nite" as he wrote in his journal, at 11 p.m. as often as possible, but many entries recorded studying until 1:30 or 2 a.m. As can be seen from the journal, on such a day, he spent 4½ hours in classes, 2½ hours traveling to and from the college, and more than 3 hours studying, including reading over a class paper while eating lunch. Not much time was left for sleep or relaxation.

Ricardo responded to a questionnaire about "self-awareness and personal planning" to overcome stress by stating: I need to start "becoming more patient to achieve goals." I need to stop "being so impatient." I need to continue "being aware of the beauty that surrounds me." The first steps I plan to take toward each necessary change are "Relax and start using time on what's ahead of present task." In response to the last response, the professor wrote: "Not first steps! You need to start more slowly—each goal can be achieved one step at a time! You have the basis for a good action plan, but you need to develop some of the questions more fully!!" "This course," Ricardo said, at the end of the semester, "showed me how to control stress in my life." He felt that he had "really learned something from that class."

For the last communications course he was taking, Ricardo wrote a paper about a film adaptation of Ernest Hemingway's "Soldier's Home." A comparison between the sections he wrote on the "plot" and the "theme" of the story clearly illustrate his analytic strength:

> Plot: This short story/film adaptation is about a young man named Harold Krebs that left his native Oklahoma to fight in WORLD WAR I. As Krebs returned from the war after it ended his fellow citizens did not recognize knowledge or show any respe t for the young man who performed his patriotic duty. This resulted in a feeling of not fitting in within his community. He found himself lying about his war experience

in order to receive some recognition or to be listened to. For Krebs lying about his experience turned into resentment about the war and about talking about it.

> [Paper also included section on Conflicts in which he wrote that Krebs had a conflict with his mother who represented the "religious, social and family values" that she wanted her son to submit to and which he rebelled against.]

> Theme: The conflict of a young man as he was maturing and the doubts that a life experience created on his value system. The different degrees that those conflicts reach and the disorientation that they create on his mind. The displacement of the old value system (imposed by family and society) and the creation of a new one (chosen and experienced by himself).

As this analysis reveals, Ricardo has been able to abstract the larger social issues represented in the film and articulate their significance.

Because much of what has been called developmental research has looked at the accomplishments of different individuals representing different levels in the academic spectrum, it has been difficult to make an argument for spending the resources and time required to demonstrate the achievements of individuals who started in ways that defined them as "underprepared." It is only through research that follows individuals over the years, hearing their voices, knowing the factors that affect their academic performance, seeing the changes that occur in their thinking and their ability to express complex ideas, and examining the instructional settings within which they function that it is possible to make some determination about the potential and actual accomplishments of such students.

As a beginning college student, 26-year-old Ricardo was more mature than the other students in my study. He had experienced personal difficulties in his family life in Puerto Rico and came to the college after working for a few years in New York determined to improve his capabilities and his ability to contribute in meaningful ways to the larger society. His second-language interference patterns in his writing caused him to be placed in an English 2 class, although his intellectual abilities were immediately evident. In his high school experience, he already had been willing to risk retaliation for activist stances, and this behavior continued throughout his college years, although he learned to temper his language in his formal writing assignments so that his views would become more persuasive to his readers.

Ricardo developed note-taking and writing strategies that made it possible for him to succeed in difficult courses. By writing first and analyzing later, he was able to sort out the important concepts when he had enough time to devote to studying. His life was consistently complicated by the necessity to work long hours, but he never allowed that difficulty to overwhelm him. Instead, he made rational decisions at appropriate times that would permit him to accomplish his goals. Even though his writing continued to evidence sentence-level problems throughout his college years, he found support and encouragement for his ideas and his values from his instructors, while they simultaneously urged him to work at improving the formal correctness of his papers. Because he had a powerful social agenda, Ricardo was able to benefit from the advice he received to support his views with sustained evidence to increase their credibility.

Disillusioned with the quality of equipment and concerned that faculty he admired might leave the college, Ricardo decided to fulfill the requirements for a physician assistant program, delaying the completion of the requirements for his major. The poor job market in communications also influenced his decision. In his writing, Ricardo became more committed to finding solutions to difficult problems, not just describing them. As he became more knowledgeable about world affairs, he came to believe even more strongly that education was the essential means for beginning to overcome social injustices. His personal struggles made him aware of how difficult it was to achieve such goals at a time when the society devalued education and reduced its commitment to supporting students with little or no financial resources. His ethical values were also strengthened as he came to see greater complexities in issues that had a moral basis. By finally completing the difficult science requirements for his new career choice, Ricardo demonstrated how hard work and solid values could carry him to a successful conclusion.

Ricardo is indeed a person to be respected for his accomplishments. His writing over the years developed to enhance his ability to defend the social and political views he cared so strongly about. The setbacks in his personal life (difficulties with his wife at one time, continuous financial distress, lack of family support or encouragement at crucial stages in his life) did not deter him from working and working and working to achieve his self-defined goals—always committed to helping others.

Joan

Joan is an African-American woman who was 18 years old when she started in the English 2 class. All of her preparatory schooling was in the Bronx, although she moved from an essentially "White" area to the "projects" when she was 10 years old. She lived with her mother on the 15th floor of a building where the elevator frequently broke down. She told me in an interview in February 1993 that she felt that she could not bring friends home. "I've been surviving without friends so far, and I guess I will continue to do so," she said.

Joan was certainly unprepared for the level demanded of college writing. She had not been taught how to take notes in high school, and her writing tasks had been mostly creative ones, such as writing about "what it felt like to be an orange until about the tenth grade." Most of the labels Haswell (1991) listed about underprepared students might have been attached to Joan: She was initially "slow" and only, over time, learned to regulate herself to plan ahead to carry out her assignments; she was indeed a "novice," in need of support and expertise, and she could be labeled "developmental," with the need to catch up on what she had missed in reading, writing, and mathematics, all serious problems for her.

Joan was literally disabled, having been in an accident at the age of 2 when she lost 70% of the vision in her left eye. She received therapy at the age of 4 and her eyesight got better. In high school, she pushed herself too hard, and the muscles in both eyes were weakened. She resisted letting the college label her "disabled," but, by the fall of 1991, when she was having academic difficulties with intense reading assignments in her upper level courses, she sought out that formal designation. It later served a crucial role for her, allowing her to be given extra time to complete the college's Reading Assessment Test and to be excused from the fourth required semester of foreign language study.

Joan's family history would hardly have predicted any likelihood of success for her. In a paper for her freshman composition course in the spring of 1990, Joan wrote: "My family has a history of early teenage pregnancies, going back to my great grandparents. Everyone seemed to bear their first child at age seventeen. Seventeen seemed to be the magic number. During these times talk of having an abortion was immoral, demeaning, and unheard of." She described how her mother had her first child at the age of 17, noting that her mother "struggled through many years, but she didn't do too bad considering that she was raising her children as a single parent during this time." Joan's mother married her father and then had 6 of her 10 children with him, Joan being the last. Her father was an alcoholic and philanderer that made "things too complicated to bare [sic]" for her mother. In 1968, Joan's mother moved her children to New York "to start a new life." In an interview in December 1992, Joan told me more about her family background: Her oldest brother was 43 and had had 2 years of college, as did one older sister. One sister was addicted to drugs and alcohol and had children. Two brothers were homeless and were also addicted to drugs. One other sister was an alcoholic and still another sister was a fanatic on religion. After making mistakes with her other children, Joan's mother had taken time with her and Joan felt pressured by the family to succeed.

But none of the labels applied to underprepared students could truly be said to characterize Joan's outstanding characteristic: tenaciousness. Success in college meant everything to Joan. It was her whole life. In an interview in December 1993, Joan's fifth year at the college, she told me that "the most significant thing that happened in the past year was that I was able to pull off working at Radio City Music Hall, working at the clinic in my internship, and doing my schoolwork without going crazy. I can handle these things because I have nothing else. This is the only thing I have to look forward to." She also told me that the most important thing she learned during the past year was that "you have to love yourself to get things done or you'll never get anywhere. It was a change for me to learn to love myself." Shutting down the outside world and abandoning her boyfriend who had adopted religious beliefs that "expected women to be subordinate," Joan's entire world consisted of her life at the college. She would do anything necessary to achieve the bachelor's degree that would open her to a better life.

After 6 years at the college, Joan graduated in the spring of 1995 with a bachelor's degree in psychology. In a telephone interview in September 1995, she told me she had accepted a position as a counselor at the hospital where she had done her internship. Earning $25,000 a year in a unionized job, more than anyone in her family had ever earned, Joan was now able to move her mother out of the projects into an apartment where, for the first time in her life, she would have "a room or her own."

So, how does a "slow," "developmental," "disabled," "outsider," "novice" come to succeed in college? And what does success mean? For Traub, who wrote about Joan under another name in his book *City on a Hill: Testing the American Dream at City College* (1994), Joan's progress did not mean that she had become an "educated person" by his standard (p. 132): "[Joan] had not developed intellectual discrimination, and she certainly knew virtually nothing of philosophy and history" (p. 132). Traub spoke with Joan independently of my interviews over one semester, and, with her permission, had access to the papers she had written during her first 4 years at the college. What he failed to understand completely was that her difficulties and her life experiences, combined with her college learning, prepared her to contribute meaningfully in the larger society. In fact, Joan told me that her family history helped the hospital that hired her to consider her for the counseling position in a methadone clinic: "I came from a family where most members of my family had problems [with drug and alcohol abuse], so living through it gives you an indirect experience with families with these problems. I was a victim, and that gave me empathy, which is what the people in the clinic want." So, although Joan may have barely passed her philosophy course and was an average student in her history [world civilization] courses, she did become a useful, functioning part of society where the combination of her life experiences and her knowledge would prove useful to others.

Joan told me in her first semester at the college that she found the college demands extremely different from the high school requirements "which made things a little difficult to adjust to, but I can say it was a challenge for me." She had taken only the minimum amount of mathematics required at her high school and passing the Math Skills Assessment Test before the completion of her 60th credit became a tremendous hurdle for her. In the fall of 1993, her fifth year at the college, she told me that she had not been asked to do much writing in junior high school. She basically had to take tests. In her English courses, she had written summaries, but not much else.

She received 90s for her work. This led her to believe that she had been properly prepared for writing demands when she came to college. "But I really wasn't," she said. Like Linda, instead of creative writing in high school, Joan now wished that she had "had more writing that made a lot of sense."

In her writing placement test, Joan presented a traditional organizational pattern, an introduction, two paragraphs of development, and a conclusion. The best guess for the reason for failure is that there were a few grammatical errors (e.g., a comma after the word "but" instead of before it, a missed possessive apostrophe, the confusion of "loose" with the verb "lose," and the use of "took" as a past participle. Missed by the readers were Joan's thoughtful comments on the topic of whether students should be expelled from courses if they are late more than three times. Joan noted that students become disadvantaged when they are late because, "most lessons given by teachers or college professors are started out with an aim which sometimes revolves around the lesson itself. By the student being late, he or she is totally lost because they have missed the whole meaning of the lesson which could be the beginning of the end for a student." Although certainly not stated clearly, Joan had identified an important reason why students should be prompt in attendance, one unmentioned by most takers of the WAT.

Joan took the test again at the end of her first semester and passed it. For each of the points she made on the assigned topic, she included a personal experience as a point of development. Since this paper contained fewer grammatical errors than her previous attempt, the readers, instructors of other sections of English 2 that semester, found her response adequate. That semester she was also enrolled in the College Skills class, and she had to take the Reading Assessment Test again. She failed this test, possibly because her vision problems prevented her from completing it in the allocated time.

In the papers she wrote for the English 2 course, Joan frequently alluded to family problems. For example, in one paper, she described how her father wanted a son instead of a daughter when she was born. She felt that her being a girl helped cause the rift between her father and mother: "Every time they spoke, they would argue about me. Then I would hear 'If this was my son.' I often heard this phrase and I tried to ignore it, but every time I heard it would hit me right in the heart. I've held back my feelings for many years."

Joan wrote several drafts of a paper comparing her experiences with those of an anthropologist in a foreign country. In her final draft, she wrote, "As I enter through the college doors, I began to feel more and more uncomfortable because I was surrounded by many people who were much different than me. . . . People sensed my fear as soon as I walked through the doors. They knew that I was a freshman who know nothing about college life." Reminiscent of Belenky et al.'s (1986) stage of "silence," Joan seemed strongly intimidated by the college environment. But, in an earlier draft of the paper, she had included a section suggesting a hope that she might be able to overcome these fears: "At City College, I also became angry and frustrated because I felt a sense of isolation and self-consciousness in the college atmosphere. Also I felt very afraid and lost. But, later on I began to realize that as I learn a little more about college life at City College, it will be much easier to adjust." A pattern began to emerge in her writing that suggested she dealt more fully with ideas and emotions in early drafts than in final papers. Perhaps she felt constrained to deal more narrowly or neatly with ideas in her final papers.

Another paper she wrote in this course revealed how central the quality of persistence was in her life. After describing Booker T. Washington's tenacious efforts to gain admission to Hampton Institute, she described her own attempts at finding a job:

> Job hunting takes lots of patience. I was out of work for 4 months. I had no type of income coming in. I had applied almost everywhere trying to find a job. I had no luck but I didn't give up. Until one day I had an interview with someone from Martin Luther King Health Center. I was determined to get that job. But later they told me there weren't any openings. They told me to call in everyday to check. I did this for an additional 2 months. Finally they informed me that they had a position open for switchboard operators. I filled the position.
>
> Booker T. Washington's ambition has inspired me. This is proven by the above written assignment that I've just written.

Washington may have served as a model for Joan to emulate, but her inner drive and determination were what sustained her.

By the end of her first semester, Joan had passed the WAT, allowing her to enroll in the freshman composition course. She had failed the Reading Assessment Test for a second time, and she had not yet attempted any of the basic mathematics course that would prepare her to pass the required Mathematics Assessment Test. She successfully completed the freshman orientation course and a bridge course in social sciences.

Admitted into the freshman composition course the next semester, Joan found the course not very helpful to her. She felt that too much time was spent on grammar rather than on discussion of the assigned readings. She also had difficulty understanding the comments made on her papers by her instructor, an adjunct in the English Department who at that time had little preparation for the teaching of composition. Although her instructor made copious comments on her papers, they were either too "jargon-laden" and complex for her to follow, or they failed to lead her to develop the necessary insights. For one paper, students were assigned to revise the summary of an essay by J. Black on Kafka. The instructor's comments are interpolated in brackets:

> "A Report to an Academy" by Frank Kafka is about an ape who wanted to become a human. [Why did either Kafka or Black state that the ape's first wish was to become

human?] Along with this, he wanted freedom. The ape did not want to be caged up. In order to be successful at becoming human, he had some steps to follow. [You could take the first sentences of this, remove one, and by fiddling a bit with punctuation, transition words (conjunctions and conjunctive adverbs), sentence length (perhaps combining 2), and most of all sentence order, make this opening make sense. Try.]

As a summary comment on the paper, he wrote: "Overall, you really don't get at the essential problems with Black's essay in terms of the reasoning, though you do smooth out his grammar in some places. C+." Extensive as these comments are, they do not address the specific places in the paper where Joan's analysis of Black's reasoning is lacking. In addition, the advice on reworking the introductory sentences is far too complicated for her to follow. At the minimum, the instructor might have reworked these sentences to illustrate the possibilities for Joan.

Retaking the college skills class, Joan passed the Reading Assessment Test that semester after one of the counselors gave her additional time to complete it (Traub, 1994, p. 126). In another course that semester, she had learned a formal structure for writing a term paper: introduction, subsequent sections, conclusion. She had also learned the five-paragraph theme model, with each paragraph of development to include examples. She maintained that this plan was proving useful to her and she said it helped her "to write in depth about each idea." But when she described her actual writing process at that time, it did not resemble this orderly plot. She said that sometimes she mapped out ideas, a strategy she had learned in her college skills class. "Words lead to other words, brainstorm, and then free write." She took the words "that come to mind" and put them into her essay. She organized the words (perhaps in an outline), but she did not write rough drafts. She proofread her papers, but revised only by filling in words and making editing changes. In her classes, she took careful notes and underlined definitions and important terms in her books to use for studying.

At the end of her first year, Joan was depressed and discouraged. Although she had by then passed the WAT and the Reading Assessment Test, she had failed the first remedial math course. She was uncertain as to whether or not she would return to the college in the fall. She wanted to be a psychology major, but she was afraid to be declared visually impaired and handicapped. She had a cataract and found that reading put a lot of strain on her eye. Taking fewer courses each semester seemed to be the best possibility for her in the future.

Joan did return in the fall. She said that in the previous year she had learned to use writing to better understand the material in her courses by "taking notes in all classes, taking out the important terms from those notes, and using them as the basis for study." She underlined definitions and important terms in her books. This strategy of referring carefully to authorities was also implemented in her writing, where she underlined key terms. She was working that semester at a telemarketing company, doing market research. She had cut back her working hours to 13 per week because she wanted to get better grades. At the first interview about 5 weeks after the fall semester began, Joan told me that her most difficult class was the world civilization course, which she eventually withdrew from. (She took it again the next semester with a different instructor and passed with a "C.") She was enjoying the world arts course, making sculptures, drawings, and collages. She said she was "good with her hands." Joan was also enrolled in psychology and sociology courses that semester.

In the writing in her sociology course, Joan's papers were full of definitions with authorities for each carefully provided. Although this approach was initially successful for her, in examinations Joan's responses were not sufficiently analytical. Definitions alone were inadequate when differences between concepts were asked for. Received knowledge could not carry her very successfully when analysis was required. She received a "D" in this course. For her first paper in the sociology course, Joan defined terms such as *sociology, interaction, action, basic research, applied research*, etc. An example from her paper illustrates how she defined terms carefully: "*Sociology* is referred to as the systematic and objective (scientific) study of human society and social interaction. Sociology is more or less the study of interactions within groups in society. A sociologist never studies an individual. He or she may observe or study an individuals interaction within a group or groups." When Joan attempted to supply definitions as responses to examination questions, her instructor was dissatisfied, requiring analysis, asking, for example, that she explain the difference between *role strain* and *role conflict*. In her comments on the examination, the instructor told Joan that she needed to provide the sources of differences in terms and better examples to illustrate her points. Received knowledge would not carry her to a successful outcome here.

Citing authorities, providing definitions, and discussing causes of problems were more successful for her in her psychology class, and she received a "C" in the course. Joan liked the readings and found the class discussions helpful in clearing up ideas presented in the lectures. In a paper titled "Impotency in Males," Joan defined and discussed many possible causes and treatments of impotence. In the conclusion, she stated, "Moreover, I have gathered information based on my own knowledge and life experiences which have helped shed light on the subject itself." This assertion had no basis in the paper itself, and the instructor noted beside this sentence, "Which ones?" apparently asking about which of Joan's life experiences had been referred to. This may be an example of Joan unconsciously internalizing her own experiences in her presentation without delineating them specifically. In any case, this statement is an example of "subjective knowledge" as described in the *Women's Ways of Knowing* (Belenky et al., 1986) category system.

By the end of that semester, Joan felt that writing helped her remember much more: "If I write when I'm reading, it sinks in more." Her work load had increased, and she was working double shifts from 7:15 a.m. to 11:30 p.m. 3 days a week. "I'm tired," she said. She had learned the importance of planning ahead, and she said she "liked it when teachers gave a syllabus and advance notice." Clearly, such materials helped students like Joan, who had time-consuming outside commitments, to handle the planning of their academic work in a better way.

Like Linda, Joan had more difficulty with courses that required multiple choice exams than those in which she could write papers. She was passing these courses with grades of "C," but she felt that that was not good enough for her. She found multiple choice exams difficult because the answers were "debatable" and she had difficulty choosing among the options. She was starting to plan ahead more for her courses and beginning necessary research sooner than she had in the past. Also like Linda, who tried to remove herself from those in the community around her, Joan was resentful of her sisters who had children and had "gotten lazy." She was beginning to feel burned out, with demands being made on her by her schoolwork, her job, and her family. She felt that she was always "cramming," no matter how hard she tried to plan ahead. People in her community in the Bronx, mainly Hispanic and Black, although living in a high crime area, seemed to have more respect for her now that she was a college student. They left her alone and did not "pester her to do things."

Continuing in her psychology major, although expressing some reservations about this "if the courses become too difficult," Joan found that writing helped her mind to flow more, allowing her to put her thoughts on paper. She was still using the mapping strategy learned in her college skills class in her writing and taking careful notes in her classes and from her textbook assignments. She read over her notes every day, trying to accumulate information over time so that she would be prepared for her exams.

In the spring semester of 1991, Joan was taking a psychology course, an art course, a speech course, and taking the world civilization course for the second time. Her hardest course was the psychology course. She found the language "very technical with difficult words." She was concerned that she was having so many problems in understanding and carrying out the assignments since this was her major field. She received a "C" in the course. Her easiest courses were art and speech. During this semester she was working at Radio City Music Hall as a page and a hostess, conducting tours and giving speeches. This experience made her feel comfortable in the speech class, and she earned an "A" in it. She was working from 4 to 12 hours during the week, and from 2 to 30 hours on the weekends, depending on the show that was playing. With this schedule, Joan felt that the working hours were not interfering with her schoolwork.

In the classroom observation of Joan's psychology class, the professor started by asking students questions about a research assignment. The students responded well, with the professor directing their attention to problems in doing research. The remainder of the class period was spent with the professor lecturing, actively using the blackboard to illustrate his points, and asking students to illustrate the concepts he had been presenting. The professor made an effort to see that his lecture was understood by the students, and more than half of the 13 students present participated in the discussion.

Joan did not have to do much writing that semester. Most of her courses required essay examinations or lab reports in which she had to follow a specific step-by-step method. I do not have copies of these materials. The shut down of the college during the spring semester because of the student protests disrupted Joan's pattern of studying, and she said "it took awhile to get back into the swing of things." She didn't drop any courses as a result of the shut-down, and she passed all her classes, receiving an "A" in the speech class, a "B" in the art class, and "C's" in psychology and the first level world civilization course.

By the end of her second year at the college, Joan had passed three psychology courses, had started to fulfill the core course requirements of the college, and had only the Math Assessment Test looming before her. She had learned how to use periodicals for research, and she was committed to continuing at the college with a major in psychology. Getting the job at Radio City Music Hall had allowed her to cut down on her working hours, thus freeing her to spend more time on her school work, at least for the time being.

By the fall of 1991, Joan felt that her writing in her psychology courses was improving. She was able to apply insights from a psychologist's model of child development to observations of a particular child, and the instructor approvingly wrote "very good" or "good" five times on her paper. She received a "B+" on this paper and the instructor remarked at the end, "Your thinking is rather scientific and systematic," an acknowledgment of the approval that received knowledge garners. Joan saw writing at that point as providing her with "a chance to elaborate on ideas." She received a "B" in this course. But Joan was having more problems with her world civilization and French courses. Having failed the first two pop quizzes in the world civilization course (multiple-choice and objective questions), Joan finally asked for the official designation of "disabled" that she had avoided for so long. She realized that she needed to take more time for the reading in the world civilization course, and she was troubled because she "forgets what [she] is reading" and her "mind wanders in class." She managed to pass the world civilization and French courses with "C" grades, but she received a "D" in French the next semester and eventually asked for exemption from the final required fourth semester French course on the basis of her disability.

During that semester, she also passed the first level remedial mathematics test, but she had not yet passed the Math Assessment Test.

Joan's predilection toward presenting "received knowledge" in her papers prevented her from accomplishing her professors' demands for more analytic writing. In the second level world civilization course, Joan wrote a paper on a novel by Chinua Achebe. The instructor commented on the paper that she had "recounted much of the novel rather than analyzing it." Only in the last paragraph did she express an opinion about the book: "I believe that Achebe when writing this novel, expressed the point very well." The instructor wrote in the margin, "What point?" Her paper continued: "Moreover, I believe that the tribe justified their actions. 'An eye for an eye and a tooth for a tooth' simply means that two lives had to be sacrificed in order to stop a war that could wipe out a whole generation. Idemefuna's life was taken to save others." The instructor was again puzzled by these statements, commenting in the margin, "not the way I understand the saying." When Joan briefly deviated from presenting received knowledge to provide her own interpretation, she failed to convince her instructor that she was analyzing the novel appropriately.

By the end of the semester, Joan said that having to work long hours had made her sluggish and she was not eating well. The day before the interview in December 1991, she had worked from 7 a.m. to 5 p.m., getting up at 4 a.m. to fulfill all her responsibilities. At this point, she had become more committed to her psychology major.

In the spring of 1992, Joan was writing papers in her abnormal psychology course that her professor liked, commenting "Terrific job," at the end of one of them and giving her a "B+" on the paper. But her grade in the course was dragged down by her performance on the two examinations that counted for two thirds of the course grade, and she received a "C" in the course. Once again, where exams were weighted more heavily than papers, students who benefited from the reflection provided in writing were disadvantaged. In that psychology course, Joan had been told explicitly by the instructor that students were not to give opinions or say "I feel" in their papers. Answers were to be based on facts. Prevented then from expressing ideas related to her own knowledge or experiences, Joan was in an environment where "subjective knowledge" had been devalued. By this time she had recognized that her habit had been to let things pile up so that she "had to work under pressure." But now, she said, "You must think ahead. If you apply yourself and do homework, the semester will go smoothly." She also said she had learned she had to "take really good notes."

Joan had described her course in abnormal psychology that semester as her most difficult one. She said that the professor was complex and the course seemed more like a philosophy course. The teacher supplemented the textbook and other assigned readings with his lectures. The major writing assignment for the course was the review and analysis of pertinent articles in the field of abnormal psychology. Students were expected to apply theories learned in the course to the situations described in the articles. The professor emphasized in the description of the writing assignment that the students were to present conclusions related to the facts of the article and how the article related to the field of abnormal (behavior) psychology.

Discussion of the midterm exam filled the first 15 minutes of the class observation period for this course. After presenting an overview of the topic for the balance of the class, the professor lectured, but he interrupted himself to ask questions or respond to student questions, creating a comfortable environment. Then, in a darkened room in which it was impossible to take notes, slides were shown, with the professor lecturing in a rather monoto-nous tone. The atmosphere brightened in the remaining moments of the class when the professor raised the topic of drug abuse.

In her paper for the abnormal psychology course, Joan used a format that was common to almost all her formal papers, including what she called "a proper introduction and a proper conclusion." What is interesting about the conclusions to her papers is that she almost always included a statement saying that she hoped the reader found the paper interesting. In the conclusion to this paper, she wrote:

> The purpose of this paper has been to introduce the various articles that I have chosen to discuss relating to Abnormal Psychology. I have stated my reasons for choosing these articles. I've discussed those theories and concepts from the textbook that applied to each individual as I gave my psychological profile. Moreover, I have given various research studies and findings that have been done on these topics to the best of my ability. I hope that you've found this research report interesting.

Indeed, her instructor did find her paper interesting. Not only did she receive an "A" on her report, he wrote at the end: "Needless to say, I do. Terrific job." This pattern of personal statements in the conclusions of her papers had begun with her paper the previous semester when she had written about the case study of the 2½-year-old child. The final statement in that paper bears a strong resemblance to the one in the abnormal psychology paper: "I hope that you've found this case observation to be useful and interesting." Here again, she had been deemed successful and awarded a "B+" on the paper.

These kinds of comments suggest that Joan was firmly entrenched in the category of received knowledge in that she had confidence that she could reproduce knowledge in an acceptable manner. Her paper for the abnormal psychology course presented a variety of cases with psychological interpre-tations grounded firmly in research that Joan had studied. In her analysis of the first case of a doctor who inseminated his patients with his own sperm, she described this condition as, "an individual having a superiority complex about his/herself. These individuals believe that they are so perfect that he or she has no thoughts or consideration of others. These individuals suffer from low self-esteem and may go through great lengths to demonstrate their self-worth by making themselves the center of attention." Joan had clearly understood the parameters of the assignment and was capable of fulfilling them.

At this stage, Joan recognized that writing helped her understand where she stood "with theories and materials as well as grades." She felt that exams did not show everything without writing assignments. She said, "In a writing assignment, a teacher can point out problems and misunderstandings." In other words, she could *learn* from the responses of her instructors to the writing. In exams, students only found out whether they were right or wrong but not always why.

That same semester, Joan was enrolled in the first level world humanities course. She was very much impressed with the professor, who she described as a "warm and worldly woman." Although there were stringent reading requirements, eight books during the semester, Joan did not complain about these assignments. There were no papers required for the course; the only writing was essay questions on the final examination. Joan said that she had learned to define a word in a sentence to help a reader understand her meaning. This professor appeared to become a serious role model for Joan. She received an "A" in this course.

Thus, at the end of her third year at the college, Joan had acquired a certain kind of academic competence. She could take insights from research and theory and apply them to individual psychological cases. She felt that responses to her writing assignments were much better guides to increasing her understanding of the materials she was working with. Simultaneously, Joan's relationships with her professors had grown in the spring semester, and this had had a very positive impact on her, as she told me at the end of the term:

> This has been one of the better semesters for me. Professors have been more giving. They work more closely with you. They're more involved with the student—more on a personal level outside of class. More available. They seem to care, too. I see Professor ____ [the humanities professor] and my math professor and psychology professor outside of class. They're helpful to me. I can see my psychology professor after the semester for medical purposes, for counseling or if I have something I want to talk about. He has left his telephone number for students.

Although during this third year she had had to accept the designation of disabled, Joan's confidence in her abilities had developed so that she was energized to continue with her studies.

The fall of 1992, Joan's fourth year at the college, found her taking courses in biology, psychology, the third level of world civilization, and the second level of world humanities. She felt that her most difficult course was the world humanities class, and she was having problems "shifting from one type to another type of reading." In a paper for this course, for the first time, Joan began to build relationships between what she was learning in one discipline to another. She applied concepts from psychology to her analysis of Voltaire's *Candide*: "Pangloss inspired Candide's Optimism because he attributed what we would call in Psychology, a Halo-effect to every experience in life, meaning there is good in everything and everyone." In another paper, on whether Nora was entitled to divorce her husband in *A Doll's House*, Joan began a thoughtful analysis of the relationship: "Torvald not only stripped Nora of her pride and dignity as a person, but he also assisted in the degrading of her character by taking advantage of her child-like ways." The instructor admired this insight and wrote "nice" in the margin. Joan presented both analytic and subjective stances to this relationship in a later section of the paper: "Moreover, to deprive a mother of contact with her children is appalling to me. Torvald phorbids [sic] his wife to even physically look at her children which is downright cruel." Joan received a "C" in this course.

In her world civilization course that semester, Joan wrote a paper in which she included the three perspectives described in the *Women's Way of Knowing* (Belenky et al., 1986) model: received knowledge, procedural knowledge, and subjective knowledge. She was able not only to cite authority, but also to analyze the views presented. She wrote, for example, "With Korean's discovery of the western culture, this country experienced having new ideas relating to their fascinating artwork, which put their old values in the back seat of society." She also provided her own reasons for admiring modern art forms. What this analysis reveals is not that the linear model proposed in *Women's Ways of Knowing* is faulty, but that these positions can exist in overlapping ways while the individual is in a state of changing perceptions—at times accepting of authority (for which students are amply rewarded in the academic environment), at times going "beyond the information given" to create original insights, and at times asserting one's own feelings and likings as a legitimate expression of knowledge.

At the beginning of this fourth year at the college, Joan found that writing had several important uses for her. She felt that she had learned to write a good paper by coming back to the point she was making, something she said she originally learned in the English 2 class I had taught. Writing was crucial in helping her understand what she was reading. She said, "I forget most of what I read, but if I have to write something about it, it becomes part of a recording. It sticks with me. I can remember what I wrote and how I wrote it." Joan was also learning to do everything early: make arrangements early, stay on top of advisement and guidance and tests, and type up papers early. She was then working 12 hours per week as an usher at Radio City Music Hall, but she felt that the hours were flexible and did not interfere with her school work as much as in the past.

Joan had an acute sense of what she could pick up from her professors that would help her. She learned to use transition words from listening to her professors. She had discovered that professors love it when students mimic them. Because her psychology professor used "moreover" and "in that," Joan learned to use those terms in her writing. She also applied this insight to papers she wrote in other courses. She told me, "I understand anything when I write it. I like writing because it gives me a chance to elaborate on a subject, not being limited in any way." She felt she was better able to explain and elaborate in writing than on multiple-choice tests, where she felt it was more difficult for her to show what she had learned. This is the same insight Linda came to, also believing writing gave her an opportunity to demonstrate to her teachers what she knew.

Joan's greatest difficulty during this semester was with the biology course. She failed the first exam, but then, following her professor's advice to read three chapters thoroughly of the 11 assigned for the next exam, she was able to pass the test. The biology exams were multiple-choice and fill-in-the-blanks types, methods of examination she had always had difficulty with. She passed the course with a "D."

Joan believed that the social psychology course she was taking that semester would be her easiest one. She had to write two papers for this course. In the class that was observed, the professor returned the multiple-choice part of the midterm exam and responded to student questions. She told the students that she had evaluated the essay part of the examination both on content and form. When students had writing problems, she wanted to meet with them individually. In her response to the essay part of the examination, Joan had defined terms carefully and provided examples from different cultures and religions to support her points. She received an "A" on the essay part of the examination, but a "C" in the course.

At the end of the semester, Joan told me more about her family life. She and her mother (who was disabled and received supplementary social security funds) lived in public housing. Joan received assistance for books from the SEEK program at the college, a Pell grant to help cover her living expenses, and tuition support from the Tuition Assistance Program. Any spending money she needed she had to earn. Clinical psychology had started to attract Joan, and she thought she would like to help troubled teens, especially those addicted to narcotics. She had promised herself that she would never turn out like her brothers and sisters. "Being at college is my life," she said. "I will not let anyone take it away from me."

In the spring of 1993, Joan was taking a required astronomy course, two psychology courses, and a course on U.S. society. Her first paper for a psychology course on theories of personality was not very successful, but the teacher's comments and suggestions provided the kind of help that Joan needed in order to improve her papers, evidence of the learning she felt could take place in response to writing that did not occur with short answer examinations. In the paper, Joan had attempted an analysis of a young man suffering from what she called "anti-social personality disorder." Joan had written that the subject's behavior "is demonstrated by this individual many times in the many schools and facilities where he was placed." Her instructor cited specific details from the case study that Joan should have considered and analyzed more carefully (e.g., information that "this [moving around] should have explained some of the truancy and misbehavior and alerted them to get the mother in and interview her carefully"). From these comments, Joan could see that she had not included enough of the details from the case study to provide the required in-depth analysis.

Joan's next paper in the course was more productive, as she speculated on the causes of the behavior of the individual she was analyzing. In a paper titled, "The Man in the Shell," Joan asserted a greater degree of self-confidence that she had evidenced in her earlier papers. Although she continued to frequently cite authorities, she brought to bear her own analysis of the subject's problems: "Here is a man with many negative thoughts, a slim build, and extremely low self-esteem. One does not need a scholar to figure out this individual has an intense phobia or fear of people, activity, and/or pleasure." She followed this expression of her view with a series of speculative questions about how the subject might behave in situations not described in the case study data, in the conditions she postulated. Even though the instructor had a different view from the one expressed by Joan, Joan was not punished for taking a risk. She received a grade of 8 out a possible 10 on the paper, and the instructor wrote "good" beside the grade marking. Her grade in the course was a "C."

The classroom observation that semester was for Joan's other psychology course, Introduction to Human Development—Adolescence. Students were required to take four in-class multiple-choice exams and write one paper of about 12 to 15 pages on approved fieldwork or an interview project with prior approval from the instructor. Alternatively, they could complete a take-home final that would be handed out in class. The final grade in the course was determined by a complex formula in which the average of the four exams was doubled and the grade on the final paper was added. This total was then divided by three. The observer stayed for the first hour of the 2-hour class. During this time, the professor helped the students to prepare for the midterm exam that they would be taking at the next class meeting. The professor offered advice about how the students could best learn for the exam: "First read the introduction, second the summary, then, the chapter. Never read the whole chapter at one time. At the end of each chapter, take notes. Reading alone does not work." This was the only time that a professor was observed explicitly recommending to students that they combine writing with reading as a way of learning. During the lecture, students gradually became more active in asking questions, and the professor was especially sensitive to the needs of students for whom English was a second language. The professor gave examples of the types of questions that would be on the examination.

Joan also received helpful advice in her U.S. society course. She wrote a paper on the experiences of Jean Baptiste in Haiti and the United States, integrating his experiences of growing up in Haiti with the economic conditions of that country. In her summary conclusion, Joan presented her own views on Jean Baptiste's determination to improve his life: "It is said that most Americans donot [sic] realize what it really takes to succeed because the red carpet is always rolled out for them to step on. Jean Baptiste believes that things must be taken away in order to really appreciate and preserve what we often take advantage of 'the good life.'" There was a strong sense here that Joan identified with these struggles. Her instructor commented both that he "liked this paper. It's got a solid theme" and alerted her to the fact that she needed to learn how to rearrange the elements in her paper so that they more clearly told the story she wanted to relate. If she would be able to make such changes, he said, "Then you'll have an A paper." This was exactly the kind of positive encouragement that Joan profited from.

Joan could surely have benefited from collaborative learning activities in courses that she had difficulty with, but she persisted as a loner, wistfully telling me of study groups working on the math problems in an astronomy course she was having trouble understanding. She failed the astronomy course, but passed it with a "D" in the fall of 1994. Although the two psychology courses she was taking were difficult, she passed both with "C" grades and received a "B" in the U.S. society course. She said she had learned that "if [she] really wants something, [she] really has to work hard for it." During this semester, the most important thing that had happened to her was that she had finally passed the Math Skills Assessment Test. She had had a tutor in math for 3 weeks and then she had reviewed previous tests. When she took the actual test, she even managed to finish the questions 5 minutes early. Thus, at the end of her fourth year at the college, she would now be permitted to register as a junior and removed from "Skills Assessment Test-Warning" designation.

Whereas in the past she had talked about writing primarily as a means of helping her remember the material better, now Joan saw writing as giving her an opportunity to elaborate on ideas and to give her personal opinion. In words strikingly similar to those that Linda had used, Joan said that "writing papers gives me an opportunity to prove what I have learned or if I have learned." Her papers allowed her to combine received knowledge with subjective knowledge. She had had a difficult semester, with personal problems, household problems, problems at work, and problems with "people I thought were my friends, but weren't." Feeling that she was depressed, she had gone "to talk with someone," and now she was feeling better. She was planning for the future, thinking about an internship she would like to have in the next semester.

When asked in what ways she felt that she was now a different person from the one she was when she started at City College, Joan said that she was really starting to understand that "business is business." She was "no longer laid back like I was in high school." "At first, I was into materialistic things at the college," she said. "I liked the building, the cafeteria, the lounge, the music. Now I believe that that was taking away from what I'm really at the college for. Now, I am into concrete things that the college offers, like films, or things that will help me get extra credit for my classes." She knew that she had to get her grade point average up. She said, "I'm really here to obtain a degree and get a job. I started to wake up in '91. My GPA was higher at first, but now I'm taking more difficult courses."

Joan said she had also learned things about her relationships with other people. She felt she was more tolerant of people than she had been initially at the college. "I had an attitude," she told me. "I was really stubborn. I've matured. If I didn't like a person, now I see it isn't a personal thing—just get what you can from the person." This comment was likely made in reference to instructors with whom she had not had good relationships. She said that she had left one course in the past because of such a difficult relationship and she had received an "F." She would no longer treat problems that way. She said, "I would let the professor know if there's a personal problem between us." She said she would not let that interfere with her work now; instead, she would take a more mature approach.

Recognizing that her visual disability slowed her down in undertaking complex writing tasks, Joan had learned by the fall of 1993, the beginning of her fifth year at the college, when I collected a writing profile from her, that she had to try to start her assignments a week before the due date. "Sometimes I drag [delay], sometimes I get on the ball." If she needed to do research for the paper, she went to the library. If she already knew something about the topic and she was interested, she would do an outline and introduction. But if the paper was on a more technical topic, she found all the information she could and took from it what she needed. She then wrote one or more rough drafts. In the more technical papers, she had to be sure of the facts. With easier papers, she wrote one draft and then made corrections. The more technical papers reflected a strong dependence on outside authority, the "received knowledge" described by Belenky and her co-authors in *Women's Ways of Knowing* (1986). Joan said that the writing process became distressing if she could not find the necessary information. She did not want to write from hearsay. The influence of authority was very strong for her, unlike for Ricardo who was determined to shape his own perspectives. The "easier" papers for Joan were in what Belenky et al. called "subjective knowledge."

Joan wrote her papers at a night stand in her mother's room where the lighting was bad, using a blue ball-point pen ("black is blah and makes me uncomfortable"). She used paper with big lines, probably because of her vision problems, but she said the "college ruled paper makes me feel cramped and prevents me from loosening up." She took her handwritten draft to a computer at the college and typed it in. She noted that as she was typing, "something may not sound right or I find a better way to say it. I do some changing at the computer or type in different stuff." So, although Joan may not formally call this process revising, this was what was occurring, although in a less conscious way than with Linda's awareness of the capabilities of revision with a computer.

Although she had passed the Math Assessment Test, Joan found that the required statistics course was her most difficult class that fall. In her world arts course, Joan talked with another student in my study who had also been in her English 2 class, Delores. Delores had been very successful at the college and had been accepted into the combined BA/MA program in psychology. Delores offered to tutor Joan in statistics. Joan passed the statistics course with a "D" and the philosophy course, where she had decided to avoid arguments when she found her own beliefs questioned, with a "C." She was now working part time, 3 days a week in an internship at a health center, doing counseling and clerical work.

Joan again strongly reiterated that writing papers was helpful to her in that "it tests what I know. If there are mid-terms and finals only, you don't get tested. I'd rather write papers. It gives me a hands-on of what I know and confirms what I know. If I just take a multiple-choice test, it limits your ability to express what you know." Joan recognized that writing served to alert her as to how well she understood the material in her courses. She said, "I fear that if I don't get writing, I don't have a grasp of where I'm going in the course. I have had more trouble with courses that don't require writing." She was still using mapping to help her with her writing. She said, "Mapping helps me find my thoughts. I use one word and look for another word that relates to it."

In her writing this semester, Joan once again drew on her knowledge of psychology to assist her in the analysis of materials. In a paper on the film version of *The Joy Luck Club* for her world arts course, she wrote: "The filmmaker wants us to empathize with the mother, by observing her, not as an antagonist, but a victim of circumstance, as she had no choice but to abandon her children, hoping that someone would have the heart to return them." Had Joan taken this world art core course earlier in her academic program, she would not have had these psychological terms and perceptions to assist her in her analysis. Her instructor was pleased with this insight and wrote "good" in the margin of the paper. In her analysis of the family relationships in the film, Joan emphasized the importance of love within a family, even when such love might lead to problems: "We all need love to keep us together as a family. Sometimes we can love someone so much that we take away what that person loves the most." Such commentary suggested a reflection on her own family history, perhaps in trying to deny drugs or alcohol to family members when she saw the destructive behavior that followed their use. The conclusion to the paper reinforced Joan's commitment to the importance of sustaining family in her own life. "Moreover, I went on to explain what I've learned, which was, that we must look beyond the realms' of pain and discomfort, in order for us to see the purposes of sacrifice, THE FAMILY." In this paper, Joan's insights from psychology combined with her real life experiences to allow her to see the events in the family's life in The Joy Luck Club as ambiguous and internally contradictory, as the family searched for solutions to complex problems. Here she had been able to see knowledge and experience as contextual and she was able to value both subjective and objective knowledge. (It is the same combination that she would bring to her position as a counselor in the methadone clinic after her graduation.) Her instructor in the world arts course was pleased with the paper, commenting: "You've worked very hard on this paper—it's quite apparent!—and have made some excellent insights into the themes, connecting the subplots. Very good." Joan received a "B+" on the paper and a "B" in the course.

During this fall 1993 semester, Joan had been taking three core courses (world art, philosophy, and political science), courses usually taken by students in their freshman and sophomore years. Having taken many courses in psychology by this time, her fifth year at the college, she felt more confident enrolling in some of the more abstract core courses such as philosophy. She had essay exams in the philosophy course and did sufficiently well to pass the course with a "C." In the two other core courses she took, she received a "B" in world art and a "C" in political science. She received a "D" in the psychology statistics course.

On a personal level, Joan told me "I have lost a good friend, but I felt that it was the best thing that happened since the person was no good anyway." Possibly this was a reference to her boyfriend, because she never mentioned him again in later interviews. Traub (1994) described Joan's difficulties with her boyfriend who had joined a Muslim community. He had told Joan that he expected women to be subservient.

In the spring of 1994, Joan returned to grappling with another persistent problem, passing the required two years of a foreign language. She had last taken a French course two years earlier and squeaked through it with a "D." She still needed two more semesters of French to complete the foreign language requirement. Her easiest course that semester was her world humanities course that focused on Black American studies. Her professor, a woman, talked about slavery and stereotypes in the course. Joan had read a good deal in this field, so she did not find the course difficult. In her voice as an African American, in one of her papers, Joan asserted a prime value of education for herself: "In closing, reading The Narrative of the Life of Frederick Douglass, one can conclude, education was, and still remains, the key element involved in overcoming oppression. One should never forget that knowledge is the one tool that can be used to overpower the white man." Inside Joan, not evident in her quiet demeanor, resided the pride that had carried her throughout the difficulties of her personal life and her college life to this point of achievement, within grasp of earning her undergraduate degree in the next year. She received a "B" on the paper, and in her comments, her instructor supported her and prodded her to think more deeply about some of the issues she had raised. She earned a "B" in the course. (Joan told me that she could only give me one paper from that course because her book bag had been stolen while she was in a restaurant.)

The classroom observation that semester was of a psychology class, Sex, Marriage, and the Family. There were three textbooks for the course, plus additional assigned readings. Students were evaluated on the basis of a midterm exam, a final, and a research paper. The syllabus described the intention of the course, "to discover the extent to which the behavior of men and women is biologically determined, and the extent to which it involves cultural learning. Material to be covered includes studies of both non-Western and Euro-American societies of the past and present." (In an interview at the end of the semester, Joan commented on how she had learned that things could be done in different ways in different cultures.) The class discussion was concerned with sex roles in different cultures. The professor introduced the term *femininity* as it was used in certain cultures and older civilizations. When she asked questions about the assigned readings related to the topic, some students responded to the questions, but it appeared that others had not done the reading. The professor then explained some of the rituals of the Muslim and Greek cultures, and students provided examples from their own cultures. After a further presentation on marriage rituals in different cultures, students were again asked to provide examples from their own cultures. There was good interaction between the professor and the students. She pointed out to the students that they needed to read the assigned text materials more carefully.

Toward the end of the semester, Joan got a throat and eye infection that she could not shake. As a result, she was not able to do the required reading for her courses and she fell behind in her preparation for final exams. She had to miss the final in the French course, and she failed the course. During this semester, Joan also worked at an internship in a psychiatric–mental health clinic at a hospital near her home in the Bronx.

Joan came to another realization about the role of writing during this spring term. She said that "Writing helps me put ideas into my own words—makes me think how things can be put more simply than in textbooks sometimes." This conscious realization of the value of putting ideas into her own language is a crucial insight for Joan. It was an insight mentioned by most of the students in my study, although the insight occurred at varying times in the students' academic experiences.

During her fifth year at the college, Joan successfully completed most of the required core courses, and she managed to pass the difficult statistics course. With the exception of the French course that she had failed, she was passing her other courses with "B's" and "C's." Writing had become the primary way she kept her grades up, as she continued to experience difficulty with short-answer examinations. She was increasingly able to apply the insights from her psychology classes to readings and concepts in other courses.

In order to graduate from the college, Joan needed to pass the English Proficiency Test, another writing test similar to the WAT. She took this examination in the fall of 1994, her sixth and last year at the college. One of the options provided for the English Proficiency Test allowed students to pick up a reading which would serve as the basis for some of the questions on the test. Students could select a question based on the reading or select one of the other questions that were presented "cold" to them as had been the questions on the WAT. Taking the exam in the fall of 1994, Joan selected a topic about the hardships facing arrivals in a new country either as immigrants or students. She wrote an outline, including in the introduction the three aspects she would develop in the paper. In her outline, she set out in the second section to consider *why* these were hardships, a significant cognitive move for her. This would be followed by a conclusion. In the exam paper, Joan focused on the hardships of Asian immigrants, drawing from the reading she had been supplied with. In each paragraph of development, she stated the point she wanted to make, established its significance (because . . . in order that . . .), and concluded with an example to illustrate her point. Her conclusion lays out the format she had used successfully for her readers: "In the essay, that you have read, I have stated some of the hardships, faced by Asian immigrants moving to America. I have examined why these specific things prove to be hardships. Moreover, I have touched base with specific examples which help to better understand why these specific tasks carried out by those individuals, are considered hardships." Despite her difficulty, still, with comma use and an occasional verb-form lapse, the organization and content of Joan's exam carried her to a successful conclusion. She had waited until her senior year, her sixth year at the college, to take this exam, and her exam book noted on the cover that she was a "graduating senior."

Passing the proficiency test was an omen of the generally good semester Joan was having. Although she was under a lot of pressure, she told me that she "didn't feel extra anxious." She said, "I go through motions one day at a time. I see other people with problems." During that semester, she was working 2 to 3 days a week in 4-hour stints at her internship in the drug and alcohol unit of the hospital that eventually hired her full-time. In the internship, she conducted group therapy sessions and felt very dedicated to her field work. She was also working 10 to 14 hours a week at Radio City

Music Hall. She was enjoying courses in family psychology and speech. In the latter course, she was polishing up her diction and articulation. She found it interesting to give presentations and the experience was useful to her when she had to speak to groups of individuals with drug and alcohol addictions in her internship.

The hardest course Joan was taking that semester was a sociology course titled "Magic, Witchcraft, and Religion." She said that it was being taught from "an anthropological perspective," and that "there was a lot of material to cover in the course." The syllabus for the course described the one required text and a sizable group of recommended readings. Course evaluation was determined by midterm and final exams, that would each count for 30% of the grade, a 10-page original research paper that would count for 30% of the grade, and class participation that would make up the remaining 10%. According to the syllabus, the course would "explore the relationship between social behavior and ideas about supernatural forces" such as the origin of religion in society, practices of witchcraft and magic in different societies and ethnic groups, and interpretations of ritual symbols and mythology. During the class meeting that was observed, students were explaining their final paper topics to their classmates. The professor commented that he thought it was "cowardly" that many students were absent and not telling others about their topics. Students gave their names, their topics, and a two sentence precis about their papers. The professor praised students as they presented their topics, valuing original research and saying, "In anything of investigation, learning directly is preferable." He also suggested that students bring their topics "up to modern times." The professor was supportive of the reports throughout, and at one point commented, "As you can tell, we have some hot papers."

In her paper on stuttering in the speech course, Joan used the pattern that had been successful for her in the past, summarizing her points in her conclusion. Students were required to use at least five references in preparing the paper, and Joan drew on outside authoritative knowledge, although her instructor commented at the end of the paper that "an encyclopedia is not the best reference for a technical topic" and "more up-to-date references would also help." Joan presented evidence that had been clearly gathered through her research, but she did not always document her sources carefully enough. Her background in psychology appeared to add additional evidence to her discussion, but since the documentation was so sparse, it was difficult to tell from reading the paper what came from the actual sources listed and what came from her background in psychology. A paragraph from the paper illustrates this confusion. Her instructor's comments are interpolated in brackets.

> In children, bashfulness may be present in their lives as being normal, but it is often [said that bashful children] develop a fear for speaking out. This can contribute to

stuttering (5) [a reference number]. A second speculated cause of stuttering is [low] self-esteem. This is the feeling that the individual has about him or her self to speak or communicate with others. Children often need to be given a chance to speak. If you as a parent, never let them voice their opinions literally, insecurity and low self-esteem will result, causing the child to stutter. Constant interruptions within a child's conversation are said to cause a paralysis of the tongue, causing the throat to tighten [References?].

Joan appended a statement directly to her reader that resembled one she had also used in previous papers: "I hope you've found this research paper to be most informative and interesting." She received a "B" on the paper and a "B" in the course.

By the time I saw Joan again at the end of the semester, Traub's book, *City on a Hill* (1994), had been published. Traub had written an entire chapter about Joan, calling her a "A Miraculous Survivor," but seriously denigrating her accomplishments. When she first read the chapter about her, Joan told me she had been deeply depressed. (I saw one of the counselors in the SEEK program to whom Joan had also talked, and she confirmed that Joan had been troubled and disillusioned by her experience with Traub.) Joan told me that at first she had worried about her family's reaction to Traub's discussion of her life and work, but "they didn't have much of a reaction." She felt that her degree was confirming for her that she was capable of doing what she wanted to do. The most important thing she had learned from her experience with Traub was "You just can't be nice to everybody. You can't trust everyone." She had been surprised by the book, apparently expecting a more sympathetic treatment of her experiences and accomplishments. Furthermore, she told me that Traub had been inaccurate in some of the things that he reported about her life. Since the book was published so close to the time that Joan would be graduating, it probably had less of an effect on her than it might have had if it had been published earlier. She had gained enough pride in her accomplishments that she could rather quickly overcome the immediate distress she felt when she first read the book. She still faced the dilemma of the foreign language requirement. She planned to take the third semester of French in her final semester and request exemption from the fourth semester because of her visual disability. She passed the French course with a "D" and was exempted from the fourth semester, enabling her to graduate.

In this last year, Joan was more conscious than ever of the ways in which writing had helped her to learn. She said, "I used to have trouble getting my thoughts together—how to get away from paraphrasing and putting thoughts into my own words. I stick to my concepts; it helps keep the thoughts well organized, in a structure. When I write papers, it helps me get better grades. I might have a mid-term 'C+,' but a paper gives me a chance to develop my own thoughts and prove myself more." This constant reitera-tion by the students of how writing gave them an opportunity "to prove themselves" reinforced the significance of including writing opportunities that allowed students, first of all, to learn for themselves and, secondly, to demonstrate their knowledge and understanding to others.

In her last semester at the college, Joan struggled with the required experimental psychology course, in which use of statistics was essential. The course was evaluated on the basis of short laboratory reports and a final exam. Joan still suffered from courses that required complex quantitative analysis, and she received a "D" in the course. The class session that was observed was scheduled to last for 3½ hours. It included both class lecture time for the first half hour and then 3 hours of experimental work in the computer lab. The teacher began the class by drawing a graph on the blackboard, commenting that for these graphs students would need to have a ruler, because anything other than a straight line would be unacceptable. The professor asked students to comment on problems with the graph as he added information to it. He illustrated some problems by drawing a graph that had appeared in *The New York Times*, and he explained what was wrong with it. He advised students that captions of graphs should not be too long as they were part of a communication skill. Most students were listening carefully and drawing copies of the graphs.

In the computer lab, the social science lab assistant who usually had the computers ready for the class was absent that day. There were 16 available computers, so students had to work in shifts. The professor distributed disks and gave instructions on how to enter the program into the computer. The students worked at their own pace, while the professor walked around the room checking on how they were doing. The students were told to be sure to write their findings down at the bottom of the screen, or they would have to do the work over again. When the students finished their work, they brought their information to the teacher's desk and wrote it on a chart that he would make copies of for everyone to have for use in making their graphs. There were two programs for the students to complete. While the students interacted with the professor, there was little to no interaction among the students.

Although Joan said that writing helped her "regurgitate" back what she had learned, she qualified this statement by explaining that she learned "not to mimic back to a professor but to apply what you learned from readings." "Writing helps me remember things," she explained, "because I have to apply concepts."

Joan had not come to City College as a very confident student. Burdened with complex physical, family, and economic problems, she slowly strengthened her resolve to complete her academic studies successfully. In her early years of study, she depended on authoritative knowledge to support her assertions. While this approach brought her to enough success to pass many of her courses, she increasingly found a demand for thinking that was more analytic. Like other students who had started in basic skills classes, Joan found that writing gave her better opportunities to demonstrate the learning she had achieved than did her performance on short-answer examinations. When given the opportunity to write research papers, Joan became able to apply psychological principles and theories not only to cases presented in her psychology classes, but also to literary works she was being asked to interpret. Quantitative studies plagued her throughout her years at the college, and she struggled to pass required college skill tests and academic courses like astronomy, statistics and experimental psychology. Because she had to work many hours at outside jobs to earn spending money, Joan forced herself to bring better planning skills to her commitments and to organize the time needed to fulfill her academic assignments more carefully. Over time, she came to see her professors as her allies, and she became comfortable seeking out their help. Writing became an essential means of learning, as she recognized that reading alone was not an adequate tool for understanding the complex materials she was encountering. Writing after reading helped her to remember material better and to comprehend meanings. Through her internships, she became increasingly committed to her work in psychology, and she felt that her coursework, her outside jobs (such as taking visitors to Radio City Music Hall on tours), and her family experiences had built her knowledge and confidence to a point where she could succeed both as a student and a professional person.

So here is Joan, graduating after 6 years, hired as a full-time counselor in a methadone clinic, reveling in her achievements after long and difficult years of stress and hardship. She told me in a telephone conversation in September 1995 that she was earning $25,753.36 (she knew the amount to the last penny) in a union job with full benefits, including 20 days' vacation ("since it is such a stressful job"), 12 sick days, 8 holidays, and 4 personal days. After 90 days, she expected to get a raise, and she would get annual raises thereafter. Her brother helped her realize that she was "making more money than anyone else in the family has." She would be using some of this money to move her mother out of the projects, and, for the first time, she would have "a room of my own."

Joan had been hired even though she had had no experience in this particular field because she "had done so well" as an intern in the drug and alcohol abuse program. She felt rewarded to have found a job so quickly. She said, "I was sort of like a mediocre student—it was hard, and I thought grades would count a lot. I was worried about who would hire me. A BS in psychology doesn't carry a lot of weight. But I was hired for a union position." She told me that her life experience helped her get this job. "I come from a family where most members of my family had problems [drug and alcohol abuse], so living through it gives you an indirect experience with families" with these problems. "I was a victim, and that gave me empathy, which is what the people in the clinic want." Clearly, her positive evaluations in her previous work experience at the clinic along with her life experience combined to outweigh an evaluation based solely on academic performance. Joan was extraordinarily proud of this accomplishment, having a real professional position with her own office, "considering where I came from in the past." She was writing up case history reports, and her supervisor told her that she was "a pretty good writer."

Joan was advised by the director of the SEEK program at City College to work for a few years and try to impress the people she worked with so that they would write favorable recommendations for her for graduate school. This was a special concern of Joan's because she knew that her undergraduate grades were not high. Her final cumulative grade point average was 2.24.

After 6 years of arduous school responsibilities, work responsibilities, and family responsibilities, Joan was not a "miraculous survivor," as Traub (1994) called her. There was no miracle that accounted for her success. Her accomplishments stemmed from hard work and dedication, and her most important trait: tenaciousness. She had become a contributor to the society through her own efforts.

Jacob

The prototypical "insider" in my study was Jacob, a Korean student who had received most of his elementary and all of his high school education in Australia. He was not required to take any remedial courses. He told me, in the fall of 1991, his third year at the college, that he knew exactly how to write papers for his college courses: "I read a book, make a long list of quotations, paraphrase some of them and quote others. I stick to what is in the book. I evaluate or give a critical analysis if that is what the teacher wants. I can figure out the teacher's feelings and don't cross him or her if the teacher feels strongly. I can be penalized if the teacher's opinions are different." Jacob's cynicism toward his college work is evident. But, in the same interview, he acknowledged that he was beginning to see that in order to succeed, he would have to begin working harder. He said, "I have a history of being a 'general Renaissance man' who happens to know a little about everything, but when it comes to greater depth in a specific field, I'm not so confident I can succeed." Having changed his major from architecture (when he received his first "B" in a course) to physics, he reported that his performance in the math and physics course he was now taking would help determine how successful he could be in the field of physics. He had learned from his previous history that he started out well but gradually fell behind. (He received a "B" in the math course and an "A" in the physics course and retained this major.) But, of course, his heart was not in these studies at all.

Jacob's heart was in creative writing. He once told me in an interview that if he did not have to worry about earning a living that he would like to write about Norse mythology, since it was so "dark." Because Jacob shared examples of his creative writing with me, I intersperse some excerpts from his poetry and short stories that were written at approximately the same time he was producing the required academic writing. The differences in tone and commitment are noteworthy.

As the youngest child and the only male in the family, Jacob was expected to succeed at some important endeavor. He lived with his mother and sisters (his father having remained in Australia) during his college years. After graduating in the spring of 1995, he returned to Australia for a visit, intending to return in the spring of 1996 to begin a master's program in computer science at a private university in New York City. However, when I spoke with one of his sisters in November 1996, I was told that Jacob had decided to remain in Australia for the present and that he had recently married and was "really happy." He was taking computer science courses.

Flower (1994) described "an able average student [Carter] who had learned to use the efficient strategies of knowledge-driven planning to advantage" (p. 128). Carter was shocked to discover that his "technique for fast text production no longer worked" (p. 128). Nevertheless, he continued to focus on content, "on the presence or absence of ideas and on the quality of correctness of his coverage of an assigned topic. The road to successful writing appear[ed] to lie in better knowledge telling" (p. 128). But, in the particular classroom setting Flower described, the knowledge-telling strategy was not what was expected. The student would have "to change some of his goals for writing, to alter his process and habits" (p. 129). The freshman writing class was a new discourse community for Carter and he would have to adjust to its different expectations. The question remained, though, whether the knowledge-telling strategy would work for Carter when he enrolled in other academic courses that focused not on writing strategies but on the often expected regurgitation rather than transformation of knowledge. When Carter tried his last-minute writing without substantial content, the strategy he used in high school failed in college. He told a writing partner in his freshman composition class that the previous semester he had written "five or six pages on nothing, but I included the words *African nationalism* in there once in a while. I thought, why this is just like high school, I can get away with doing this. I got the paper back, and it was a C– or a C, or something like that. It said 'no content.' And I was introduced to the world of college writing" (p. 153). Although this example indicated that the student could not get away with a last-minute draft that said nothing substantial, it was not evidence that the content-driven strategy would not have worked for him if he had included enough substantive information, the strategy that Jacob developed.

Jacob had received strong preparation for his undergraduate work in his studies in Australia, although he had been denied the opportunity after his elementary school years to write creatively. He had compensated for this by "making up" novels he was to review in high school or writing creative pieces outside of school. In the middle of his first semester, he told me that English was his most difficult course so far. He said, "I don't feel as certain about the ground I'm standing on and I often feel as though I'm just being carried on by the current instead of making my own waves—that is, I'm not sure exactly what I've learned." The importance of the creative dimension in Jacob's writing wasn't clear to me during that first semester, but I believe that he wished that the course had offered him more opportunities to express his ideas in imaginative ways. Geared as it was to preparing the students for the analytic demands of future courses, I can see that the class appeared to Jacob to be a continuation of the types of writing that had previously been required of him.

Jacob's analytic abilities were firmly in place by the time he began the freshman composition course. In an early paper on an essay by Mario Puzo, Jacob wrote:

> I feel that Mario Puzo had two major intentions in writing the essay "Choosing a Dream: Italians in Hell's Kitchen." The first of these was motivated by the desire that the story of the poor immigrant Italian should be told. And being both a writer and a child of such Italians, he felt that the responsibility for this fell on his shoulders. In telling the reality behind these people, he tried to dispel the superficial, and rather indulgent attitude that outsiders might have had about Italians. Namely the euphemistic clichés of the "lovable Italians, singing Italians, happy-go-luck Italians." At first the "coarse, vulgar and insulting" truth offended Puzo and made him feel contempt, and then pity. What he is telling us now, and what he has discovered for himself, is that the harsh truth glorifies those poor, illiterate, coarse and ultimately heroic people, not belittles them. . . .

Jacob's second point in the paper was that Puzo reached a point of "self-admonishment," for "not having seen the true value of his family and people" and for thinking himself superior to them. Jacob concluded his paper by writing, "The two [intentions] are obviously entwined, since the act of telling the story of the heroic Italians in a way compensates for his initial contempt, and makes his self-chastisement more meaningful." As these excerpts reveal, whether written in one or several drafts, Jacob was able to select appropriate evidence and develop appropriate implications from them.

Having read a series of essays and narratives about immigrant and minority experiences, in another paper Jacob compared the success of individuals from these backgrounds in the educational system. His thesis emphasized the role of the family: "The real factor behind the relative failure of minorities in the educational system as compared to the immigrant lies in the internal realm of the family rather than the looming external forces." In comparing his experience with that of a Vietnamese immigrant, he wrote:

> When we see the family environment too, we are aware of a contrast that supports the educational discrepancy. In a 1988 article titled "The Model Minority Goes to

School," a 10th-grade Vietnamese immigrant to the U.S. describes the pressures she faces from her family to excel in class. I can personally vouch for the accuracy of the description of the push for Asian immigrants at least to not only do well, but to beat everyone else. Not necessarily so in my own family, Koreans in general that I see around me, push their children without mercy from the beginning. Success not only brings personal glory, but is said to improve the image of the community of Koreans as a whole, a need to prove ourselves in our new home. . . .

Although Jacob here denied that personal pressure has been exerted on him, in interviews over the years, he made it clear to me that his mother had the highest expectations for him, particularly since he was the only son. In the conclusion to his paper, Jacob acknowledged that family influence was not the only factor in the relative success or failures of individuals, but he noted, "I am merely offering a new perspective in the old quandary." My comment on this paper encouraged his willingness to take risks, noting: "This is a very thoughtful paper with an original perspective. You use the evidence from the readings and from your own experience very well to support your points."

In a short paper asking students to assign themselves to a category system devised to assess immigrants' degrees of assimilation to the American society, Jacob described his own situation as follows:

I think that the category I most closely belong to, from the three established by Gordon, is the Anglo-Conformity model. In that all my acquaintances outside of the family are white and I do not participate in the "society within a society" of expatriate Koreans. However, Gordon's definition for my individual case could need to be modified, for I have not been so totally "absorbed" as to have lost all allegiances to my past. I still identify with Koreans to an extent, participate in some traditional Korean ceremonies with my family, eat ethnic Korean food and mix up my english (at home) with a splattering of odd Korean words. I would therefore fit into a more lenient version of Anglo-Conformity, not totally isolated from my native culture but basically "Westernized."

Because most of Jacob's life, since he was 8 years old, was spent in the "westernized" cultures of Australia and the United States, it is not surprising that he characterized himself in this way. And, because he also frequently spoke of himself as a "loner," he did not seek out the comfortable presence of others who had a similar cultural background in the available immigrant communities and organizations.

Having been placed directly into the freshman composition course on the basis of his writing on the WAT, Jacob was permitted to enroll concurrently in the required core courses. In his first semester, he was taking the initial core courses in world art, world civilization, and world humanities as well as a math course and the freshman writing course. He told me that was disappointed that he had to enroll in these "preliminary, general, non-architecture courses first" because he had wanted to go straight into his architecture major.

The easiest course for Jacob that first semester was the world humanities class. He said, "We do no work except for the exam-essays, which are easy because they are open-book and we can do it over the weekend." In an excerpt from one of the open-book essay examinations for the course, Jacob wrote about a quotation from *Oedipus the King*:

> "Oh light—now let me look my last on you!
> I stand revealed at last—
> cursed in my birth, cursed in my marriage,
> cursed in the lives I cut down with these hands!"

> . . . We must remember that *Oedipus the King* is not a story about a man who kills his father and couples with his mother, it is the story of a man who *finds* out he has killed his father and married his mother. And when again we ask ourselves what Oedipus' fault was that led to his tragic discovery, we find, surprisingly, that it was not his fault, but his virtues that damned him. Namely, his compassion for his people, his hunger for the truth, his determination, and his perseverance. There is a prophetic sense when he tells Creon: "I grieve for these, my people, far more than I fear for my own life." It is in fact all the qualities we admire in him which brings about his downfall. So where is justice?

Jacob's instructor wrote "Excellent" on his paper and gave him an "A."

Despite his early reservations and later cynicism about his writing, by the end of his first semester, Jacob had established himself as a proficient writer. As he later told me, the concepts in introductory courses were not difficult for him, and he quickly evolved strategies for carrying out his writing assignments. Although he dropped the noncredit freshman orientation course, he succeeded in all his other courses, earning a straight-"A" record.

In his second semester, Jacob enrolled in the second-level world humanities and world civilization courses and a more advanced philosophy course than the introductory core course. He was disenchanted with the world humanities instructor, saying that the "teacher doesn't really want to have students have different opinions." He felt that the best thing for him to do was "tell them what they want to hear." Jacob said that he "didn't go to the class too often;" rather, he read the material on his own. He received his first "B" at the college in an examination in this course, but he got an "A−" on a paper, and an "A" in the course. He had midterm and final essay examinations as well as papers in this course.

In an essay for the world humanities course on the "problem/presence of money in one or more works" read by the class, Jacob concluded his essay on *Candide* by reflecting on what real wealth was:

> *Candide* is a story of undulating fortunes, of passing states of both luck and suffering, and it is in the midst of this chaos that Candide searches for enduring happiness. He finds however that things such as appearance and wealth are temporal (as demonstrated in the case of Cunegonde who loses both through the course of the novel) and

nobility nothing but a useless shell in the absence of property. They therefore cannot be the solution to human woes, though no alternatives are offered till the very end. Candide however spends much of the time pursuing both, and thinks himself finally successful when he accidently comes upon the fabulously wealthy haven of Eldorado. The irony is that he DID finally come upon enduring and meaningful happiness, yet he was blind to the real wealth before his eyes and chose to see only the glitter of the gold and precious stones.

This paper again illustrates Jacob's ability to identify major themes and to draw implications from the evidence he finds in the material he is analyzing.

Jacob felt that the philosophy course was his easiest course because he "didn't have to learn anything new." "It's all logic," he said, "but you really have to learn logic by living." He told me both at the beginning and the end of the semester that he was learning how to "cope with his philosophy professor." He said that he got into arguments with the professor and he told the teacher when he "really disagreed" with him. He said that the short essays he had to write for the class "were not likely to get [him] into much trouble." In one of the essays, he had an opportunity to use his imaginative powers. The task was to "write a letter to a legislator as a lobbyist arguing against the planned building of a new airport in the city whilst committing as many fallacies [of logic] as possible through the emotional appeal." Jacob started by threatening the use of militant activities similar to those used by some antiabortion activists, then moved on to express concern about the possibilities of airplanes "falling on top" of homes near the expanded airport, and then concluded by suggesting that celebrities were opposed to the planned building. His final paragraph read as follows:

> Instead of being a dyke [sic] holding back the tide of human compassion and mercy, why do you not champion the cause instead? Believe me that the majority of people support our fight, the people who care and are intelligent enough to see into the future; some join this majority of better people and thwart the machinations of the mean few who would deprive us of the right to live! Let me assure you that I have personally discussed this problem with several CELEBRITIES in both sports and the pictures, and their overwhelming opinion seems to be to get this new airport off the drawing board and into the sewer. I believe that you are a reasonable man, and as a reasonable man will see my reasons and be convinced of the rightness of my protest. I furthermore hope that your convictions will lead to swift action to kill the newborn evil in its crib before it is too late for all of us.

The instructor wrote "good" as a marginal comment to each of the paragraphs, and "good work" at the end of the paper. Jacob received 18 of 20 possible points for the paper with a notation that 2 points were taken off for the paper being late.

In a paper on Kuhn's *The Structure of Scientific Revolution* for his world civilization course that semester, Jacob again demonstrated his academic vocabulary and his ease in synthesizing complex materials. In the introduction to his paper, he wrote:

As a partaker in the continuation of the Western tradition (i.e. West European) in learning, and with a background in theoretical physics, social sciences and philosophy of sciences, Kuhn speaks of the attributes and peculiarities of the nature of Science (and Scientific Revolutions) with the confidence of a native speaking his own tongue. His perspective is essentially one of an insider, and despite Kuhn's claims of going against the grain of society's norm, he is really fulfilling his part in the ongoing practice of his society in finding novel or rechurned perspectives of their past development (Kuhn's is no definitive interpretation by any means and contains as many holes as he professes is a part of scientific paradigms)—and what better aspect to focus on than Science when implicitly studying the European development?

After an extensive discussion of the concept of paradigm shift, Jacob notes that "the main point of Kuhn [is] that Science is ultimately not cumulative." In his conclusion, Jacob is critical of Kuhn's ideas and his expression of those ideas:

> I must state here that fundamentally I disagree with Kuhn, but some of the individual points he makes are fair and well handled. Unfortunately I found him much too repetitive and unable to express himself refreshingly—a necessity when writing a reasonably lengthy and scientifically orientated book for lay readers (of which I am one).

Jacob's instructor commented on the paper that it was "Excellent, well-written and perceptive essay!" He received an "A" on the paper and an "A" in the course.

Jacob's comments on Kuhn's style were of particular interest to me because this was the semester that Jacob first shared some of his creative writing with me. At the end of the semester, he gave me copies of two poems, one titled "Dying" and the other "Crypt." I told him that I would read them and then send him a note with my reactions. I reminded him that I was not a literary scholar, so I could only share a reader's response and reaction. The poem, "Crypt," composed in August 1989, just before he started at the college, read as follows:

> The gleam in the distance doth freeze into ice,
> Spawning a void of a cruel appetite.
> As forth from the nectar the bees chide delight,
> It snatches with passion our new paradise.
>
> Our pains come but one more than does our relief,
> Deliverance does no more than prolong our ordeal.
> My soul is stifled by a mountain of grief,
> That only the odiferous Death can heal.
>
> Each fleeting new hope doth show up but empty,
> Or transpire into sirens with hair of pure gold,
> And a voice like velvet, a smile oddly cold,
> Who from the deep, to the rocks doth tempt me.

> I fear the very waves that lap the shore,
> I fear the earth, that colossus at my feet,
> I fear the expanse the heavens meet
> But secure am I, in my crypt, in the core.

My reaction to Jacob's poems, written in late May 1990, engendered a long letter of response from him. I had written, in part:

> I'm touched by your poems—but I'm saddened by them too. The poem, "Dying," has a somewhat more hopeful feeling with the wish to continue living.
> In my comments, please remember that I am not a poet nor an expert in poetry. . .
> In the poem, "Crypt," I am puzzled by your use of archaic words like "doth." I very much like the images of the gleam in the distance freezing into ice. Does the "it" in the 4th line refer to "the gleam?" In the third stanza, I am a little puzzled by the second line where the sirens "transpire." I'm not sure what "transpire" means here. I am also a little unsure, in the 4th stanza, about how the speaker can have so many fears and yet be secure in the crypt at the same time. . . .

I will excerpt here passages from Jacob's lengthy response to my letter:

> I am writing (typing?) to thank you for taking the time to read and comment on my poems. I had not shown them to anyone besides the youngest (older than me—remember?) of my sisters before, even though perhaps it is more of an ordeal than a privilege! I want to assure you that I do not count your feelings any less simply because you are not an "expert" on poetry. Just as philosophers are the last people to see Life past their nose, and psychologists are too busy luxuriating in their assumed knowledge to learn about people, I am most cynical when it comes to anyone who professes to have acquired in examinations a talent that is largely inherent.
> Anyway, before I go off on yet another of my anti-everything tirades (as you have had some experience with!), I would like to respond to your criticisms. First of all I would like to say that I am overwhelmed that you were touched and saddened by the poems; the most gratifying aspect of art (whether it is writing or painting) is the idea of emotionally affecting some audience (or an individual) I believe. And even though I have no illusions about me overflowing with talent, it is wonderful nevertheless to have such a sympathetic reader as yourself! . . .
> Finally you question how one who has so many fears can be secure in the crypt. In response, I ask you, who else would feel secure in a crypt? The crypt isn't a material entity, the way that the sea, the earth and the heavens are, in fact the three examples given of the things I fear were specifically designed to encompass ALL material entity, ALL existence. The "crypt" isn't a positive notion like a home where I feel secure despite the fears, it is the RESULT of my fears, a surrendering, a kind of death (therefore a "crypt"), a deadening of all the senses that connect me with the elements, with the world. It is as much a negative notion as there can be and the word "secure" is said with a great deal of cynicism—since it sounds rather incompatible with the idea of crypt (to all but necrophiles!).
> . . . I thank you again and I wish you a happy summer. Perhaps one day (over the rainbow) when I might be able to publish a poem or two, I would dedicate them to you as a reader who helped me get some self-confidence!!

This remarkable letter revealed depths to Jacob's thinking that I had not encountered before. His passionate commitment to his creative writing stands in strong contrast to his disdain for "academic knowledge," which he sees as far removed from the needs of real people in the real world. I felt privileged to participate in this dialogue with him.

In that same semester, however, Jacob had risked letting his expository writing be evaluated by outside readers. He had asked me to submit an essay he had written for the freshman composition course on "Stereotypes and Racism" to the English Department's Awards and Prizes competition. One of the categories in this competition was called "The Mina Shaughnessy Memorial Basic Writing Award," and papers written in basic writing or freshman composition sections that year could be submitted. Jacob's thesis was that "A stereotype need not be always of a racial nature, however, racial attitudes depend on stereotypes designed to justify and perpetuate racism." He did not win the prize.

At the end of his first year, Jacob said that he was glad he was doing well; he felt an "intellectual or cultural challenge would be good, but I'm not really looking for reasons to work harder. I'm not self-motivated." In the second semester, Jacob had again received all "As" in his courses. He said that he hoped "architecture would be okay" when he got to it. He had deliberately chosen art courses over science courses although he had taken both during the first year because architecture combined these fields. He said he was "indifferent at this time" and had chosen architecture "just to make a living." His path at the college had been set by the end of this first year; he would do what he needed to do to get by. He had recognized that his writing style was adequate to receive the high grades demanded by his mother. He had agreed to select some field "to make a living," and, as it could not be creative writing, he felt no commitment to any profession. This lack of commitment led to his several changes of majors over the years.

Jacob said he had been "feeling lazy" that semester and that he wanted "to use the least effort." He felt under pressure to get high marks, but he did not really feel the college was the place to learn. He preferred to read novels on his own. In the previous semester, he had learned how to cope with pressure and exams. He had also learned "to write essays when you have nothing on your mind—with a little material, spread it out." He acknowledged one strength of writing, that "it forces you to be more clear about what you are studying." He added that writing, for him was "easily effortless; ideas occur while writing," emphasizing, perhaps unintentionally, the creative aspect of all types of writing. He proudly declared that he did not "write second drafts—they make [the paper] worse." His writing strategies at that point consisted of the following: (a) thinking of a beginning and go on; (b) if it is an important essay, developing points to raise; and (c) no drafts, just one gets you by.

During the subsequent summer, Jacob took the first course directly related to his major in architecture, a course in aesthetics. He was disillusioned by the course and the instructor, telling me in the fall that she had been "inconsistent, disrespectful, and too admiring of herself without any reason." He had felt that the assignments were unclear and that the professor did not provide helpful comments. He received his first "B" at the college. The highlight of his summer had been the completion of a short, 180-page, novel written in a fantasy genre. He felt that he still wanted to work on it more, perhaps converting it to a screen play. He said that he had enjoyed writing papers on individual books during his first year at the college, because "writing makes you aware of the ideas of the book when you look for a central idea or focus." If he did not have to write, he would have been a "passive reader."

The next level in aesthetics was Jacob's most difficult course in the fall of his second year. The course was to cover architectural history, but he felt that the readings were too general or too specific, and he had trouble hearing the lectures. He felt that he did not really know what the course was about. The introductory biology course was his easiest one that semester, even though some of the terminology differed from what he had learned in his courses in Australia. A writing strategy he had adopted was to use the ideas that came to him while he was reading, take notes and write down page numbers, come up with a general idea, and then select relevant material for his papers.

At the end of the semester, Jacob received a "B" in the aesthetics course and "A's" in all his other courses, biology, sociology, and world art. He passed both the freshman orientation course and one of the required semesters in physical education. I do not have copies of any of the papers he wrote during that semester.

Jacob had temporarily declared himself a sociology major, but he found himself not doing well in the sociology course he was taking that spring, so he was planning to change his major to physics. Because of his then-declared major in sociology, he was placed into an introductory physics course and an introductory core course section of astronomy. He found these his easiest classes because he had an adequate background in mathematics for both. He was less satisfied with the sociology and anthropology courses he was taking, feeling, for example, that the sociology teacher was not making the requirements for the course clear to the students. The entire grade of the course would be determined by a paper written as a group report, and Jacob said his group "didn't work out." Because he was so accustomed to working by himself, it is not surprising that the experience in the sociology class turned him away from the field, and at the end of the semester, he said the most important thing he had learned was "not to take more sociology." The decision to major in physics was satisfactory to Jacob because he said he liked the concepts in the field and they "helped him to see the world in a different way." He had been disappointed by the courses in the architecture major because he had expected them "to be 50% art and 50% science, but they were 95% art, and too subjective."

Writing for Jacob meant he "had to know it to write about it." He said that he "could hide problems in writing, because writing was more planned." "I can pick a calculated way to present ideas without editing," he added. Writing a paper in one draft, without prior planning, "just plunging in," had become "a matter of pride" for him. In his classes, he was taking notes and then rewriting them in a more compressed form. He then read over the compressed notes to study for exams.

The physics class that was observed was primarily a lecture, with the students asking questions. The professor began the class by explaining what would be covered that day and reviewing material from the previous class. He drew diagrams on the blackboard and demonstrated principles through the use of appropriate apparatus. The professor responded to questions and drew additional diagrams and formulas on the blackboard. The students took careful notes, often referring to their textbooks as they did so. Students took four examinations in the course, with both quantitative questions and short essay questions included. Occasionally, the professor included more extensive essay questions on the exams that asked students to incorporate their own thinking and experiences with what was being learned in the class. One such question illustrates this approach: "Beliefs die hard. This is true for beliefs in the sciences, and often even more so in social, political, and religious affairs. Why do beliefs die hard? What is the relation of the belief to the person that makes it hard to give up, and hard to replace with a new one that may be knocking at the door with the 'sound of truth'?" This kind of openness in the field of physics was attractive to Jacob and encouraged him to adopt this field as a major. He said he had had very little writing to do for his courses that semester, and he did not share any papers with me. He was almost halfway through a final draft of his novel, and he hoped to finish it during the next summer. He was also writing short stories and poems.

During that semester, he told me about his schooling in Australia. He had gone to a Church of England grammar school, a prestigious school for which students had to take exams to be admitted. Ninety-eight percent of the students from that school went on to higher education. In New York, he was living in a section of Brooklyn where there were not many Asians. Most people in the community were German and Hispanic, and he said that the groups got along. Being a college student did not affect his relations with others because he said he was "mostly a private person."

This second semester of his second year was also a successful one for Jacob, and once again he received "A's" in all his courses. Thus far, he had received "B's" only in the two aesthetics courses. To this point, then, Jacob's academic strategies had carried him to successful conclusions, and he had been reinforced in his decision to change his major to physics.

As mentioned earlier, it was in the fall of 1991, Jacob's third year at the college, that he first expressed reservations about his confidence to "automatically" succeed in his courses. He was waiting to see how he would perform in the math and physics courses that semester before deciding whether to retain his major in physics. His most difficult course that semester was the math course, and since he said that he did not enjoy mathematics, this was giving him doubts about continuing this major, but he believed he would stay with it so that he could graduate in two more years. His change in majors had already bought about a 1-year delay in his graduation. He felt more comfortable, however, with physics and math, because they were more "objective," whereas he felt that English and architecture courses were more subjective.

Jacob reported that the third level of the world civilization course he was taking that semester, on Asian studies, would be his easiest because there would be only one major essay and a final examination. He said that he could take any topic he wanted for the paper, and since it was due in December, he would wait until early December to start writing because he "felt comfortable writing essays." He told me: "I feel more comfortable writing than taking notes—my mind is medium when I'm taking notes—I don't know what's going on. I'm not thinking." "But," he added, "when I'm writing an essay, I'm more actively involved with the subject. I have to know the subject, but I can cloak ignorance by choosing where to go—giving the teacher a guided tour. I can fool the teacher, make the most out of the least. I need a certain cynical attitude to cope. This is a practical skill. I only develop a limited interest in the topic—remain a dispassionate observer."

Although this approach to writing was successful for Jacob in his academic writing, he had found less success that summer and fall with his creative writing. He had completed the final version of his fantasy novel and sent off three chapters along with a proposal to two potential publishers. He had received no encouragement from the publishers and had decided to shorten the first chapter before sending it out again. Jacob said that he had felt that it would be easier to have a "genre fiction" piece like his fantasy novel accepted than his more individualistic short stories and poems. He had hoped that acceptance of the novel would lead to acceptance of these other pieces.

In a take-home midterm exam for his U.S. society course that fall, Jacob responded to two questions. The second question was: "What was it that made it possible for the U.S. to succeed as a new nation in the years after 1790?" After considering the importance of the inclusion of the Bill of Rights, the powers of the Supreme Court, the raising of national revenue, and the ability to negotiate successful international treaties, he addressed the issue of the voting population:

Another important factor that contributed to the success of the nation was the change in the political scene. For a democracy to succeed there has to be a broad political involvement by the ordinary people, but the Federalists who dominated the early political scene did not bother with trying to reach the masses. For them the government was merely a collection of the best people—"those whose education, wealth, and experience marked them as leaders. For candidates to debate their qualifications before their inferiors—the voters—was unnecessary and undignified." The success of the Republicans who did not share these scruples and did away with the pompous garb of the congressmen, inspired imitation in campaigning for active popular support. The end result was greater public participation. In some states where both Republicans and Federalists campaigned, more than 90% of eligible voters participated between 1804 and 1816.

Jacob received a score of 91% on this exam and earned a "B" in the course.

At the end of the semester, Jacob told me that he had frequently missed his 9 a.m. physics class because it took him 80 minutes to commute to the college, and he "couldn't get" himself up at 6:30 a.m. He said that even though he had missed many classes, he was doing "okay on the exams." He said he had used to study 9 to 10 hours on the weekends, but now he was "worn out with studying." He had not developed relationships with any of his professors nor had he been active in any student organizations. Jacob told me he preferred the "impersonal" atmosphere of the college where he could be "anonymous and concentrate on studying." He felt this would lead to his being "less likely to make enemies." "Sometimes," he added, "I instinctively hate someone and they hate me. My logic is different from others, and I'm not really communicating with them."

During that same semester, Jacob wrote two short stories that he shared with me. In one of his stories, "Null and Void," two shipwrecked men struggle to a deserted island where they find fresh water but no food. After several days, they discover a deep well filled with fruits and meats. ("something beyond belief"). The only way to recover the food is for one man to go down into the well, gather the food, and then be pulled up by his companion. The last two paragraphs of the story convey the despairing tone of Jacob's creative writing:

> Thus the issue was decided and the plan carried out. Before too long the Weak One was at the bottom of the well, staring goggle eyed at the culinary wealth around him. Snapping himself out of his inactivity, he proceeded to fill his pockets with the food, every now and then pausing to stuff his mouth with a handful of meat. "Hurry up—I am starving!" called out the Strong One. "What's taking you so long?" "Stop being so impatient, I'll be right up!" "You are eating already, aren't you!!" roared the Strong One accusingly, "I can tell by the sound of your voice that your mouth is stuffed as you speak!" "Stay your anger buffoon! It is no hardship for you to wait a few more seconds, and besides I am done already and waiting to be pulled up." "All right then, but we must deduct what you have eaten from your share." Now it was the Weak One's turn to be angry, "How dare you!! I should have received more than fifty fifty in the first place anyway! All YOU do is pull on the rope. I not only collect the food, but I thought up our plan!" "This is an outrage!! I have to pull and strain till sweat

beads my temple while you stuff your face like a pig below! My part is far more demanding and valuable than yours and thus I deserve more!"

The face of the Weak One crinkled in devious contemplation for a while, hidden from his brother by the darkness of the well. "If your part is so valuable, then why is it that if I merely withdraw my own humble services, you are left to starve to death!? I gather the food and without me you die!" Silence answered his challenge long after the echoes had died down, and when finally the reply came it was spoken in a measured voice that chilled the listener. "Call me a buffoon? Trivialize my efforts? You may have the food but I hold the key to your prison, were I to decide so I could leave you trapped within the suffocating confines of the well, better than any dungeon." The Weak One shuddered, but he knew that he also held a winning hand and he decided to call the bluff. "Remember, turn your back on me and you starve!" More silence . . . Suddenly, abruptly, a slithering shadow falls down and hits the Weak One across the face. Wincing, he reaches up and feels it in his hand—it is the rope.

In talking with me about this story, Jacob said that he felt that in many works of fantasy, "everything turns out too well." In his own writing, he wanted to change fantasy writing, "try to make it more unpredictable." He wanted to "delay the reader knowing how things will turn out."

By the end of the semester, Jacob had performed well enough in the math and physics courses, earning a "B" and an "A" respectively to retain his physics major. He also received a "B" in his world civilization course, thus, for the first time, earning three "B's" and only one "A." Apparently his concerns about how he would fare in upper level courses were well-founded. Of course, his disillusionment with studying also contributed to his performance.

In the spring of 1992, Jacob enrolled in the introductory philosophy course (even though he had already completed a more advanced course), chemistry, earth sciences, math and physics. In the philosophy course, one of his papers was on the topic: "Using Bertocci's notions of 'personality,' 'will-agency,' and 'will power,' choose one aspect of your personality that you would like to change but cannot. Does it prove anything for either freedom or determinism?" In this paper, Jacob demonstrated his ability to articulate complex ideas clearly and apply them to his own situation. He presented the aspect of his personality under consideration by writing: "I have in the past found myself lamenting my introversion and inclination towards a hermit existence. Upon deciding to break from this pattern of behavior, I was seeking to free myself of the shackles of my traditional personality. . . . Ultimately my endeavor was to fail." In a later discussion in the paper, Jacob related his efforts to the theoretical issues under consideration:

Before we discuss the other reason, let us draw a distinction between what Bertocci calls "will-agency" and "will-power." Will-agency is our free will, whilst will power refers to our effectiveness in overcoming the many obstacles in realizing one alternative over another. The latter is not necessarily proportional to the actual amount of will we can exert, since the level of obstacles we face varies depending on the nature of the choice and the circumstances. Therefore will power is "the ability of will-agency to overcome opposition." Now if we were to say that the ability of wind to move objects lay in its strength, then the fact that in one instance an object was too heavy for the wind to move does not necessarily mean there was no wind. In the same way, the fact that my will power was insufficient to meet the various obstacles does not mean that I have no will-agency.

Our free will is not limitless. If it were so, then there would be nothing gained from developing good habits nor in eschewing bad ones, since at any point in time we are equally capable of doing both. However within those limits, determined by all the hereditary and environmental factors around us, we have real free will. Just as some of the choices we make may restrict our freedom further in the future, others can break the mold and help us remain free. Though my will power was insufficient at the moment to disrupt my introvert habits, I was still able to will myself to think about the options and to make a decision to try and change my ways. The difference between one who possesses no will agency and my own experience lies in the effort and the battle that occurred within myself. . . .

At the end of the paper, Jacob's instructor wrote: "This is again excellent work—clear and well organized. 100." Jacob received "A's" in all his courses that semester, except for the physics course, in which he earned a "B."

By the end of this third year, Jacob had reassessed his abilities, still having confidence in his strength in writing academic papers, but recognizing that complex materials would not necessarily come easily to him. The objectivity of the science courses pleased him, while he felt less sanguine about the subjectivity of some courses in the arts and humanities. He was continuing his creative writing, and he gave me another short story to read at the end of the spring semester. This is the most macabre of the stories he shared with me. The story begins as follows:

the 12th of May

It happened half a dozen times though I recall not when it began, only that on each occasion the passage of events would follow this general course. I would be sound asleep when, without warning, a touch of a hand would awaken me, but no matter how swiftly I opened my eyes—my reaction heightened by the tangible presence of real fear—there was never a cause to be revealed. The only remnant of the experience, and that which convinced me it had not been a dream, was the coldness on my cheek where those deathly fingers had been pressed. Needless to say I was deeply affected, oh how I was indeed! Little that words convey could allow you, the reader, to live through those nights as I have. Fearful to sleep lest the hand return and fearful to remain vigilant lest I should see its owner. . . .

This very day there has been a disturbing twist to my predicament which I discovered earlier this morning while looking into the bathroom mirror. It appeared that an outline of a hand had been imprinted upon the right side of my face, and the skin within was visibly whiter than the remaining areas yet untouched. Drunk with anxiety, I had reached up and touched the spot and not without hesitation. The thing was cold to the touch, and the nerves were dead so that it was as if I were touching the face of another. What was perhaps the most unsettling thing of all was when, quite by chance, I discovered in the process of my investigation that my own hand fitted perfectly the mark so mysteriously made. Such a chill rushed down my spine then that for a moment my whole body died, and it was a while ere the relentless beating of my heart could pump blood back through my veins and life into my eyes. I can see now the handwriting on the wall, but I do not understand yet its full portent, nor whether perchance it is written in my own hand. Perhaps future events will clarify the nature of my fate. . . .

As the story continues, over the next few days the protagonist decided that since his own hands were the "culprit," he would wrap them as tightly as he could with a pair of cords. Experiencing excruciating pain from this, he found in the morning that his hands had "promptly dropped off." Then, he asked a friend who kept "all manner of ghastly things" to lock up his hands and write his tale as he dictated it. He found himself tormented the next night and his hands mysteriously reappeared in his bed. He then asked his friend to take the hands far away after he had completed typing this part of the story. After one peaceful night's sleep, the narrator decides to venture out to a local tavern because he "was free, free at last!" He is disappointed that his friend and neighbor is not at home. While sitting in the bar, he is approached by a police sergeant who first confronts him with the stumps of his hands and then tells him that he is charged with the murder of his friend:

From what I could glean at the police station I discovered that my friend had been found in the other side of town, dead. Apparently he had been strangled, and the finger prints on his neck matched those of the amputated hands which were found in the vicinity of the crime. The sergeant who had found me had been on his way to the home of the victim with evidence in hand, and while taking an unofficial detour to the tavern, had seen me with my stumps and put two and two together. . . . The state version of the story was that I had myself removed them in order to destroy the damning evidence of the fingerprints. And though this story hardly held water, it was deemed far more satisfactory than my own account of the events as I knew them. . .

The story ends as the writer awaits his hanging. His posthumous "request was that the hands be burnt like the rest of my body, at least then I would have had a measure of revenge against my own hands." This eerie tale stands in direct contrast to the analytical stances Jacob took in his academic writing.

By the beginning of his fourth year at the college, Jacob was enrolled entirely in science and math courses, two in physics, two in chemistry, one in math, and one in biology. He told me that in the physics courses, "everything is math." He said that as the professors talked and wrote notes on the blackboard, he copied them and hoped to make sense of them later, the same strategy that Ricardo had adopted in some of his classes. Rewriting the notes later helped him understand the materials better. He said, "To write it out you must organize it in your head. The process of writing itself forces you to understand—you have to have some idea yourself." He also mentioned that he would "read a bit" in the textbook, find the relevant section in the text, then find the related part in the notes, and rewrite his notes. Jacob told me that he put "a lot of effort into answering a few questions." This caused him to "get behind in other courses." He was thinking about trying to get tutoring help. He was finding the biology and chemistry courses somewhat easier. Jacob reported that the previous semester he had come to understand that physics would be a difficult field. In this semester, his prediction had come true, especially now that he was in classes that were specifically for physics majors.

In the middle of the semester, Jacob stopped in to see me to tell me that he had learned that the English Department gave awards for creative writing (part of the same awards system to which he had submitted his freshman expository essay several years before). He said that he planned to enter several of the categories, such as poetry and short fiction. His primary motivation seemed to be the possibility of earning some award money, and this had overcome his aversion to allowing his work to be evaluated by creative writing "experts." (As City College had an extensive creative writing program for both undergraduates and graduate students, the competition for these awards would be intense.) He also told me at that time that he had submitted sample chapters of his novel to three publishers, but had been told by all of them in a formulaic way (perhaps in a form letter) that the work was not appropriate for publication. He felt that without an agent to represent him, his work would not get a serious reading.

At the same time, Jacob stated that he was doing well in math and was considering going on for a PhD in physics so that he could become a college professor. He indicated that he "wasn't much interested in the field, but it was a way of making a living." He did not think that his mother would approve of his changing majors again, so he would "stay in physics and write on the side." The pieces that were cited earlier were among those he submitted for the creative writing awards. He did not win in any of the categories.

The class observation for that semester was for one of the physics courses in the area of mechanics. The small class of 12 students, all physics majors, was intently interested in the professor's lecture and explanations. The class began with the professor returning corrected homework and discussing problems with the students. He told them that in future exams, they would be permitted to bring their notes, for he saw "no use in memorizing formulas that could be looked up." The professor added, "I just want to know whether you know how to apply the formulas." He then began his formal lecture, frequently repeating and simplifying formulas. The students were very active in responding to questions. The professor carefully responded to student questions, providing everyday examples to clarify his points. He was extremely concerned that students followed his points. During the last part of the class, he provided a handout and went over it step by step.

At the end of the semester, Jacob told me that learning about the English awards had "brought meaning to my life." (The results of the award competition were not to be announced until the spring semester.) He had

had time to write only intermittently because of the pressures of his courses. Now he was somewhat more pessimistic about his future in physics. He said that when he had tried to catch up in one course, he had fallen behind in others. Because he had changed majors twice before, he now needed to take six courses so that he could graduate in 1½ more years. He was still planning to go on to graduate work in physics, and he said he would "persevere." He did not have to do any writing in his courses. When asked what the most interesting thing was that had happened to him that semester, he replied, "Nothing interesting happens to me." He earned "As" in one of the physics courses, one of the chemistry courses, the biology and math courses. He received a "B" in the other chemistry course, and a "C" in the other physics course, the one that had been observed.

In the spring semester of his fourth year, Jacob was enrolled in four physics courses, one math course, and one biology course. One of the physics courses was a continuation of the one in which he had received a "C" the previous semester, and he had the same instructor. Jacob's "read" on the class differed sharply from the impression garnered by the research assistant who had observed one of the class sessions the previous semester. Jacob claimed that he "couldn't understand the teacher. He was very smart, but not a good teacher. He didn't encourage student questions." Because the observation was of only one class session, it is not possible for me to come to a clear determination as to what precisely the learning environment was, but regardless of the differing interpretations, it is clear that the pedagogical approach had not worked for Jacob. At the beginning of the semester, he told me that this follow-up course was his most difficult one. (He received a "C" in this course.) He was also having difficulty with the required biology course, because he had to dissect animals and he "didn't have the stomach for that." (This from the writer of ghoulish fantasy stories.) He said he had no easy courses that semester, and that he was still "trying to do the most work with the least effort." "I often let things go to the last minute," he added. "That was one of my problems with one of the physics courses last semester." That was the course he had received the "C" in. At the same time, he said that he realized he "has to study more—I need to keep up." He said he was trying to do that more than in the last semester. He was finding the physics course on relativity interesting, and he said, "That's one of the reasons I became interested in physics. The ideas seem so different."

Jacob was using the same strategy of condensation that he had developed earlier with note-taking. He described his method: "I copy notes, condense them and rewrite them. My class notes are messy and not organized. I take the relevant text notes and put them together and try to organize them." An indication of his indifference to his college studies was his revelation that he had missed the first week of classes that semester because "the registration material didn't come and I didn't inquire."

The class observation that semester was for a course called Modern Physics. This was another small class with only six students present. The professor announced the next exam for the following week, indicating the chapters in the textbook for which students were accountable. He then began his lecture, writing formulas, graphs, and sentences on the blackboard. He explained ideas clearly, giving examples from everyday life. Students appeared to follow and understand the lecture and responded immediately to questions.

Near the end of that semester, Jacob told me that he "understood the field of physics better but was less interested because [he] knew more about it." He still felt that he would have to go to graduate school and was considering the field of astrophysics because he had taken an astronomy course and "found it interesting." He said that his life was "dull," and that he was going to have to go overseas that summer to get the appropriate student visa he needed since he hadn't applied for one when he first came to the United States. His life was a "waste," he said, and he "learned nothing." He was hoping he could get by without learning much about physics—"just enough to get by in class." "Real learning," he emphasized, "is something you feel enriched by." His final grades that semester included "A's" in one physics course and the biology course, "B's" in two physics courses and in math, and the "C" already discussed in the fourth physics course.

When asked whether he felt he was a different person than when he had started at the college, Jacob gave a long and revealing reply:

> I'm more disillusioned. When I started, the whole idea of college was a more exciting prospect, but it hasn't turned out that way. My own failure, because I didn't respond to it the way I thought I would. I'm more tired, more depressed, more irresponsible. It has to do with the fact that I'm not interested in anything. I'm trying to find a niche—maybe some obscure subject in this world.
>
> If I were financially independent, I might major in art, easy and quick, for cultural things, if I didn't have to have a job. I would live in Iceland and write about Norse mythology. I like cold weather, rural life. . . . Norse mythology is less well-known but is more satisfying. Norse people believe in the end that darkness will triumph and that the bad side will win. The important thing is not winning or losing but how hard you fought. Characters are more complex. I would like to use these heroes or characters—to popularize Norse mythology. I need to read more in it. . . .
>
> Everything in the future seems dark but I hope for some "divine intervention" that will change things. My family believes in fortune tellers and a prediction was that I would become sick and recover (it happened), but they also predicted that I would attain greatness, but I am skeptical. It's very important what the individual dreams and what his mother dreams. She dreamed she was seeing a beautiful sunrise—something nice, a gift from God. There's added importance because I am the only son. The son should be successful, a great figure in whatever he chooses.

The pressures on Jacob from his family can be clearly seen in this telling monologue. Ironically, he states that the son should be a great figure in whatever "he" chooses, but in his case, the choice has not been left up to him. So, after four years in college, Jacob could be described as an able student, but more importantly as a perfunctory one, completing the demands made by others while neglecting the internal ones so central to his real sense of a life.

In the fall semester of 1993, Jacob's fifth year at the college, he was taking three physics courses, a math course, and a Spanish course, to fulfill the college's foreign language requirement. All of the physics courses were difficult, but he said that the hardest was an advanced level lab course. He complained that the "labs were unstructured" and it "was not clear what he was supposed to do." He said that some of the "handouts have missing pages." This course was clearly a problem for him, reflected in the fact that he received a "C" in it while earning "A's" in the other two physics courses, as well as in the math and Spanish courses. In contrast to his difficulty with the physics lab course, he described his math class, the highest level physics math course, as "lucid and clear." He had had the instructor for previous math courses and had found that the tests covered material that had been presented in the lectures. In his physics classes, he was still writing everything down that was said in the lectures and "figuring out later what was important." He was using his process of selection afterward because he "couldn't tell during the lecture what was important." In preparation for exams, he was "rewriting his notes more succinctly, reading them on the train before the exam, and then regurgitating it all out" in responding to the questions.

This was the semester that I collected the writing profiles. Jacob said that when he started his college courses, he had found the writing assignments easy to carry out and he disdained revising his writing, developing a one-time draft strategy that worked well for him. Here is his description of how he worked through his writing assignments at the college:

> I found it so easy. Even though I don't have a lot of information, I just type away. I'm good at expanding and including a lot of rubbish. I guess it's just a natural gift. If I have a week, I have five days free because I can do it in one sitting. For example, in a history essay, I have certain information to give to the reader and I find whatever extra words are needed. I can belabor a point and expand the paper to a respectable length. I have gotten good marks, so I have no incentive to change.

If a paper required library research, he also had a formula for carrying out those assignments. He went to the library, selected about three books related to the assigned topic and took them home. He waited until close to the deadline when the paper was due and then read one of the books more thoroughly so that it could serve as the main guideline for his paper. He used the other books for minor points so he could include them in the bibliography. His first draft might be rubbish and he might need to write a second draft. When he got explicit guidelines for a format, he followed them carefully. He wrote on a word processor at home in his bedroom/study, usually during the day when it was quieter. He took advantage of the flexibility of the computer to move or insert information. He expanded the information to fit the required length for the paper. A paper that did not require research was the easiest kind for him. He said, "I wait until the last minute, look at the question to get ideas, have some vague notion, let my mind go blank, and then my fingers follow my meditation. It's usually very easy for me."

This picture of Jacob writing contrasted sharply with the energy and effort expended by the students who started at basic writing levels. Jacob's prior preparation and skill permitted him a cynicism toward his college work that was impossible for students with weaker backgrounds. Already in his second semester at the college, Jacob thought he had "psyched out" the appropriate response to the academic demands being made on him. He told me, "Teachers don't really want to have students have different opinions. The thing to do is tell them what they want to hear." He said that he realized this was a cynical position, but he saw it as a pragmatic one if he wanted to succeed. That fall, he also told me that in high school he had had to write essays and book reviews. For one class, he had made up a book and reviewed it. He received an "A" on this paper and was apparently delighted to be able to both do creative writing (something discouraged in the English courses) and fool his teacher. At the college, he continued to pride himself on writing papers at the last minute, belaboring points and expanding the paper to what would be considered a reasonable length. He told me that he knew that he could write more concisely, but since this would lead to bad grades, he did not attempt to do so. Earning high grades was crucial for him and also for his family's pride.

The classroom observation that semester was of the second-level modern physics course. Grades were determined by two exams, a midterm and a final. The class was basically a lecture on properties of light and waves, and the students frequently asked questions, with the professor responding by putting formulas on the blackboard and constructing models to illustrate his points. He encouraged students to use "keen observation" when they did their laboratory experiments. Students followed the lecture carefully, taking notes and responding to the professor's questions.

The one sample of writing that I have from Jacob's science courses is an examination booklet from one of his physics courses. The booklet is nearly entirely comprised of formulas and equations. One of the equations is supplemented by this brief discursive section:

> A blackbody is both a perfect emitter & an absorber. It absorbs everything (i.e. no reflection) and emits everything (at equilibrium).
> A frying pan is an approximate black body because it absorbs most of the heat (and reemits it to cook food).

An astronaut in space shouldn't wear a spacesuit made of perfect blackbody material because it would absorb all the radiation it encounters.

Jacob received a –2 for this question and 89 of a possible 100 on the exam. This exam was written in one of the physics courses in which he received an "A." Clearly such limited writing opportunities provided no outlet for his creative spirit.

The only sustained piece of writing I have from Jacob's last year at the college is his response to the Proficiency Test Writing Examination. (He had waited until the last possible semester to take it, obviously not expecting any difficulty in passing it.) For that paper, Jacob chose the topic of what it means to be the first-born child in a family. After noting that the first-born experiences "a shift of affection or at least of attention" when the next child is born, he described his experience in his own family:

> One might discard this point [about the shift in affection and attention] by saying that both children get their share of demonstrative love, only at different times. However there is a crucial difference: one child experienced someone taking his or her place in the center of the parents' lives and the other suffered no such abrupt change. In my own family of 4, I am the youngest. Everyone has, to different degrees, suffered through this hurt of sibling jealousy, except me. As the youngest child, I was the recipient of effusive care and attention well past the normal age for such treatment. Of course this may also be a double edged sword, for one needs that certain detachment from one's parents in order to mature as an adult. However, how one responds to this situation, I believe, is largely due to the individual. Some might welcome the benefits and eschew the pitfalls, while others might fall right in.
>
> On several occasions my mother has told me how she learnt valuable lessons in parenting her earlier children and was able to avoid many mistakes with her later ones. This points to another disadvantage of being the first born, for no amount of preparation can equip one to raise a child like prior experience. . . .

Jacob's facile writing skills were clearly in evidence here, and he had no difficulty passing this test.

During that semester, Jacob's mother left for Korea, planning to spend 1 or 2 years there to attempt to sell some real estate she owned. Jacob was then living with his sister, which he said was "not so easy." For the first time, he was working at a part-time job cleaning apartments for 4 to 5 hours over the weekends. His mother wrote to him every day.

By the end of the semester, Jacob had changed his mind about studying for a PhD in physics and instead had decided to pursue a master's degree in computer science. He had become interested in robotics and artificial intelligence and he was reading on his own in the field of computer science. He asked me to write a letter of recommendation for him to the graduate school to which he intended to apply. I did so, and later learned that he had been accepted into this program.

Jacob also had decided to study the college's *Bulletin* to see what courses he needed to graduate. His physics advisor told him that he did not need all the courses listed and that he could graduate in the next semester. Part of Jacob's decision to pursue graduate work in computer science was determined by his having read a job market book that indicated that there were few jobs for physicists, but growing opportunities for computer science majors. He said he thought this field would be interesting to him because he had found "the ideas in the modern physics courses interesting." He had tried over this semester to become more responsible, as, for example, in taking the initiative to talk with his physics advisor. He now regretted that he had not majored in computer science.

Jacob described himself at that point as "just plodding along doggedly." He said that he was "an even-keeled personality—without real highs or lows in his life." He was now beginning to plan for his future after graduation.

For his last semester, Jacob enrolled in two physics courses, a computer science course, and the required Spanish course. His most difficult course was a continuation of the modern physics classes, and he was not pleased with the instructor, whom he had had in a previous course. He said that the professor lectured in a monotone, and sometimes corrected himself at the end of a class, making it necessary for Jacob to rewrite his notes. He had made a photocopy of the textbook, with some tops and bottoms of pages missing.

The classroom observation that semester was of this physics class. The professor was late. He then announced that he would be away for a few days, so he discussed dates with the students when they could make up the classes. There were ten students present. The professor then provided an overview of the lecture and introduced a discussion of electrons. He wrote formulas and charts on the blackboard to illustrate his points. Students took notes, and some asked questions for clarification. When students offered examples to illustrate the principles, the professor corrected them when necessary. The lecture continued with a few students being outspoken and demanding further clarification and explanations.

Jacob's easiest course that semester was an introductory computer science course. He felt that he had an aptitude for that field; in addition, the course was geared to students who did not have the depth of knowledge about mathematics or computers that Jacob had. He had learned one computer language, and his sister and brother-in-law, who were computer programmers, had promised to teach him another one.

The writing strategy of combining textbook notes and classroom notes continued. Jacob noted that he could "read without thinking, but when writing, you read while you're writing." He continued to condense notes to make his studying more efficient.

As his graduation neared, Jacob told me that he had found "everything in physics useless—only the math background is useful." He said that when he chose physics as a field, he did not know what area to go into. But because there were few projects in physics to go into, and computer science was "growing faster," that would be a better area for him. He continued to be interested in robotics and artificial intelligence. He was still planning to go to graduate school for a master's degree in computer science.

Jacob said that he had done no writing that semester. He was "not going to push to be a writer—just relax and see what would be a natural outflow." He added that he was considering branching out to write children's stories.

Jacob's experiences at the college contrasted sharply with those of the other case study students presented in this chapter. With his rigorous academic background from his education in Australia and his natural affinity for writing, Jacob had been overprepared for the introductory courses he took in his first 2 years at the college. Because of his facility with writing and the lack of intellectual challenge, he evolved strategies for completing his academic writing assignments with the least amount of energy and commitment possible. This hardened his already cynical approach to college studies until he found himself confronted with more rigorous courses and more rigorous demands. Even then, when the science and mathematics courses became difficult, he did the minimal amount of work required to complete the courses. Denied the opportunity to spend his life writing creative pieces, Jacob acquiesced to his mother's demands that he pursue a profession that would bring pride to the family. But, in this acquiescence, he lost all motivation that might have made it possible for him to make meaningful contributions in a professional life. Perhaps his interest in robotics and artificial intelligence will grow, and he will sustain a sufficient commitment to do meaningful work in the field of computer science.

Jacob's approach to his writing tasks is disheartening both to composition specialists and disciplinary instructors. That a student who had both strong analytic skills and strong writing skills should use these talents to "fool" his instructors by providing the minimal amount of work and thinking, padding and stretching out small amounts of information to fulfill length requirements, is disheartening not only for the lack of respect it indicates for the student's instructors, but also for the loss of learning that the student experienced himself. Jacob may have thought that he was fooling his teachers, and perhaps in some cases he did; but, more truly, he fooled himself by not using the opportunities he was given to challenge his own thinking and allow himself to grow conceptually and personally. Certainly his academic writing demonstrated that he was capable of clear, analytic thinking, but he denied himself the opportunity to probe more deeply into issues than his initial responses led him to.

In September 1995, a year after Jacob graduated, I spoke by telephone with his sister who told me that Jacob was in Australia taking computer courses. He had been accepted into a master's program in computer science at one of the private colleges in New York City and intended to return in time to begin that program in the spring of 1996. But, in November 1996, when I tried to contact Jacob to learn whether he had started the master's program, his sister told me that he had decided to remain in Australia and that he had recently married. "He's really happy," she said. He was taking computer science courses there.

What a mixed tale Jacob could write about his own life, past, present, and perhaps future. He had been neither stimulated nor challenged by anything he cared about in his 5 years of college. He had mastered a cynical approach to success in his writing tasks, and only in his last years at the college did he begin to sense the learning that could take place through writing. Perhaps the future will bring us serious writing from Jacob, but it seems safe to predict that its message will be dark and despairing.

CONCLUSION

As these case studies reveal, there was no clear linear pattern of writing development that occurred in the college experiences of these students. But the centrality of writing as a means of learning dominated the students' observations of how they acquired knowledge and mastery of concepts. The students shared critical experiences, leading to appropriate methods of inquiry, although the particular facilitating events may have occurred at different times during their college years. Students learned the significance of translating academic jargon from lectures or textbooks into their own language; students learned to distinguish between "fact-gathering research" and "interpretation of material learned" (Spack, 1997, p. 50), the movement from reliance on authoritative sources to analysis; and students learned to adapt to the demands of specific tasks and specific instructors. By examining what happens to student writing *over time* it is possible to make the argument that even the weakest students benefit by appropriate instructional prodding to achieve the levels required for academic success.

Translating Concepts Into One's Own Language

The critical importance of being able to translate difficult concepts into the students' own language has been documented throughout this book. The case study experiences bring the significance of this developmental milestone to life. Although Joan articulated this understanding directly only in her fourth year at the college, she gradually began to move away from the strict definitions she presented in her first and second year writings, characteristic of the "received knowledge" of Belenky et al. (1986). As she developed more expertise in the field of psychology, she applied concepts from that field to readings in other disciplines, creating original connections for herself. As cited in earlier chapters of this book, many other students in the study also came to this crucial realization, among them, Delores, Donald, and Linda.

The Movement From Fact Gathering to Analysis

From the very beginning of their college courses, writing assignments were designed to move students from a bare recitation of facts to a more analytic stance. In her first psychology course, taken in her second semester at the college, Linda was prompted to link the evidence she presented to the larger conceptual issue addressed in the task, the relationship between a specific incident and the prejudice it purported to manifest. Through instructor comments on her papers, Linda recognized that her writing had to become more substantive, more formally correct, and more analytic. Research papers had initially made Linda "nervous," but she gradually worked her way into the "deep thinking" she knew was being required. In addition to overcoming her reluctance to undertake extensive research projects, Linda found herself able to apply psychological concepts to her interpretation of readings, thus providing an appropriate tool for analysis. Her growing confidence led to the ability to design and undertake original research projects, and she began to realize that an essential part of her learning was for herself.

Analysis was a given component of Ricardo's style from his earliest writing. He had to learn to modify his confrontational language and strengthen the evidentiary part of his papers to become an effective advocate for his ideas. Learning to question authority and backing up his positions with sustained evidence became the central focus of his educational experience.

Like Linda's early writing, Joan's was also mainly narrative and descriptive. She provided adequate details for her readers to understand the content, but she did not easily interpret or analyze the events under consideration. Although in some courses, citing authorities and providing definitions were accepted, in other classes, greater demands were made for analysis. By the beginning of her second year, she came to recognize that writing reinforced reading in important ways for her, allowing her to retain more of what she had read. Over time, Joan was able to apply psychological concepts to case study observations, and even to apply these concepts to literary figures. Like Linda, Joan achieved better results in courses that included writing assignments, because she could learn how to improve from her professors' suggestions. Examinations that consisted of multiple-choice questions troubled her throughout her college years, and her grades suffered when such examinations counted for a substantial portion of the grade evaluation. She became an acute observer of her instructors' language, and she began to model her own formal language on the patterns she noted. Because she was not consistent in her use of evidence nor in her use of analysis, Joan found herself frequently reminded by her teachers that she needed to provide more details and/or more in-depth analysis. But, at the same time, writing papers gave Joan the best opportunity to demonstrate what she had learned. She remained dependent on authoritative sources in what she called "more technical papers," but her ability to apply psychological theories, in particular to literary works as well as psychological cases, provided her with the insights that successfully moved her to analytic writing.

Like Ricardo, Jacob's ability to analyze complex materials was never in question. But, unlike, Ricardo, he came fully equipped with the proper style of language to handle complex reasoning tasks. Because so many of the students at City College had come from less privileged academic backgrounds, Jacob found little competition from others in his early courses. This ease of success reinforced his cynical posture that he could accomplish great success with little effort. Although he only contributed perfunctory efforts to his essays and examinations, his insights were credible and thoughtful.

Adjusting to Demands of Specific Tasks and Specific Instructors

Courses that required memorization and that were evaluated through short-answer examinations were the most difficult for students who began at basic writing levels. Linda, for example, had more difficulty with the science courses than in the humanities and social science courses in which she could write her way into better understandings of complex concepts. These opportunities were not always panaceas guaranteeing her success, but they provided her with better opportunities to work through the complexities. Her professors' comments on her papers helped her learn the strategies expected in college writing, the marshaling of evidence to support her points and the analysis of that evidence. But, as samples of Linda's writing in this chapter reveal, this development did not occur in a neat, linear fashion. The revelation of personal and family experiences seemed to deter analysis, as if she were reluctant to probe too deeply behind the facts that were offered.

Ricardo and Jacob shared a common trait—sensitivity to how their instructors would respond to their ideas—but they had diametrically opposing ways of responding to this awareness. Ricardo felt deeply committed to the viewpoints he espoused, whereas Jacob was entirely indifferent to the positions he presented in his papers. Ricardo learned that he would have to temper his language and bolster the evidence he presented to receive a fair hearing. On the other hand, Jacob assumed whatever noncontroversial position he felt his professor would accept, and then he gathered the minimal amount of evidence he could get away with, stretching it as necessary to fulfill paper length requirements. Both these students were successful in garnering praise from their instructors, but only Ricardo had really learned anything from these writing experiences. Because he was committed to social and political perspectives, he mastered the necessary conventions of presenting evidence so that his ideas would be accepted. Since Jacob had no investment in the topics the academic writing addressed, and since he possessed facile writing skills, he could achieve success with the least amount of effort. But, Ricardo, too, at times, recognized that it served his best interests to adopt dispassionate postures in settings where too much activism would not be tolerated, as in the objective stance he took in writing papers for the broadcast seminar course.

Through his course in ethics, Ricardo came to recognize that there was significant complexity in moral and social issues, and he developed a wider perspective than he had originally brought to such questions. He also began to develop a propensity to see that social issues could be addressed through legal social activism, rather than through student takeovers or demonstrations. (He told me that during the takeover of the academic buildings in the student protests of 1991, he had left the occupied buildings because he felt that the leaders of the student protests were not acting in rational ways in response to administrators' attempts at reconciliation.) In the play he wrote for one of his communications courses, his professor had urged him to have his protagonist seek out options for responding to the injustices he observed, and Ricardo rewrote the play's conclusion so that Diego could play a constructive rather than a destructive or detached role.

Jacob's difficulties with conceptual matters did not arise in the courses in which he had writing assignments, especially the entry-level humanities and social science core courses he was required to take. In these latter courses, he carefully selected evidence to support his thesis and analyzed that evidence for appropriate implications. Since he remained distanced from the demands of these courses, he had time to explore his true passion, creative writing. His dark poems and short stories, written concurrently with his dry academic papers, portray the depth of his feelings, hidden so carefully from almost everyone, as his reluctance to share this writing demonstrated. His last years at the college were consumed with the math and science courses his physics major required, and because they were conceptually more difficult than his courses in the earlier years, he had no time for creative writing nor was analytical writing asked for. Only through his method of condensation in note taking, the strategy also used by Ricardo, could Jacob have been said to do any writing.

Joan's movements among courses were the most varied of the case study students presented in this chapter. Although writing provided her with the best opportunity to demonstrate what she had learned, she was uneven in her ability to handle requested analyses. In particular, quantitative studies plagued her, and in writing laboratory reports for the experimental psychology course, she struggled with clarity of expression. Joan was most successful when she had opportunities to apply theories gleaned from her psychology courses to analyses in other disciplines.

IMPLICATIONS

In this very long chapter, detailed pictures of four students' academic and personal life experiences have been presented. It is not the purpose of this chapter or this book to draw neat generalizations from the portraits that have been drawn. Rather, it is critical to note how long it takes to really acquire a complete and honest picture of an individual's capabilities. The three students who started at developmental levels, Linda, Ricardo, and Joan, persisted in having sentence-level problems in their writing through all their 5 or 6 years at the college. However, their growth in handling complex reasoning tasks was not inhibited by their second-dialect or second-language interference patterns. Their most significant development occurred through the opportunities given to them for writing in their academic courses and through the constructive criticism this writing generated. The students benefited from comments that urged more substance, more evidence, more analysis, and clearer writing. No such feedback was provided through the taking of multiple-choice or short answer examinations. Rather than seeing learning as an accretion of facts, the students themselves recognized that writing promoted the truest method for learning. Even Jacob, who practically scorned the academic writing tasks, came to acknowledge that writing focused attention and promoted understanding.

In the first chapter of this book, the relationship between writing and learning was posited as having three aspects: (a) to help in remembering, (b) to help in analyzing, and (c) to help in constructing knowledge new to the individual. These case studies demonstrate that all of these ways of experiencing learning were acquired by the students and that writing was the key element in this happening.

As the title of this book, *Time to Know Them*, suggests, students must not be judged on their early accomplishments (or lack of them) in the academic setting. Consideration must be given to their previous preparation for academic demands, their experience with the formal language and thinking required in the college setting, and, yes, the other demands being made on them in their complex lives. This latter factor is crucial if economically less well-off students are to have a chance to succeed. I am not arguing here for any lowering of standards but instead for the recognition that either additional financial resources have to be supplied so that students can do their best work without having to choose between eating and learning, or else the colleges and universities must be more hospitable to part-time schedules, offering required courses at different times of the day to accommodate working schedules. For students like those pictured in this chapter, the college experience and gaining a professional education were their whole life. Such individuals should be valued, encouraged, and honored through societal policies.

8

Implications for Instruction and Research

In the preceding chapters, I have not emphasized my own role in the interactions with the students because I thought it was important to let them speak with their own voices. But, in this final chapter, I attempt to draw implications from their personal development and their academic work that I believe are crucial to developing appropriate educational policies. If one believes, as I do, that a major function of education is to foster questioning, then the interviews and writing samples presented in this study can be seen as evidence that the students developed this ability *over time*. Many started with the acceptance of "facts" that were presented to them in their discipline studies. But, all were able to move beyond such automatic acceptance to recognize that new insights could be provided that might alter some unexamined assumptions in their fields.

The role of writing in this transformation has been crucial. Repeatedly, students reported that reading alone or listening to lectures alone did not engage them deeply enough for them to remember facts and ideas nor to analyze them. Only through writing, perhaps through the condensation and analysis of classroom notes or through the writing of drafts of papers that required them to integrate theory with evidence, did they achieve the insights that moved them to complex reasoning about the topic under consideration.

Although the student population in this study was skewed to multicultural backgrounds that may not be replicated in many institutions of higher education, their experiences do not differ markedly from those of all students who come to college disadvantaged by their previous educational histories and/or their socioeconomic status. The students in this study, in bringing their world views to bear on the issues presented in their courses, demonstrated how these world views could increase their perceptions and lead them to significant analyses of accepted beliefs. Because of their backgrounds, they brought a heightened sensitivity to certain issues that contributed to their growing analytic powers. But worldviews of all students impinge on their attempts to make sense of the academic perspective and to integrate their experience into it, thus changing or modifying the existing schemas of fields as new insights are incorporated.

Having presented these general implications from the data collected in this study, it is appropriate to move on to more specific recommendations for instruction and research.

RECOMMENDATIONS FOR INSTRUCTION

The most significant central finding of this study is that students with poor academic preparation have the potential to develop the critical reasoning processes that they must bring to bear in academic writing if they are given the time. But recommendations are being made at high governmental levels that such students be denied any opportunity, even in public colleges and universities. As reported in *The New York Times* on March 18, 1997 ("CUNY Admissions Reviewed"), Governor George E. Pataki of New York State and Mayor Rudolph W. Guliani of New York City "criticized the admissions policy of City University of New York as ineffective." Such criticism led the trustees of the university to question "whether to retain the system's extensive remedial program." The argument against such support is founded on data that indicates that only 5% of CUNY community college students graduate in 2 years and only 19% in 5 years. As Lavin and Hyllegard's (1996) study demonstrated, and as this study reveals, the amount of time needed to complete degree requirements continues to grow as the economic support for poor students declines, necessitating longer time periods to complete academic programs. Yet, the social and economic benefits to the students themselves, as well as the larger society, are clear.

Early instruction in composition is critical to fostering critical reading and writing skills, but the expectation that students have become "finished writers" by the time they complete a freshman sequence or even an advanced composition course must be abandoned. As the writing and conceptual development of the students in this study reveal, over several semesters and even several years, through consistent instructional prodding both in writing and discipline area courses, students can develop an analytic stance that permits them to understand the significance of ideas in the particular field to the level where they become able to question some of the assumptions in that field. At this stage, it is not essential that they contribute new knowledge to the discipline, but it is essential that their questioning allow them to evaluate the givens in the field and determine what their own contributions can be.

What I believe this means for composition instructors is that they should foster critical reading and critical writing from the first assignments given to freshmen students. Students in basic writing classes, if such classes continue to exist, should not be treated differently from students in so-called regular composition classes. And, if integrated courses become the norm in composition teaching in the next few years, all students should be exposed to the challenges central to their development as thinkers and writers. Of course, instruction on sentence-level problems need not be abandoned, but as process models of writing have urged for many years now, these issues can be dealt with in the editing process of developing drafts. Most significantly, teachers must be informed enough to recognize that patterns exist within sets of grammatical features so that they can confront students with the specific features they need to practice rather than overwhelm them with what may appear to be many discrete errors. Furthermore, teachers need to be knowledgeable about hierarchies of language development, particularly for students whose native language is not English.

Another central finding of this study is that instructional approaches in a wide range of disciplines have the ability to use writing to foster critical thinking. Repeatedly, students said that multiple-choice and short-answer tests did not provide them with the opportunities they wished to have to demonstrate to their instructors what they had learned. And students knew that they learned more in those courses that required analytical writing, because such writing demanded their questioning of assumptions. Whether students were successful or unsuccessful in their early attempts to accomplish such writing tasks, in all cases they learned from these attempts and from their instructors' responses how to develop more successful responses. Whereas the composition teacher often asks for more specific details to support an assertion, the discipline area teacher is more likely to ask for evidence to support the claims being made in a piece of writing. The difference between details and evidence is not an irrelevant distinction; in the latter case, where students are attempting to justify positions on significant issues, they are required to support their claims with appropriate information from the particular discipline. In particular, if they wish to question conclusions that others have drawn, they find the demand increasing that they provide substantive proof or documentation that would make their claims credible.

This approach in discipline courses suggests that composition instruction could become more rigorous; writing instructors could demand that students not just give examples, for instance, to support their thesis claims, but that they use the readings in their courses as a basis for providing the reasons *why* their examples back up their topic sentence or thesis claims. In other words, at no level of instruction should facts be accepted as evidence without some statement of the significance of that information to the assertion being made. What students at all levels of instruction require is practice, practice, and more practice with meeting these demands in writing assignments.

Early in this book, I claimed that writing development occurred neither neatly nor linearly. As can be seen from the many examples presented here, student responses to writing tasks were influenced by their backgrounds or expertise at the time they approached a task, by the degree of instructional support and response they received, and by the complex factors in their lives that determined the amount of time and energy they could contribute to the task. Students who were burdened with heavy outside workloads did not ask for special consideration by any of their instructors; nevertheless, they suffered from these conditions. When students lacked sufficient background for a course, they sometimes had to repeat the course; at other times, sympathetic instructors changed the pace of instruction, without compromising academic standards. When instructors made themselves available to students outside of class or set up tutorial groups, they were providing the type of support that would make success possible for their students.

I have been very critical of the way that institutional testing impinges on the academic progress of students. In particular, students with second-dialect or second-language interference patterns were found to be heavily penalized by their placement and retention in basic level classes. I do not intend to argue that there is no role for basic writing instruction; students with the least expertise in reading and writing processes, I believe, can benefit from specific instruction in overcoming reading and writing difficulties. But most of the students who were placed both at the English 1 and English 2 levels in my study did not need specific remedial work; they would have benefited more strongly from a 1-year "regular" composition course that would have integrated reading and writing skills with a single instructor (such as the design developed by my colleagues at City College in the Enrichment Program).

The placement and evaluation process in institutional tests is so flawed by its timed, impromptu nature that no credibility can be attached to its results. When the difficulties within the testing situation itself are compounded further by the lack of knowledge of language development by the readers, then the only conclusion that can be drawn is that such testing should be eliminated or so completely redesigned that it replicates actual process writing tasks, with students being given ample opportunity for revision and editing. In addition, topics for such exams should be provided beforehand so that students have an opportunity to gather information and spend some time in reflection and information gathering before they are required to do the actual writing. It has been recognized for a long time that writing itself helps the individual know what else he or she needs to know, so some time must elapse between the writing of the first draft and the presentation of the final draft. If this description sounds as though it tells what should be happening in the instructional setting itself, I will have accomplished my purpose of proposing that placement tests essentially be eliminated. Instructors in the first 2 weeks of writing classes can easily identify those students who might require an additional period of intensive reading and writing work. An alternative to the proficiency testing graduation requirement might be the submission of a portfolio containing three papers that the student has written in upper level courses.

Instructional practices that begin with the freshman writing courses, not confounded by destructive institutional testing procedures, followed by supportive and challenging writing tasks in upper level courses provide even the students with the weakest beginning characteristics the opportunity to prove their capability. Furthermore, precisely such students bring new perspectives to their disciplines that will benefit the larger society as well as themselves. The students in my study have shown that this can happen when they are provided with enough time and support.

IMPLICATIONS FOR RESEARCH

The logistical requirements for undertaking a longitudinal study are daunting. As can be seen from the description provided in Appendix A, I had great difficulty sustaining contact with the students in my study because of their complicated living conditions—their moving often and/or having no available telephone number through which contact could be arranged. Nevertheless, the effort required to carry out such a study is justified. The findings from such studies, I believe, contribute meaningful information that can lead to the improvement of instruction and the potential success of more students.

The greatest benefit that arises from longitudinal research is the opportunity to follow intellectual growth and to be able to identify the factors that contribute to it. When students in my study found themselves in settings where received knowledge and the reiteration of facts were accepted as appropriate responses, they did not grow as conceptual thinkers. Only when instructors demanded that theory be applied to knowledge were students required to make the kinds of evaluative assessments that sharpened their critical powers. So, from class to class, and from year to year, students learned to adapt their responses to the particular demands being made on them. Almost without exception, in higher level discipline courses, the application of knowledge was the central focus of instruction. These observations are not surprising; what is significant is that *with the proper support*, all students in the study could produce the required analyses. Thus, the long-term nature of this study allows educators to see that even the apparently most educationally disadvantaged students have the potential to achieve academic success if they are given the time and support they need to demonstrate their abilities.

The trend of institutions of higher education demanding that basic level students "prove" themselves within the first year of instruction is shown to be biased against students who come from both poverty backgrounds and inadequate educational backgrounds. That combination is devastating to beginning students, but these are precisely the students that the society needs to nurture in order not only to create a more equitable society but to foster one within which individuals can believe that a fair opportunity will exist for all. Not only will these individuals have more satisfying lives, but the larger society will benefit from receiving valuable input from a segment of the society that is often denied the opportunity to make a contribution.

On a pragmatic level, I would recommend that researchers who wish to undertake longitudinal research follow some of the practices I used and substitute different approaches for some other practices. I believe strongly in the benefit of knowing the research subjects personally. Although I had originally hoped to follow a much larger population, I do not regret that conditions required me to cut down on the number of participants. Because I knew the students well, first as their instructor, and then as their "supporter," I was able to develop close enough relationships with them that they became increasingly comfortable about revealing aspects of their personal lives that helped me interpret their academic progress. I doubt that students would reveal much about their private lives if they were interviewed by a number of research assistants over the years, meeting the one whose schedule they could fit into in a particular semester. As I stated earlier, I made no attempt to pry into aspects of students' lives about which they did not feel comfortable volunteering information.

No researcher can predict which students will continue throughout the period of a study, so it is essential to collect the most complete information possible from each participant from the very beginning. Researchers should expect a dramatic falling off of student participation in the study after the first year, and then again after the second year. Some students' lives become more complicated with school and possibly work responsibilities; others will transfer or drop out of the college; still others will lose interest in the project. (Although I know of some researchers in concurrent longitudinal studies who have had financial resources for paying students to participate, I do not personally believe that this arrangement will lead to the best relationship between the researcher and the participants.) The researcher should decide what he or she feels would be the appropriate number for a final study population and triple that with the initial population. Having no previous studies to provide such data for my study, I started with the 53 students enrolled in the three levels of composition I taught and ended with full data for only 9 students. Although I would have preferred a larger final number, I would advise future researchers that analyzing the data for even that number of students is enormously time consuming. (In addition to the 6 years of data collection, I have spent almost 2 years writing this book, reviewing my student files extensively.) Clearly, this is not a project to be recommended for a nontenured faculty member or perhaps even one waiting for promotion.

The problem of remaining in contact with the students is one that will have to be handled on a local level. Although I had transcripts telling me which classes students were enrolled in each semester, I made a conscious decision not to pursue them to their classes to urge them to continue in the study. I felt that there should be no level of coercion to continue. Occasionally, I ran into a student who had not come to see me for a semester or two, and I asked that student if he or she would be willing to make an appointment with me. Too embarrassed to say no, they made these appointments, but they almost never kept them. In smaller communities or in on-campus living situations, students may not move around as much as students in large urban areas, so keeping in touch may not be so difficult. Telephone contact seems the essential way of maintaining a connection.

Having institutional and research support is essential to carrying out a longitudinal study. If the researcher wishes to collect copies of student papers, the sheer time spent in copying the papers can be overwhelming, particularly in the early stages of the study when there are more participants. Having a research assistant do this copying and draw up transcripts for the students allows the researcher to spend valuable time in the actual interviews with the students.

In my research design, I had the research assistants over the years do the classroom observations. I would make two changes in this procedure in a future study. First of all, I would have classes observed from the very first semester of the study, and I would certainly include all composition sections, particularly if the researcher is not the instructor of the students in the study. Secondly, I believe the researcher should do some of the classroom observations. In that way, the researcher will have a more direct insight into the instructional strategies used in the different disciplines, rather than relying solely on the reports of the research assistants. I am not recommending that the researcher do all the classroom observations, but the researcher should do enough to have some contact with the range of approaches being presented to the students.

Longitudinal research is complex to carry out. But no other methodology gives such a complete picture of the factors that influence student development and demonstrate the crucial role that writing plays in this development.

CLOSING COMMENTS

The problems that I have emphasized throughout this book regarding the lack of support for financing public higher education have not diminished. Indeed, a recent editorial in *The New York Times* ("The Governor's Divisive Cuts," January 16, 1997, p. A16) reported on Governor George Pataki's new budget proposals for New York State: "Also unwise are Mr. Pataki's proposed cuts for both the City University and State University systems. These would be offset by increasing tuition by $400 for students at both systems, making them less affordable for the poor and working class." A follow-up article by Karen W. Arensen in *The New York Times* on January 27, 1997 ("Aids Cuts Put College Assistance Beyond Reach of Poorest Students") described how "tuition at public institutions is likely to continue rising as financial aid shrinks, moving college further beyond the reach of poor students," according to education experts. Students have reported that previous and proposed tuition increases "strain their personal budgets." The article goes on to report that public universities are "increasingly pricing themselves beyond the means of the poorest Americans." Simultaneously, Federal Pell Grants that help cover costs other than tuition and state support are both declining. Already, tuition increases and cuts in state aid have contributed to a sharp drop in enrollment at City University of New York, with 4,500 fewer students enrolling in 1995 than in 1994. The "double whammy" of higher costs and less support for remedial instruction will continue to prevent students from less-prepared backgrounds and poorer economic resources from having the opportunity to demonstrate their capabilities and achieve their educational and social potential.

As the students in this study have demonstrated, they are willing to devote all their energies to achieving academic and professional success, but they should not be increasingly punished simply because they lack the financial resources of more affluent individuals. These students have demonstrated that they have the potential to succeed; it is time to reward their efforts by making it possible for them to focus on their studies and shorten the amount of time required to earn a degree so that they can begin to make their valuable contributions to the larger society.

It is difficult to believe that this study has drawn to a close. I have been living so close to it for so many years that it has become a constant companion to me. The desire to share the students' experiences and perceptions, however, has become a strong impetus for drawing it to a conclusion. I hope the readers will feel that they have come to know the students as I have and to feel the same enormous sense of pride that I feel in their accomplishments.

Appendix A:
Study Methodology
and Questionnaires

METHODOLOGY

During the early weeks of the first semester of the study, students in the three levels of composition I was teaching were invited to participate in the longitudinal study. They were assured of confidentiality and told that their real names would not be revealed in any publications. Students agreed to come to my office for interviews during the subsequent semesters and to provide copies of papers and examinations written in their courses. An initial demographic questionnaire, including a consent statement, was distributed and filled out in class during the first semester.

Students were interviewed twice each semester with the same beginning and ending questionnaires used each semester. Additional questionnaires were developed over the years to which students were asked to respond. Because I had inadequate resources for transcribing tapes of the interviews, I took detailed notes at each session, trying as much as possible to capture the exact language the students used. Students brought original copies of papers they had written for classes or examinations they had taken. Often these material had instructor comments and grades on them. A graduate assistant made copies of papers, and the originals were returned to the students. Sometimes students provided "extra" copies of papers they had written using a computer, and these papers did not have responses on them.

Beginning with the second year of the study, students were asked if they would be willing to have one of my research assistants observe one of their classes, preferably a course in their major field. Students recommended courses for the observations. All instructors of these classes were contacted prior to the observation to obtain their consent. They were asked to provide syllabi and other appropriate course materials. Faculty were very supportive and cooperative, and many made these materials available.

Other material that was collected included transcripts each semester to keep up with students' academic progress and copies of all writing examinations required by the college.

The most perplexing problem in undertaking a study of this nature is the problem of keeping in contact with the students. The City College students moved frequently, without providing the college with an appropriate forwarding address. Telephone numbers changed or were unlisted, or students had no telephones. (College transcripts failed to provide current informa-tion.) In the first two years of the study, when more students remained involved, I tried to contact students by mail to set up appointments. These attempts mostly failed, and I began more consistently to try to reach the students by telephone. These efforts were also frequently frustrated, and so my ability to retain contact with the students diminished over the years. Some were very conscientious about letting me know how I could reach them, writing me or calling me to tell of changes in their addresses and telephone numbers. Occasionally, I "ran into" a student whom I had been trying to contact, and I made an appointment to see that student. Of course, additional students were lost to the study when they left the college either to transfer to another school or to abandon their studies.

INITIAL DEMOGRAPHIC QUESTIONNAIRE

Date _____

Please write your student ID in the space below

_____ - _____ - _____

Name _____ _____

Address _____ Apt. No. _____

City_____ State _____ Zip Code _____

Telephone _____ - _____
       (Area Code)   (Number)

Date of birth _____
        (Month)   (Day)   (Year)

1. Please put <u>date</u> of semester, e.g., "Fall 1987," beside <u>each course</u> you have taken in a previous semester:

    English 1 _____ ESL 10 _____
    English 1 _____ ESL 10 _____
    English 2 _____ ESL 20 _____
    English 2 _____ ESL 20 _____
    English 110 _____ ESL 30 _____
    English 110 _____ ESL 30 _____

2. Number of times SKAT exam taken _____ [Writing Assess-ment Test]

    Date SKAT exam passed _____

3. Are you a U.S. citizen? Yes _____ No _____

4. What is your country of birth? _____

5. Language history
   What was your first language? _____
   At what age did you first study English? _____
   Where did you first study English? _____
   How old were you when you came to the U.S.? _____
   What language is spoken at home most of the time? _____

6. Educational history: <u>Name of school</u> / <u>City</u> / <u>State</u> / <u>Country</u>
   Elementary_____
   Middle _____
   Junior High_____
   High School_____

7. Which of the following groups do you use to describe yourself?
   <u>Check only one</u>.
   American Indian _____
   Asian-American/Oriental/Pacific Islander _____
         Country _____
   Asian-East Indian _____
   Black/African-American _____
         Country_____
   Mexican-American/Chicano _____
   Puerto-Rican _____
   Other Hispanic (please specify) _____
         Country _____
   White _____ Country _____
   Other (please specify) _____ Country _____

8. Did you receive a GED or a high school diploma?
   GED _____ Year _____
   High school diploma _____ Year _____
   Other (please explain) _____

9. What is the highest level of formal education obtained by your
   parents? Check one for each parent.

	<u>Father</u>	<u>Mother</u>
Grammar school or less	_____	_____
Some high school	_____	_____
High school graduate	_____	_____
Business or trade school	_____	_____
Some college	_____	_____
College degree	_____	_____
Some graduate school	_____	_____
Graduate degree	_____	_____
Don't know/not applicable	_____	_____

10. What is your current employment status? Complete one of the following:
    a. Employed full-time _____Number of hours/week _____
    Description of job _____
    b. Employed part-time _____Number of hours/week _____
    Description of job _____
    c. Not employed outside home _____
    d. Seeking employment _____ What type of job _____

11. What is the current employment status of your parents? Check one for each parent.

	Father	Mother	Occupation
Employed full-time	_____	_____	_____
Employed part-time	_____	_____	_____
Not employed outside home	_____	_____	_____
Seeking employment	_____	_____	_____
Retired	_____	_____	_____
Don't know/not applicable	_____	_____	

12. Do you have any brothers or sisters?
    No _____   Yes—how many? _____

13. If yes, how many or your brothers and sisters have reached each of the following educational levels? Count each sibling only once and include him/her in the highest educational level that he/she has achieved. Do not include yourself.

	Number
Graduated from college	_____
Attended college but did not graduate	_____
Now attending college	_____
Graduated from high school but did not attend college	_____
Now attending high school	_____
Not yet reached high school age	_____

14. What is your current marital status?
    Unmarried/single_____
    Married or living with partner_____

15. How many dependent children do you have?
    None _____
    I have _____ dependent children. Ages: _____

16. With whom do you live right now? Check all that apply.
    Parent(s) _____
    Brother(s)/sister(s) _____

Spouse _____
My children _____
Roommate _____
I live alone _____

17. Do you receive financial support from any family member or friend?
    No _____   Yes _____
    If yes, from whom do you receive support? Check all that apply.
          Parent(s) _____
          Spouse _____
          Other—please explain _____

18. I am enrolled as a
    Full-time student _____ No. of credits this semester _____
    Part-time student _____ No. of credits this semester _____
    Courses I am taking this semester:
          Course number   Title   No. of credits
    _____
    _____
    _____
    _____

19. Please write your intended major or area of study at City College
    _____

20. What degree are you currently working toward at City College
    and what is the highest degree you ultimately hope to earn?

	Current	Ultimate
Not seeking a certificate or degree	_____	_____
Certificate	_____	_____
Bachelor's degree	_____	_____
Graduate degree	_____	_____
Other—please explain	_____	_____

I give permission for the information gathered for the Writing and Learning Study to be used for research and curriculum development purposes. I understand that I will not be identified by name in publications resulting from this study.

_____
Name Printed

_____
Signature

_____
Date

FOLLOW-UP QUESTIONNAIRE AT BEGINNING OF EACH SEMESTER

Date _____

Name _____

Student ID _____

1. What is your most difficult course so far this semester? Why?

2. What is your easiest course so far this semester? Why?

3. List the courses other than English composition that have writing assignments required (e.g., lab reports, reading exercises, short papers, term papers)

   <u>Course title</u>   <u>Types of writing assignments</u>

   _____
   _____
   _____
   _____

4. What type of outside job do you currently hold?

   _____

   How many hours a week are you currently working?

   _____

5. How much time do you spend commuting <u>one way</u> to City College?

   Less than 30 minutes   _____
   30–60 minutes   _____
   60–90 minutes   _____
   More than 90 minutes   _____

6. How many credits are you currently taking? _____

   Have you dropped any courses since the beginning of the semester?
   Yes _____   No _____
   If yes, list course(s) that were dropped and reason for dropping
   <u>Course</u>   <u>Reason</u>

   _____
   _____

7. What do you feel that you learned last semester that was most valuable to you?

8. What are you learning this semester that seems valuable to you?

9. Have you decided on a major? Is this a change from an earlier decision?

10. Has writing helped you to understand any of the material in your courses better? How? Why?

11. Are you doing any writing on your own to help you better understand any of the materials in your courses?

12. Have any particular writing strategies been helpful to you in any of your courses? What strategies? Which courses?

13. Would you be willing to let me ask any of your instructors in any of your courses if I could come to visit a class? [Students were told that a research assistant would carry out the observation.]

FOLLOW-UP QUESTIONNAIRE
AT END OF EACH SEMESTER

1. Are you planning to continue at City College next semester?

2. What seems to be the most significant thing that has happened to you during this past year?

3. What are the most important things you learned during this past year?

4. What role has writing played in your learning of your subjects this year?

5. What kind of preparation do you wish you had had (in high school or at the college) that would have helped you academically?

6. What is the most interesting thing that happened to you during this year?

7. Have any big changes occurred in your life during this past year?

ADDENDUM TO FALL QUESTIONNAIRES

1. Did anything especially important or interesting happen to you over the summer?

2. What do you think were the most important things you learned in your courses last year?

3. Did writing papers in any of your courses help you to understand the materials or ideas in the courses better? What courses? In what ways?

4. Do you think the freshman writing courses should emphasize any different things that would be helpful to you in your courses?

EFFECT OF STUDENT TAKEOVER OF CAMPUS BUILDINGS THAT DISRUPTED CLASSES FOR 3½ WEEKS (END OF SPRING SEMESTER, SECOND YEAR)

1. Describe how your studies at the college were affected by the student take-over during the spring of 1991.

2. During the disruption of classes, did you work extra hours? Are you continuing to work extra hours?

3. Did you drop any classes as a result of the disruption of classes? If so, why?

4. Did the disruption of classes affect a decision to drop out of school for this semester? If so, why? If so, do you plan to return in the fall?

5. Are you getting any help with your writing for your courses? Which courses? If so, from whom? From professors? From friends? From the Writing Center?

QUESTIONNAIRE ON EXPERIENCES AT THE COLLEGE (END OF FALL SEMESTER, THIRD YEAR)

1. Have you developed a relationship with any of your professors or administrators so that you see or talk with them outside of your classroom situations?
2. Have you been active in any student organizations? Have you held any leadership positions?
3. Have you served on any college or departmental committees?
4. Have you been active in any varsity or collegiate sports? Have you earned any athletic letters?
5. Do you think that the size of City College has affected your college experiences in any way?
6. Do you think that having to commute to the college has affected your college experience in any way?
7. Do you think that having to work has affected your college experience in any way?
8. Do you think that the skills courses at the college helped you?
   College Skills 1 and 2 [basic reading courses]
   English 1 and 2

9. Do you think that your commitment to your academic studies has changed over the years?
10. Do you expect to return to the college next semester?

PERCEIVED CHANGES OVER TIME
(END OF SPRING SEMESTER, FOURTH YEAR)

In what ways do you feel you are a different person from the person you were when you started City College? Why?

WRITING PROFILE
(BEGINNING OF FALL SEMESTER, FIFTH YEAR)

[The questions used in this writing profile were adapted from an article by Cleary (1991).]

Previous Writing Experiences

1. What has writing been like for you from the time you first remember until the present?
2. What do you remember of writing before you began school?
3. How did you learn to write?
4. What was writing like for you in elementary school?
   What was writing like for you in middle school or junior high?
   What was writing like for you in high school?
5. Who helped you with writing (parents, neighbors, grandparents, siblings, peers, others)?
6. Was the help useful?
7. Tell me about a time when writing was really good or bad for you.
8. What has writing been like for you thus far in college?

Present Writing Experiences

1. What is writing like for you right now?
2. What are all the kinds of writing you do inside and outside of school?

3. How do you go about school writing from the time you first receive an assignment until you hand in the finished paper? What is the process like for you?

4. When is the process easy, satisfying, exciting, hard, worrisome or distressing?

5. How do other people help or hinder that process?

6. If I had a picture of you writing at home or at school, what would it look like? Where do you write, when, how, with what?

7. What sense do you make of your experience with writing? That is, given your experience with writing in the past, what sense do you make of the way you go about writing today?

Appendix B

The City University of New York
Freshman Skills Assessment Program

WRITING SKILLS ASSESSMENT TEST
EVALUATION SCALE [WAT]

6   The essay provides a well-organized response to the topic and maintains a central focus. The ideas are expressed in appropriate language. A sense of pattern of development is present from beginning to end. The writer supports assertions with explanation or illustration, and the vocabulary is well suited to the context. Sentences reflect a command of syntax within the ordinary range of standard written English. Grammar, punctuation, and spelling are almost always correct.

5   The essay provides an organized response to the topic. The ideas are expressed in clear language most of the time. The writer develops ideas and generally signals relationships within and between paragraphs. The writer uses vocabulary that is appropriate for the essay topic and avoids oversimplifications or distortions. Sentences generally are correct grammatically, although some errors may be present when sentence structure is particularly complex. With few exceptions, grammar, punctuation, and spelling are correct.

4   The essay shows a basic understanding of the demands of essay organization, although there might be occasional digressions. The development of ideas is sometimes incomplete or rudimentary, but a basic logical structure can be discerned. Vocabulary generally is appropriate for the essay topic but at times is oversimplified. Sentences reflect a sufficient command of standard written English to ensure reasonable clarity of expression. Common forms of agreement and grammatical inflection are usually, although not always, correct. The writer generally demonstrates through punctuation an understanding of the boundaries of the sentence. The writer spells common words, except perhaps so-called "demons" with a reasonable degree of accuracy.

3   The essay provides a response to the topic but generally has no overall pattern of organization. Ideas are often repeated or undeveloped, although occasionally a paragraph within the essay does have some structure. The writer uses informal language occasionally and records conversational speech when appropriate written prose is needed. Vocabulary often is limited. The writer generally does not signal relationships within and between paragraphs. Syntax is often rudimentary and lacking in variety. The essay has recurrent grammatical problems, or because of an extremely narrow range of syntactical choices, only occasional grammatical problems appear. The writer does not demonstrate a firm understanding of the boundaries of the sentence. The writer occasionally misspells common words of the language.

2   The essay begins with a response to the topic, but does not develop that response. Ideas are repeated frequently, or are presented randomly, or both. The writer uses informal language frequently and does little more than record conversational speech. Words are often misused and vocabulary is limited. Syntax is often tangled and is not sufficiently stable to ensure reasonable clarity of expression. Errors in grammar, punctuation, and spelling occur often.

1   The essay suffers from general incoherence and has no discernible pattern of organization. It displays a high frequency of error in the regular features of standard written English. Lapses in punctuation, spelling, and grammar often frustrate the reader. Or, the essay is so brief that any reasonable accurate judgment of the writer's competence is impossible.

References

Ackerman, J. M. (1993). The promise of writing to learn. *Written Communication, 10*(3), 334–370.

Anson, C. M. (1989). Response styles and ways of knowing. In C. M. Anson (Ed.), *Writing and response: Theory, practice, and research* (pp. 332–336). Urbana, IL: National Council of Teachers of English.

Arensen, K. W. (1997, January 27). Aids cuts put college assistance beyond reach of poorest students. *The New York Times*, p. B-1.

Aronson, A. (1992, March). *Outsiders within: Identity conflicts in non-traditional student writers.* Paper presented at the annual meeting of the Conference on College Composition and Communication, Cincinnati, OH. (ERIC Document Reproduction Service No. ED 346 464)

Bartholomae, D. (1980). The study of error. *College Composition and Communication, 31*, 253–269.

Bartholomae, D. (1993). The tidy house: Basic writing in the American curriculum. *Journal of Basic Writing, 12*(1), 4–21.

Beach, R., & Anson, C. M. (1988). The pragmatics of memo writing: Developmental differences in the use of rhetorical strategies. *Written Communication, 5*, 157–183.

Beckham, E. F. (1997, January 5). Diversity opens doors to all. *The New York Times*, p. 58.

Belenky, M. F., Clinchy, B. M., Goldberger, N. R., & Tarule, J. M. (1986). *Women's ways of knowing: The development of self, voice, and mind.* New York: Basic Books.

Berlin, J. (1988). Rhetoric and ideology in the writing class. *College English, 50*(5), 477–494.

Bizzell, P. (1986). What happens when basic writers come to college? *College Composition and Communication, 37*, 294–301.

Bleich, D. (1986). Gender interests in reading and language. In E. Flynn & P. P. Schweickart (Eds.), *Gender and reading: Essays on readers, texts, and contexts* (pp. 234–266). Baltimore: Johns Hopkins University Press.

Bleich, D. (1995). Collaboration and the pedagogy of disclosure. *College English, 57*(1), 43–61.

Bloom, A. (1987). *The closing of the American mind.* New York: Simon & Schuster.

Bradford, A. N. (1983). Cognitive immaturity and remedial college writers. In J. N. Hayes, P. A. Roth, J. R. Ramsey, & R. D. Foulke (Eds.), *The writer's mind: Writing as a mode of thinking* (pp. 15–24). Urbana, IL: National Council of Teachers of English.

Brandt, D. (1992). The cognitive as the social: An ethnomethodological approach to writing process research. *Written Communication, 9*, 315–355.

Britton, J., Burgess, T., Martin, N., McLeod, A., & Rosen, H. (1977). *The development of writing abilities* (pp. 11–18). Urbana, IL: National Council of Teachers of English. (Original work published 1975)

Brodkey, L. (1989). On the subjects of class and gender in "The literacy letters." *College English, 51*(2), 125–141.

Bruner, J. S. (1973). *Beyond the information given: Studies in the psychology of knowing.* New York: Norton.

Chin, E. (1994). Redefining "context" in research in writing. *Written Communication, 11*(4), 445–482.

Chiseri-Strater, E. (1991). *Academic literacies: The public and private discourse of university students.* Portsmouth, NH: Boynton/Cook-Heinemann.

Cleary, L. M. (1991). Affect and cognition in the writing process of eleventh graders: A study of concentration and motivation. *Written Communication, 8*(4), 479.

Connors, R. J., & Lunsford, A. A. (1988). Frequency of formal errors in current college writing, or Ma & Pa Kettle do research. *College Composition and Communication, 39,* 395–409.

Connors, R. J., & Lunsford, A. A. (1993). Teachers' rhetorical comments on students' papers. *College Composition and Communication, 44*(2), 200–223.

Copeland, K. A. (1985, November). *The effect of writing upon good and poor writers' learning from prose.* Paper presented at the annual meeting of the National Council of Teachers of English, Philadelphia, PA. (ERIC Document Reproduction Service No. ED 276 993)

Corder, S. P. (1981) *Error analysis and interlanguage.* Oxford: Oxford University Press.

CUNY admissions reviewed. (1997, March 18). *The New York Times,* p. B-3.

Dickson, M. (1995). *It's not like that here: Teaching academic writing and reading to novice writers.* Portsmouth, NH: Boynton/Cook-Heinemann.

Durst, R. K. (1987). Cognitive and linguistic demands of analytic writing. *Research in the Teaching of English, 21,* 347–376.

Elbow, P. (1991). Reflections on academic discourse: How it relates to freshmen and colleagues. *College English, 55*(2), 135–155.

Emig, J. (1971). *The composing processes of twelfth graders.* Urbana, IL: National Council of Teachers of English.

Ericcson, K. A., & Simon, H. A. (1984). *Protocol analysis: Verbal reports as data.* Cambridge, MA: MIT Press.

Fishman, J. (1984). Do you agree or disagree: The epistemology of the CUNY writing assessment test. *Writing Program Administration, 8,* 17–25.

Flower, L. (1994). *The construction of negotiated meaning: A social cognitive theory of writing.* Carbondale: Southern Illinois University Press.

Flower, L. S., & J. R. Hayes. (1981). Plans that guide the composing process. In C. H. Frederikson & J. F. Dominic (Eds.), *Writing: Process, development and communication* (pp. 39–58). Hillsdale, NJ: Lawrence Erlbaum Associates.

Flynn, E. A. (1989). Learning to read student papers from a feminist perspective, 1. In B. Lawson, S. S. Ryan, & W. R. Winterowd (Eds.), *Encountering student texts: Interpretive issues in reading student writing* (pp. 49–58). Urbana, IL: National Council of Teachers of English.

Fox, H. (1994). *Listening to the world: Cultural issues in academic writing.* Urbana, IL: National Council of Teachers of English.

Fox, T. (1993). Standards and access. *Journal of Basic Writing, 12*(1), 37–45.

Freedman, A., & Pringle, I. (1980). Writing in the college years: Some indices of growth. *College Composition and Communication, 30,* 311–24.

Freire, P. (1993). *Pedagogy of the oppressed.* New York: Continuum. (Original work published in 1970)

Geisler, C. (1994). *Academic literacy and the nature of expertise: Reading, writing, and knowing in academic philosophy.* Hillsdale, NJ: Lawrence Erlbaum Associates.

Gilligan, C. (1982). *In a different voice: Psychological theory and women's development.* Cambridge, MA: Harvard University Press.

Gleason, B. (1995). *Messing with Mr. in-between: Interlanguage development theory and writing instruction.* Unpublished manuscript.

Gleason, B. (1997). When the writing test fails: Assessing assessment at an urban college. In C. Severino, J. C. Guerra, & J. E. E. Butler (Eds.), *Writing in multicultural settings* (pp. 307–324). New York: Modern Language Association.

Hairston, M. (1992). Diversity, ideology, and teaching writing. *College Composition and Communication, 43*(2), 179–193.

Hamill, P. (1989, April 2). Gorgeous autos, but can anyone do the repairs? *The New York Post.*

Harlston, B. W. (1987). *The legacy affirmed: A report from the president*. New York: The City College of New York.

Haswell, R. H. (1991). *Gaining ground in college writing: Tales of development and interpretation*. Dallas: Southern Methodist University Press.

Haswell, R. H., & Wyche-Smith, S. (1994). Adventuring into writing assessment. *College Composition and Communication, 45*, 220–236.

Hayes, C. G. (1990, May). Using writing to promote reading to learn in college. Paper presented at the Annual Meeting of the International Reading Association, Atlanta, GA. (ERIC Document Reproduction Service No. ED 322 499)

Hays, J. N. (1983a). The development of discursive maturity in college writers. In J. N. Hays, P. A. Roth, J. R. Ramsey, & R. D. Foulke (Eds.), *The writer's mind: Writing as a mode of thinking* (pp. 127–144). Urbana, IL: National Council of Teachers of English.

Hays, J. N. (1983b, October). An empirically-derived stage model of analytic writing abilities during the college years: Some illustrative cases. Paper presented at the Annual Meeting of the Northern Rocky Mountain Educational Research Association, Jackson Hole, WY. (ERIC Document Reproduction Service No. ED 247 553)

Hays, J. N., Brandt, K. M., & Chantry, K. H. (1988). The impact of friendly and hostile audiences on the argumentative writing of high school and college students. *Research in the Teaching of English, 22*, 391–416.

Hirsch, E. (1988). *Cultural literacy: What every American needs to know*. New York: Vintage.

Hoetker, J., & Brossell, G. (1986). A procedure for writing content-fair essay examination topics for large-scale writing assessments. *College Composition and Communication, 37*, 328–335.

Holloway, K. F. C. (1993). Cultural politics in the academic community: Masking the color line. *College English, 55*(6), 610–617.

Horner, B. (1996). Discoursing basic writing. *College Composition and Communication, 47*(2), 199–222.

Hull, G., & Rose, M. (1989). Rethinking remediation: Toward a social–cognitive understanding of problematic reading and writing. *Written Communication, 8*(2), 139–154.

Jones-Royster, J. (1992). Looking from the margins: A tale of curricular reform. In S. Batchelder (Ed.), *Diversity and writing: Dialogue within a modern university* (Monograph series no. 2, pp. 1–12). Minneapolis, MN: Center for Interdisciplinary Studies of Writing.

Keating, A. L. (1995). Interrogating "whiteness," (de)constructing "race." *College English, 57*(8), 901–918.

Kogen, M. (1986). The conventions of expository writing. *Journal of Basic Writing, 5*(1), 24–37.

Krater, J., Zeni, J., & Cason, N. D. (1994). *Mirror images: Teaching writing in black and white*. Portsmouth, NH: Heinemann.

Kutz, E., Groden, S. Q., & Zamel, V. (1993). *The discovery of competence: Teaching and learning with diverse student writers*. Portsmouth, NH: Boynton/Cook-Heinemann.

Langer, J. A. (1986). Learning through writing: Study skills in the content areas. *Journal of Reading, 29*, 400–406.

Langer, J. A., & Applebee, A. N. (1987). *How writing shapes thinking: A study of teaching and learning*. Urbana, IL: National Council of Teachers of English.

Langstraat, L. (1995, March). *Gender literacy in the cultural studies composition classroom: Fashioning the "self" through an analysis of popular magazines*. Paper presented at the annual meeting of the Conference on College Composition and Communication, Washington, DC. (ERIC Document Reproduction Service No. ED 384 879)

Larsen, N. (1928). *Quicksand and passing*. D. McDowell (Ed.). (1986). New Brunswick: Rutgers University Press.

Lavin, D. E., Alba, R. D., & Silberstein, R. A. (1981). *Right versus privilege: The open admissions experiment at City University of New York*. New York: Free Press.

Lavin, D. E., & Hyllegard, D. (1996). *Changing the odds: Open admission and the life chances of the disadvantaged.* New Haven: Yale University Press.

Lees, E. O. (1983). Building thought on paper with adult basic writers. In J. N. Hays, P. A. Roth, J. R. Ramsey, & R. D. Foulke (Eds.), *The writer's mind: Writing as a mode of thinking* (pp. 141–151). Urbana, IL: National Council of Teachers of English.

Loban, W. (1963). *The language of elementary school children.* Champaign, IL: National Council of Teachers of English.

Lu, M.-Z. (1992). Conflict and struggle: The enemies of preconditions of basic writing? *College English, 54*(8), 887–913.

Lunsford, A. (1979). Cognitive development and the basic writer. *College English, 41,* 38–46.

Martinez, J. G. R., & Martinez, N. C. (1987, April). *Are basic writers cognitively deficient?* Paper presented at the Western College Reading and Learning Association, Albuquerque, NM. (ERIC Document Reproduction Service No. ED 285 179)

Marshall, J. D. (1987). The effects of writing on students' understanding of literary texts. *Research in the Teaching of English, 21*(1), 30–63.

Martin, N., D'Arcy, P., Newman, B., & Parker, R. (1976). *Writing and learning across the curriculum* (pp. 11–16). London: Schools Council Publication for Ward Lock Educational.

Newell, G. E. (1984). Learning from writing in two content areas: A case study/protocol analysis. *Research in the Teaching of English, 18,* 265–287.

Newell, G. E., & Winograd, P. (1989). The effects of writing on learning from expository text. *Written Communication, 6*(2), 196–217.

Ogbu, J. (1978). *Minority education and caste: The American system in cross-cultural perspective.* New York: Academic Press.

Oliver, E. (1993, November). *Let the writing speak for itself: Assessing the composing skills of inner-city African-American students.* Paper presented at the annual meeting of the National Council of Teachers of English, Pittsburgh, PA. (ERIC Document Reproduction Service No. ED 381 803)

Onore, C. (1989). The student, the teacher, and the text: Negotiating meanings through response and revision. In C. M. Anson (Ed.), *Writing and response: Theory, practice, and research* (pp. 231–260). Urbana, IL: National Council of Teachers of English.

Penrose, A. M. (1992). To write or not to write: Effects of task and task interpretation on learning through writing. *Written Communication, 9*(2), 465–500.

Penrose, A. M. (1993). Writing and learning: Exploring the consequences of task interpretation. In A. M. Penrose & B. M. Sitko (Eds.), *Hearing ourselves think: Cognitive research in the college writing classroom* (pp. 52–69). New York: Oxford University Press.

Perry, W., Jr. (1968). *Forms of intellectual and ethical development in the college years, a scheme.* New York: Holt, Rinehart & Winston.

Perry, W., Jr. (1981). Cognitive and ethical growth: The making of meaning. In A. W. Chickering (Ed.), *The modern American college* (pp. 76–116). San Francisco, CA: Jossey-Bass.

Phelps, L. M. (1989). Images of student writing: The deep structure of teacher response. In C. M. Anson (Ed.), *Writing and response: Theory, practice, research* (pp. 37–67). Urbana, IL: National Council of Teachers of English.

Reinharz, S. (1984). *On becoming a social scientist.* New Brunswick, NJ: Transaction.

Ritchie, J. S. (1990). Confronting the "essential" problem: Reconnecting feminist theory and pedagogy. *Journal of Advanced Composition, 10*(2), 249–273.

Rose, M. (1983). Remedial writing courses: A critique and a proposal. *College English, 45,* 109–128.

Rose, M. (1985a). The language of exclusion: Writing instruction at the university. *College English, 47,* 341–359.

Rose, M. (1985b). *When a writer can't write: Studies in writing block and other composing processes.* New York: Guilford.

Rose, M. (1988). Narrowing the mind and page: Remedial writers and cognitive reductionism. *College Composition and Communication, 39,* 267–302.

Rosenthal, G. (1993). Reconstruction of life stories: Principles of selection in generating stories for narrative biographical interviews. In R. Josselon & A. Lieblich (Eds.), *The narrative study of lives* (Vol. 1, pp. 59–91). Newbury Park, CA: Sage Publications.

Schumacher, G. M., Klare, G. R., Cronin, F. C., & Moses, J. R. (1984). Cognitive activities of beginning and advanced college writers: A pausal analysis. *Research in the Teaching of English, 18,* 169–187.

Schumacher, G. M., & Nash, J. G. (1991). Conceptualizing and measuring knowledge change due to writing. *Research in the Teaching of English, 25,* 67–96.

Shaughnessy, M. (1975). Basic writing. In G. Tate (Ed.), *Teaching composition: Ten bibliographical essays* (pp. 142–167). Fort Worth: Texas Christian University Press.

Soliday, M. (1994). Translating self and difference through literacy narratives. *College English, 56*(5), 511–526.

Soliday, M. (1996). From the margins to the mainstream: Reconceiving remediation. *College Composition and Communication, 47*(1), 85–100.

Spack, R. (1997). The acquisition of academic literacy in a second language: A longitudinal case study. *Written Communication, 14*(1), 3–62.

Spear, K. L. (1983). Thinking and writing: A sequential curriculum for composition. *Journal of Advanced Composition, 4,* 47–63.

Steinberg, L. (1996). *Beyond the classroom: Why school reform has failed and what parents need to do.* New York: Simon & Schuster.

Sternglass, M. S. (1974). Close similarities in dialect features of black and white college students in remedial composition classes. *TESOL Quarterly, 8*(3), 271–283.

Sternglass, M. S. (1988). *The presence of thought: Introspective accounts of reading and writing.* Norwood, NJ: Ablex.

Sternglass, M. S. (1993). Writing development as seen through longitudinal research: A case study exemplar. *Written Communication, 10*(2), 235–261

Stotsky, S. (1986). On learning to write about ideas. *College Composition and Communication, 37,* 276–293.

Straub, R. (1996). The concept of control in teacher response: Defining the varieties of "directive" and "facilitative commentary." *College Composition and Communication, 47*(2), 223–251.

Stygall, G. (1994). Resisting privilege: Basic writing and Foucault's author function. *College Composition and Communication, 45*(3), 43–61.

Sullivan, P. A. (1995). Review: Social constructionism and literacy studies. *College English, 57*(8), 950–959.

Swartzlander, S., Pace, D., & Stamler, V. L. (1993, February 17). The ethics of requiring students to write about their personal lives. *Chronicle of Higher Education,* p. B1–2.

Tabor, M. B. W. (1996, August 17). Comprehensive study finds parents and peers are most crucial influences on students. *The New York Times,* p. A12.

The governor's divisive cuts. (1997, January 16). *The New York Times,* p. A16.

Traub, J. (1994). *City on a hill: Testing the American dream at City College.* Reading, MA: Addison-Wesley.

Trimbur, J. (1993). Response to Maxine Hairston: "Diversity, ideology, and teaching writing." *College Composition and Communication, 44*(2), 248–249.

Vygotsky, L. S. (1978). *Mind in society: The development of higher psychological processes.* (M. Cole, V. John-Steiner, S. Scribner, & E. Souberman, Eds.). Cambridge, MA: Harvard University Press.

Walvoord, B. E., & McCarthy, L. P. (1990). *Thinking and writing in college: A naturalistic study of students in four disciplines.* Urbana, IL: National Council of Teachers of English.

Warnock, T. (1989). An analysis of response: Dream, prayer, and chart. In B. Lawson, S. S. Ryan, & W. R. Winterowd (Eds.), *Encountering student texts: Interpretive issues in reading student writing* (pp. 59–72). Urbana, IL: National Council of Teachers of English.

White, E. M. (1996). An apologia for the timed impromptu essay test. *College Composition and Communication, 46*(1), 30–45.

White, E. M., & Thomas, L. L. (1981). Racial minorities and writing skills assessment in the California State University and Colleges. *College English, 43*(3), 276–283.

Whitla, D. K. (1981). *Value added and other related matters.* (ERIC Document Reproduction Service No. ED 228 245)

Widdershoven, G. A. M. (1993). The story of life: Hermeneutic perspectives on the relationship between narrative and life history. In R. Josselon & A. Lieblich (Eds.), *The narrative study of lives* (Vol. 1, pp. 1–20). Newbury Park, CA: Sage Publications.

Wilkinson, A., Barnsley, G., Hanna, P., & Swan, M. (1980). *Assessing language development.* Oxford: Oxford University Press.

Wolcott, W. (1994). A longitudinal study of six developmental students' performance in reading and writing. *Journal of Basic Writing, 13*(1), 14–40.

Wood, R. G. (1993). Response to Maxine Hairston: "Diversity, ideology, and teaching writing." *College Composition and Communication, 44*(2), 249–250.

Zamel, V. (1995). Strangers in academia: The experience of faculty and ESL students across the curriculum. *College Composition and Communication, 46*(4), 506–521.

Author Index

Subject Index